IFA1, CF1, CeFA®1

UK FINANCIAL SERVICES, REGULATION AND ETHICS

2006/07 tax year edition

Study Text

IFA/Cert FP/CeF/

This **Study Text** provides full coverage for:

- Paper 1 *Financial Services, Regulation and Ethics* of the Securities and Investment Institute's IFA Qualification

- Paper CF1 *Financial Services, Regulation and Ethics* of the Chartered Insurance Institute's® Certificate in Financial Planning

- Module 1 *Financial Services, Regulation and Ethics* of the Institute of Financial Services' Certificate for Financial Advisers (CeFA®)

Visit www.bpp.com/financialadvisers for more information

PROFESSIONAL EDUCATION

Contents

First edition May 2006

ISBN 0 7517 2628 1

British Library Cataloguing-in-Publication Data

A catalogue record for this book
is available from the British Library

Published by

BPP Professional Education
Aldine House, Aldine Place
London W12 8AW

www.bpp.com

Printed in Great Britain

We are grateful to the SII, CII® and *ifs* for permission to
reproduce syllabuses.
*Chartered Insurance Institute® and CII® are registered
trademarks. The CII® does not endorse, promote, review
or warrant the accuracy of the products or services
offered by BPP Professional Education.*

Using this Study Text

Standards for examinations in *UK Financial Services, Regulation and Ethics* are prescribed by the Financial Services Skills Council and form the FSSC's Appropriate Examination Standards ApEx1. This Study Text has been written to cover all of the required topics for ApEx1 *UK Financial Services, Regulation and Ethics*.

This Study Text has been written for candidates sitting one of the following examinations, all of which meet the FSSC requirements.

- Paper 1 *UK Financial Services, Regulation and Ethics* of the Securities and Investment Institute's **IFA Qualification**

- Paper CF1 *UK Financial Services, Regulation and Ethics* of the Chartered Insurance Institute's® **Certificate in Financial Planning**

- Module 1 *UK Financial Regulation* of the Institute of Financial Services' **Certificate for Financial Advisers (CeFA®)**

The Study Text contains:

- A list of topics covered in each Chapter
- Clear, concise topic-by-topic coverage
- Examples and Exercises to reinforce learning, confirm understanding and stimulate thought
- A roundup of the key points in each Chapter
- A quiz at the end of each Chapter
- A bank of practice questions, with answers

We recognise that most students have only limited time for study and that some study material available on the market can be very time-consuming to use. BPP Professional Education has prepared study material which provides you with what you need to secure a good pass in your exam, while making effective use of your time.

Updates to this Study Text

There is a free Updating Service for users of BPP's *Financial Adviser Series*. For information on Updates to this Study Text, go to our website at **www.bpp.com/financial advisers**. If you do not have Internet access, please telephone our Customer Service Team on 020 8740 2211 for further information about available Updates.

Plan your exam practice and revision

How can you give yourself the best chance of success in your exam? As well as studying the material in this **Study Text** fully, plan your **exam practice** and **revision**.

BPP's long experience in preparing students for exams shows that **question practice** is a vital ingredient in exam success. Question practice will improve your exam technique and help to build confidence for tackling the exam itself. It can highlight problem areas and remind you of key points. BPP's **i-Pass CDs** each include a bank of questions for you to try at a computer. Feedback is given on answers, and there are flexible ways of using the question banks.

The syllabuses for your examination, which are based on the standards for Appropriate Examinations published by the Financial Services Skills Council, are wide-ranging. In your **revision** during the run-up to the exam, you will want to focus your revision on ensuring that you recall what you have studied. BPP's **Passcards** present key facts for your subject in a visually appealing style, to remind you of key points.

To order **Financial Adviser Series** Study Texts, i-Pass CDs and Passcards, call 0845 0751 100 or order online at **www.bpp.com/financialadvisers**.

Syllabuses

Syllabus references are set out below for the *UK Financial Services, Regulation and Ethics* examinations of the **Securities and Investment Institute (IFA Paper 1)**, the **Chartered Insurance Institute (CF1)** and the **Institute of Financial Services (CeFA Module 1)**.

In the **CeFA** syllabus references, '**U**' denotes the requirement to demonstrate **Understanding** while '**Kn**' denotes the requirement to demonstrate **Knowledge**.

UK Financial Services, Regulation and Ethics

IFA syllabus reference	CF1 syllabus reference	CeFA 1 syllabus reference	
1.1	**1**	**1 U1**	**Understand the purpose and structure of the UK financial services industry**
1.1.1	1.1	1 U1.1	The function of the financial services industry in the economy – transferring funds between individuals, businesses and government - risk management
1.1.2	1.2	1 U1.2	The main institutions/organisations – markets, retail institutions, wholesale institutions
1.1.2	1.3	1 U1.3	The role of the EU and of the UK government - regulation, taxation, economic and monetary policy, provision of welfare and benefits
1.2	**2**	**1 U2**	**Understand the main financial asset classes and their characteristics, covering past performance, risk and return**
1.2.1	2.1	1 U2.1	Cash deposits
1.2.2	2.2	1 U2.2	Government securities and corporate bonds – fixed interest and index-linked
1.2.3	2.3	1 U2.3	Equities
1.2.4	2.4	1 U2.4	Property – residential and commercial
1.3	**3**	**1 U3**	**Understand the main financial services product types and their functions**
-	3.1	1 U3.1	Direct investment – cash, government securities and corporate bonds, equities and property
1.3.1	-	-	Investment services – discretionary managed accounts, managed funds accounts, funds supermarkets, wrap platforms, execution-only products
1.3.2, 1.3.4	3.2	1 U3.2	Collective investments – structure, tax and charges – OEICs/unit trusts, investment trusts and companies, life assurance contracts, offshore funds
-	3.3	1 U3.3	Derivatives – their structure and purpose
1.3.3	-	-	Structured products – guaranteed growth and income products
1.3.5	3.4	1 U3.4	Mortgages and other loans – personal and commercial

BPP PROFESSIONAL EDUCATION

IFA syllabus reference	CF1 syllabus reference	CeFA 1 syllabus reference	
1.4	**4**	**1 U4**	**Understand the purpose of the main areas of financial advice**
1.4.1	4.1	1 U4.1	Budgeting [and expenditure planning]
1.4.2	4.2	1 U4.2	Protection
1.4.3	4.3	1 U4.3	Borrowing
1.4.4	4.4	1 U4.4	Investment and saving
1.4.5	4.5	1 U4.5	Retirement planning
1.4.6	4.6	1 U4.6	Estate planning
1.4.7	4.7	1 U4.7	Tax planning
1.5	**5**	**1 U5**	**Understand the process of giving financial advice, including the importance of regular reviews of the consumer's circumstances**
1.5.1	5.1	1 U5.1	The relationship between the client and the adviser – agreeing client goals, and the adviser's responsibilities with regard to confidentiality, trust, consumer protection and regulatory requirements, ie terms of business, statutory status disclosure
1.5.2	5.2	1 U5.2	Fact finding – gathering the information needed to provide financial advice
1.5.3	5.3	1 U5.3	Identification of needs and possible solutions – factors determining how to match solutions with consumer needs and demands
1.5.4	5.4	1 U5.4	Assessment of affordability and suitability
1.5.5	5.5	1 U5.5	Communication skills – giving advice and adapting advice to customers with different capacities and needs
1.5.6	5.6	1 U5.6	The importance of regular reviews of the consumer's circumstances and arrangements to monitor the continuing position and advise on appropriate changes
1.5.7	5.1	1 U5.7	The information consumers must be given under the current regulatory requirements: fees and commission statement (menu), initial disclosure document, statutory status disclosure
1.6	**6**	**1 U6**	**Understand the legal concepts relevant in financial advice**
1.6.1	6.1	1 U6.1	Legal identity – individuals, wills, intestacy, personal representatives (and administration of estates), trustees, companies, limited liabilities, partnerships, limited liability partnerships
1.6.2	6.2	1 U6.2	Contract, capacity
1.6.3	6.3	1 U6.3	Agency
1.6.4	6.4	1 U6.4	Types of property [real property, personal property] and its ownership
1.6.5	6.5	1 U6.5	Powers of attorney and enduring powers of attorney
1.6.6	6.6	1 U6.6	Insolvency and bankruptcy

IFA syllabus reference	CF1 syllabus reference	CeFA 1 syllabus reference	
1.7	7	1 U7	**Understand the UK taxation and social security systems and how they affect personal financial circumstances**
1.7.1	7.1	1 U7.1	UK income tax system – liability to income tax, allowances, reliefs, rates, grossing up interest and dividends, employed and self-employed income, priorities for taxing different classes of income
1.7.2	7.2	1 U7.2	Capital gains tax – liability to CGT, disposals, death, deductions, losses, main exemptions, indexation relief, taper relief, basic calculation of chargeable gains
1.7.3	7.3	-	Inheritance tax [– liability to inheritance tax, liability on gifts during life and on death and common exemptions]
1.7.4	7.4	1 U7.3	[Stamp duty, Stamp Duty Land Tax], Stamp Duty Reserve Tax on securities
1.7.5	7.5	1 U7.4	National Insurance
1.7.6	7.6	1 U7.5	Social Security benefits
1.8	8	1 U8	**Understand the impact of inflation, interest rate volatility and other relevant socio-economic factors on personal financial plans**
1.8.1	8.1	1 U8.1	Definition of inflation
1.8.2	8.2	1 U8.2	The difference between fixed and variable interest rates and how they affect the affordability, suitability and performance of financial products in both the long and short term
1.9	9	2 Kn1	**Understand the main aims and activities of the Financial Services Authority (FSA) and its approach to ethical conduct by firms and individuals**
1.9.1	9.1	2 Kn1.1	The Financial Services and Markets Act 2000
1.9.2	9.2	2 Kn1.2	The FSA's main objectives, role and activities
1.9.3, 1.10.5	9.3	2 Kn1.3	The FSA's principles for businesses and approved persons – how they reflect the need for ethical behaviour by firms and approved persons, FSA guidance [for example, Treating Customers Fairly]
1.9.4	9.4	2 Kn1.4	Arrangements, systems and controls for senior managers
1.9.5	9.5	2 Kn1.5	The fit and proper test for approved persons
1.9.6	9.6	2 Kn1.6	The prevention of crime, including market abuse and insider dealing
1.10	10	2 U1	**Understand the FSA's approach to regulating firms and individuals**
1.10.1	10.1	2 U1.1	Authorisation of firms
1.10.1	10.2	2 U1.1	Regulated activities and regulated investments
1.10.1	10.3	2 U1.1	Different types of financial adviser, their main responsibilities and restrictions
1.10.2	10.4	2 U1.2	Capital adequacy
1.10.3	10.5	2 U1.3	FSA supervision and the risk- [and principle-]based approach
1.10.4	10.6	2 U1.4	Discipline and enforcement, including notification requirements

IFA syllabus reference	CF1 syllabus reference	CeFA 1 syllabus reference	
1.11	**11**	**2 U2**	**Understand the effect of the FSA's rules on the control structures of firms and their relationship with the FSA**
1.11.1	11.1	2 U2.1	Approved persons and controlled functions
1.11.2	11.2	2 U2.2	Advertising and financial promotion rules
1.11.3	11.3, 12.14	2 U2.3	Reporting and record keeping
1.11.4	11.4	2 U2.4	Training and competence rules
1.11.5	11.5	2 U2.5	Specific rules for [whole-of-market and] independent financial advisers
1.12	**12**	**2 U3**	**Understand how the FSA's Conduct of Business Rules apply to the process of advising clients**
1.12.1	12.1	2 U3.1	Types of customer
1.12.2	12.2	2 U3.2	Terms of business, client agreements [and client money]
1.5.7	12.3	2 U3.2	Initial disclosure document and fees and commission statement (menu)
1.12.3	12.4	2 U3.3	Scope of advice and the range of advice for advisers
1.12.4	12.5	2 U3.4	Advice and know your customer rules
1.12.5	12.6	2 U3.5	Suitability of advice
1.12.6	12.7	2 U3.6	Execution-only sales
1.12.7	12.8	2 U3.7	Charges and commissions
1.12.8	12.9	2 U3.8	Cooling off and cancellation
1.12.9	12.10	2 U3.9	Product disclosure
1.12.10	12.11	2 U3.10	Proposals for simplified advice on the stakeholder suite of products
1.12.11	12.12	2 U3.11	Regulatory rules for mortgage advice – MCOB
1.12.12	12.13	2 U3.12	Regulatory rules for general insurance advice – ICOB
1.13	**13**	**2 U4**	**Understand how the Anti-Money Laundering rules apply to dealings with private and intermediate customers**
1.13.1	13.1	2 U4.1	Proceeds of Crime Act 2002 [and purpose of Joint Money Laundering Steering Group guidance]
1.13.2	13.2	2 U4.2	Proceeds of crime - definition
1.13.3	13.3	2 U4.3	Money laundering offences [– MLRO, three stages of money laundering, recognising, reporting and preventing suspicious transactions, penalties]
1.13.4	13.4	2 U4.4	Client identification procedures
1.13.5	13.5	2 U4.5	Record keeping requirements
1.13.6	13.6	2 U4.6	Reporting procedures
1.13.7	13.7	2 U4.7	Training requirements
1.13.8	13.8	2 U4.8	Enforcement

IFA syllabus reference	CF1 syllabus reference	CeFA 1 syllabus reference	
1.14	**14**	**2 U5**	**Understand the rules for dealing with complaints and compensation**
1.14.1	14.1	2 U5.1	Firms' internal complaints procedures
1.14.2	14.2	2 U5.2	The Financial Ombudsman Service (FOS)
1.14.3	14.3	2 U5.3	The Financial Services Compensation Scheme (FSCS)
1.15	**15**	**2 U6**	**Understand how the Data Protection Act 1998 affects the provision of financial advice and the conduct of firms generally**
1.15.1	15.1	2 U6.1	Definitions in the Data Protection Act
1.15.2	15.2	2 U6.2	The data protection principles
1.15.3	15.3	2 U6.3	Enforcement of the Data Protection Act
-	16	2 Kn2	**Understand the relevance of other non-tax laws and regulations to firms and to the process of advising clients**
-	16.1	2 Kn2.1	The Office of Fair Trading
-	16.2	2 Kn2.1	The Consumer Credit Act 1974
-	16.3	2 Kn2.2	The Pension Regulator's rules with respect to pension schemes
-	16.4	2 Kn2.5	CAT (Charges, Access, Terms) standards and stakeholder standards
-	16.5	2 Kn2.3	Unfair Contract Terms
-	16.6	2 Kn2.4	EU directives
1.16	-	-	**Demonstrate a knowledge of ethical codes of conduct**
1.16.1	-	-	The background to the SII Code and Principles

Web site links

Organisation	Information included	Website address
Association of British Insurers	Insurance topics	www.abi.org.uk
Association of Investment Trust Companies	Investment trust data	www.aitc.co.uk
BPP Professional Education	Study material and Updates	www.bpp.com/financial advisers
Chartered Insurance Institute®	Cert FP exam information	www.cii.co.uk
Debt Management Office	Details of gilts	www.dmo.gov.uk
Department for Work and Pensions	State benefits	www.dwp.gov.uk
Financial Services Authority (FSA)	Regulatory information	www.fsa.gov.uk
FTSE	FTSE indices	www.ftse.com
HM Revenue & Customs (HMRC) – practitioners' area	Technical tax information	www.hmrc.gov.uk/practitioners
HMRC	Child Trust Funds	www.childtrustfund.gov.uk
Institute of Financial Services	CeFA® exam information	www.ifslearning.com
Investment Management Association	Unit trust and OEIC/ICVC data	www.investmentfunds.org.uk
National Savings and Investments	NS&I products	www.nsandi.com
Office for National Statistics	Demographic, economic and other statistical information	www.statistics.gov.uk
Pension Service (part of DWP)	Information on state pensions and other benefits	www.thepensionservice.gov.uk
Pensions Regulator	Regulation of work-based pensions	www.thepensionsregulator.gov.uk
Securities and Investment Institute	IFA Qualification exam information	www.sii.org.uk
Standard and Poor's	Fund databases and ratings	www.funds-sp.com

Examination formats

Each examining body – the SII, the CII and the *ifs* – uses multiple choice questions for the examination. The examination formats used are described below.

SII's IFA Paper 1

The **duration** of the examination for the *IFA Qualification* Paper 1 is **90 minutes**.

There are **two parts** in the Unit 1 examination.

Part A: Introduction to UK Financial Services (45 minutes) – comprising 37 Multiple Choice Questions:

- All 37 questions testing **comprehension**

Part B: The Ethical and Regulatory Framework (45 minutes) – comprising 37 Multiple Choice Questions:
- 6 questions testing **knowledge**
- 31 questions testing **comprehension**

What is meant by knowledge and comprehension?

These terms indicate **levels of attainment**, defined in terms of the cognitive skills required to achieve learning outcomes. The table below shows successive levels of attainment, the **abilities** needed to reach each level and the **action verbs** that might be used to frame examination questions and tasks.

Level of attainment	Abilities	Action verbs (examples)
Knowledge	Recall (eg, facts, rules, definitions)	List, State, Define, Outline
Comprehension	Interpret, translate ideas, extrapolate	Explain, Describe, Discuss, Interpret, Identify
Application	Apply general principles/rules in new situations	Demonstrate, Apply, Operate, Illustrate, Employ
Analysis	Break down information and make clear the nature of the component parts and their relationship to each other	Distinguish, Investigate, Analyse
Synthesis	Assemble a number of components in order to generate a new statement or plan	Design, Create, Organise, Plan
Evaluation	Judge the value of methods or materials by comparison with external criteria	Judge, Evaluate, Appraise, Assess

BPP)))
PROFESSIONAL EDUCATION

CII's Paper CF1

The **duration** of the examination for CF1 is **two hours**.

The examination consists of **100 Multiple Choice Questions**.

Each question will consist of a problem followed by four options, labelled A, B, C and D, from which you are asked to choose the one correct or best response. One mark is awarded for each correct response. No marks are deducted for incorrect responses.

Pay particular attention to words in the question that are emphasised in **bold** type, for example: **maximum**, **minimum**, **main**, **most**, **normally** and **usually**. Negative wording is emphasised by the use of capital letters, for example **NOT** and **CANNOT**.

Calculators can be used during the examination, but must be silent battery or solar-powered non-programmable models.

The CII states that the nominal **pass mark** for the CF1 exam is **70%**. There is no pre-defined quota of passes, but the actual pass mark may be varied depending on the difficulty of the question paper, to ensure that a consistent standard is applied.

The CF1 examination will be based on the legislative position in England **eight weeks** before the date of the examination.

The CF1 syllabus requires the ability to fully comprehend the subject matter, including the underlying factual knowledge. Each **learning outcome** in the syllabus begins with **'Understand'**, which encompasses two levels of cognitive skill.

- **Knowledge**. Candidates are required to be able to recall factual information. Typically questions may ask 'What', 'When' or 'Who'.

- **Understanding**. Candidates must be able to link pieces of information together in cause and effect relationships. Typically questions may ask 'Why'.

  Questions set on an 'understand' learning outcome can test either knowledge or understanding or both.

ifs CeFA Module 1

The **duration** of the examination for *CeFA* Module 1 *UK Financial Regulation* is **two hours**.

The paper includes a total of **100** separate **Multiple Choice Questions**.

Normally there are:

- 50 questions on Unit 1 *Introduction to Financial Services Environment and Products*, and
- 50 questions on Unit 2 *UK Financial Services and Regulation*

Tackling MCQs

Multiple choice questions (MCQs) each contain a number of possible answers. You have to **choose the one option(s) that best answers the question**. The incorrect options are called distracters.

There is a skill in answering MCQs quickly and correctly. By practising MCQs you can develop this skill, giving you a better chance of passing the exam.

You may wish to follow the approach outlined below, or you may prefer to adapt it to suit your own learning style and needs.

Step 1. **Note down how long** you should allocate to each MCQ. For example, if you have 100 questions to answer in 120 minutes, you have approximately 1.2 minutes on average to answer each question. For a group of 10 questions, you have 12 minutes. You will probably not spend an equal amount of time on each MCQ. You might be able to answer some questions instantly while others will take more time to work out.

Step 2. **Attempt each question**. Read the question thoroughly. A particular question might look familiar to you, but be aware that the detail and/or requirement may be different from any similar question you have come across. So, read the requirement and options carefully, even for questions that seem familiar.

Step 3. Read all the options and see if one matches your own answer. Be careful with numerical questions, as the distracters are designed to match answers that incorporate **common errors**. Check that your calculation is correct. Have you followed the requirement exactly? Have you included every stage of the calculation?

Step 4. You may find that none of the options matches your answer.

- **Re-read the question** to ensure that you understand it and are answering the requirement

- **Eliminate any obviously wrong answers**

- **Consider which of the remaining answers** is the **most likely** to be correct or best and select that option

Step 5. If you are still unsure, **continue to the next question**.

If you are nowhere near working out which option is correct after a couple of minutes, leave the question and come back to it later. Make a note of any questions for which you have submitted answers but you need to return to later.

Step 6. **Revisit questions** you are uncertain about. When you come back to a question after a break, you may find that you are able to answer it correctly straight away. If you are still unsure, have a guess. You are not penalised for incorrect answers, so **do not leave a question unanswered!**

Part A:
Introduction to UK
financial services

Financial services and the economy

1 The function of financial services

1.1 The monetary economy

Money is the main **medium of exchange** in our society. In a **barter economy**, goods and services are exchanged one for another. If someone works to harvest corn, and is given corn in payment for their labour, this is a barter exchange. The use of money as a medium of exchange creates much flexibility in economic transactions. If the harvester is paid in money instead of corn, he may be able to use that money to buy cooking pots and meat. He cannot subsist only on corn.

Most measures of 'money' include balances (eg at banks and building societies) as well as notes and coin. Money functions as a medium of exchange because:

- It is **divisible** into small units (pounds and pence, dollars and cents)
- There are **sufficient quantities of money** to use for transactions
- Money is **generally accepted** by all parties in transactions

The modern **monetary economy** involves a huge variety of types of transactions involving money. Because money is a recognised medium of exchange among people, it is accepted that debt relationships between people, and claims by one person or institution over another, can be expressed in monetary terms.

The **financial services industry** covers various activities within our monetary **economy**. At the national level, we have the economy of the United Kingdom, with its own currency, the pound sterling. The financial services industry also operates within an international framework, resulting from both the multinational nature of many financial services activities and from various international agreements and regulatory influences. As a member of the **European Union (EU),** the United Kingdom is subject to EU legislation.

In this first Chapter, we look at the place of the financial services industry within the economic system, and at the main institutions and markets within the industry. We examine also the roles of the national government and the EU.

1.2 The flow of funds in the economy

The **flow of funds** in an economy describes the movement of funds or money between one group of people or institutions in the economic system and other groups.

If we begin by ignoring the country's imports and exports of goods and services and foreign investments, we can start to build up a picture of the flow of funds by identifying three sectors in the economy.

(a)   The **personal sector** - mainly individuals or households

(b)   The **business sector** (or industrial and commercial sector) - ie companies and other businesses

(c)   The **government sector** - ie central government, local government and public corporations

Within each of these three sectors, there are continual **movements of funds**.

(a)   Individuals will give money or lend money to other individuals.

(b)   Companies will buy goods and services from other companies, and may occasionally lend money direct to other companies.

(c)   Central government will provide funds for local government authorities and loss-making nationalised industries.

As well as movements of funds within each sector, there are flows of funds between different sectors of the economy.

These flows of funds can be shown in a diagram.

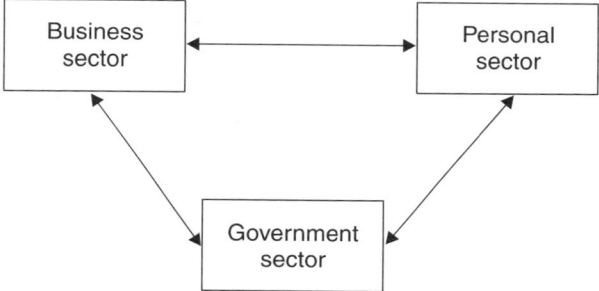

Flow of funds ignoring financial intermediation

But reality is not quite so simple, and our analysis of the flow of funds in the UK should also take account of two other main factors.

(a)   The **overseas sector** comprises businesses, individuals and governments in other countries. The UK economy is influenced by trade with the foreign sector and flows of capital both from and to it.

(b)   **Financial intermediaries** – see below

1.3 Financial intermediation

An intermediary is a go-between, and a financial intermediary is an institution which **links lenders with borrowers**, by obtaining deposits from lenders and then re-lending them to borrowers. Such institutions can, for example, provide a link between savers and investors.

The role of **financial intermediaries** such as banks and building societies in an economy is to provide means by which funds can be transferred from **surplus units** (for example, someone with savings to invest in the economy to **deficit units** (for example, someone who wants to borrow money to buy a house. Financial intermediaries develop the facilities and **financial instruments** which make lending and borrowing possible.

If no financial intermediation takes place, lending and borrowing will be direct.

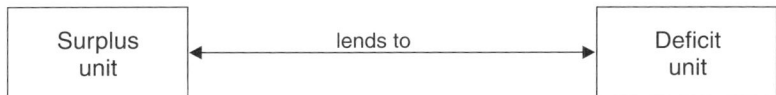

If financial intermediation does take place, the intermediary provides a service to both the surplus unit and the deficit unit.

For example, a person might deposit savings with a bank, and the bank might use its collective deposits of savings to provide a loan to a company.

Financial intermediaries might also lend abroad or borrow from abroad, and a fuller version of a diagram depicting the flow of funds is thus as follows.

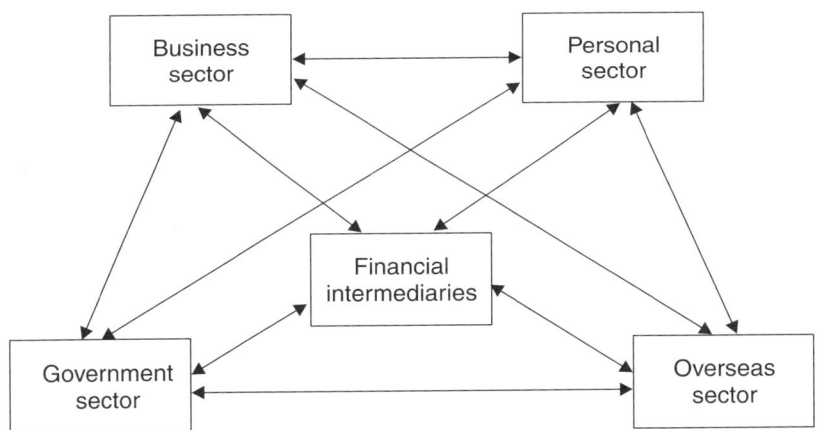

Flow of funds in an open economy, showing the role of financial intermediation

A **financial intermediary** is a party bringing together providers and users of finance, either as a broker facilitating a transaction between two other parties, or in their own right, as principal.

UK financial intermediaries include the following sectors of the financial services industry:

(a)   Banks
(b)   Building societies
(c)   Insurance companies, pension funds, unit trust companies and investment trust companies
(d)   The Government's National Savings & Investments (NS&I)

In spite of competition from building societies, insurance companies and other financial institutions, banks arguably remain the major financial intermediaries in the UK.

The clearing banks are the biggest operators in the retail banking market, although competition from the building societies has been growing in the UK.

There is greater competition between different banks (overseas banks and the clearing banks especially) for business in the wholesale lending market.

Financial intermediaries can link lenders with borrowers, by obtaining deposits from lenders and then re-lending them to borrowers. But not all intermediation takes place between savers and investors. Some institutions act mainly as intermediaries between other institutions. Almost all place part of their funds with other institutions, and a number (including finance houses, leasing companies and factoring companies) obtain most of their funds by borrowing from other institutions.

1.4 Benefits of financial intermediation

Financial intermediaries perform the following functions.

(a)   They provide obvious and **convenient** ways in which a **lender can save money** to spend in the future. Instead of having to find a suitable borrower for their money, lenders can deposit money. Financial intermediaries also provide a ready **source of funds for borrowers**.

(b)   They can aggregate or 'package' the amounts lent by savers and lend on to borrowers in different amounts (a process called **aggregation**). By aggregating the deposits of hundreds of small savers, a bank or building society is able to package up the amounts and lend on to several borrowers in the form of larger mortgages.

(c)   Financial intermediaries provide for **maturity transformation**; ie they bridge the gap between the wish of most lenders for liquidity and the desire of most borrowers for loans over longer periods. For example, while many depositors in a building society may want instant access to their funds, the building society can lend these funds to mortgage borrowers over much longer periods, by ensuring that it attracts sufficient funds from depositors over this longer term.

By pooling the funds of large numbers of people, some financial institutions are able to give small investors access to professionally managed **diversified portfolios** covering a varied range of different securities through collective investment products such as unit trusts and investment trusts.

Risk for individuals is reduced by **pooling**. Since financial intermediaries lend to a large number of individuals and organisations, losses suffered through default by borrowers or capital losses are pooled and borne as costs by the intermediary. Such losses are shared among lenders in general.

1.5 Management of risk

For most people, **risk** means the chance that something will go wrong. Taking a risk means doing something that could turn out to be damaging, or could result in a loss.

Individuals can face various risks, such as a risk of physical injury, ill health or death, a risk of damage to property or theft of property, a risk that an investment will lose money, a risk that their bank or other financial institution may fail, and so on.

Insurance, of various kinds, offers ways of reducing various risks, by transferring the risk to an insurer who bears risks for many others in exchange for premiums collected from each insured party.

Various financial instruments made available through the financial services industry allow individuals to expose themselves to **investment risks** that they may wish to run, in the hope of a positive return on their investment.

Businesses, likewise, face various risks. A business may lose customers or key staff, its products may fail, changes in the law may curtail its activities, and so on. A company is owned by its members – that is, its **shareholders**. When a company is exposed to risks, this will affect the value of the shareholders' stake in the company. However, there are other stakeholders in a company who may stand to lose from the risks that a company is exposed to: these other **stakeholder groups** that could be affected include providers of debt finance (often, banks), employees and directors. As with individuals, insurance offers a way in which businesses can manage various risks.

Financial products offer ways in which individuals and businesses can **manage** risk.

It is not the aim of **risk management** to eliminate risks entirely. The aims of risk management can be formulated as follows.

- Make an assessment of risk when taking decisions, and keep investment risk within acceptable limits

- Avoid unnecessary risks and prevent unnecessary losses

- Reduce the frequency of adverse outcomes when the risk probability is high, and reduce the impact of adverse outcomes where the severity of the risk is high

Risk cannot be totally eliminated, for either individuals or businesses. The Financial Services Authority (FSA), as regulator of the financial services industry, asserts that it sees it as both **impossible and undesirable to remove all risk** and failure from the financial system.

Exercise: Risk

Set out some reasons why it could be undesirable to remove all risk from the financial system.

Solution

If there was no risk in the financial system, companies would not be able to raise finance through the system for risky ventures such as developing new medicines or investing in innovative technologies.

People may wish to take risks with money that they can afford to lose, to give the possible prospect of high returns if an investment turns out well.

Many of the things that people would like to do, such as buy their own home, are subject to market forces that inevitably involve risks: house prices might fall, so that someone with a mortgage might find that the house comes to be worth less than the mortgage loan on the house.

Removing all risk from transactions could mean that excessive resources are spent on bureaucracy to regulate institutions and markets. Alternatively, a 'risk-free' financial system might involve the State effectively 'underwriting' all the risks that an individual might face: this suggests an economic system with a very high level of State control, which many would consider to be undesirable.

2 Markets and institutions

2.1 Capital markets and money markets

The capital markets and the money markets are types of market for dealing in capital.

(a) **Capital markets** are financial markets for raising and investing largely **long-term** capital.
(b) **Money markets** are financial markets for lending and borrowing largely **short-term** capital.

2.2 Long-term and short-term capital

What do we mean by **long-term** and **short-term** capital?

- By **short-term capital**, we mean capital that is lent or borrowed for a period which might range from as short as overnight up to about one year, and sometimes longer.

- By **long-term capital**, we mean capital invested or lent and borrowed for a period of about five years or more, but sometimes shorter.

- There is a **grey area** between long-term and short-term capital, which is lending and borrowing for a period from about 1-2 years up to about 5 years, which is not surprisingly referred to as **medium-term** capital.

2.3 The Stock Exchange

The **London Stock Exchange** (LSE) is an organised **capital market** which plays an important role in the functioning of the UK economy. The LSE provides the main way for larger companies to raise funds through the issue of **shares** (equity). It makes it easier for large firms and the government to raise long-term capital, by providing a market place for businesses seeking capital and investors to come together.

The **Alternative Investment Market** (AIM), which opened in 1995, is a market where smaller companies which cannot meet the more stringent requirements needed to obtain a full listing on the Stock Exchange can raise new capital by issuing shares. It is cheaper for smaller company to be on the AIM than to meet the requirements for a full listing. Like the Stock Exchange main market, the AIM is also a market in which investors can trade in shares already issued. The AIM is regulated by the Stock Exchange.

2.4 Banks

Banks can be approached directly by individuals (**retail** business) and businesses for medium-term and long-term loans as well as short-term loans or overdrafts.

The major clearing banks, many investment banks and foreign banks operating in the UK are often willing to lend medium-term capital, especially to well established businesses.

2.5 The gilt-edged market

The **gilt-edged market** is a further major capital market in the UK. The government borrows over the medium and longer term by issuing government stocks (called 'gilt-edged stock' or 'gilts'). Trade in second hand gilts will continue until the debt eventually matures and the government redeems the stock.

The **primary** gilts market is the market for the sale of new gilt issues. There is an active **secondary** market in second-hand gilts with existing holders selling their holdings of gilts to other investors in the gilts market.

2.6 Providers of capital

Providers of capital include **private individuals** in the retail sector. This includes those who buy stocks and shares on the Stock Exchange, and those who deposit money with banks, building societies and National Savings & Investments (NS&I). NS&I is a government institution set up to borrow on behalf of the government, mainly from the non-bank private sector of the economy.

There are also important groups of **institutional investors** which specialise in providing capital and act as financial intermediaries between suppliers and demanders of funds. Many financial services organisations now have diversified operations covering a range of the following activities.

(a) **Pension funds**. Pension funds invest the pension contributions of individuals who subscribe to a pension fund, and of organisations with a company pension fund.

(b) **Insurance**. Insurance companies invest premiums paid on insurance policies by policy holders. Life assurance policies, including life-assurance based savings policies, account for substantial assets, which are invested in equities, bonds, property and other assets.

(c) **Investment trusts**. The business of investment trust companies is investing in the stocks and shares of other companies and the government. In other words, they trade in investments.

(d)   **Unit trusts and Open Ended Investment Companies (OEICs)**. Unit trusts and OEICs are similar to investment trusts, in the sense that they invest in stocks and shares of other companies. A unit trust comprises a 'portfolio' - ie a holding of stocks or shares in a range of companies or gilts, perhaps with all the shares or stocks having a special characteristic, such as all shares in property companies or all shares in mining companies. The trust will then create a large number of small units of low nominal value, with each unit representing a stake in the total portfolio. These units are then sold to individual investors and investors will benefit from the income and capital gain on their units - ie their proportion of the portfolio.

(e)   **Venture capital**. Venture capital providers are organisations that specialise in raising funds for new business ventures, such as 'management buy-outs' (ie purchases of firms by their management staff). These organisations are therefore providing capital for fairly risky ventures.

2.7 Overview of capital markets

The role of financial intermediaries in capital markets is illustrated in the diagram below.

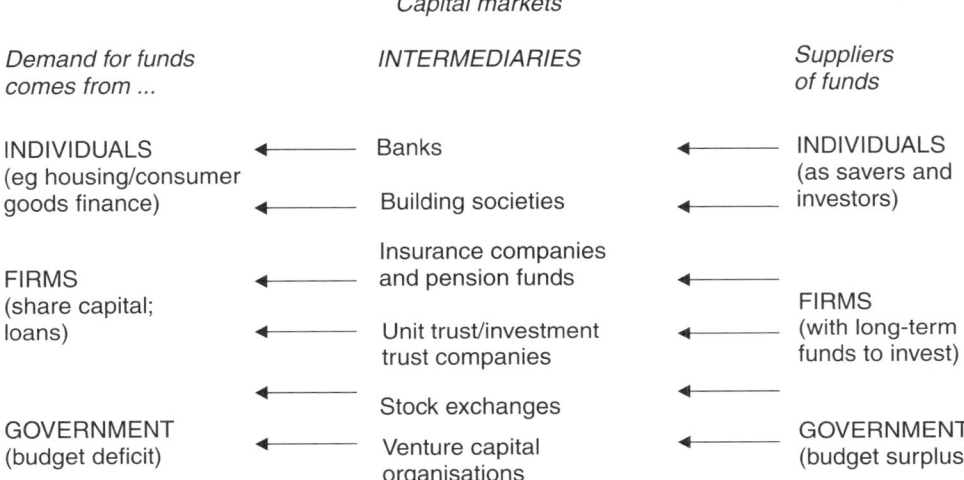

2.8 Competition

Competition for business between financial institutions for business is fiercer than it has ever been. Building societies have emerged as competitors to the banks, and foreign banks have competed successfully in the UK with the big clearing banks. Banks have changed too, with some shift towards more fee-based activities (such as selling advice and selling insurance products for commission) and away from the traditional transaction-based activities (holding deposits, making loans).

2.9 The money markets

The UK **money markets** are operated by the banks and other financial institutions. Although the money markets largely involve **wholesale borrowing and lending** by banks, some large companies and the government are also involved in money market operations. The money markets are essentially shorter term debt markets, with loans being made for a specified period at a specified rate of interest.

The money markets operate both as a **primary market**, in which new financial claims are issued and as a **secondary market**, where previously issued financial claims are traded.

Amounts dealt in are relatively large, generally being above £50,000 and often in millions of pounds. Loans are transacted on extremely 'fine' terms – ie with small margins between lending and borrowing rates - reflecting the

economies of scale involved. The emphasis is on liquidity: the efficiency of the money markets can make the financial claims dealt in virtually the equivalent of cash.

2.10 The banks and the banking system

There are different types of **banks** which operate within a banking system, and you will probably have come across a number of terms which describe them. **Commercial banks** make commercial banking transactions with customers. They are distinct from the country's **central bank**.

- **Clearing banks** are those that operate the clearing system for settling payments (eg payments by cheque by bank customers).

- The term **retail banks** is used to describe the traditional High Street banks. The term **wholesale banks** refers to banks which specialise in lending in large amounts to major customers. The clearing banks are involved in both retail and wholesale banking but are commonly regarded as the main retail banks.

- **Investment banks** (which used to be referred to as **merchant banks**) offer services, often of a specialised nature, to corporate customers.

These categories are not mutually exclusive: a single bank may be a retail clearing bank, with wholesale and investment banking operations.

2.11 Building societies

The **building societies** of the UK are **mutual** organisations whose main assets are mortgages of their members. Among their liabilities are the balances of the investor members who hold savings accounts with the society. The **Building Societies Act 1986** requires that at least **50%** of a building society's funds must be raised from share accounts held by individual members.

The distinction between building societies and banks has become increasingly blurred, as the societies have taken to providing a range of services formerly the province mainly of banks, and banks have themselves made inroads into the housing mortgage market. Some building societies now offer cheque book accounts, cash cards and many other facilities that compete directly with the banks.

The building society sector has shrunk in size over the last 20 years as a number of the major societies have either converted to public limited companies and therefore become banks or have been taken over by banks or other financial institutions.

2.12 The central bank

A **central bank** is a bank which acts on behalf of the government. The central bank for the UK is the **Bank of England**. The Bank of England is a nationalised corporation.

Functions of the Bank of England

(a)   It acts as **banker to the central government** and holds the 'public deposits'. Public deposits include the National Loans Fund, the Consolidated Fund and the account of the Paymaster General, which in turn includes the Exchange Equalisation Account.

(b)   It is the **central note-issuing authority** in the UK - it is responsible for issuing bank notes in England.

(c)   It is the **manager of the National Debt** - ie it deals with long-term and short-term borrowing by the central government and the repayment of central government debt.

(d)   It is the manager of the Exchange Equalisation Account (ie the UK's **foreign currency reserves**).

(e)   It acts as adviser to the government on **monetary policy**.

(f)   The Bank's **Monetary Policy Committee (MPC)** acts as agent for the government in carrying out its monetary policies. Since May 1997, the MPC has had operational responsibility for **setting short-term interest rates** at the level it considers appropriate in order to meet the government's inflation target.

(g)   It acts as a **lender to the banking system**. When the banking system is short of money, the Bank of England will provide the money the banks need - at a suitable rate of interest.

Supervision of the **banking system** is the responsibility of the Financial Services Authority (FSA).

2.13 The central bank as lender of last resort

In the UK, the **short-term money market** provides a link between the banking system and the government (Bank of England) whereby the Bank of England lends money to the banking system, when banks which need cash cannot get it from anywhere else.

(a)   The Bank will supply cash to the banking system on days when the banks have a cash shortage. It does this by buying eligible bills and other short-term financial investments from approved financial institutions in exchange for cash.

(b)   The Bank will remove excess cash from the banking system on days when the banks have a cash surplus. It does this by selling bills to institutions, so that the short-term money markets obtain interest-bearing bills in place of the cash that they do not want.

The process whereby this is done currently is known as **open market operations** by the Bank. This simply describes the buying and selling of short-term assets between the Bank and the short-term money market.

3 Financial services in the UK

3.1 The UK's position in the world

The financial services industry is a key sector of the UK economy. The UK financial services industry employs over 1 million people and net overseas earnings from the industry were £31.2 billion in 2000 (5.1% of national output or GDP).

With a long history going back to the time of merchant adventurers who sought finance for world-wide overseas trading, the 'Square Mile' of the **City of London** is the centre for the UK financial services industry. The City is the largest centre for many international financial markets, such as the currency markets. The UK has the world's largest share in the metals market (95%), Eurobond trade (70%), the foreign equity market (58%), derivatives markets (36%) and insurance (22%).

3.2 Banking

While there are over 300 **banking** groups and building societies operating in the UK, the ten largest UK-owned banking groups hold some 70% of UK households' deposits. Building societies hold over 20% of household deposits.

The UK has the greatest concentration of foreign banks in the world. There were 481 in 2000, while the next nearest was the USA with 287. In 2000, London accounted for 19.1% of global cross-border bank lending, more than any other financial centre. The total assets of the UK banking system were £3,441 billion (August 2001) of which 55% belonged to foreign banks. The assets of UK owned banks, total £1,336 billion are dominated by around a dozen retail banks, with national branch networks serving domestic, personal and corporate customers.

The banks and building societies now form a significant part of the market for financial services. A banking institution could maintain access to a full range of products and product providers by setting up an independent arm. However, few have maintained a wholly independent stance. Most have either formed tied links to life insurance companies ('life offices') or have acquired or set up their own insurance companies which mainly or wholly offer products to clients introduced through the bank or building society.

3.3 Insurance

UK **life insurance companies** sell various products within the UK retail market, including collective investment schemes such as unit trusts, OEICs and investment trusts, pension products and individual life insurance. The development of life assurance provision by **banks** is known as **bancassurance** or **all finanz**. The Association of British Insurers (ABI) defines **bancassurers** as 'insurance companies that are subsidiaries of banks and building societies and whose primary market is the customer base of the bank or building society'.

The UK has a major **general insurance** and **reinsurance** market ranging from personal motor insurance to insurance for space satellites. Reinsurance is a process by which a company – for example, a life office writing new business – can sell or pass on the risks on its policies to a third party **reinsurer**.

The UK insurance business generated premium income in the UK insurance market was almost £174 billion in 2000. This was the third largest in the world, exceeded only by the US and Japan. The London market – centred on **Lloyds** of London – is the global market leader in aviation and marine insurance, with market shares of 31% and 19% respectively.

Lloyds acts as a major reinsurer for life assurance. Lloyds is a long-established market in which **underwriting syndicates** operate independently. Syndicates are made up of companies and individuals (**Lloyds 'names'**) who provide capital and assume the risk of liabilities they insure or reinsure. Syndicates are run by **managing agents** who appoint **underwriters** to write (assess) risks on behalf of the syndicate. Although the Financial Services Authority (FSA) has overall regulatory responsibility for Lloyds, much of the regulatory work is delegated to the Council of Lloyds.

3.4 Pensions

With a rapidly ageing population, there is a **pensions crisis** worldwide. Many countries are passing the burden for pensions provision from the state sector to the private sector.

Domestically, the UK pensions market is of great importance, and a higher proportion of pension payments are provided by the private sector in the UK than in nearly any other country.

3.5 Fund and asset management

Collective funds like unit trusts and investment trusts need to be managed. In the **fund management** sector, the value of assets under management increased by 40% between 1995 and the end of 1998 to £2.5 billion. 23% on these funds were managed on behalf of overseas clients. The UK fund management sector offers liquid markets, with the opportunity to trade in large blocks of shares, and a relatively liberalised operating environment combined with protection against abuse. More funds are invested in the London than the ten top European centres combined. Edinburgh is the UK's second major fund management centre and is the sixth largest in Europe.

3.6 Securities and currency markets

As well as having a substantial domestic market in **equities** (company shares) and **bonds** (interest-bearing securities), the UK is a major international centre for trading in the Euromarket, which is the market for debt denominated in other currencies – not just the euro. Eurobonds account for the majority of all bonds issued and the UK issues 60% of them and has a 70% share of the secondary market.

More **foreign companies** are traded on the London Stock Exchange than on any other exchange (475 such companies were listed at the end of 2000). Turnover in these companies' shares in London represented 48% of global turnover in foreign equities in 2000.

The UK has 31.1% of the global market in **currency trading**, making London the leading world centre for foreign exchange ('forex') trading.

4 The role of the UK Government

4.1 Introduction

There are various ways in which Government actions impinge on people's lives and on the activities of businesses. Legislation introduced by Parliament often gives authority for Government departments to introduce secondary legislation in the form of additional regulations. Government agencies and local authorities affect our lives in many aspects, whether for example through taxation or in the services they provide to us.

The extent to which the Government influences what we do reflects the type of economic system we have. The economic system of the UK and of the wider European Union to which the UK belongs can be described as a **mixed economy.** A mixed economy involves some degree of State intervention in economic activity, while mostly markets are allowed to operate as freely as possible so long as intervention is not needed in the public interest. This type of economy stands between the two extremes of a *laissez-faire* **free market economy** in which market forces are allowed to reign, with minimal State intervention, and of a centrally planned **command economy**, such as that of the former Soviet Union and other Communist-ruled states, in which the government controls most industries and regulates many prices and wages, possibly with a rationing system to distribute scarce goods and services.

There are various laws or pieces of legislation that affect the provision of financial services in the UK, and the regulation of the industry under the Financial Services Authority (FSA) is of key importance. In this section, we also outline the Government's role in taxation, economic policy-making and the promotion of welfare and the provision of benefits.

4.2 Regulation of the financial service industry

Consumer protection in the financial services industry and other consumer markets became an increasingly important aspect of UK Governments' policy from the 1970s onwards. The Financial Services Act 1986 (FSA 1986) was brought in to replace the system of **self-regulation** which had previously prevailed in the UK financial sector.

The FSA 1986 brought a new system of **'self-regulation within a statutory framework'**, with financial services firms authorised by Self-Regulatory Organisations (SROs).

When the Labour Party gained power in 1997, it wanted to make changes to the regulation of financial services. A series of **financial scandals**, including those involving the Maxwell Group, Barings Bank, BCCI and pensions mis-selling, had added weight to the political impetus for change, leading to the establishment of the Financial Services Authority.

4.3 The Financial Services Authority

The **Financial Services Authority** (**FSA**) was set up as the single statutory regulator of the financial services industry, under the **Financial Services and Markets Act 2000 (FSMA 2000)**. This Act brought together the regulation of investment, insurance and banking. Giving **financial advice on investments** became a regulated activity under the new statutory regime from 1 December 2001 (a date known as 'N2').

The FSA is not a government agency, but it carries out the work of statutory regulation. It is a private company limited by guarantee, with **HM Treasury** (a Government department) as the guarantor. The FSA is financed by compulsory levies paid by financial services firms. The Board of the FSA is appointed by the Treasury. The **Chancellor of the Exchequer** is ultimately responsible for the system of regulation for the financial services industry.

4.4 Voluntary codes and statutory regulation

In some areas, financial services providers are subject to **voluntary codes**, which an industry sector develops itself, rather than rules imposed through the law (statutory rules). The area of banking can be taken as an example. The FSA regulates banks' status as authorised deposit-taking institutions and supervises the banks' liquidity position and capital adequacy. (This supervisory role used to be undertaken by the Bank of England.) However, banks and building societies follow a voluntary code (the **Banking Code**) in their relations with personal customers in the UK.

Clearly, if the Government wishes, it can extend statutory regulation to areas previously governed by voluntary codes. For example, **mortgage advice and selling**, previously governed by the voluntary Mortgage Code, came under FSA regulation from 31 October 2004. **General insurance** regulation followed on 14 January 2005.

4.5 Fiscal policy

A government's **fiscal policy** concerns its plans for **spending, taxation and borrowing**.

These aspects of fiscal policy reflect the three elements in public finance

(a)   **Expenditure**. The government, at a national and local level, spends money to provide goods and services, such as a health service, public education, a police force, roads, public buildings and so on, and to pay its administrative work force. It may also, perhaps, provide finance to encourage investment by private industry, for example by means of grants.

(b)   **Income**. Expenditure must be financed, and the government must have income. Most government income comes from taxation, bit some income is obtained from direct charges to users of government services such as National Health Service charges.

(c)   **Borrowing**. To the extent that a government's expenditure exceeds its income, it must borrow to make up the difference. The amount that the government must borrow each year is known as the **Public Sector Net Cash Requirement (PSNCR)** in the UK. (This used to be referred to as the Public Sector Borrowing Requirement (PSBR).)

Government **spending is an injection** into the economy, adding to the level of overall demand for goods and services, whereas **taxes are a withdrawal**.

A government's **'fiscal stance'** may be **neutral, expansionary** or **contractionary**, according to its overall effect on national income.

(a)   **Spending more money** and financing this expenditure by borrowing would indicate an expansionary fiscal stance. Expenditure in the economy will increase and so national income will rise, either in real terms, or partly in terms of price levels only: the increase in national income might be real, or simply inflationary.

(b)   **Collecting more in taxes** without increasing spending would indicate a contractionary fiscal stance. A government might deliberately raise taxation to take inflationary pressures out of the economy

The impact of changes in fiscal policy is not always certain, and fiscal policy to pursue one aim (eg lower inflation) might for a while create barriers to the pursuit of other aims (eg employment).

Government planners need to consider how fiscal policy can affect savers, investors and companies.

(a)   The tax regime as it affects different savings instruments will affect **investors'** decisions.

(b)　**Companies** will be affected by tax rules on dividends and profits, and they may take these rules into account when deciding on dividend policy or on whether to raise finance through **debt** (loans) or **equities** (by issuing shares).

The formal planning of fiscal policy usually follows an annual cycle. In the UK, the most important statement is **the Budget**, which takes place in the Spring of each year. The Chancellor of the Exchequer also delivers a Pre-Budget Report each autumn. The Pre-Budget Report formally makes available for scrutiny the government's overall spending plans.

4.6 Monetary policy

Monetary policy is the area of government economic policy making that is concerned with changes in the **amount of money** in circulation – the **money supply** – and with changes in the **price of money – interest rates**. These variables are linked with **inflation** in prices generally, and also with **exchange rates** – the price of the domestic currency in terms of other currencies.

4.7 Setting interest rates

Since 1997, the most important aspect of monetary policy in the UK has been the influence over interest rates exerted by the **Bank of England**, the **central bank** of the UK. The **Monetary Policy Committee (MPC)** of the Bank of England was charged with the responsibility of setting interest rates with the aim of meeting the government's current inflation target of 2% based on the **Consumer Prices Index (CPI)**, also known as the Harmonised Index of Consumer Prices (HCIP).

The **UK inflation objective** was originally formalised in the 1998 Bank of England Act. That Act states that the Bank of England is expected 'to maintain price stability, and, subject to that, to support the economic policy of HM Government including its objectives for growth and employment" (Bank of England Act 1998).

The MPC decides the short-term **benchmark 'repo' rate** at which the Bank of England deals in the money markets. This will tend to be followed by financial institutions generally in setting interest rates for different financial instruments. However, a government does not have an unlimited ability to have interest rates set how it wishes. It must take into account what rates the overall market will bear, so that the benchmark rate it chooses can be maintained. The Bank must be careful about the signals it gives to the markets, since the effect of expectations can be significant.

The monthly minutes of the MPC are published. This arrangement is intended to remove the possibility of direct political influence over the interest rate decision.

The Bank of England **reducing** interest rates is an **easing** of monetary policy.

(a)　Loans will be cheaper, and so consumers may increase levels of debt and spend more. Demand will tend to rise and companies may have improved levels of sales. Companies will find it cheaper to borrow: their lower interest costs will boost bottom-line profits.

(b)　Mortgage loans will be cheaper and so there will be upward pressure on property prices.

(c)　Values of other assets will also tend to rise. Investors will be willing to pay higher prices for gilts (government stock) because they do not require such a high yield from them as before the interest rate reduction.

(d)　Interest rates on cash deposits will fall. Those who are dependant on income from cash deposits will be worse off than before.

The Bank of England **increasing** interest rates is a **tightening** of monetary policy.

(a)　Loans will cost more, and demand from consumers, especially for less essential 'cyclical' goods and services, may fall. Companies will find it more expensive to borrow money and this could eat into profits, on top of any effect from reducing demand.

(b)   Mortgage loans will cost more and so there will be a dampening effect on property prices.

(c)   Asset prices generally will tend to fall. Investors will require a higher return than before and so they will pay less for fixed interest stocks such as gilts.

(d)   Interest rates on cash deposits will rise, and those reliant on cash deposits for income will be better off.

4.8 Exchange rate policy

The **exchange rate** of the national currency (pounds sterling) against other major currencies (such as the US dollar, the euro and the Japanese yen) is another possible focus of economic policy.

The Government could try to influence exchange rates by buying or selling currencies through its central bank reserves. However, Government currency reserves are now relatively small and so such a policy might have to be limited in scope.

Another way the Government might wish to influence exchange rates is through changes in **interest rates**: if UK interest rates are raised, this makes sterling a relatively more attractive currency to hold and so the change should exert upward pressure on the value of sterling. As we have seen, interest rate policy is now determined by the MPC. Interest rate policy is decided in the light of various matters apart from exchange rates, including the inflation rate and the level of house prices.

If the UK joined the **single European currency**, the **euro**, interest rates would effectively be determined at the European level, by the European Central Bank, instead of at the national level as now. It would not be possible for interest rates in different eurozone countries to be much out of line at any one time, since differences would encourage money flows to seek the higher rates available in a particular country, and borrowers would seek the best rates available. The forces of supply and demand would lead to an approximate equalisation of rates.

At the time of writing (March 2006), the Government has no plan to initiate a new assessment on whether the UK should join the euro.

4.9 Welfare and State benefits

Maximising the **welfare** of its citizens is, on the face of it, a good objective for a Government to have. But how is this to be achieved? Is it desirable to have policies which attempt to equalise welfare levels among the population, or should market forces be allowed to operate freely even if this results in a relatively unequal distribution of wealth between people?

We have outlined the **mixed economy model** of countries like the UK. In such a system, should the State provide a '**safety net**' to protect those who are least advantaged? If so, how can the Government provide **benefits** in such a way that people's incentive to work or to save is not removed by the benefit system of benefits?

The UK underwent great change with the introduction of the so-called **Welfare State** after World War II. Health care for all was provided through the National Health Service. Benefits have been provided for the jobless, now called **Jobseekers Allowance**.

Child benefit is not subject to a means test: that is, it is paid irrespective of the recipient's income or wealth. Other benefits include **incapacity benefit** and **disability benefits**.

Income Support exists as a top-up of the income of those under 60 whose income from all sources is below a minimum threshold level set by Parliament. **Working tax credit** and **child tax credit** are also available. We cover State benefits in more detail later in this Study Text.

A basic **State pension** is paid to those who have paid sufficient National Insurance contributions and is supplemented by **pension credit** for those with limited means.

The **State Second Pension (S2P)** is aimed at providing improved pensions, particularly for the lower paid, compared with the **State Earnings Related Pensions Scheme (SERPS)** which S2P has replaced. Employees can opt out or '**contract out**' of S2P through low-charging stakeholder pensions which the bulk of employers are required to make available to their workforce. From 2006, the S2P benefit will become a flat rate benefit, to continue to encourage contracting-out. Note that **self-employed** individuals do not accrue S2P benefits.

In spite of the Government's wish for people to make their own retirement provision and not to rely wholly on State provision, there are still many who have not made any private pension arrangement.

Financial advisers need to be aware of the availability of State benefits as part of the overall financial circumstances of clients, and a later Chapter in this Study Text covers many of the types of benefit available.

5 The European Union

5.1 Introduction

The **European Union** (**EU**), formerly called the EEC or the European Community (EC) is one of several international economic associations. Its immediate aim is the integration of the economies of the member states. A more long-term aim is political integration. The association dates back to 1957 (the Treaty of Rome) and the EU now has 25 members including the UK, following the admission of ten new countries in 2004.

5.2 UK sovereignty and EU membership

UK Statute law is made by Parliament (or in exercise of law-making powers delegated by Parliament). Until the United Kingdom entered the European Community in 1973, the UK Parliament was completely **sovereign**.

In recent years however, UK membership of the EU has restricted the previously unfettered power of Parliament. There is an **obligation**, imposed by the Treaty of Rome on which the EU is founded, to bring UK law into line with the Treaty itself and with EU directives. Regulations, having the force of law in every member state, may be made under provisions of the Treaty of Rome.

5.3 The Single European Market

Under the Single European Act 1986, the EC heads of government committed themselves to the progressive setting up of a **Single European Market**. The Act defines a single market as 'an area without internal frontiers in which the free movement of goods, persons, services and capital is ensured in accordance with the provisions of this Treaty'. The process of establishing the single market is ongoing. Some aspects of change, such as the envisaged harmonisation of tax rates between member countries, have moved only slowly.

5.4 EU law

EU legislation takes the following three forms.

- **Regulations** have the force of law in every EU state without need of national legislation. Their objective is to obtain uniformity of law throughout the EU. They are formulated by the Commission but must be authorised by the Council of Ministers.

- **Directives** are issued to the governments of the EU member states requiring them within a specified period (usually two years) to alter the national laws of the state so that they conform to the directive. Until a directive is given effect by a UK statute it does not usually affect legal rights and obligations of individuals.

- **Decisions** of an administrative nature are made by the European Commission in Brussels. A decision may be addressed to a state, person or a company and is immediately binding, but only on the recipient.

The Council and the Commission may also make recommendations and deliver opinions, although these are only persuasive in authority.

Key chapter points

- **In this chapter, we have looked at the place of the UK financial services industry in the national economy, and at wider influences on the industry exerted by government.**

- **Financial intermediaries such as banks and building societies take deposits from savers and re-lend to borrowers. Financial intermediation brings benefits from aggregation and maturity transformation.**

- **Financial services products can help people manage risk, for example by pooling risks (insurance) and by offering access to diversified portfolios of assets at relatively low cost.**

- **Capital markets, such as the Stock Exchange, are markets for long-term capital. Money markets are shorter term debt markets in which banks and other financial institutions deal mainly with each other, on a wholesale basis.**

- **The UK financial services industry employs over 1 million people in the UK and accounts for around 5% of national output. Key areas are banking, life insurance, general insurance, pensions, fund and asset management, currency markets and securities markets.**

- **The UK Government has established the Financial Services Authority (FSA) as the overall regulator of the financial services industry.**

- **European Union legislation is increasingly important, and takes precedence over UK law.**

Chapter Quiz

1   Identify the three main sectors of the domestic economy... (see para 1.2)

2   Outline the benefits of financial intermediation. ....(1.4)

3   Distinguish between capital markets and money markets. ....(2.1)

4   State four functions of the Bank of England. .... (2.12)

5   Under what Act of Parliament is the Financial Services Authority established? ....(4.3)

6   What is fiscal policy? ....(4.5)

7   Describe the mechanism whereby short-term UK interest rates are set in line with Government policy. ....(4.7)

8   What are the three types of EU legislation? ....(5.4)

Asset classes and direct investment

1 Financial asset classes

1.1 Main asset classes

The main **classes of financial asset** can be set out most simply as:

- **Cash**
- **Bonds**
- **Equities**
- **Property**

Cash generally refers to cash deposit accounts which earn interest, and in which the capital invested is normally preserved.

Government securities ('**gilts**' in the UK) and **corporate bonds** comprise various different kinds of security on which fixed or inflation-linked interest may be paid. The value of the capital invested may rise or fall in value, as the price of the security fluctuates. Collectively, these are called **bonds**. Some building societies and other institutions give the name 'bond' to a different type of product: for example, a fixed rate deposit over a term of one or two years, for which there is no fluctuation in capital value. The two uses of the word should not be confused.

Equities are the ordinary shares of private companies.

Property includes **residential** property – houses and apartments/flats – and **commercial** property – retail shops and stores, office buildings and industrial factories and warehouses.

1.2 Exposure to asset classes

An investor will be affected by changing fortunes of asset classes through whatever **exposure** the investor has to the different classes of asset. This 'exposure' could be **direct** or **indirect**. For example, exposure to equities as an asset class could be through direct share ownership by the investor, or through a collective investment vehicle such as a unit trust, an OEIC or an investment trust. Exposure to bonds could be through owning units in a bond fund rather than through owning the bonds themselves. Likewise, there are various 'indirect' ways of being exposed to property as an asset class, rather than being the direct owner of the property.

Financial institutions may adjust their exposure to different asset classes at times, and the effects will flow through to investors and customers, depending on the financial products they have bought. For example, at the end of 2002, life insurers' holdings of equities accounted for about 30% of their total assets, compared with 49% at the end of 2000. The life insurers had reduced their exposure to equities significantly. Falls or rises in the general level of equity (share) prices would therefore, by 2002, have had less effect on the value of the insurers' assets (including their 'with-profits' policyholders' funds) than two years previously.

In this Chapter, we are concerned with **direct investment** in the four main asset classes. In the following Chapter, we explain some **indirect** ways for an investor to become exposed to the markets in these different types of asset.

1.3 Asset classes in a portfolio

In investment terms, a **portfolio** is a set of investments collected together for a specific purpose. The asset classes in a portfolio should suit the purpose of the portfolio.

Before constructing an investment portfolio, an adviser will already have undertaken a considerable amount of **fact-finding** work. He will have talked to the client, and above all, listened to the client's needs. He should understand the client's attitude to risk and long-term financial ambitions. The information collected enables the adviser to construct a portfolio that will fit the particular client's needs.

2 Direct investment: cash deposits

2.1 Reasons for holding cash deposits

The most tangible forms of money are banknotes and coins. Keeping money 'under the mattress' (or in a secure safe) as notes and coin is one option for someone with money saved. However, inflation will erode the purchasing power of the money, and no interest will be earned. There would be a risk of loss or theft. An alternative is to deposit the money with a sound financial institution.

Apart from earning **interest**, important reasons for holding money as **cash deposits** are **security** and their **accessibility**.

Cash deposits are generally characterised by a high level of **security**. The money value of the capital invested will be preserved, unless the deposit-taking institution is unable to meet its obligations to repay depositors and defaults. The purchasing power of capital held on deposit will, however, be eroded by inflation. Against this, there is the reward of any interest receivable, and the rate of interest may exceed inflation, resulting in a real rate of return for the investor.

An important advantage of cash deposits, particularly when held on call in 'instant access' accounts, is their **accessibility**. Every investor could have a need for cash at short notice, and so should hold some cash on deposit to meet possible needs and emergencies.

2.2 Rates of interest on cash deposits

Cash deposits earn for the investor a **reward** in the form of **interest** paid regularly, normally at a percentage rate on the capital invested, at rates of interest prevailing from day to day, or alternatively at rates fixed over certain periods.

The performance of cash as an investment can be measured as a **'real' rate of return** by comparing the interest rate with the rate of inflation.

Approximately:

Rate of interest – Rate of inflation = Real rate of return

An investor will want to compare the interest rate **net of tax** with the inflation rate. For example, if annual interest is paid at 4% (net of tax), and the rate of inflation is 2.5%, then the real rate of return is approximately 1.5%. The purchasing power of the cash investment is increasing at 1.5% per year.

Interest rates on cash deposits will generally move approximately in tandem with **rates of interest on borrowing**: deposit takers obtain income from the difference between deposit rates and their lending rates. Interest rates generally will move in line with the short-term 'base' rate of interest set by the Bank of England's Monetary Policy Committee. This will be set according to various economic conditions. If the economy appears to be 'overheating', with people finding credit and borrowing easy to obtain and afford, interest rates may be raised to discourage borrowing. Over the period since 1988, the base rate has varied between 15% and 4%.

Deposit taking institutions are in competition with one another and so the interest rates set on different deposit products will reflect these market conditions.

2.3 Past performance

A study by Barclays Capital shows that £100 invested in cash deposits since 1899, with income reinvested, would have grown to £14,940 by the end of 2002. The same £100 invested in equities (shares) with dividends reinvested would have grown to £815,000 over the same period.

Stripping out the effects of inflation to leave only real returns, £100 invested in 1899 grew to £14,850 in equities and £272 in cash deposits by the end of 2002.

However, over shorter term periods, such as years in which share prices fall, then cash deposits may outperform equities. The lower risk of cash deposits can be an important consideration for investments over short periods particularly.

2.4 Risks

Cash deposits involve:

(a)   Very low **capital risk,** since capital will be lost only if the deposit taker defaults

(b)   **Inflation risk**, since inflation could exceed the interest payable. While an investor is locked in at fixed interest rates, inflation might race ahead due to unforeseen economic conditions, and the purchasing power of the investor's capital could fall.

(c)   **Interest risk,** if the rate of interest paid is less than could otherwise be obtained on other low-risk investment products, or the investor is locked in at a fixed rate for fixed terms, when he might otherwise have been able to take advantage of rising interest rates available in the market.

The **capital** on a deposit investment is secure in that the original capital is returned when the deposit is withdrawn, or the account matures, subject to any penalties which will have been made explicit in the terms and conditions of the account.

Another aspect of **capital risk** for the depositor is the chance that the deposit taker fails and goes into liquidation. This happened with the Bank of Credit and Commerce International, which collapsed in 1991.

If a UK deposit taking institution fails, the depositor will have recourse to the **Financial Services Compensation Scheme (FSCS),** which is administered by the Financial Services Authority (FSA).

2.5 Financial Services Compensation Scheme limits

The FSCS will pay the following compensation following default by a bank or building society:

- 100% of the first £2,000 deposited
- 90% of the next £33,000 deposited

Therefore, the maximum compensation will be £2,000 + £29,700 = £31,700.

These FSCS compensation limits:

- Apply only to UK sterling deposits held at a UK branch of the deposit taker

- Apply to each depositor, and not to each individual account

- Apply separately to each joint account holder: therefore, two joint account holders each could receive up to £31,700, for a joint account in which £70,000 was deposited

2.6 Spreading risk across different deposit takers

The **ceiling on compensation** available through the FSCS leads some investors to consider **spreading** their capital among a number of banks and building societies in order to reduce the overall risk. The benefit of spreading the risk in this way should be weighed against the possible disadvantage of lower rates of interest that may be earned because of the investor missing out on higher rates offered for larger deposits.

2.7 Principal deposit takers

The principal UK **deposit takers** are:

- Banks
- Building societies
- National Savings & Investments (NS&I) – a government agency, previously called 'National Savings'

Supervision of the prudential soundness of banks and building societies is the responsibility of the Financial Services Authority.

A **building society** is a mutual organisation, owned by its members. The members are the holders of savings accounts – often called share accounts – and borrowers. Members of the Society have voting rights.

Banks are listed public limited companies, owned by their shareholders. The rights of account holders are limited to the terms and conditions of the account.

Deposits held with **National Savings & Investments (NS&I)** are guaranteed by the government and therefore can be considered to be completely secure. As a Government department, NS&I is not a licensed deposit taker as banks and building societies are.

2.8 Instant access accounts

As the name implies, an **instant access account** allows the investor immediate access to funds. The investor will want to keep some funds available on instant access, for emergency purposes. At the time of writing, some deposit takers are

offering around 4% interest for instant access funds, before tax. This rate provides a small real rate of return for a basic rate taxpayer. Some accounts give instant access **subject to restrictions**. For example, an account might allow only two withdrawals per year.

2.9 Notice accounts

With a **notice account**, the investor must give, for example, 30, 60 or 90 days notice of withdrawal unless he wishes to lose interest. There may be a higher rate of interest available to compensate for the requirement to give notice. However, the investor should be careful to weigh the advantage of any higher rate offered against the disadvantage of the loss of liquidity and the costs of penalties if the money needs to be withdrawn earlier than planned.

Example: Notice account

Meena has a sum of £10,000 to place on deposit. She can place it in an Instant Access account for which interest is paid annually at 3.5% (variable).

Alternatively, Meena can place the money in a Notice account, subject to 90 days notice, and will then receive a rate of 4.0% (variable) annually. For immediate withdrawal, there will be a loss of 90 days' interest.

At the current rates:

- The Instant Access account will pay £350 annually, before tax.
- The Notice account will pay £400 annually, before tax.

If Meena needs to withdraw her funds in an emergency after one year, she will be lose interest before tax of:

$$£10,000 \times 4.0\% \times 90/365 = £98.63$$

In that event, the total interest received on the Notice Account will be £400 − £98.63 = £301.37. This is lower than would have been received on the Instant Access account.

Check that you can see how it will take approximately two years for the Notice Account to begin to out-perform the Instant Access account, if the money is required without notice being given.

2.10 Monthly interest accounts

Interest paid monthly will generally be slightly lower than on an instant or notice account which pays interest annually because of the increased frequency of payment of interest. When interest is credited month after month, then the interest itself will begin to earn interest as soon as it is credited.

Example: Monthly interest

An account pays interest at an annual rate of 3.6%. Interest is credited monthly.

$$3.6\%/12 = 0.3\% \text{ will be paid monthly.}$$

The annualised rate of interest is:

$$100 \times ((1 + 0.036/12)^{12} - 1) = 100 \times ((1.003)^{12} - 1) = 100 \times (1.0366 - 1)$$

$$= 3.66\%$$

This shows that the account pays the same return as an annual interest account paying 3.66%.

2.11 Regular savings accounts

Some accounts allow for **regular savings** to be made each month, possibly with some access to funds without penalty.

2.12 Time deposits

Time deposits or **term accounts** offer investors terms that involve tying up the deposit for a fixed period, often at fixed rates. The period may range from 7 days to several years, and there may be a fairly high minimum for such arrangements.

Time deposits may be offered as **bonds**. The bond offer may be open for a specified period, or the deposit taker may reserve the right to withdraw the offer at any time. The bond could run for a fixed term: 1, 2, 3, 4 or 5 years, with severely restricted access subject to a penalty, or no access at all.

Interest may be **tiered.** For example, a five year 'step-up bond' might offer a gross rate of interest of 3.0% in year one, 3.25% in year two, 3.50% in year three, rising to 4.0% in year four and a final 4.5% in year five.

2.13 Tax treatment of cash deposits

A UK resident will be subject to tax on bank and building society deposits in the tax year in which the interest is paid at one of the following rates:

- 10% starting rate
- 20% lower rate
- 40% higher rate

Interest on bank and building society accounts is generally **paid net** of 20% income tax. The deposit taker pays the tax deducted to HMRC.

- **Non-taxpayers** can reclaim all tax deducted. (If someone expects their total income to be less than their personal allowance, they can submit **Form R85** to HMRC, so that the interest is received gross instead.)

- **Starting rate (10%) taxpayers** can reclaim a partial refund, as their liability is 10%.

- **Basic rate (22%) taxpayers** have no more tax to pay in addition to the 20% deducted at source.

- **Higher rate (40%) taxpayers** pay the additional 20% tax due, through their annual tax assessment.

In the case of accounts with a minimum of **£50,000 held on fixed deposit** for a maximum of five years, interest can be paid **gross.**

As there is no **capital** appreciation on a deposit investment, there is no charge to **capital gains tax**.

2.14 The ISA wrapper

For UK residents aged 16 or over, up to £3,000 can currently be invested each year in a Cash mini-ISA (**Individual Savings Account)** or in the **cash component of a maxi-ISA.** The ISA is a tax-advantaged 'wrapper' and interest received will be free of tax. When cash is withdrawn, the tax advantage is lost.

Cash mini ISAs are available from National Savings & Investments (NS&I). A large number of deposit taking institutions also provide cash mini-ISAs and various financial institutions provide maxi-ISAs which may, or may not, include a cash component.

3 Direct investment in gilts and corporate bonds

3.1 Introduction

The term **fixed interest** or **'fixed income' securities** is sometimes given to securities that pay a pre-specified return, in the form of capital and income. Following US usage, such securities are also collectively called **bonds**. Gilts (UK government securities), corporate bonds, loan stock, debentures and loan notes are names given to types of bonds. Index-linked gilts, where the interest payment ('coupon') is linked to the rate of inflation, are available.

Bonds are loans, with the investor as the lender. The holder of the bond – that is, the investor – will be due to receive any interest payment (the coupon), and normally repayment of capital on maturity of the bond.

3.2 Features of fixed interest securities

Fixed interest securities generally have:

- A fixed **redemption value** which the issuer/borrower will repay to the holder of the bond on maturity (alternatively called the **face value**, **par value** or **nominal value**)

- A fixed rate of **interest** (the **coupon**), expressed as a percentage of the par value

- A pre-specified **redemption date** (or maturity date)

The **issuers** of bonds include:

(a) **Government (Government bonds – 'gilts'** in the UK), and
(b) **Companies (corporate bonds)**

Treasury bills are short-term government bonds. The term **corporate bonds** is used broadly to describe bonds issued by any entity other than the Government. Many corporate loan stock pays interest six-monthly, as with government stocks, although some pay annually.

Examples: Loan stocks

Issuer	Coupon	Maturity date
Lloyds TSB	10.625%	2008

In this example, for £1,000 nominal of the stock **Lloyds TSB 10.625% 2008**, Lloyds TSB plc will pay £53.12 interest every six months until 2008. (The dividend dates for this stock are 21 April and 21 October.)

This loan stock happens to mature on 21 October 2008, when holders will be repaid the face value.

Tesco 6% 2008 is another example of a corporate bond. This bond pays interest once yearly. On £1,000 nominal stock, Tesco plc pays interest of £60.00 on 13 June each year. The par value of £1,000 will be paid on 13 June 2008.

Bond **prices** are quoted at the price for £100 nominal value of the stock. For example, a price of 96 means that £960 must be paid for £1,000 nominal of the stock.

A bond usually cannot be encashed (redeemed) before the specified maturity date. However, the holder of a bond can usually sell it in the stock market at any time. That is, the bond is **negotiable**.

The price at which the bond holder can sell will fluctuate according to supply and demand for the bond. Therefore, the holder cannot be sure of the price he would obtain by selling in the market before the bond matures. Note however that, if he holds the bond to maturity, the return is known.

A holding of a bond is normally described in terms of the **nominal value**: for example, a holding of £5,000 of a stock refers to stock with a nominal value of £5,000.

Where a **government stock** is **quoted with two dates**, this means that the Government (not the bond holder) has the option to redeem the stock at any time between the two dates. For example, Treasury 12% 2013-2017 could be redeemed at any time between 12 December 2013 and 12 December 2017.

3.3 Influences on market prices

The **income (coupon)** from a bond remains the same through its life. However, during the life of the bond, there are factors that can make the bond more or less attractive to investors. These factors lead to the **price of bonds** changing.

If investors see **interest rates** tending to **rise**, the prices of bonds will generally **fall.** The reason for this can be seen if we appreciate that investors will **require** a particular level of return, depending upon rates of interest generally. If interest rates rise, investors' required rate of return rises. That means that they will be prepared to pay less for a particular bond with a fixed rate of interest than they were prepared to pay previously. If interest rates generally **fall**, then investors will be prepared to pay more for a fixed-rate bond than previously, and bond prices will tend **rise.**

This mechanism can be appreciated more clearly by thinking of **investors' required return** determining the **yield** they expect from bonds. Yield is a measure of the rate of income paid out as a proportion of the bond price. The rate of income does not change, but the bond price changes, and thus the yield changes.

Investors will generally require a higher return if the **expected rate of inflation rises.** Therefore, prices of fixed-rate bonds will tend to fall with rising expectations of inflation. However, **index-linked bonds** have a coupon that is linked to the inflation rate, with the result that the price of index-linked stock will tend to rise as higher inflation is expected.

Changes in economic prospects can lead to changes in interest rates and therefore to changes in bond prices.

Bond prices are influenced by the market's perception of the **quality of bonds**. A perception that a bond issuer might default on the bond will depress its value.

(a)   Bonds issued by major **governments** (such as the USA and the UK) are of the highest security and therefore the lowest risk. Governments can generally raise more money through taxation or they can increase the money supply (by 'printing money') rather than default on a bond. However, the perceived quality of the debt of different countries varies, affecting the price of government debt. In the recent past, capital and income defaults on the 'sovereign' (government) debt of some countries has been a problem.

(b)   **Corporate bonds** are generally perceived as more risky than the debt of major governments. Therefore, investors seek a higher rate of return from corporate bonds generally, and the price will typically be lower than for a government bond with a similar coupon and maturity date.

(c)   **Ratings** are available that assess the **creditworthiness of bond issuers**. Such ratings can help to indicate the risk in holding the bonds of different issuers. **Changes in creditworthiness rating** can have an effect on the prices of the issuer's debt in the market. In turn, this will affect the ability of organisations to raise new debt. If the creditworthiness of a company declines, the market will expect a higher yield from the debt. Therefore, it will be more expensive for the company to raise new debt.

3.4 Tax treatment

Interest received from fixed interest securities is taxed as savings income, in the tax year in which it is paid, for **income tax** purposes. Depending on the band in which the taxpayer's income falls, this means it will be taxed at:

- The starting rate of 10%
- At 20% (for basic rate taxpayers), or
- At the higher rate of 40%

Interest on government stocks (gilts) is paid gross, unless:

- The investor elects to have 20% tax deducted at source, or

- Tax has deducted at source for a gilt purchased before 6 April 1998 and the investor has not elected for gross payments

On other bonds, interest may be paid net of 20% tax.

Where 20% tax is deducted at source, non-taxpayers and starting rate taxpayers will be entitled to a refund. Higher rate taxpayers will have additional tax to pay.

Gilts and corporate bonds with at least five years to maturity when acquired can be purchased within a stocks and shares **ISA** or existing Personal Equity Plan (**PEP**). They will then be entirely tax-free.

No stamp duty is charged on buying and selling corporate bonds or government stock.

Individuals pay no **capital gains tax (CGT)** in respect of direct holdings of:

- Gilts
- Qualifying corporate bonds

Qualifying corporate bonds comprise:

- All **company loan stock and debentures** (except loan stock convertible into shares) that are issued in sterling and bought by the investor after 13 March 1984

- **Permanent Interest Bearing Shares (PIBS)**, which are issued by building societies

While gains are not taxed, it is also the case that losses cannot be set against other taxable gains.

3.5 Gilts

UK government securities are known as **gilts** or **gilt-edged securities**. A gilt is an investment in the form of a loan to the Government.

British Government securities are called gilt-edged because they were initially indeed gilt-edged documents, backed by a promise from the government. The government first borrowed from the City of London in the sixteenth century but the secondary market only became fully developed in the nineteenth century.

The issue of gilts helps the government to fund its borrowings, and in turn to replace the capital from maturing issues. The size of the gilt market depends on the government's borrowing needs. At some times the government is in a position to repay maturing issues without the need to borrow more. At such times, the gilt market reduces.

Gilts are issued by the government at various times for different terms and rates of interest. Therefore the investor has a wide choice of securities to meet individual needs.

Gilts are classified in groups depending on their term to redemption. (As indicated below, the classifications used by the Government's **Debt Management Office (DMO)** differ from those you may find in the financial press.) Examples given are as at March 2006.

(a) **Shorts**: gilts with up to seven years to redemption according to the DMO classification (sometimes 'shorts' refers to gilts with up to five years to redemption, in the financial press).

   Example: Treasury 4¾ % 2010

(b) **Mediums**: gilts with between seven and fifteen years to redemption (five to fifteen years, in the financial press).

   Example: Treasury 4% 2016

(c) **Longs:** gilts with a period in excess of fifteen years to redemption.

Example: Treasury 6% 2028

During its life, a long-dated gilt will, of course, move through the categories, so the Treasury 6 pc 2028 will become a medium-dated gilt, and eventually a short-dated gilt.

(d) **Undated**. These gilts have no stated redemption date, but the Government promises to pay the interest indefinitely.

Example: War Loan 3.5%

War Loan is unlikely to be redeemed. The only situation in which the Government would repay this stock is if interest rates fell below 3.5% and they could refinance the borrowing at a lower coupon.

(e) **Gilts with a spread of redemption dates**. As already mentioned, some gilts have a spread of redemption dates.

Example: Treasury 5½% 2008-12

This designation states that the government can repay the gilt at any time between the years 2008 and 2012. They will only repay it if they can replace the borrowing with a new issue with an interest rate below 5½%. If not, they will hold on until the last possible moment.

A further category of gilt is **index-linked gilts.**

3.6 Index-linked gilts

The first **index-linked gilt** was issued in 1981. Originally, only pension funds could purchase them. However, from 1982 onwards index-linked gilts became available to all investors. Index-linked gilts have their income and redemption payments linked to the Retail Prices Index (RPI).

It is the RPI figure **eight months before** each payment that is used in the calculation. The figure in brackets after the description of the stock shows the RPI base for indexing purposes.

The indexation multiplies the coupon and capital payment by:

$$\frac{\text{RPI eight months before coupon or capital payment is due}}{\text{Base RPI for the stock} (= \text{RPI eight months before issue})}$$

Example: Index-linked 2% Treasury 2006 (69.5)

How does **index-linking** work?

Suppose that an index-linked gilt is issued at a coupon of 2½% over a five year period. Over this period the RPI rises by 30%. Then, at redemption, the investor who has held the gilt since issue will receive a capital return of £130 for every £100 invested. The interest on the investment will also have risen by 30% to 3¼%.

3.7 Features of gilts

The **coupon** (rate of interest) on a gilt reflects the rate of interest the government needed to offer at the time of issue in order to attract funds. For example, Treasury 2015 was issued at 8%, at a time when interest rates were much higher than they are today.

In the case of all gilts except 3½% War Loan, the stock moves from **ex-dividend** to cum-dividend **seven business days** before the interest payments. For 3½% War Loan, the ex-dividend period is **ten business days.**

The usual form of **description of a gilt** is similar to that of other fixed interest securities.

For example the description **Treasury 5% 2012** means that the Government will pay the investor £5 per annum interest for every £100 of stock held. With interest on gilts being paid half-yearly, £2.50 will be paid at each 'dividend date'. The DMO website **www.dmo.gov.uk** shows that the dividend dates for this stock are 7 March and 7 September.

The nominal or **par value** of the stock is the price at which the stock is issued and will be redeemed. So, in the above example, each £100 of stock will be repaid at a pre-specified date in the year 2012 by a payment of £100. The DMO website shows that the redemption date for this stock is 7 March 2012.

During the term of the gilt the market value of the gilt will change according to demand. Suppose that the price of this gilt on a particular date was £105.08. If you were to buy the gilt at that price, you would buy 100/105.08 = £95.16 nominal of stock for £100. Therefore at redemption you would suffer a loss. You would have paid £100 but only receive back £95.16.

Suppose that, on the same day, you could instead have purchased the long gilt Treasury 4$^{1}/_{4}$% 2032, price £93.41. You would then receive £107.05 nominal of stock for £100 invested. At redemption you would receive £107.41 in return for an investment of £100. You would make a gain on redemption, in 2032.

The specific **name** of a gilt – eg, 'Treasury' or 'Exchequer' – is of no consequence.

Most gilts are **registered securities**: this means that the security is held in the name of the investor. If the word 'loan' appears in the title, it denotes a **bearer stock**. Such a stock is not registered in an individual's name and the only proof of ownership is the possession of the certificate.

3.8 Influences on gilts prices

As with markets generally, the price of gilts is affected by **supply and demand**. If investors want to buy gilts, the prices will tend to rise (surplus demand). Similarly prices are likely to fall if a government is running a big deficit and issuing a large number of new gilts (surplus supply).

Short-dated gilts are very sensitive to changes in prevailing **interest rates**. We have already seen how, as interest rates rise and fall respectively, the prices of fixed interest securities have an inverse relationship to the interest rate change, and the prices fall and rise respectively. Suppose that the Government issues a 4% gilt with 6 years to redemption. Suppose that in the following year the Government wish to increase their borrowings by the issue of a further gilt but, because of prevailing market conditions, this time they need to pay an interest rate of 5% for a gilt with the same redemption date. Then the first issue must by now be less attractive and a new investor will wish to pay less than £100 for every £100 of the 4% stock issued earlier.

The price of **long-dated gilts** is not so directly influenced by short-term interest rate changes. The holders of long-dated gilts are concerned about possible changes in Government or economic policies and the effect that such factors may have on inflation and interest rates. If investors believe there is likely to be a change in government and that a future government may not be able to control inflation, then the price of long-dated gilts may be depressed because of this.

Gilt prices may be affected by changes in **exchange rates**. If sterling is weak against other currencies, interest rates may to rise, and again and gilt prices will be kept down.

Sometimes the state of the **equity market** (company shares) can have a direct effect on gilt prices. In 1987, after the stock market 'crash', gilts offered higher returns than equities. Many investors switched into gilts and consequently gilt prices rose.

3.9 Corporate bonds

As already explained, negotiable fixed interest securities can be issued by corporate entities as well as governments. The **corporate bond** market enables companies and other entities to borrow money at fixed rates of interest. In mid-2002, the market was worth approximately £280 billion, and there were approximately 380 issuers.

The investor considering purchasing corporate bonds may be concerned that the profits of the company could be insufficient to pay the interest and repay the debt. There is, therefore, a higher risk than with a government security and investors will expect to receive a higher return in compensation. Large companies that are financially secure will not need to offer an interest rate much above that offered by the Government. Smaller companies will have to offer very attractive rates to persuade investors to take the risk.

As with other fixed interest securities, the investor in a corporate bond takes the risk that interest rates will rise while he is locked in. He can then sell the bond in the market but the price will have fallen as the yield has become less attractive.

Differences between corporate bonds and gilts:

- The corporate bond market is generally less liquid, at least for lower quality bonds. This can be a problem in adverse market conditions especially, when it may be difficult to sell stock.

- Corporate bond values can be affected by changes in the issuing company's creditworthiness.

- As a result of the above factors, corporate bonds are generally higher-risk than government stock, and corporate bond yields are generally higher as a result.

- Prices of corporate bonds are generally more volatile than prices of government stock.

- The spreads between buying and selling prices are usually greater for corporate bonds, and may be as high as the range 7% to 9%.

3.10 Fixed interest securities as investments

Fixed interest securities such as **gilts** and **highly rated (AAA) corporate bonds** can provide a level of income over a long period, which could be useful for an investor with a known liability or regular expenses to meet each year.

Although the income payments and the final redemption values are fixed, the capital value may fluctuate during the life of the bond as long-term interest rates vary. As with cash, inflation can erode the real value of a bond. If the investor is sure that they will hold a bond until maturity, the eventual (redemption) value and therefore the overall returns will be known.

As **long-term** investments, the return even on highly rated bonds such as gilts has been poor. Including reinvestment of gross income, the real return on gilts was 1.3% annually over the period 1900 to 2000.

Index-linked gilts offer a low-risk investment that can be suitable to as a 'hedge' against inflation over the longer term, generating a relatively low real return. With inflation at approximately 2.5%, the return available from index-linked gilts held to redemption is around 2%. Index-linked gilts can therefore offer a low-risk investment over the long term.

Investment grade corporate bonds offer higher potential returns than government bonds, but are more volatile and there is an increased **risk of default**, if the issuer gets into financial trouble.

Sub-investment grade ('junk') bonds, whose issuers have a low credit rating, form a relatively small part of the bond market. The higher risks and potential returns from this section of the market make them more like investment in **equities.**

3.11 International bond issues

The markets for corporate bonds are international, with many foreign entities issuing bonds on the London market.

Eurobonds are fixed interest securities issued by governments or major companies in a currency other than that of the country or market in which they are issued. Do not be misled by the 'euro' part of the term, which does not refer to the 'euro' currency. Such bonds may be issued in various currencies. For example, **Eurodollar bonds** are denominated in US dollars.

Bulldog bonds are bonds issued by foreign entities, offered in the UK and denominated in pounds sterling. **Yankee bonds** are US-dollar denominated bonds of non-US entities, issued in the USA. There are other nicknames, such as **samurai bonds**, in the case of Japan, and **Matilda bonds**, in the case of Germany.

4 Direct investment in equities

4.1 The nature of equities

The term 'equities' refers to the ordinary shares of companies. The ordinary shareholders of a company are its owners. The directors of the company are seen as having the task of maximising the wealth of the ordinary shareholders.

A company may or may not also have preference shares in its capital structure. A preference share pays a fixed rather than variable amount of dividend, normally half-yearly. Thus, preference shares are similar to loan stock. With loan stock, the interest must be paid even if the company is losing money. With preference shares, the dividend is only paid if there are enough post-tax profits to pay it. Preference shares do not usually carry voting rights unless the dividend payments fall into arrears.

When we discuss equities and shares generally, we are usually referring to ordinary shares.

Many smaller 'Limited' companies are private companies, which may be owner-managed and cannot offer their shares to the general public. The use of the term 'limited' indicates that shareholders have limited liability: if the company fails, shareholders can lose their entire investment in the company but the company's creditors cannot pursue the shareholders for any further money.

To offer shares for sale to the public, a UK company must be a 'plc' (public limited company).

- Such a company can seek a full listing on the main market of the London Stock Exchange (LSE), or
- It may join the less closely regulated Alternative Investment Market (AIM) that is also operated by the LSE.
- There is also 'OFEX', comprising companies whose shares are traded 'off-exchange', with much less liquidity: that is, buying and selling at any particular time may be difficult.

Both UK and foreign equities are bought and sold by private investors, by large institutions such as life assurance companies and pension funds, and by foreign investors. The investor buys ordinary shares for two main reasons:

- To receive dividends from the company's earnings stream (income)
- To gain from increases in the price of the share (capital gain)

4.2 The value of a share

Investment theory tells us that the value of an equity share to the investor is the net present value (that is, the value adjusted to current day terms) of all the anticipated future dividend payments arising from the share. If future growth in earnings and consequently dividends is anticipated, this will be reflected in the share value. Because the future is extremely difficult to predict and because our perceptions of the future will change based on the information we have at any time, the perceived value of a share can fluctuate with sometimes great volatility.

A company's earnings (profits) can be used either to pay dividends, or to re-invest within the business. Some companies do not pay dividends, for example because they have not yet made profits, or because they choose instead to retain their earnings and to re-invest them.

To take one example, the American corporation Microsoft, which has been a highly profitable company for many years, has only very recently started to pay any dividend at all. The company's shares have risen in value over many years and are currently worth around $60 billion. How then does such a company command a high stock market valuation, if the value of a share is the net present value of its future dividends? The answer is that such a company has the prospect of paying out significant dividends at some stage in the future. Its re-investment of earnings enhances its ability to generate eventual future dividends. (In 2004, Microsoft did announce that it would distribute substantial funds to shareholders.)

For some companies, a return to shareholders may be achieved when the company is sold for cash in a **takeover**, instead of through payment of dividends.

4.3 Influences on share prices

As with markets generally, the main determinants of the prices of shares are the **supply** of and **demand** for those shares. The prices of equities move continually during Stock Exchange trading hours. Whatever value an investor places on a share, the market provides a picture of how the balance of buyers and sellers in the market are valuing a share in the current **share price**. At any time, a share price will reflect what active buyers are prepared to pay and the price that active sellers require.

Share prices can change as a result of information becoming available to investors about various matters, including:

- The earnings prospects and asset values of individual companies
- The membership of the Board
- Adverse factors affecting companies, such as legal action against it, or action by a bank to call in loans
- Industry and economy surveys, for example about levels of retail sales, or productivity
- Macro-economic developments, for example: the expected level of interest rates, or where an economy appears to be located in the business cycle
- Changes in government policy, for example on taxation and monetary policy
- Movements in other stock markets around the world, such as the USA and Japan
- Global economic and political developments

Investors follow the public statements made by the company through the LSE's **Regulatory News Service (RNS)**. RNS statements cover matters such as results announcements, major developments, and purchases or sales of the company's shares by its directors. If the company warns that profits will be lower than anticipated (a **profit warning**), there is usually a sharp drop in the share price.

Many companies aim to present a stable and steadily rising pattern of **dividend payments** from year to year. Sharp changes from the usual pattern may be taken by investors as a **signal** of a change in the company's fortunes, which may cause a shift in the share price.

Trading in shares by anyone with **insider information** about the shares that has not been made public is illegal.

Investors will look for evidence of the **quality of a company's management**, although such evidence can be difficult to obtain in practice. Do the directors have the competence and motivation to drive the business forward in the interests of the shareholders, making any changes necessary to adapt to future developments? Changes in Board membership can affect investors' assessment of a company's prospects and the share price may move as a result. If a director resigns, investors will be interested in the reason for the resignation. If new directors are appointed, their experience and past track record will be of interest.

The prices of some companies' shares are affected more by the **state of the economy** than others. For example, because house purchase decisions are influenced by mortgage rates, house building companies will be particularly sensitive to interest rate changes. If people are moving house less as a result of interest rate increases, businesses such as DIY ('do it yourself') and carpeting may also face a downturn in demand and therefore earnings.

Given the increasing interdependence of national economies through trade (**globalisation**), share prices can be heavily affected by economic news from around the world, particularly from the world's largest economy, that of the USA.

Share prices are also affected by:

- **Supply and demand conditions** affecting a particular share (for example, a shortage of the share relative to the current demand for it)
- **Changing investor sentiment** and the speculative motives of investors

Speculative motives can drive share prices spiralling higher. If investors may buy particular shares in the hope of taking advantage of a rising trend in prices. As more investors buy, prices are driven higher still and this may encourage still further buying. The process cannot continue indefinitely and eventually the 'bubble' may burst when prices fall back and there is a sudden change in sentiment. The fall in prices can then be as steep as the original rise and those who bought at the highest prices will suffer losses.

The **buying (offer) price** of a share will generally be higher than the price at which an investor can sell **(bid price)**. The difference **(spread)** earns an income for **market makers**, who deal in the stock and maintain market liquidity.

4.4 The performance of equities

The main reason for choosing **equities** instead of other asset classes is to take advantage of their long-term growth potential.

Equities have produced the **best real (inflation-adjusted) returns** of all the main asset classes we are reviewing in this Chapter over the long term. The long-term growth seems spectacular when we consider that £100 invested in a broad portfolio of equities in 1899, with income reinvested, would have grown to £815,000 by the end of 2002 (as shown in Barclays Capital studies). Over the long term, global equity returns might be expected to be in the order of 5-6% above the rate of inflation. The excess of around 3% over returns from **cash** and **gilts** reflects what is sometimes called the **risk premium** that accrues to equity investors to reflect the **higher risks** of a loss. The ability of equities to produce these returns above inflation partly reflects the fact that **economic growth** produces growth in companies' earnings, which benefit shareholders.

Consider also though, that the same £100 from 1899 mentioned above would have grown to £1,200,000 when stock markets peaked in 1999. The riskiness of equity investment is highlighted if we note that an investment of £10,000 made at the market peak in 1999 would have lost about 33% of its value by the end of 2003, over the space of four years. The value would have fallen in value to approximately £6,700. That investment then needs to grow by 50% for the investor to get back to their starting position of £10,000: this could take many years.

This illustration underlines the possible downside effects on an investor's capital from the volatility of share prices. There have been periods in which sharp falls in stock markets have occurred – for example, in the USA in 1929, in the UK in 1973-74 and in Japan after 1989.

What lessons are there for investors seeking exposure to equities? One point is that spreading investment over a period can reduce some of the effects of market volatility. If, instead of a single investment of £10,000 made in 1999, our investor had invested perhaps £2,000 per year over a five year period, the investment would not all have been made at the market peak when equities were most expensive.

However, equity investment is not necessarily simply a matter of gaining exposure to the stock market as a whole. The investor who makes direct investment in individual shares may seek to do better than the broader market. He or she might do this by engaging **professional advisers** to manage the investments. Alternatively, the investor might apply his or her own **stock selection** knowledge and skills in trying to select equity investments that will outperform the broad market indices of share prices such as the **FTSE 100 Index** ('the Footsie').

A further approach, particularly for investors with relatively small sums to invest, is to gain exposure to equities through **collective investment vehicles** such as unit trusts, OEICs/ICVCs or investment trusts. These vehicles may themselves consist of actively managed portfolios of equities, and the investor hopes that the skills of the **fund manager** are above average, so that the fund will outperform the broader stock market. (Collective investment routes are a subject of the next Chapter.)

4.5 Equities as part of a portfolio

Direct holdings of ordinary shares could be appropriate in a **portfolio** for an investor who obtains advice on an ongoing basis or who wishes to spend the time researching has own investments. Over the short term, capital values (as reflected by share prices) can fluctuate greatly, although dividend payments are more stable than capital values. Over the long term – for example, over most five-year periods – the share market has been found to out-perform the general rate of inflation, fixed interest securities and deposit funds.

Investors with smaller amounts to invest and who do not wish to build their own portfolio can gain exposure to equity markets through **pooled investments** such as unit trusts, open ended investment companies (OEICs – also called Investment Companies with Variable Capital or ICVCs) or investment trusts (covered in the next Chapter of this Study Text).

Direct purchase of ordinary shares should only be considered if the client is well aware of the risks associated with individual company share ownership. The investor must be aware that there is no guarantee of dividends or of return of capital. Particularly with more speculative investments, it is possible that the whole investment in a particular share will be lost. **Diversification** into different shares helps to reduce the risk of substantial losses.

The extent to which adding new shares to an existing portfolio will reduce the volatility of the returns on the portfolio will depend in part on how the share typically behaves, compared with the share market as a whole. Portfolio managers sometimes use measurements of the **beta factor** of a share for this purpose.

- A share with a **beta factor of 1** moves in line with the market. If the market (for example, as indicated by a share price index such as the FTSE-100) moves up 5%, the price of this security is likely to move up 5%.

- A share with a **beta factor greater than 1** varies more widely than the market. If the market moves up 5%, the price of a security with a beta of 2 is likely to move up 10%.

- A share with a **beta factor of less than 1** fluctuates less than the wider market. If the market moves up or down 10%, the price of a security with a beta of 0.5 is likely to move up or down respectively by 5%.

An investor in equities should generally always have other assets that can be realised more easily. Although equities may be sold relatively quickly, the price might be unfavourable at the time funds are required.

It is often said that an investor ought not to invest money in shares that he or she cannot afford to lose.

4.6 Tax treatment

Dividends paid to equity shareholders are paid on the basis that there is a **10% tax credit**.

- A non-taxpayer cannot reclaim the tax credit.

- There is no further tax to pay for a basic rate or starting rate taxpayer.

- A higher rate taxpayer has a liability to pay 22.5% tax on the gross dividend in addition to the 10% tax credit.

The gross dividend (including the tax credit) can be calculated as: Dividend received x 100/90

The position for a dividend received of £100 for different types of taxpayer is summarised in the table below.

	Non-taxpayer	**10% taxpayer**	**22% taxpayer**	**40% taxpayer**
	£	£	£	£
Dividend	100.00	100.00	100.00	100.00
Tax credit	11.11	11.11	11.11	11.11
Additional tax due	Nil	Nil	Nil	25.00
Total tax suffered	11.11	11.11	11.11	36.11*
Net income	100.00	100.00	100.00	75.00

* The effective rate for higher rate taxpayers is (36.11/111.11) x 100 = 32.5%.

If the investor makes a capital gain on the realisation of a share it may be subject to capital gains tax.

The basic calculation for **capital gains tax** is:

Profit = Proceeds (less sale expenses) less original investment less indexation allowance up to April 1998, less taper relief from April 1998

The profit thus calculated could become subject to capital gains tax if:

- After taking into account the capital gains tax indexation allowance and taper relief, the individual's gain is in excess of the annual exemption (£8,800 for 2006/07), or

- The gain is below the annual exemption but the investor has already made use of this in other transactions

There are methods of reducing the capital gain.

- The investor may have other capital losses including losses brought forward which could be offset.

- The investor may consider transferring the holding into a spouse's name prior to sale if the spouse has not used up their annual exemption.

4.7 Buying and selling shares

Equities are bought and sold through a stockbroker. The stockbroker can deal for the client in one of three ways.

- **Execution only dealing service**. In this case the broker simply carries out the client's instructions. The client has agreed that he chooses not to receive advice on his investments.

- **Advisory or non-discretionary service**. In this case the broker makes recommendation but the client makes the final decision.

- **Discretionary service**. In this case, the stockbroker will have authority to buy and sell without reference to the client. A carefully worded agreement will lay down the parameters for transactions, for example, the amount of risk the client wishes to take or the types of securities he wishes to consider.

5 Direct investment in property

5.1 Property markets

In the UK, a substantial proportion of **residential property** is owned by its occupiers. Home ownership has been promoted by tax incentives, including exemption from capital gains tax for the taxpayer's own principal private residence. Mortgage Interest Relief At Source (MIRAS) for private homebuyers was another significant incentive in past years, but this relief was phased out and abolished in 2000 (except for certain pre-existing **home income plans**).

The rented sector has seen the rise of '**buy-to-let**' ownership of property by many new private landlords during the 1990s and early 2000s. More easily obtainable mortgage finance for buy-to-let and rising house prices have fuelled the buy-to-let boom. By 2003, almost 5% of total mortgages outstanding were buy-to-let loans, up from under 1% five years earlier. The expansion in buy-to-let could make residential property values more volatile, as buy-to-let landlords may be more likely sellers than owner-occupiers, if there is a housing market downturn.

The market in **commercial property** – retail, offices and industrial units – has tended in the past to be dominated by investment by insurance companies and pension funds. These institutions may act as property developer and, once the property is built, the landlord. More recently, more private investors have been making direct investment in commercial property. Some have made investments via their own Self-Invested Personal Pension Plans (SIPPs).

Commercial property is typically let on **long leases**. In the past this could be as long as 99 years. Now it is likely to be a maximum of 25 years, with three or five year rent reviews. **Factories and warehouses** tend to produce the highest yields in the property sector and shops typically produce the lowest yields.

The value of commercial property is normally calculated as a **multiple** of the rental income. For example, a property might be purchased at 18 years multiple of the rent. The owner of the property obviously hopes that the rental income from his property will increase. A property price set at a high multiple may reflect expectations of strong future rental growth.

The rental receivable (calculated either gross, or net of expenses) as a percentage of a property's value is the **yield**.

As **property prices increase** significantly, **yields** generally **fall** as the value of property rises, eg for residential property during a housing 'boom', yields will tend to fall as rents typically do not increase as much as the rising property prices.

5.2 Gearing of property investments

Given their substantial size and the fact that a lender can usually be given security in the form of a legal charge on the property, property investments are often made with help from borrowed funds. That is, the investment is '**geared**'.

The **gearing effect** of borrowing for property purchase can be severe if prices start to fall, and **negative equity** can even result in some cases where the loan is a high percentage of the property value.

Example: Effect of house price falls

An investor obtains a mortgage of £80,000 and pays £20,000 of her own money to buy a property for £100,000.

The investor then has equity of £20,000 in the property.

Interest rates rise and prices in the local property market fall by 10%.

If the investor wishes to sell, the price will be around £90,000.

Ignoring the original purchase costs and the selling costs, and loan capital repayments, the investor will have £10,000 after repaying the loan of £80,000. Her equity has fallen by 50% from the original £20,000 investment.

5.3 Long-term returns

Research shows that, over the long run, investment in property has provided real returns ahead of the returns on cash and gilts and slightly below that of equities. The annualised nominal (money) return for **commercial property** was 11.6% over the 30-year period to the end of 2001 (IPD estimates). Returns from equities were 13.5% over the same period. The commercial property market has undergone 'crashes' from time to time: between 1989 and 1992, following a period of significant levels of speculative development in London, some office rent levels halved. Property yields have recently seemed attractive on income grounds compared with the relatively low yields from government bonds.

The **residential property** market tends to move in cycles different from those of the commercial property market, and it is influenced by economic factors such as disposable incomes and interest rates. A major slump in the residential market followed substantial rises in interest rates in the years following 1989. A shortage of building land and planning restrictions contributes to rising prices in some areas, particularly the South of England.

Some commentators believe that, in late 2004, residential property is significantly over-valued in the market, and that a **housing market** correction is likely. Over the long run, a fairly stable relationship between real incomes and house prices can be expected: this implies that, as the economy grows, positive long-term real returns are likely. Over shorter periods, expectations and buyer psychology play a part: a widespread belief that property prices will continue to rise can become a self-fulfilling prophecy over shorter-term periods as buyers pile in to the market, pushing prices higher.

5.4 Advantages and disadvantages

Advantages of residential property ownership

- Many investors participate in residential property ownership by owning the home in which they live. One of the attractions of **owner-occupation** is psychological: most owner-occupiers like the security of a permanent home they own, even if it is subject to a mortgage.

- Over the long term, UK property values have out-stripped general price inflation, although the property market is susceptible to cyclical fluctuations.

- It is possible to use a property as part of an investor's retirement fund. He or she can decide to sell a large house, moving to a smaller one on retirement and using the surplus funds to invest and create income.

- If for some reason the owner cannot live in a property for a period, for example when working abroad, a property can be let and used to create an income.

- Similarly, if a client owns a holiday home, this can be let for part of the year. The rental income will, hopefully, offset general running expenses.

- Residential property can be used as collateral security for a loan.

- Including property as an asset class provides diversification for the investor who also has investments in other asset classes such as fixed interest securities and equities.

- 'Buy to let' investment – discussed further below – offers the prospect of rental yield plus a potential capital gain.

Disadvantages of residential property ownership

- One of the main disadvantages of owning property is **illiquidity**. The property can only be sold when a buyer can be found, and this may take weeks or months. Most properties cannot be easily divided up into smaller units, so that either the whole of the property must be sold, or it must be retained.

- As well as agents' and legal costs, purchases of property are subject to stamp duty land tax. Taken together and depending on the purchase price, these costs may add up to several percentage points to the cost of a purchase.

- Often the sale of a property can be protracted and the vendor may be incurring expenses during this period.

- If a property is leased out, there may be times when a suitable tenant cannot be found. In addition there are charges involved in letting property. A letting agent may be needed to vet suitable tenants, collect rents and oversee the upkeep of the property.

- If house prices fall, capital values of residential property investment will suffer. The gearing effect of loans will amplify the effect on the investor's stake (or 'equity') in the property.

Advantages of commercial property as an investment

- The **capital value** of commercial property, which does not follow the residential property market, may keep pace with inflation, although this is not guaranteed.

- Tenants in commercial property must continue to pay their rent even if they are making trading losses. The **rental income stream** is thus more like that from fixed interest securities than from shares (equities). This insulates the landlord from some cyclical economic changes, provided the property does not fall vacant.

- Property can produce an **increasing rental income** if good tenants can be found and maintained.

- Property can provide a balance in the investment **portfolio** particularly as the performance of property may be directly opposed to the performance of the stock market. Thus, if the stock market is doing well, property may perform relatively poorly, and *vice versa*.

Disadvantages of commercial property as an investment

- From time to time, there will be **slumps** in the property market and these may be protracted.

- Commercial property may remain untenanted for 'void periods' of many months or even years during which time there is no rental income and the underlying value of the property may also have fallen.

- As with residential property, legal, survey and other **buying costs**, together with stamp duty land tax, may add up to several percentage points to the cost of a property purchase.

- Property can be **expensive to manage**. The buildings have to be kept up to a high standard if suitable tenants are to be found and retained. The owner will have the expense of an agent who will be in charge of the day-to-day running of the property and finding and vetting suitable tenants. Other professional advisers will need to be employed from time to time such as surveyors and lawyers to draw up suitable leases and contracts.

- Properties must usually be **purchased as a whole**. Because there are relatively few property sales and the sums involved are usually large, commercial property can be difficult to research as an investment area.

- Commercial property is very **illiquid**. It may take many months or even years to sell a property.

- **Diversification** into different properties in different areas will only be possible for a portfolio of substantial value.

5.5 Tax treatment of property investments

Profits from rent – whether from residential or commercial property – are treated as follows for tax purposes.

- Profit will be taxed at the taxpayer's marginal rate of 10%, 22% or 40%.
- Each year's profit is taxed in that tax year.
- Mortgage interest and certain other expenses relating to the property being let can count as a deductible expense to set against the letting income.

If the landlord is **non-UK resident**, the tenant or letting agent must deduct basic rate tax from the property income before remitting rent to the landlord. A landlord may apply to HMRC to come within the self assessment regime in order to receive gross payments of rent.

If the investor owns **furnished holiday accommodation** which is let out on a frequent basis (at least 70 days in a 12 month period) he may if he satisfies the following criteria, be able to treat the letting **as a trade**. In this case he may obtain other reliefs and allowances.

- The property must be situated in the UK.

- The property must be run on a commercial basis.

- The property must be furnished.

- The property must be available to let for not less than 140 days per fiscal year.

- The property must not normally be occupied by the same person/people for more than 31 days for at least seven months within a twelve-month period.

If a property is the investor's **principal private residence**, the sale of the property will be exempt from capital gains tax.

A gain on eventual disposal of a property that is not the taxpayer's principal private residence (for example, a buy-to-let property) is liable to **capital gains tax**. The base cost will be the cost of acquisition plus subsequent improvement expenditure that has not been allowed for tax. Non-business asset taper relief will apply.

5.6 Stamp duty land tax

Stamp duty land tax (SDLT) is a tax payable on buying property, and is payable by the buyer at the rates set out below (**2006/07**) on the purchase consideration (price).

Note that the rate is applied to the total price paid. The tax is rounded up to the next multiple of £5.

Consideration	Rate (2006/07)
Up to £125,000 (up to £150,000 in Disadvantaged Areas and on commercial property)	Nil
£125,001 – £250,000 (£150,001 – £250,000 in Disadvantaged Areas and on commercial property)	1%
£250,001 – £500,000	3%
£500,001 +	4%

Exercise: Stamp duty land tax

What is the difference in the stamp duty land tax (SDLT) payable on a house which sells for £249,000 and the SDLT on a house which is sold for £251,000?

Solution

£5,040.

Sale at £249,000: £249,000 x 1% = £2,490

Sale at £251,000: £251,000 x 3% = £7,530

Difference: £7,530 - £2,490 = £5,040

This calculation shows the significant effect of the SDLT threshold levels arising from the SDLT charge being levied on the total price paid. A purchase at a little above £250,000 will cost the buyer approximately £5,000 more in SDLT than a purchase slightly below £250,000.

Key chapter points

- The main broad asset classes are cash, bonds, equities and property.

- Rate of interest – Rate of inflation = Real rate of return

- Studies show that, over the long term, the return from equities has exceeded that of other asset classes. Property shows the next highest long-term return, followed by gilts and then cash deposits.

- An investor can hold cash on deposit with a sound financial institution. There is only a small risk of loss of capital, if the institution were to default. Deposits are covered within certain limits by the Financial Services Compensation Scheme.

- The term 'bonds' covers fixed interest securities, including government securities (gilts, in the UK) and corporate bonds. With gilts, the risk of default is insignificant. Corporate bonds vary in quality: where the risk of default is high, the bonds can be a higher risk investment.

- The capital value of fixed interest securities fluctuates with the general level of interest rates. The ultimate redemption value is known, and so holding the securities to maturity removes the risk of these fluctuations.

- Direct ownership of company shares (equities) can involve a significant level of risk. Share prices can be volatile under the influence of various factors and stock markets are susceptible to wide swings arising from changes in investor sentiment.

- Diversification of shareholdings across a number of companies can reduce the potential downside from failure of particular companies.

- Owner-occupiers are direct investors in residential property. Buy-to-let investors represent a growing sector in the UK property market. Some investors make direct investments in commercial property, such as shops or factory units.

- Direct investments in property are relatively illiquid and buying and selling costs are significant. Many property investments are geared (assisted by loans).

Chapter Quiz

Collective investments and derivatives

1 Collective investments

1.1 Introduction

A **collective** or **pooled** investment is a scheme by which the money of a large number of investors can be pooled to purchase shares or other securities and investments. By participating in a collective investment, investors can participate indirectly in a pool of investments that would be more difficult to own directly as an individual.

1.2 Advantages and disadvantages of collective investments

Advantages of collective investments

- An individual can invest relatively small amounts, perhaps on a regular basis.
- The pooling of investments enables the fund to make purchases of securities at lower cost than would be possible for an individual.
- The time involved in directly managing one's own portfolio is saved.

- The funds are managed by professional fund managers. A fund manager with a good past performance record may be able to repeat the performance in the future.

- A wide diversification between different shares and sectors can be achieved: this can be impractical and costly in dealing charges for a small portfolio held by an individual.

- Risk is reduced by exposure to a widely diversified spread of investments in the underlying portfolio.

- Specialisation in particular sectors is possible.

- The investor can gain exposure to foreign stocks, which can be costly and inconvenient for an individual who holds shares directly.

- Different funds provide for different investment objectives, such as income or growth, or a combination of both.

Disadvantages of collective investments

- The individual can only choose baskets of investments selected by fund managers, not by himself, and this will not suit all investors.

- Although the individual does not have to pick individual securities, he still has to choose the fund manager, and different managers' performance can vary widely.

- Although 'star' fund managers can have a successful track record with a fund, such 'star' managers may switch jobs, making future management of the fund less certain.

- Larger collective funds find it more difficult to invest in shares of companies with a relatively small capitalisation, because of the small quantities of stock available.

- Successful collective funds investing in smaller companies can become a victim of their own success if more funds are brought in, as a greater fund size can make it more difficult for such a fund to follow their successful strategy.

1.3 Types of collective investment

The following are types of **collective investment**:

- Open Ended Investment Companies (OEICs), which are also termed Investment Companies with Variable Capital (ICVCs)

- Unit trusts

- Investment trusts

- Life assurance based schemes

The term 'funds' is often used to refer to unit trusts and OEIC/ICVCs collectively.

1.4 Open-ended and closed-ended funds

Unit trusts and **OEICs/ICVCs** are normally **open-ended** funds. This means that the trust can create new units when new investors subscribe and it can cancel units when investors cash in their holdings. This makes unit trusts and OEICs different from **investment trusts**, which are **closed-ended**: new investors buy investment trust shares from existing holders of the shares who wish to sell.

1.5 Fund supermarkets

Funds supermarkets are a concept in internet-based financial services (**e-commerce**). Funds supermarkets offer funds from various different providers, particularly for holding in an **Individual Savings Account (ISA)**.

A full online fund supermarket may provide:

(a)   The ability to **'mix and match**' funds from different providers within a single ISA or other account without incurring the extra charges normally associated with self-select ISAs. However, only **unit trusts** and **open-ended investment company** investments can be held, so that investors wanting a selection of individual shares or investment trusts will still need to choose a self-select ISA

(b)   The facility to **deal online** by credit card or debit card in real time without the need to download and print an application form

(c)   The facility to **track and manage** the account online

(d)   The ability to switch between funds within the service at minimal cost

Discount brokers operating on an **execution only** basis are sometimes referred to as fund supermarkets, but they do not normally offer the same mix and match facility and switches.

Discounts may be offered on funds' initial charges, and the fund supermarket may hope to generate revenue from ongoing trail commissions from customers who use their service. Fund supermarkets hope to win customers by offering the convenience of **consolidating** the availability of different funds through a single agency.

With funds supermarket **consolidation services**, it is possible to invest with several different fund managers and have all transactions summarised on a single statement, electronic or paper. Distributions can be aggregated and paid by a single cheque and in many cases, regular withdrawals of capital from the whole portfolio can be automated to 'simulate' an 'income'. As well as having a wide choice of funds it is possible to switch between funds at low cost and avoid a high proportion of the initial charge.

Most fund supermarkets specialise in unit trusts and OEICs, but there are similar services for onshore and offshore life assurance funds and also pension funds.

When choosing which fund supermarket to use, there are a number of factors to take into account:

- The number of fund managers accessible
- The number of funds accessible
- Costs involved in switching funds
- Whether access is available on a regular premium basis
- Any minimum investment
- How income is taken from the funds. Some funds allow a programmed series of monthly withdrawals to allow a larger and more regular income (particularly effective to make use of the annual CGT exemption)
- Additional services available (such as data and information or access to make switches and make new contributions via internet)

1.6 Wrap accounts

A further development is the introduction of **'wrap' accounts**. These allow a wider range of assets to be held including:

- Unit trusts/OEICs – based on a 'supermarket'-type arrangement
- ISAs and PEPs
- Pension investments from a SIPP or SSAS
- Life Assurance Bonds

- Child Trust Funds
- Shares, held in a nominee account

The ability to analyse all these assets from a single source allows management of funds under a range of different arrangements as part on a single portfolio.

The holdings are all shown in a single account, which can usually be accessed online. The investor can view the value of his or her assets and asset allocation, based on up-to-the-minute data.

1.7 Structured investment funds

Structured products are available that link repayment of capital to the investor by a pre-determined formula to the performance on an index such as the FTSE 100 Index (most commonly), or to other factors or combinations of factors.

Some funds make use of derivatives in order to make a guarantee of a return of capital to the investor (which might be in the range 85% to 100% of the original investment, for example). A **fixed period** often applies to the investment. Returns may be specified in a proportion of the rise of an index. Many share price indices, including the normally quoted version of the FTSE 100 Index, do not reflect dividends paid out by companies. In making comparisons of the investment performance of structured products based on an index, this should be taken into account.

Such structured funds may be located **offshore** (ie, outside the UK mainland).

2 Unit trusts and OEICs

2.1 Funds available

The buyer of an OEIC/ICVC or unit trust buys into a particular **fund** that is managed by a particular **fund manager**. The fund will have particular characteristics.

There are OEIC and unit trust funds to meet various different investment objectives. Some **income funds** principally target **immediate income**, while others aim to achieve **growing income**. **Growth funds** which mainly target **capital growth or total return** are distinguished from those that are designed for **capital protection**. **Specialist funds** form a further category. Some funds are **index-tracking funds**, which mechanically 'shadow' a particular share index such as the FTSE 100 Index rather than being actively managed by fund managers.

Although unit trusts and OEICs are often thought of particularly as providing exposure to **equity** markets, note that the following types of fund are also available.

- **Bonds funds**, investing in fixed interest securities including government bonds, corporate bonds and convertibles.

- **Cash funds**, which enable the investor to have the advantage of wholesale rates on cash deposits. An investor might use a cash fund to hold money before it is switched into other funds.

Funds may be **UCITS schemes**, meaning that they conform to the European **UCITS Directives** and can be marketed throughout the European Economic Area (EEA), which comprises the EU plus Norway, Iceland and Liechtenstein.

2.2 Unit trusts

Unit trusts have been available in the UK since the 1930s. Taking unit trusts together with **Open Ended Investment Companies (OEICs),** funds under management now exceed £200 billion.

With a **unit trust**:

- Investors can buy **units**, each of which represents a specified fraction of the trust.
- The trust holds a **portfolio** of securities.
- The assets of the trust are held by **trustees** and are invested by **managers**.
- The investor incurs **annual management charges** and possibly also an **initial charge**.

An authorised unit trust (AUT) must be constituted by a **trust deed** made between the manager and the trustee.

The basic principle with AUTs is that there is a single type of undivided unit. This is modified where there are both **income units** (paying a distribution to unitholders) and **accumulation units** (rolling up income into the capital value of the units).

The trustee's primary duty is to protect the interests of the investors. The **investor in** a unit trust owns the underlying value of shares based on the proportion of the units held. He is effectively the beneficiary of the trust.

The **trust deed** of each unit trust must clearly state its **investment objectives**, so that investors can determine the suitability of each trust. The limits and allowable investment areas for a unit trust fund are also laid out in the trust deed together with the investment objectives.

2.3 Unit trust charges

The **charges** on a unit trust must be explicit in the trust deed and documentation. They should give details of the current charges and the extent to which managers can change them.

Charges need to be made to cover the following **costs**.

- Managing the fund
- Administration of the fund
- Marketing
- Regulation and compliance costs
- General administration
- Direct marketing costs
- Commissions for intermediaries

These charges can be taken in one or more of three ways, via an **initial charge**, an **exit charge** or through **annual management charges**.

The **initial charge** is added to the **buying price**. So, the buyer incurs the cost of both the difference (spread) between the buying and the eventual selling price, and the initial charge. Managers might make an initial charge of 3.0-6.5% on **equities**, and less on **gilt** and **fixed interest funds** (1-4%) because of their lower dealing charges. Other funds with lower charges include **index tracker funds** and **cash/money market funds**, where the lower price reflects the lower burden of management. Where an initial charge is small or non-existent, there may be a further charge on exit.

Fund managers may offer **discounts** on the usual initial charge, particularly for direct sales or sales through low-cost 'fund supermarkets' which generally conduct their business on the Internet.

Exit charges are typically invoked where the investor sells the investment within a set period of time, eg five years.

An **annual management charge** of around 0.5–1.5% of the underlying fund will generally be made to cover the ongoing cost of the investment management of the trust. In some cases part of the annual management charge is paid to intermediaries as **renewal commission**, typically at a rate of 0.5% per annum. The cost will vary with the level of management required on a fund. **Offshore funds** require more management and costs are likely to be **higher**. **Tracker funds** require less management and costs will generally be lower. Some funds will have several tiers of management and will allow access to a wide range of investment managers via a single management company. In this case, each tier of management will need to recoup its costs and, in these cases, annual management costs will be higher.

2.4 Unit trusts taxation

Authorised unit trusts are **exempt from tax on gains** made within the fund, giving them an advantage, for instance, over life funds. Any income (other than dividend income from UK companies, which is not taxable) is taxed to corporation tax at **20%**. Foreign withholding tax on dividends will be offset against the tax charge, subject to double taxation treaties.

Management expenses can be offset against income from **non-UK equities.**

Unit trusts do not pay tax on gains from options or futures.

The tax treatment of distributions parallels the tax treatment of direct holdings of equities and interest.

If the trust holds more than 60% of its investments in **interest bearing securities**, the income is deemed to be interest then the distribution is made net of 20% tax, which can be reclaimed by non-taxpayers. 10% taxpayers can reclaim 10%, while basic rate taxpayers have no further liability. Higher rate taxpayers must pay 20% more in tax.

For equity unit trusts, the distribution is made with a 10% tax credit. The tax treatment for different types of taxpayer is then as for dividends from shares held directly. The tax credit cannot be reclaimed by non-taxpayers. The tax credit satisfies the tax liability for a basic or lower (10%) rate taxpayer, but higher rate taxpayers will be liable to an additional 22.5%. Non-taxpayers cannot reclaim the tax credit.

The individual is liable to **capital gains tax** on disposals of unit trust investments.

There is **no stamp duty** to pay on purchases of UK unit trusts.

2.5 OEICs/ICVCs

Open Ended Investment Companies (OEICs) / Investment Companies with Variable Capital (ICVCs) are managed, pooled investment vehicles set up as companies. They invest in securities with the objective of producing a profit for investors. Unlike unit trusts, the OEIC structure is recognised throughout Europe. The possible prospect of UK participation in economic and monetary union (EMU) and the single European Market helped to drive the UK to adopt this form of pooled investment, in addition to the unit trust. Regulations made under the European Communities Act brought OEICs into existence in the UK in 1997.

If it is marketed to the public in the UK, an OEIC must be **authorised** by the Financial Services Authority (FSA).

Classes of shares within an OEIC may include **income shares**, which pay a dividend, and **accumulation shares**, in which income is not paid out and all income received is added to net assets.

An OEIC has an **Authorised Corporate Director (ACD)**, who **may be the only Director**. The responsibilities of the **ACD** include the following.

- Day-to-day management of the fund
- Pricing of the fund
- Management of the investments
- Dealing in the underlying securities
- Preparation of accounts
- Compliance with regulatory requirements

In order to ensure that the **ACD** acts in the interests of **investor protection**, there is a **separate, independent** depository. The responsibility of the **depository** is similar to that of a trustee with a unit trust.

For the investment industry, an advantage of OEICs is that they are **widely recognised throughout Europe**.

2.6 OEICs/ICVCs taxation

OEICs themselves face a tax regime similar to that faced by **unit trusts**. Interest, rent and foreign dividends not taxed at source will be subject to a 20% corporation tax charge. UK dividends received will suffer no further tax other than the 10% deducted at source. Capital gains within an OEIC are exempt from CGT.

Distributions (dividends) paid to investors in an OEIC are taxable in the same way as the distributions from unit trusts. Dividends are paid with a **tax credit** of 10% that satisfies the **tax liability** for basic and lower rate taxpayers. **Higher rate taxpayers** are liable to an additional 22.5%. Fixed interest funds pay interest with 20% tax deducted, which satisfies the liability for basic rate taxpayers. Higher rate taxpayers must pay 20% more and starting rate taxpayers can reclaim 10%. **Non taxpayers** may **reclaim** tax on interest distributions, but not equity distributions.

For investors' OEIC holdings outside a tax-advantaged wrapper such as an ISA, **capital gains tax** will be chargeable on disposals.

There is no UK stamp duty for the investor to pay on purchases of OEICs.

Where an OEIC is based **offshore**, the distributions will **not be taxed** internally. This can be helpful for non-taxpaying investors, and can offer a cashflow advantage to tax paying investors.

2.7 OEICs/ICVCs charges

Unlike unit trusts, OEICs are **single priced**. This means that there is no difference (spread) between quoted buying prices and selling prices. The buying price reflects the value of the underlying shares, with any **initial charge** reflecting dealing costs and management expenses being disclosed separately.

As with unit trusts, **discounts** may be offered on the usual initial charge, eg for direct sales or sales through fund supermarkets.

The charges with **OEICs** may be lower than for unit trusts, particularly in respect of **cost of entry (setting up)** and **exit (encashing the investment)** due to single pricing.

Annual management costs are not set out as a separate charge as they are with unit trusts. It is however possible to quantify the costs by looking at the **total expense ratio (TER)** of the company. Figures for this are available in the public domain, allowing investors to make comparisons between investment managers.

3 Investment trusts

3.1 Introduction

Investment trusts are a type of professionally managed collective investment with a long history in the UK. The Foreign and Colonial Investment Trust was the first to be founded in 1868 with the aim of 'giving the investor of moderate means the same advantage as the large capitalist'. The investment trust provided a way for the small investor to have some exposure to investments in overseas stocks that it would have been impractical for the investor to buy individually. By mid-2003, there were 371 trusts in total, with total assets in the region of £50 billion.

Investment trusts are generally accessible to the individual investor, and investment trust shares are also widely held by institutional investors such as pension funds.

Investment trusts are **public limited companies** (plcs) listed on the London Stock Exchange. Whereas other companies may make their profit from manufacturing or providing goods and services, an investment trust makes its profit solely from investments. The investor who buys shares in the investment trust hopes for **dividends** and **capital growth** in the value of the shares.

3.2 Comparison with unit trusts and OEICs/ICVCs

Investment trusts have wider investment freedom than unit trusts and OEICs/ICVCs. Investments trusts can:

- Invest in unquoted private companies as well as quoted companies
- Provide venture capital to new companies or companies requiring new funds for expansion

The conventional corporate structure of an investment trust gives it a further advantage over unit trusts and OEICs because it can raise money to help it to achieve its objectives. The ability to **borrow** allows an investment trust to 'gear up' returns for the investor. However, this **gearing** increases the volatility of returns.

Investment trusts are **closed-ended** investments. The number of shares in issue is not affected by the day-to-day purchases and sales by investors. An advantage of the closed-ended capital structure is that it allows the managers to take a **long-term view** of the investments of the trust. With an open-ended scheme such as a unit trust or an OEIC if there are more sales of units or shares by investors than purchases, the number of units is reducing and the fund must pay out cash. As a result, the managers may need to sell investments even though it may not be the best time to do so from a long-term viewpoint.

The **price of shares** of the investment trust **rises** and **falls** according to **demand** for and **supply** of the shares of the investment trust, and not directly in line with the values of the company's assets, ie **the underlying investments**. In this way, investment trust prices can have greater **volatility** than unit trusts and OEICs, whose unit prices are directly related to the market values of the underlying investments.

Because prices are **dependent on supply and demand**, the price of the shares can be **lower** (at a **discount**) or higher (at a **premium**) than the **net asset value (NAV)** of the assets underlying the investment trust share.

Some investment trusts are set up with a **limited life.** Provision is made for shareholders to vote on whether to wind up the trust at the end of the specified period. As with all companies, the shareholders can in theory vote to wind up an investment trust at any time.

A **split capital investment trust** is like other investment trusts in that it has a single portfolio of investments. A split capital trust however involves a number of different classes of share, with holders of the different classes having different entitlements to returns of capital or income from the trust.

3.3 Management

As a company, an investment trust has a **Board of Directors**. The **objective** of a company is to **invest** the money of the shareholders, so decisions on **investment strategy** are very important. These decisions might be made by the directors (in a **self-managed trust**), or may be delegated to an external fund management company. In all decisions, the directors of the company should act for the **benefit** of the shareholders.

Decisions made by the management of the company are open to scrutiny by shareholders, who may act if they are **not satisfied** with the performance. One sanction for shareholders is to **sell** their holding, which could affect the share price. If the share price falls significantly, the company could become a takeover target for other trusts or 'asset strippers' who may buy the shares in order to press for it being wound up.

Special resolutions, and those passed at the annual general meeting, will be subject to a vote by the shareholders. This will include **election of directors** and **appointment of professional advisers**. Some investment trusts also buy in other specialist services such as investment or registration services and the appointment of these will be subject to a shareholder vote.

3.4 Regulatory aspects

An **investment trust** is a listed company, governed by the Companies Act and Stock Exchange regulations. As with other companies, it is bound by the rules set out in its Memorandum and Articles of Association, which are set up when the company is formed. An investment trust is not a trust in the legal sense of that term.

The trust is also subject to the rules of the **Financial Services Authority**, the overall regulator of the financial services industry.

3.5 Pricing and dealing

The quotation of the price of investment trust shares is similar to that for equities generally, and a dealer will give two prices.

- The higher price is the **offer price**, at which an investor can buy the shares
- The lower price is the **bid price**, at which a holder of the shares can sell

In a newspaper, a single price may be given: this is the **mid-market price**, between the offer and bid prices.

The difference between the offer price and the bid price is the **spread. Marketmakers,** through whom a broker makes deals in the stock, make their profit from this spread, which will vary through time as different marketmakers move their quoted offer and bid prices in competition with each other. The spread for less liquid shares will generally be wider than for more frequently traded and liquid stocks.

Shares in investment trusts can be bought through a **stockbroker**, who is likely to charge the same level of commission as for other equities.

An investor can usually **deal through the investment trust managers** instead of through a broker, and may incur lower charges by doing so. Small investors who do not have an account with a broker may prefer to deal through the managers. However, the managers may only deal on a daily basis, while a broker will be able to quote an up-to-the-minute price and a deal can be made instantly by telephone.

The major trust management groups also operate **regular savings schemes**, through which an investor can make monthly investments.

- 'Drip-feeding' an investment through such a scheme means that the investor spreads purchases over different time periods, when the prices may fluctuate widely. (A single lump sum investment might offer bad value if the price was relatively high at the time of purchase.)

- Typically, such schemes will have a minimum investment of £25 or £50 per month.

- **Charges** are typically in the range 0.25% to 1% of the initial investment. Dealing may be at no extra charge.

- **Dividend reinvestment** (in further shares) may be available as an option for investors who do not require income.

- **Financial advisers** may be paid **commission** through such schemes. Investors may agree for up to 3% to be deducted from lump sum investments to pay an adviser.

3.6 Charges

Charges incurred on investment trust holdings can be compared with the alternatives. Some **unit trusts and OEICs** have **initial charges** of around 5%. Initial charges may be much lower than this (at around 0.25%) for some investment trust savings schemes. However, there may be charges on selling investment trust holdings.

There are **internal charges** applied within the fund. These include funds' annual management charges, which generally range between 0.25% and 1.5% of the fund's total value.

Certain other costs, such as auditors' fees, custody fees, directors' remuneration, secretarial costs and marketing costs, may be charged in addition. They will normally be charged against the income of the trust, or in some cases against capital. Such charges will normally be disclosed in the investment trust company's annual report and accounts.

There has been a growing trend for collective investment funds to introduce **performance-related fees** for fund managers. The basic principle is to reward outperformance against a selected benchmark, as specified by the Board of Directors.

There are also charges that are **external** to the fund which the investor may incur.

(a)   The **spread** is the difference between buying and selling prices, as set by marketmakers.

(b)   **Dealing charges,** including **commission** and **stamp duty**, are payable to the broker carrying out the transaction.

(c)   **Product wrapper charges,** usually administration charges, may be charged by the manager of a wrapper' such as an ISA used to hold the investment in the collective fund.

(d)   **Charges for advice** may be incurred in addition if the investor takes financial advice. An Independent Financial Adviser (IFA) may charge a fee for advice. An up-front **initial commission** may be paid to an IFA, and there may also be a periodic **trail commission** payable to the adviser. Some advisers may agree to rebate part or all of commission received against fees for advice.

3.7 Taxation of the investment trust

Investment trusts can seek **HMRC approval** under section 842 of the Income & Corporation Taxes Act 1988. With this approval, the taxation of investment trusts is similar to that of **unit trusts**.

- The trust pays **no tax on gains** made from selling investments in their portfolio.

- They trust is not liable to tax on dividends from UK companies (**franked investment income**)

- The trust is liable to corporation tax at 30% on **unfranked income** (which includes foreign dividends, gilts and bank interest, and underwriting commission). Interest paid on borrowings and management fees can be set against unfranked income, with the result that a trust may not have to pay any tax at all.

To obtain approval by HMRC, the investment trust:

- Must be a UK-resident company, with its ordinary shares quoted on the London Stock Exchange
- Must not be a 'close' company (which means broadly that it cannot be controlled by five or fewer persons)
- Must get 75%+ of its income from shares and securities
- Must have no more than 15% of its assets invested in one company
- Must not distribute its capital gains (except for Venture Capital Trusts)
- Must distribute ≥ 85% of its gross income from shares and securities

Some **offshore-registered** investment companies that are managed in the UK and listed on the London Stock Exchange have s842 ICTA 1988 approval.

3.8 Taxation of the investor

Investors are liable for **income tax** on **dividends** in the same way as they would be with shares in any other company, and will be liable for **capital gains tax** on **disposal of shares**. There will be CGT to pay on any gain if the individual has exceeded his or her annual CGT exempt allowance.

The dividends received from shares in an investment trust are like any other dividend on shares and carry a tax credit of 10%. (As set out in the previous Chapter in respect of equities generally, a non-taxpayer cannot reclaim the tax credit;

there is no further tax to pay for a basic rate or starting rate taxpayer; a higher rate taxpayer has a liability to pay 22.5% tax on the gross dividend in addition to the 10% tax credit.)

The investor is subject to CGT on disposal of shares.

As with unit trusts and OEICs held in ISAs and PEPs, CGT and additional (higher rate) income tax on dividends will be avoided where the shares are held in an **Individual Savings Account (ISA)** or in an existing **Personal Equity Plan (PEP)**.

Stamp duty reserve tax (SDRT) of 0.5% is charged on purchases of shares in investment trusts, as for other UK equities.

4 Life assurance contracts

4.1 Protection and investment

The term **life assurance** implies some form of protection relating to death. There are broadly two types of life assurance contract:

- Contracts that are only for **protection** (insurance) purposes (for example, term assurance, which pays out only on death and only if death occurs within a fixed term)
- Contracts with both **protection and investment** elements

Here, we are concerned particularly with life assurance policies as **investment** products.

We should bear in mind that, particularly as tax relief is not available on premiums on new policies, alternative investments such as ISAs and unit trust and OEIC savings schemes tend to be more tax efficient and/or less costly in charges. Advisers are of course expected by regulators to take these factors into account.

With a policy that has both protection and investment elements, part of premiums paid must go towards providing for the **life insurance cover** element. The premiums required for this cover will be based on actuarial assumptions based on mortality statistics.

Some policies, such as **single premium bonds**, have a relatively low life insurance element and are primarily designed for **investment**. For example, the life insurance cover may be only slightly above the level of premiums paid and then almost all of the premiums will be attributable to the investment element of the policy.

4.2 With-profits policies

The investment element of life assurance products originally developed as a method of distributing underwriting profits to **with-profit** policyholders. In the 1970s, new forms of life assurance investment were developed based on **unit-linking**. Unit-linked funds are effectively **open-ended investments**, where the value of the unit is directly related to the underlying assets of the fund.

With-profits investors with policies in mutual insurers have ownership rights in the life office, and may gain from a windfall distribution from reserves if the company **demutualises**. However, demutualisation is not often more than a possibility and so should not generally influence the investor's choice of policy.

The market for with-profits policies is now mainly in **unitised with-profits** policies.

4.3 Conventional with-profits policies

The traditional non-unitised type of with-profits policy has received criticism in recent years because of the lack of transparency inherent in the **bonus** system that applies to such policies. The policy will specify a **minimum sum assured**, generally payable on death or on maturity, with bonuses payable in addition.

A **conventional with-profit policy** is set up for a **fixed term** and the return is in the form of an increase in capital value between purchase and maturity. This increase in value is based upon the sum assured of the policy and the bonuses added during the life of the policy.

Annual ('reversionary') bonuses are declared and added to the policy (for example, at a 3% compound rate). Annual bonuses broadly reflect the income yield from investments. **Terminal bonuses** are paid when a policy matures or on death. Their level is more variable because it depends more on the capital growth of the underlying investment funds.

Bonus type	When payable
Reversionary/ Normal bonuses	Paid **annually** in arrears: once added, they cannot be removed.
Special bonuses	These are declared under **extraordinary circumstances** (eg on demutualisation or takeover), or to reflect an unexpected exceptional increase in funds.
Interim bonuses	These are paid where **death** occurs between reversionary bonus payments and are proportional to the unpaid bonus.
Terminal bonuses	These are paid at the **end of the term (or on death)** and reflect the growth of the underlying assets over the term of the policy, over and above those previously distributed.

An **advantage** of a conventional with-profits policy is that the investor is aware of bonuses building up towards maturity. However, the declared bonuses are not likely to be paid in full if the policy is surrendered and so the bonuses do not indicate the current value of the policy.

The size of bonuses is set to reflect the performance of the underlying investments over the long term, rather than over a single year. This system is intended to '**smooth**' the effects of fluctuations in underlying investment values and profits. For mutual insurers, the with-profits policyholders are the owners of the business and so are affected by fluctuations in the profits of the business arising from its other insurance business, including profits from its unit-linked business. For insurers that are public limited companies rather than mutuals, there are shareholders to whom dividends will be paid from profits.

The smoothing effect of bonuses means that investors will not see the total of bonuses applied to the policy fall when the stock market falls, but it also means that bonuses applied will not rise greatly in periods when the stock market is booming.

The level of bonuses declared is set by the insurance company's Actuary. Because of relatively poor stock market performance in recent years, the level of bonuses has fallen. This has caused problems for many who have held endowment policies which they had expected would repay interest-only mortgages at the end of their term: many are now expected to show a shortfall below the amount required to repay the mortgage.

Investments underlying the with-profits funds of the company are likely to include a range of asset classes, including equities, fixed interest securities, property and cash. The typical asset allocation is similar to that of unit-based '**managed funds**', which are explained further later in this Chapter. Some companies have however made significant shifts of their allocation in or out of equities in recent volatile stock market conditions.

The performance of a **with-profit investment** will depend on:

(a) The performance of the **underlying investments**, for example equities, fixed interest securities, cash and property

(b) Whether the company is **mutual or proprietary**: proprietary companies must distribute some profits to shareholders

(c) Profits from **other areas of the business** (particularly for a mutual company)

(d) The **strength of the company** (the level of reserves, measured by the free asset ratio) affects the company's ability to continue bonus payments when investment performance is low

(e) The **reserves**, which affect the ability of the company to increase the proportion of equities in the fund as life companies are required to have certain minimum levels of liquidity

If these investments are encashed (**surrendered**) before maturity, the **surrender value** will be calculated by the life company actuary. The value is likely to be significantly less than the accumulated value of the sum assured and bonuses. The amount returned may even be less than the original investment, particularly in the early years. An alternative to surrender is to sell a policy on the **traded endowment policy (TEP)** market.

The insurer generally reserves the right to make a **market value reduction (MVR),** alternatively known as a **market value adjustment (MVA),** to **with-profits policies** if they are surrendered early. This is applied if market conditions are adverse and is intended to protect those remaining with the fund. If there has been a recent severe drop in performance, then an adjustment made to those withdrawing their policies should protect those who remain in the fund and should make surrender values more closely reflect the actual performance of policies. An MVR will not usually apply on death or on maturity of the policy.

4.4 Unitised with-profits

With a **unitised with-profits** policy, the policy value is shown in units, each of which has a specified initial value. Bonuses are declared annually and are added proportionately to each unit. Normally, unlike other types of unit-linked fund, the price of units will never fall. The underlying principle of unitised with-profits investments is similar to that of conventional with-profits policies in that returns are 'smoothed': the surplus returns from good years are held in reserve to enable unit price increases to be made in bad years.

Advantages of unitised with-profits:

- The investor can more easily appreciate the value of the investment, and has the reassurance that the price of units will not normally be reduced.

- Switches can be made to or from unit-linked funds of other types (although a **market value adjustment** may be made, to reflect the fact that with-profit units do not have their value cut when investment markets fall).

4.5 Unit-linked funds

A life assurance policy may have its value linked to the performance of unit-linked funds selected by the investor. Instead of the 'smoothed' bonuses that accrue to a with profits policy, a unit linked policy is exposed more directly to market conditions. The unit price reflects directly the underlying value of investments when the price is quoted, in a similar way to unit trusts.

Through their unit-linked funds, **insurance companies** aim to cater for a wide range of investment objectives that an investor may have. The investment vehicle can be employed to satisfy a requirement for **income** (distribution funds) or for **capital growth**.

The insurance company may also offer unit trusts operated by other companies that investors may select for their policies.

The value of the policy is determined by the number of units allocated to it and their price. There will be a spread between the buying and selling prices of units which will typically be around 5%. This spread means that the surrender value immediately after the policy is commenced will be lower than the initial premium paid. There may also be additional surrender penalties. During the life of the policy, its value will fluctuate according to the prices of the units on which it is based.

Many **unit-linked** funds are similar to non-assurance based funds or are the same as unit trusts and OEIC funds run by the same financial institution. However, the following types of fund are generally found only in life assurance based investments.

- With-profits funds
- Property funds holding direct property investments (rather than property shares)

- 'Managed funds' containing a balanced mix of different asset classes such as equities, fixed interest securities, property and cash deposits.

Like unit trusts and OEICs, unit-linked prices are based on valuations (daily, in the case of equities) of the underlying assets.

The **unit-linked funds** underlying the investment can be **changed** at the request of the investor. A **switch** will change the units already purchased to other available units, whereas a **redirection** changes the funds in which future contributions will be invested. To make a complete change from one fund to another, **switching and redirection** is combined. For example, with a switch from a company's European fund to the Managed fund, the switch exchanges existing European units for Managed fund units while the redirection ensures that future contributions buy Managed fund units. Redirection is often free and many companies offer unlimited free switches. In contrast, switches between investment trusts or unit trusts in non-life assurance based investment plans would incur charges and constitute a chargeable transfer for capital gains tax purposes.

4.6 Endowment policies

The **with-profits endowment policy** is a regular premium savings policy for a fixed term. The term may be between 10 and 25 years. There is very little new business in the category of with-profits endowment policies. Such policies are most likely to be encountered as existing policies, which may be traded as second-hand policies.

Premiums will be paid monthly, quarterly, half-yearly or annually. Only policies taken out before 14 March 1984 benefit from **Life Assurance Premium Relief (LAPR)** on the premiums paid. The premiums are paid net of life assurance tax relief at 12.5%.

The with-profits endowment policy offers the investor a guaranteed sum assured. This is normally quite low as the main aim of the policy is to provide a savings medium.

A bonus is added each year to the sum assured: this is the reversionary or annual bonus. Once added this bonus cannot be taken away. On maturity or earlier death an additional bonus, known as a vesting or terminal bonus, is added to the accrued sum assured and reversionary bonus. The terminal bonus can be a high percentage of the total return.

Before declaring **reversionary bonuses**, the insurance company values its life fund and declares a surplus for the year. The actuaries then recommend how much of the surplus can be allocated to the with profit policyholders with the balance going to reserves. (In the case of a proprietary office provision will need to be made for the shareholders' dividends.) Although the performance of the life fund can vary from year to year depending on investment performance, nevertheless by calling on reserves, if necessary, the insurance company should be able to declare a smooth pattern of bonus over the years. The **terminal bonus** reflects more directly the insurance company's returns in its life fund close to the maturity of the policy.

The Financial Services Authority (FSA) allows insurance companies to quote the projected returns on endowment policies assuming **growth rates** of 4%, 6% and 8% pa. Because providers use this common set of assumed growth rates, different companies' quoted returns based on these assumptions will only differ to the extent that their charges differ.

4.7 Unit-linked endowment policies

The features of unit-linked endowment policies are as follows.

(a)   It is a fixed term policy into which regular premiums are made.

(b)   Most contracts have minimum life cover – simply 75% of the premiums paid over the term of the policy. This level is set to maintain the qualifying status of the policy.

(c)   Some policies are designed only to accept large premium payments, say over £100 per month with the minimum amount of life cover to keep the policy qualifying. These policies are known as maximum investment policies.

(d)   Whatever the size of the premium, the investor has a choice of funds into which his premiums can be invested, including for example UK Equity, Property, European, Pacific, America, Fixed Interest and Cash.

(e)   The premium is invested in the chosen fund or funds and units are then cancelled to pay for the life assurance and charges. The choice of fund will of course depend on the client's attitude to risk.

(f)   Switches between funds are possible. Typically there is one free switch allowed in each policy year and subsequent switches might be possible at a small cost such as £10 or £20.

4.8 Whole of life and endowment policies

Endowment policies normally have payment term of at least ten years, with an option to extend them if required. At the end of the ten-year period, or at a later date, a lump sum can be taken equal to the bid value of the units.

Although the endowment type is more common, a unit-linked savings plan can be written as either an **endowment policy** or a **whole of life policy**. After an initial period, of perhaps ten years, premiums can continue to be paid indefinitely, or the units can be encashed at their bid value at any time.

Unit-linked savings plans usually have enough life cover to make sure that they are qualifying policies (qualifying policies are explained further later in this section). Accordingly, there is typically a guaranteed sum assured of 75% of the premiums payable over the whole term, or up to age 75 in the case of a whole of life policy.

4.9 Charging structure

There is a different charging structure depending on whether a life insurance contract is **with-profits** or **unit-linked**.

The advent of commission disclosure requirements has been one of the factors leading to many insurance companies abandoning traditional **with-profits** policies. This is because of the problem of having to quantify the costs of the policy to the policyholder in the Key Features Document.

As a savings vehicle, the traditional endowment policy is relatively expensive, given the hidden charges. Additionally, the policyholder is paying for life assurance which he may not need. A simpler method is to separate out an individual's protection and savings needs. Protection can then be provided by term assurance and regular investment could be by a regular contribution to an ISA or a unit trust or investment trust savings plan.

The charges on a **unit-linked** policy are more transparent. There is typically a 5% – 6% bid/offer spread on the purchase of units, a monthly policy fee, which may be indexed, and an annual management charge, of perhaps 1%. Insurance companies have used the following methods to extract setting-up charges.

(a)   Low allocation of units for the first 12 to 24 months.

(b)   The use of initial and accumulation units. The first 12 or 24 months premiums are used to purchase the initial units, which carry a heavier charge. Thereafter premiums are invested in the accumulation units.

4.10 Risk

The investment risk involved in a **with-profits** endowment policy is relatively low. The policyholder has a guaranteed sum assured to which a reversionary bonus is added and, once added, cannot be removed, however poor future performance may be. There are however the risks that future bonus rates will drop and that the terminal or vesting bonus may be low or non-existent.

There is also a risk of a poor return on early encashment. The surrender or paid-up values will include penalties which cannot easily be assessed in advance. With many with-profits policies, there will be no surrender value at all if the policy is surrendered within the first year or so. There could also be a tax implication on early encashment of such a policy.

4.11 Purchase, surrender and sale

Endowment policies may be purchased from an insurance company following a recommendation from a company direct salesman, a tied agent or an independent financial adviser.

The products are designed to be held to maturity. Early encashment brings penalties which normally cannot be quantified until the time of withdrawal. The **surrender values** for traditional with profit policies are calculated by the actuary at the time of request. As an alternative to surrender, the policy may be sold on the **traded endowment policy (TEP) market**. The amount obtained from selling could be around one-third more than the surrender value quoted by the insurance company. However, the ease with which a quote can be obtained depends on the demand for TEPs at the time.

4.12 Investment bonds

Insurance companies offer various products that are lump sum investment vehicles. Such non-qualifying policies are variously advertised as 'investment bonds', 'property bonds' or '**single premium bonds**'.

With **investment bonds**, a single payment is made and units are purchased in a fund or funds of the investor's choice.

The investor has the choice of a typical range of **unit-linked funds**. Bonds based on **unitised with-profits funds** are also available. The bond normally allows the investor to spread his capital between a number of funds and to switch between funds. The charges to use the switch facility are nominal. Typically the investor may be allowed one free switch per annum and subsequent switches are at a flat charge of, say, £25.

The investor can withdraw his money from the bond at any time, normally without penalty. There may be a restriction imposed on withdrawal from a property fund, because of the relative illiquidity of the underlying assets of property funds.

The investor can simulate an income from his investment bond by making use of a **withdrawal facility**. Such a facility allows for up to 5% of the original investment to be withdrawn each policy year with no immediate tax charge. The withdrawals are taken into account when calculating any tax on the final gain when the bond is encashed.

For unit-linked policies, there is normally an **up-front charge** which is a 5% bid/offer spread. In addition there will be an **annual management charge** typically of around 0.75% to 1.0% of the value of the fund.

Advisers should take care when recommending a bond rather than, say, an investment trust, OEIC or unit trust. They should be aware of the **compliance requirement** that 'you must not advise a client to buy a packaged product if you are aware of a generally available packaged product which would *better* meet his needs and circumstances'. The charges levied on an investment bond are generally higher than for unit trusts or investment trust. In addition the insurance company pays capital gains tax within the life fund whereas unit trusts and investment trusts do not. The performance of an investment bond may be inferior to a similar unit trust or investment trust for these reasons.

An investment bond offers certain tax advantages for a higher rate taxpayer. The insurance company fund pays tax at 20% on its investment income whereas the client would have a personal tax rate of 40%. The client can take advantage of the 5% withdrawal facility to defer taxation until, possibly, a time when he is a basic rate taxpayer. If an investment bond is held by a higher rate taxpayer and his or her spouse is a basic rate taxpayer, consideration should be given to assigning the policy to the spouse prior to encashment.

The **Trustee Act 2000** permits **trustees** to invest in investment bonds and other life assurance policies. Under the previous Trustee Investment Act 1961, these were only permitted investments for trustees if the trust deed gave appropriate powers to the trustees.

4.13 Guaranteed income bonds

A **guaranteed income bond** is a single premium investment scheme. The level of income is guaranteed and so too is the return of the original investment.

The bond can be constructed in a number of ways, as follows, although the outcome for the investor is much the same.

- A **single premium investment bond**.

- A **series of non-qualifying endowment policies**. Using this method, one bond is encashed each year to pay the income and the encashment of the final bond repays the capital.

- A **combination of a temporary annuity and a deferred annuity**. Using this method the temporary annuity pays the income and the deferred annuity repays the capital at maturity. This method may have advantages for non-taxpayers, basic rate and higher rate taxpayers.

Whichever construction method is used, a guarantee of the return of the original investment on death must be incorporated in the bond.

The bond runs for a fixed term, say one to five years. The investor selects the term to suit his needs. The bond guarantees a fixed rate of income for the selected period. The income is normally paid annually in arrears although some bonds offer a monthly income.

The **income** from the bond is paid net of basic rate tax, so there is no further tax liability for an investor who is a basic rate taxpayer. A non-taxpayer cannot reclaim the tax. The 'gross equivalent' rate of return can be compared with current National Savings & Investments (NS&I) and building society rates in order to make a fair comparison.

The bond guarantees the return of the capital at the end of the selected period.

There is no explicit **charging** structure. The insurance company's charges are taken into account before declaring the interest rate to be offered on the income bond.

The **risk** the investor takes is that interest rates will rise, in which case he is locked into a contract which must run its full course. Surrender values are available but are usually poor.

The bond is purchased from the insurance company. The insurance company is responsible for repaying the capital at the end of the fixed term and also paying the regular income to the client.

4.14 High income bonds

High income bonds can produce guaranteed income levels, at levels depending on market conditions when the bond is purchased. The total returns will be based on the movements in one or more equity indices. Derivatives (call options) are used to enhance income. If the indices rise, the options will generate profits. If the indices fall, the premium is lost, but the capital invested is protected.

The **guaranteed** minimum return will typically be the value of the original investment less the income paid out over the term. The typical expectation for this type of investment is to get a **return** of the original investment at the end of the term (in addition to the income paid out), but again this is **not guaranteed**. Growth on top of this may be a possibility for some bonds, but it is unrealistic to expect much.

This type of investment will appeal to those needing a high guaranteed income. The additional risks taken with this type of investment can lead to a return of the original capital as well as the income, where similar income levels with other investments would almost certainly deplete the capital.

4.15 Guaranteed growth bonds

Guaranteed growth bonds have features, tax treatment, charging structure, risk and methods of purchase and sale similar to guaranteed income bonds, except that the income is allowed to roll up and is paid out with the capital at the end of the term.

The net return from a guaranteed growth bond would need to be compared with the tax free return from NS&I products. The bond should only be used if the interest rate is better or the client already has the maximum holding in the current issue of NS&I Savings Certificates.

4.16 Guaranteed equity bonds

The **guaranteed equity bond** or **protected equity bond** is yet another type of investment bond.

There are various versions.

- The capital may be invested in an equity-linked fund with a guarantee that at the end of a specified period, usually five years, the investor will at least get the return of his capital. The insurance company arrange the guarantee usually by use of traded options.

- The capital may be invested in a scheme which offers a return linked to the growth in an index such as the FTSE 100 Index over the given period or return of the original capital, whichever is greater. The fixed term is usually five years.

- The capital may be invested in a scheme which offers the opportunity to lock into the growth in the FTSE 100 if the index exceeds a certain limit. These 'lock-ins' occur regularly during the term of the scheme.

As the schemes are based on investment bonds and are non-qualifying products, the return, if greater than the original investment, could be subject to tax for a higher rate taxpayer. A basic rate or non-taxpayer would have no tax to pay.

A guaranteed equity bond might be used by a cautious investor who is interested in stock market investments but wishes to restrict his risk.

Such a bond should only be used by an investor who intends and is likely to be able to hold the bond for the full term. If the investor encashes early, he or she will only receive the value of the units, which could be low.

A less cautious investor should receive a better return by direct investment into a FT-SE 100 or equity fund. With a guaranteed equity bond, the investor is paying for the guarantee in the guaranteed equity fund, which restricts the potential performance. Another disadvantage is that many schemes do not credit the investor with the income generated by the dividends paid on FTSE 100 shares, which makes a significant difference in any comparison with direct equity investments.

4.17 Taxation: qualifying and non-qualifying policies

A policy is **qualifying** if:

(a)   The policy secures a capital sum on death, earlier disability, or a date not before the tenth anniversary of taking out the policy

(b)   The premiums are reasonably even and are payable annually or at shorter intervals, ie it must be a regular premium policy, and

(c)   At least a certain capital sum is assured:

   (i)   for endowment policies, 75% of the total premiums payable.
   (ii)   for whole life policies, 75% of the premiums payable up to age 75.

In order for the payout from a policy to be tax-free, premiums must have been paid for a minimum of:

(a)   Life of the life assured

(b)   10 years, or

(c)   Three quarters of the term

4.18 LAPR

Qualifying policies taken out pre 13 March 1984 qualify for **Life Assurance Premium Relief (LAPR).** This gives relief at source on the premium payments at a rate of 12$\frac{1}{2}$ %.

Policies taken out from 13 March 1984 do not generally attract tax relief on premiums paid. (The exception is term assurance linked to a pension policy.)

4.19 Taxation of non-qualifying policies

Non-qualifying policies include what are commonly called **single premium bonds**, **investment bonds** or **property bonds**. A lump sum is invested in a life fund, a small part of which buys cover in the event of death and the balance is invested. As this is not a 'regular premium' investment, it does not meet the definition of a qualifying policy given above.

The encashment of such a policy, whether due to full surrender, sale or death of the life assured, is called a **chargeable event** for income tax purposes. Depending on the circumstances, this event may produce an additional income tax charge in the year in which the event occurs. There will also be a chargeable event if more than 5% of the capital is withdrawn in a year.

HMRC treats the resulting gain as income when the investor receives it. Since the insurance company has already paid tax on income received by the fund, those who have income in the basic rate taxpayer range (ie they pay tax at 22%) have no further tax to pay. Non-taxpayers cannot reclaim the tax, which means that this type of investment is not tax-efficient for them.

The higher rate (40%) taxpayer will be liable to tax at 20% on the overall gain, including earlier 5% withdrawals (on which tax was deferred).

Example: Qualifying and non-qualifying policies

A 20 year endowment policy is taken out. Decide whether the policy will be qualifying or non-qualifying in each of the following circumstances.

(a)   Life assured dies after seven years

(b)   Policy is surrendered after seven years

(c)   Policy is surrendered after 12 years

Solution

(a)   Qualifying (premiums paid for life of life assured)

(b)   Non-qualifying

(c)   Qualifying (premiums paid for at least 10 years)

Any gain on the policy in (b) above would be taxed under the non-qualifying policy rules (see below).

4.20 Friendly Society tax-exempt plans

Friendly societies were established in the 18th and 19th centuries as mutual organisations and they were awarded exemption from tax. The friendly societies offer **savings plans** with investment into a **tax exempt** fund, which may be cash-based, unit-linked or with-profits.

The friendly society's total **tax exemption** on their business in such policies potentially increases the rate of return to policyholders. (Ordinary life assurance companies have to pay corporation tax. However, friendly societies cannot reclaim the 10% dividend tax credit after 5 April 2004.) In spite of the societies' tax exemption, the generally high **charges** on the policies may significantly erode the tax advantage.

The normal maximum total premium which an individual may pay in a 12 month period on all his friendly society policies is **£270**. However, if premiums on a policy are payable **more frequently than annually**, only 90% of the premiums are taken into account for the purposes of the limit, so £25 a month can be paid in: £25 × 12 × 90% = £270, (ie contributions of **£300 pa** can be made).

The friendly societies generally offer 10-year plans. The plans include life cover equal to 75% of total premiums, thus ensuring that they are qualifying policies. The life cover element may be paid for by periodic cancellation of some units.

The Financial Services Authority (FSA) allows friendly societies to provide quotations showing returns of 5% and 9% pa. This is higher than the usual 4% and 8% because of the assumed effect of the societies' tax exemption.

Parents can take out friendly society policies for their children, and the profit will **not** be taxable income of the parent (or the child).

4.21 Offshore bonds

Features of **offshore bonds** are as follows.

(a)   UK life offices, such as Standard Life, Scottish Widows and Sun Life who have offshore subsidiaries, issue insurance bonds from their offices in the Channel Islands, Isle of Man, Dublin and Luxembourg.

(b)   The bonds they issue are non-qualifying life policies with similar facilities to onshore policies.

(c)   The advantage of the offshore bond is that the underlying life funds suffer little or no tax (gross roll up) compared with UK life funds which are taxed at 20%. This tax situation could be advantageous for UK higher rate taxpayers.

(d)   However, the costs of offshore products are typically higher than onshore because the insurance company is unable to offset expenditure against income for tax purposes. A typical charging structure could be 6% initial charge with 1.5% annual management charge.

(e)   An offshore bond should be maintained for as long a period as possible. Because of the charges it can take five years for the value of the offshore fund to start to edge ahead of the UK fund for a basic rate taxpayer and longer for a higher rate taxpayer.

(f)   Withdrawals of up to 5% of the original investment may be taken for 20 years without an immediate tax liability. If the 5% allowance is not used in one year it can be carried forward to the next.

A non-taxpayer might use an offshore bond. In this case money could roll up in a virtually tax-free fund and on encashment any chargeable gain will not be subject to tax. However this may not be a worthwhile exercise because the high charges imposed on the bond may wipe out the tax advantage.

5 Offshore funds

5.1 Introduction

The term **'offshore fund'** refers to funds run from low tax areas. These include the Channel Islands, the Isle of Man, the Cayman Islands, Hong Kong and Bermuda. In recent years, Luxembourg and Dublin have become more significant also, as 'tax havens' within the European Union.

Many offshore funds are run by companies associated with large UK unit trust groups and most of the countries involved now have their own regulatory framework.

Since 1979 when currency exchange controls were abolished, it has become relatively easy for the UK resident to invest his money abroad in equities, bonds or pooled investments such as bonds, UCITS (Undertakings for Collective Investments in Transferable Securities) and OEICs (Open Ended Investment Companies).

There may be income and capital gains tax advantages for **UK expatriates who are non-UK resident** and for **non-UK domiciled UK residents**. For non-UK domiciled persons, there may be inheritance tax advantages. However, investment in offshore funds may be not be as advantageous for **UK residents** as they think, particularly from a tax point of view.

In most cases, the tax benefit is limited to a possible **deferral of tax payments** resulting from income being paid gross.

There can be tax disadvantages, particularly if the offshore fund invests in UK shares.

5.2 Authorisation of offshore funds

S 238(1) of the Financial Services and Markets Act 2000 (FSMA 2000) prohibits any authorised person from promoting any collective investment scheme in the UK unless it is an authorised unit trust, an authorised OEIC, or a recognised scheme. The Financial Services Authority recognises the following offshore pooled investments.

(a) Funds categorised as **Undertakings for Collective Investments in Transferable Securities (UCITS)**, which are constituted in other European Economic Area member states. These funds are automatically recognised by the Financial Services Authority and can be marketed freely in the UK.

(b) **Funds authorised in designated territories**, that is non-EU territories such as the Channel Islands, Bermuda and the Isle of Man. The FSA recognises that certain countries in which investments are based offer a similar regulatory authority and investor protection to that afforded to the UK investor onshore.

(c) **Individually recognised overseas schemes funds**. The FSA also provides for the recognition of overseas schemes on an individual basis.

Non-regulated and non-recognised funds are subject to severe marketing restrictions in the UK. Prospectuses and details can only be forwarded to investment professionals such as stockbrokers and Independent Financial Advisers.

5.3 OEICs/ICVCs

OEICs/ICVCs are the most common form of pooled investment in Europe. OEICs are based on the European type of ICVC known as Société d'Investissement à Capital Variable (**SICAV**). Unit trusts, in contrast, are more like what are known in Europe as Fonds Commun de Placement (FCP).

(a) The attraction of the OEIC is that it can issue any number of types of shares. As we saw earlier in this Chapter, an OEIC is 'open-ended', because the total amount invested in the scheme can be increased.

(b) The ability to offer a wide number of types of shares led to the concept of umbrella funds. With umbrella funds, there are many types of share under one management. Each type of share can invest in a different international sector.

(c)   There is a wider range of funds offered to the investor through an offshore OEIC than an onshore unit or investment trust. The funds include UK Equity, International Equity, International Emerging Markets, International Managed, America, Europe, Japan, Latin America, India, Korea, Hong Kong, Australia, Commodities and Currency funds (in all the major currencies) and Fixed Interest funds (in all the leading currencies: eg yen, sterling, euro, US$).

5.4 UCITS

UCITS are not a separate type of investment, but a classification for existing investments such as unit trusts that can be marketed throughout the European Economic Area, as explained earlier in this Chapter.

UCITS were created as a result of the UCITS Directive introduced by the Council for the European Communities on 20 December 1985 (updated by UCITS II and UCITS III). The idea of the directive was that it would introduce a framework under which a fund management group could market a fund domiciled within one member state to investors resident in another member state.

Under the framework, a manager of a mutual fund certified as a UCITS in its country of domicile may not be refused permission to market the fund in another member state provided it complies with local marketing requirements.

5.5 Taxation of the fund

In general terms there will be no tax paid by an offshore fund. However, there may be withholding tax which may not be reclaimable by the fund. In addition, a fund may be subject to a small amount of local tax. Jersey funds are subject to a flat yearly corporation tax and Luxembourg funds to a tax on the asset value each year. The expenses of an offshore fund cannot be offset against its income.

5.6 Taxation of the individual

The taxation of the individual will depend upon the status of the fund whether it has **distributor** or **non-distributor** status.

(a)   **Distributor status**. Distributor funds are those which are certified annually by HMRC as pursuing a policy of distribution of income. A fund will obtain this status if it distributes at least 85% of its net income after expenses.

The distributions paid from such funds are paid gross. A UK resident will have to declare this income and pay tax as follows.

(i)   A non-taxpayer will have no liability to tax on the distribution.
(ii)   A basic or lower rate taxpayer will pay 10% tax on the distribution.
(iii)   A higher rate taxpayer will have to pay 32.5% on the distribution.

On encashment of the holding or transferring between classes of participating shares, should a capital gain arise, the investor will be liable to capital gains tax on the gain.

(b)   **Non-distributor status**. This category of fund is often referred to as a **roll-up fund**. In this instance, all income is accumulated in the fund. If a fund is not certified with distributor status, on receipt of a distribution or on total encashment a charge to income tax arises. A charge to income tax on a gain rather than **capital gains tax** can be a **disadvantage**. As the charge is to income tax, there will be no annual CGT exemption.

Those not resident in the UK will pay no UK income tax or capital gains tax on an offshore holding but of course they may be subject to tax charges in their new place of residence.

5.7 Uses

Offshore pooled investments may be useful for those who require a wider choice of funds than is available onshore. Offshore funds are particularly attractive to investors who wish to use currency funds.

A fixed interest fund with **distributor** status may be useful for a non-taxpayer. His money will be invested in a fixed interest fund which is rolling up tax-free and he will receive a gross dividend.

With a **non-distributor** fund, the taxpayer will pay no tax while income is rolling up. If a higher rate taxpayer plans to take encashment when he will be a basic rate taxpayer later, this might work to his advantage.

The non-distributor fund may be useful for a UK resident who is anticipating retiring abroad. He can roll up his investment tax-free and encash it when he is no longer a UK resident and subject to UK tax. He should however check on the tax treatment of his investment in the country in which he is then resident.

6 Derivatives

6.1 Introduction

A **derivative** can be analysed as 'a financial instrument valued according to the anticipated price movement of an underlying asset which may be a commodity, a currency or a security'.

The FSA defines derivatives as comprising **futures**, **options** and **contracts for differences (CFDs)**.

It was after its employee Nick Leeson took on huge positions in options and futures on the Tokyo Nikkei share price index that Barings Bank collapsed in 1995. Leeson's Nikkei options were a bet on the index rising. In the event, following the Kobe earthquake of January 1995, the index fell. The size of the contracts was huge compared to the bank's total capital. Barings was unable to meet its obligations and went into receivership.

Because such huge risks can be run, derivatives are often thought of primarily as risky investments. However, derivatives offer the flexibility of taking a position (effectively, 'betting') either way with respect to an outcome. As a result, derivatives can be used to reduce ('**hedge**') risk as well as to adopt more risky positions in financial markets.

Expertise is required in using derivatives. As well as being used by professional fund managers, some individual investors use derivatives. Inexperience and lack of knowledge could result in mistakes and heavy losses being suffered by the unwary. A particular problem is that of less experienced investors taking on large risky positions without fully appreciating their size. It is easy for people to focus on the great potential for making a profit without paying enough attention to the possible downside risk if events turn out differently from how the investor hoped they would. As the example of Barings Bank shows, the results of overly large exposures can be disastrous.

6.2 Futures

A **futures contract** involves an agreement between two parties to exchange a specified item at a specified price on a specified future date.

A futures contract can be a contract to buy or sell commodities, currencies, debt instruments or indices. Financial futures are traded on the London International Financial Futures and Options Exchange (**LIFFE**).

Futures contracts are **traded** on an exchange, with the contract terms clearly specified by the rules of the exchange. The first futures market was established in the nineteenth century, in Chicago. Futures based on the prices of agricultural commodities allow farmers to be sure of the profit they will receive from the commodities, months in advance of the commodities being produced.

The contracts are of a standardised size, with standardised delivery dates. This means that it may not be possible to match the exact exposure one requires over the exact period for which it is required. For example, a requirement to buy

950,000 euros using a currency future must be dealt with by buying 8 contracts, since the contract size is 125,000 euros (950,000 euros/125,000 euros = 7.6, which is 8 contracts to the nearest whole number).

Futures can be traded on **margin,** meaning that the trader only has to spend a small amount of money, far below the value of the underlying asset, to be exposed to the price rise or fall of that quantity of the asset.

Participants in the futures markets may either be speculators, who are prepared to take risks in the hope that the market moves in their favour, or parties seeking to **hedge risks** – that is, to be more sure of the financial position they will be in, when the futures contract expires.

6.3 Options

An **option** provides its buyer with the right, but not the obligation, typically to buy or to sell a commodity, currency or security, at a set price (the exercise price) over a specified time period.

There are options in commodity futures, options in share indices, currencies, bonds and equities. There are option contracts available, with a series of exercise dates, in individual shares of leading UK companies, and in the FTSE 100 Index and the FTSE 250 Index.

In a similar way to an insurance contract, the option buyer pays a non-refundable amount (**premium**) to another party who takes the risk of a claim being made. The maximum that the option buyer can lose is the premium paid.

Payment of a premium is one **difference between options and futures**: there is no initial payment for a futures contract. Another difference is that an option need not be exercised: it confers a right but **not** an obligation. A future will run to delivery, or be closed beforehand.

Complex strategies are possible using options of different kinds and in different combinations, but basically there are two types of options:

Call option. The owner of a call option has the option to **buy** a particular commodity or security at a certain price in the future. Such an option could be purchased if the buyer takes the view that the price is going to rise.

Put option. The owner of a put option has the option to sell a particular commodity or security at a specified price in the future. Such an option could be purchased if the buyer takes the view that prices are going to fall, or alternatively to protect a profit on an investment.

Note that every option involves payment of a premium even if the option is not exercised.

An option can be used to take a **speculative** position which may be **high-risk** – in the hope of making a profit from prices movements – or as a **hedge** (reducing **risk**) – when a position is taken contrary to a risk exposure that an investor already has.

Writing a call or put. The party receiving the premium in an option contract is the writer of the contract. An investor can adopt a position as the writer of the option.

There is trade in the various standardised **traded options** available themselves and these can be bought and sold on an exchange at any time. There are standardised expiry dates for such options. On the other hand, an **'over-the-counter (OTC) option'** or **'negotiated option'** is tailor-made by a financial institution for a particular client and will not be readily tradable.

An **American-style option** is one that can be exercised at any time up to expiry.

A **European-style option** can only be exercised on expiry.

6.4 Warrants

Similarly to share options, **warrants** are instruments which a company may issue in respect of its own shares. Warrants confer the right of the holder to purchase a fixed number of shares at a specified price (the **strike price**) on a fixed date

or dates. Warrants are a security rather than a separate class of share and are transferable (that is, they can be sold in the market).

6.5 Contracts for differences (CFDs)

Contracts for differences (CFDs) are offered by many of the companies that also offer **spread betting**. Both spread betting and CFDs offer ways of taking a position on the price of, for example, individual shares or indices. Spread betting involves betting on a number, such as a share price, in a bet that is traded according to the spread between buying and selling prices offered by the spread betting company. Spread betting does not come into the official (FSA) definition of derivatives, and so we do not describe it further here.

To the person trading CFDs, there are similarities with normal share dealing. The CFD for a share is dealt at the cash price of the share, and a commission is paid. However, the trader does not become a shareholder. The company from whom the CFD is purchased might, however, choose to buy the shares in the market, so that it can pay the trader for any share price increase without incurring the risk of share price movements itself.

CFDs offers some potential advantages to an investor.

- **Trading on margin.** This means that the trader does not have to pay for the full value of the shares in which he takes a position. The margin that he must deposit could be 10% or 25% of the underlying contract value. The trader must pay interest to reflect the credit that margin trading involves, and will be credited with dividends on the underlying shares. By trading on margin, a trader can take positions in excess of his resources: gearing in this way will boost potential returns, as well as increasing the magnitude of possible losses.

- **Taking a short position.** The trader can easily 'sell' shares that he does not own through CFDs. This means that he is taking a 'short' position. (Buying a share involves taking a **'long' position**.) Taking a short position will produce a gain if the share price falls. If the share price rises, the short position loses value.

- **No stamp duty.** Unlike direct share purchases, CFDs are free of stamp duty reserve tax. Like direct share trading, CFD trading is however subject to capital gains tax (unlike **spread betting**, which is exempt from CGT).

Key chapter points

- Collective investments provide a means of investing in markets indirectly. Investors' money is pooled to provide exposure to collections of investments that could be more difficult for investors to hold directly as individuals.

- Collective investment can help the small investor to achieve diversification across different underlying investments, and to gain exposure to less accessible markets such as overseas investments.

- Open-ended fund types include unit trusts and OEICs/ICVCs. When new investors come in, new units/shares can be created. When a lot of investors sell, units/shares must be cancelled. Investment trusts are closed-ended: new investors buy shares from existing holders who wish to sell, and shares do not have to be cancelled just because investors are selling.

- There are rules to ensure that unit trusts and OEICs are adequately diversified.

- Investment trusts have wider investment freedom than unit trusts and OEICs/ICVCs.

- Life assurance contracts have protection and investment elements. With endowment policies and investment bonds, the investment element is more significant than the protection element.

- Advisers must bear in mind that the tax reliefs available on ISAs generally make them more tax-efficient than life assurance-based schemes, and clients should be advised accordingly.

- Unit-linked policies are more widely used than with-profits policies now. With profits investments accrue bonuses at rates declared by the scheme Actuary, at rates designed to smooth out the fluctuations in returns seen over longer periods. Unit-linked investments fluctuate in price with the market.

- Lump sum assurance-based contracts include single premium bonds, guaranteed income bonds, high income bonds, guaranteed growth bonds and guaranteed equity bonds.

- There is no relief on life assurance premiums on qualifying policies taken out since 13 March 1984.

- Higher rate taxpayers have additional tax to pay at 20% on maturity, or partial encashment above 5% permitted annual withdrawals, of non-qualifying policies.

- Offshore funds offer exposure in a wide variety of sectors, but only limited tax advantages.

- Futures contracts, options and CFDs (contracts for differences) are derivatives.

- Trading CFDs is very similar to trading equities, but the investor can take on greater risk because the full value of the underlying investment need not be put up. CFDs also allow short selling, for investors who take the view that a share price is likely to fall.

- Futures are standardised contracts which fix a price for a transaction to take place at a future date.

- Options can give the right but not the obligation to buy or to sell an asset at a specified price.

- Derivatives can be used to speculate, and can involve high risk. Alternatively, they can be used in a strategy that involves hedging (reducing risks to which an investor is otherwise exposed).

Chapter Quiz

1   Identify five advantages to an investor of holding collective investments. ....(See para 1.2)

2   Identify three disadvantages to an investor of using collective investments.................................... (1.2)

3   What is an ICVC?.. (1.3)

4   What is a UCITS scheme? .... (2.1)

5   What is the stamp duty position for investment trust shares? .... (3.8)

6   What are the types of bonus applying to with profits policies? .... (4.3)

7   On what growth rates are projected returns on endowment policies quoted?................................... (4.6)

8   Outline what a guaranteed equity bond is. .... (4.16)

9   What makes a life assurance contract a qualifying policy?.. (4.17)

10   What are the contribution limits for tax-exempt friendly society policies? .... (4.20)

11   What three types of contract come within the FSA definition of derivatives? .... (6.1)

11   Define a futures contract. .... (6.2)

12   Define an option. .... (6.3)

Mortgages and other loans

1 Mortgages

1.1 Introduction

For most people, house purchase is the largest type of transaction they will enter into in the course of their lives. Most home buyers are not able to finance the purchase of a home from their own capital resources and so will usually seek a loan from a bank, building society or other lender to finance the purchase.

A **mortgage** is a loan given on the **security** of a property. The borrower 'mortgages' the property: that is, the borrower creates a legal **charge** over the property to the lender, as security for the loan.

A new purchaser usually pays a proportion of the purchase price of a property – often called the **deposit** – and the balance is typically provided by the mortgage lender. The loan is normally repayable not later than the end of a fixed term which is agreed at the inception of the loan.

In return for the loan the borrower gives the lender **legal rights over the property** for the duration of the loan. While the loan is outstanding, the property remains the lender's security that the loan will be repaid. The borrower cannot sell the property without repaying the mortgage.

If the borrower does not make the required repayments on the loan ('defaults'), after going through appropriate steps **the lender can gain the right to take possession of the property**, sell it, recover the amount of the loan (assuming the

sale price is higher than the loan) and pay the balance after costs to the borrower. The borrower will normally want to avoid this happening: the borrower will incur the costs of sale, and his or her credit standing is likely to suffer, possibly making it more difficult to borrow in the future.

The lender will want to avoid repossessions occurring and, as well as obtaining information about the borrower's income, will assess the **credit status** of the borrower in reaching its decision about whether to offer a mortgage.

On the assumption that the loan is repaid according to the terms of the mortgage, the legal rights over the property revert back to the owner **at the end of the mortgage term**.

Mortgage interest payments no longer benefit from tax relief.

1.2 Mortgage providers

Providers of mortgages (lenders) include:

- Banks
- Building societies
- Insurance companies
- Mortgage corporations (eg, the Agricultural Mortgage Corporation)

1.3 Sub-prime mortgage market

The **sub-prime mortgage market** specialises in providing loans to:

- Applicants with a poor credit history
- Applicants who cannot demonstrate a satisfactory income history

Sub-prime lenders may offer mortgages on the basis of '**self-certification**', meaning that the applicant is not expected to provide evidence of their income. The expansion of this form of lending presents potential dangers if borrowers become over-stretched and unable to keep up their mortgage payments.

1.4 Main mortgage types

There are two main types of mortgage.

(a)   **Capital and interest** (also called a **repayment mortgage**)
(b)   **Interest only mortgage**, which is normally combined with a **repayment vehicle** which will repay the capital

It is possible to **combine the two types of mortgage**. For example, a borrower might borrow £70,000 on a repayment basis plus £30,000 on an interest-only basis.

The roles of the **lender** and an **insurance company** or other **savings scheme manager** providing a repayment vehicle for an interest only mortgage are distinct in the mortgage process.

(a)   The lender, bank or building society **advances the money** and each month he is paid either a repayment (capital and interest) or an amount in interest only.

(b)   If there is a **policy or savings scheme**, for example an endowment policy, ISA or personal pension plan, being used in connection with the mortgage, payments are generally made monthly to the insurance company or other repayment vehicle provider.

1.5 Capital and interest mortgage (repayment mortgage)

With a **repayment** or **'capital and interest' mortgage**, a loan is made for a specified term – say, 25 years – and the borrower repays on a monthly basis. Each monthly payment is made up of both capital and interest, in proportions which vary throughout the term of the mortgage.

In the early years, the monthly repayment pays relatively more **interest** and the **capital reduces relatively slowly**. As the mortgage term proceeds, each regular payment pays off more capital and the interest part becomes smaller. Therefore, when the borrower receives his annual statement, in the early years there will seem to be very little reduction in the loan outstanding, but as the years go by the capital begins to reduce more quickly.

1.6 Interest only mortgage

With an **interest only mortgage**, **the capital remains outstanding** until the end of the mortgage term, and the borrower pays only interest.

The borrower should normally have some **method of repaying the capital** at the end of the term. In past years, the repayment vehicle was often an **endowment policy**. However over more recent years, the tax free lump sums from **stakeholder or personal pension plans** have been more frequently adopted as repayment vehicles, or alternatively the returns from **Individual Savings Accounts (ISAs)** or existing **Personal Equity Plans (PEPs)**.

A further way of repaying the loan is through **sale of the house** on which the loan is secured. At the end of the mortgage term, the borrower might wish to start a new mortgage on a new property of a similar or higher value, or might want to 'trade down', moving to a smaller home, perhaps on retirement.

In the past, the bank or building society lending its money would insist on the endowment policy being **assigned** as collateral in the event of default of payment. This is now less often a requirement.

Some lenders make interest only mortgages available to borrowers **without seeking evidence that there is a specific savings scheme** which the borrower will use to repay the mortgage. The borrower may plan to repay the mortgage eventually out of their own resources, for example their various investments, and this may be acceptable to the lender. Given this more flexible approach by lenders, some borrowers may simply expect to repay the mortgage from the eventual proceeds of the sale of the house, when they next move. Then, they may expect to take on a similar, or perhaps larger or smaller, mortgage on their next property.

It is the borrower's responsibility to maintain any investment scheme designed to provide sufficient funds to repay the mortgage. However, an adviser should ensure that the client is being advised correctly on the investment scheme used, and its risks.

2 Mortgage features

2.1 Introduction

Repayment and interest only mortgages are available with various features, and the number of different possibilities has increased as lenders have sought to come up with new ways to attract mortgage business from competitors. We now look at the main types of feature available.

2.2 Fixed interest rates

With a **fixed rate mortgage**, the borrower is offered a **fixed rate of interest for a fixed term**. This could work to the borrower's advantage or disadvantage, relative to a variable rate mortgage, depending on how interest rates move in future.

The difference between fixed rates offered and variable rates available at the same time could depend on the lender's view of future interest rates, and the extent to which the lender wishes to offer an incentive rate to attract business. The fixed rate will remain unaltered despite changes in overall interest rates.

The **length of the fixed rate** is agreed at outset between the lender and borrower. It could be anything between a few months and five years.

The scheme has the particular advantage that the borrower knows his **exact mortgage outlay for a fixed term** and is not going to be subjected to a sudden shock of increased payment following an interest rate rise.

At the end of the fixed period, the rate may revert to the current variable lending rate, or the borrower may be offered a new alternative arrangement at a new rate.

2.3 Variable interest rates

With a **variable rate mortgage**, the rate of interest required by the lender will vary from time to time in line with the general level of interest rates. As interest rates generally rise, the lender will raise rates for borrowers, just as they must pay higher rates to depositors in order to stay competitive in the savings market.

From the borrower's point of view, there is full exposure to the effects of changes in interest rates. Obviously this could be to his advantage if interest rates fall in the future, but a disadvantage if they rise.

2.4 Cap and collar arrangements

With a **cap and collar mortgage**, the borrower is charged a current interest rate of, say, 6.0% but is given a guarantee that the rate will never rise above, say, 8.0%. This is known as the **cap**.

Conversely, the interest rate paid by the borrower might not be allowed to fall below 4.5% (the **collar**), even if overall rates fall beneath this.

2.5 Interest rate discounts

Lenders may offer a **discounted rate of interest** for a period, eg 0.5% discount below the lender's standard variable rate for a period of 12 months.

Discounted rates offered to **first time buyers** are sometimes more generous than other discounted rates, although it is less usual to single out this group for marketing purposes than used to be the case.

At the end of the discounted period, the rate of interest may **revert** to the current variable rate being charged to borrowers.

2.6 Low start mortgages

A **low start mortgage** is a type of **repayment mortgage**. In the initial period, which may be two years, only interest is paid to the building society.

In year three, the full repayment mortgage starts on the total loan and payments will increase at that stage.

2.7 Deferred interest

With a **deferred interest mortgage**, the borrower pays **only part of the interest for a period**.

At the end of the period, repayments will be higher as the loan has been increased by the **deferred and unpaid interest**.

Some lenders will allow borrowers a payment holiday for a period: for example for one or two years. Again, any interest payments are deferred.

2.8 Tracker mortgage

A **tracker mortgage** has an interest rate that follows ('tracks') a published **benchmark interest rate**, such as the London Inter-Bank Offered Rate (LIBOR), which is the interest rate at which banks lend to each other.

2.9 Flexible mortgages

The **flexibility** offered by some mortgage products may arise from the following features.

- **Irregular payments facility**. The borrower can make payments in irregular amounts, rather than paying a constant amount each month. The irregular payments can be underpayments (ie less than the regular monthly amount), overpayments or payment holidays. However, underpayments and payment holidays may be restricted by the amount of overpayments the borrower has previously made.

- **Additional borrowing facilities**. Flexible mortgages may include a facility to increase the amount borrowed. Additional borrowing facilities are agreed in advance up to a maximum loan-to-value (LTV) ratio, typically 75% to 90%.

A further aspect of flexibility is the method of **calculation of interest** on the outstanding loan. With flexible mortgage arrangements, interest is generally calculated on a daily basis. Borrowers will therefore obtain an immediate benefit from any overpayments they make. This contrasts with traditional mortgage arrangements in the past, when interest was typically added to the policy annually and the borrower might not be given credit for interest purposes if partial repayments were made mid-year.

2.10 Offset mortgages

An **offset mortgage** is a mortgage plan in which the customer has both a current account, and possibly also a savings account, with the mortgage provider. There is a facility to offset positive balances on the current account or savings account against the mortgage account balance. As a result, the customer saves on interest at the normal mortgage interest rate, to the extent of the balances maintained in the current account or savings account.

Some providers link **credit card** or **personal loan balances** with the mortgage account, with the advantage to the customer that the mortgage interest rate is charged on these balances, rather than the usually higher credit card or personal loan rates. The customer should however be wary of adding too much short-term debt to the mortgage balance in this way.

2.11 Current account mortgages

With a **current account mortgage**, the mortgage loan is debited directly to a current account. This arrangement is rather like operating a current account with a very large overdraft facility, represented by the mortgage. This means that any current account credit balance is utilised to reduce the mortgage interest payable instead of earning nil or low interest as it would in most current accounts.

2.12 Islamic mortgages

The payment of interest is against Islamic law. A mortgage set up to comply with **Islamic (Sharia) law** may operate as follows.

(a) The lender buys the property in partnership with the customer, who pays for a minority stake.

(b) The customer lives in the property.

(c) The customer pays monthly instalments to the lender, covering purchase of the lender's share plus rent for the use of the property.

The customer owns the property outright on payment of the final instalment.

This type of arrangement used to attract a double charge to stamp duty. In April 2003, the stamp duty rules were changed and the double charge abolished.

HSBC is one lender that now offers Sharia-compliant mortgages.

2.13 Further advances and remortgages

A lender may allow a borrower a **further advance**, which will represent an increase in the amount borrowed during the mortgage term. This additional loan might be for **home improvement**, or for some other purpose.

A **re-mortgage** is a loan taken out with a new lender. Someone may change from one lender to another without moving home, for example to take advantage of better loan terms. Where an additional mortgage loan is taken out with a second lender, so that there are two loans in force, the second lender will require a **second charge** on the property.

The homeowner's **equity** is the excess of the value of the home over the outstanding mortgage. Some people use the opportunity to increase their loan, or to remortgage with a different lender, in order to **withdraw equity**, which they may then use for other purposes.

3 Mortgage repayment vehicles

3.1 Endowment policies

Endowment policies have become a relatively uncommon choice of repayment vehicle for new mortgages, particularly because of concerns about:

(a) Falls in policy bonuses, with the result that many endowment mortgages taken out in the past cannot now repay the mortgage at the date originally intended

(b) Endowment policies having been 'mis-sold' in the past

(c) The charges carried by such policies

(d) The lack of transparency of the policies

(e) The general move away from with-profits investments

Assume that a client has taken out a mortgage loan of £80,000 for 25 years. The client could take out a 25 year endowment policy with a sum assured of £80,000 to repay the outstanding loan in 25 years time. In this example, there is bound to be sufficient capital to repay the loan because the guaranteed sum assured is equal to the loan. However, this would be a relatively expensive policy. In most cases, the basic sum assured will be less than the amount of the loan: it is hoped that the shortfall is made up by bonuses declared over the life of the policy. If such bonuses are below expected levels, the borrower might not have sufficient proceeds from an endowment policy at the end of the term to repay the mortgage. It is important that clients understand the risks involved.

For an indication of whether the endowment policy should repay a sufficient sum, the lender will provide projections of the eventual proceeds of the policy based on assumed rates of investment return.

The death cover under the endowment policy, whatever type, should always be sufficient to repay the loan.

Types of endowment policy

(a) **Non-profit endowment policy**. This policy will have a guaranteed sum assured sufficient to repay the outstanding loan on death or survival. However, the investment return on this type of product is unattractive and they are rarely used. Total repayments would be relatively expensive.

(b) **With-profits endowment policy**. In this case, the borrower will take out an endowment policy for the same term as the loan and a sum assured equal to the value of the loan.

Reversionary bonus and, hopefully, terminal bonus will be added to the sum assured so that at maturity there should be a surplus over the amount required to repay the mortgage. Any surplus will be returned to the borrower by the building society as a tax free cash sum.

In the event of death of the borrower, the sum assured will be sufficient to repay the outstanding loan plus a surplus depending on bonus performance.

(c) **Low cost endowment policy**. The low cost endowment policy was introduced in an attempt to keep down the cost of repayment of the outstanding loan. The policy is a combination of a traditional with profits endowment policy and reducing term life assurance (life cover).

The policy is effected for total cover equal to the loan outstanding. The cover is then split between an endowment policy and a reducing term assurance. A conservative level of bonus is assumed and the term assurance reduces each year by this amount. If the endowment sum assured has risen at the same rate then the total amount of cover required will be maintained.

If bonus rates fall, there is no guarantee that the return under this policy will be sufficient to repay the mortgage. If the reversionary bonuses are better than predicted, then there should be a surplus, which will be tax-free. (The policy will normally be a **qualifying policy** and, so long as it runs for 75% of its term or at least ten years, the proceeds will be tax-free.) Similarly, a **terminal bonus** declared by the insurance company could lead to a surplus cash sum.

There is always a guaranteed level of death benefit equal to the outstanding loan.

(d) **Unit-linked endowment policy**. A unit-linked endowment policy would be effected for the same term as the mortgage.

This policy provides a guaranteed death return equal to the outstanding loan.

Premiums are used to buy units in a chosen fund and units are then cancelled to purchase the life cover. The maturity value is dependent upon the performance of the units and therefore there is no guarantee that there will be sufficient to repay the loan.

3.2 Pension plans

With a **pension mortgage**, the borrower uses a **stakeholder pension plan** or other **personal pension plan** to repay his mortgage.

With a personal or stakeholder pension, **25% of the value of the fund** at retirement age can be taken as a tax free lump sum and it is this sum which is used to repay the mortgage. The pension plan may be a with-profits type, in which case returns are provided in the form of declared bonuses. Alternatively, it may be a unit-linked policy, in which case investment returns accrue in the form of changes in the fluctuating price of units held in the plan.

The **youngest age** that benefits can be taken from a personal pension (except in the case of approved occupations) is (currently) 50 and therefore the mortgage must run to that age so that the capital is available at the right time to repay the mortgage.

Level term life assurance for a sum assured equal to the amount of the loan and for the same term should run alongside the pension policy to provide a benefit in the event of the borrower's death. This can be taken out as pension term assurance and tax relief obtained on the premiums paid, provided that total contributions including the premiums are within overall income limits.

With a pension plan, there is the advantage that payments into the pension plan receive full tax relief, and the 25% lump sum payout is tax-free. However, since only 25% of the plan is going towards paying off the mortgage, the arrangement will only suit some borrowers. If an intending borrower is already making payments into a personal pension plan and has no other planned use for the 25% lump sum available on retirement, then he may wish to treat the plan as the repayment vehicle for a mortgage. However, if a borrower is starting a pension plan in order to act as mortgage repayment vehicle, then this needs to be considered in the context of the financial arrangements of their overall retirement planning. By setting up a pension plan so that 25% of it will pay off a mortgage, the borrower will also need to finance the remaining 75% which will eventually be paid as a pension.

The pension policy is, by law, a non-assignable contract and as such **cannot be assigned to the lender**. However, assignment of the term assurance policy may be required.

3.3 ISAs and PEPs

Individual Savings Accounts (ISAs) and existing **Personal Equity Plans (PEPs)** can be used as repayment vehicles for **accumulating capital** to pay back the capital on an interest only mortgage.

PEPs were a scheme which preceded ISAs with similar investment rules to a stocks and shares ISA, and some clients may have capital in PEPs which they can utilise as a mortgage repayment vehicle.

Up to £7,000 per tax year (6 April to 5 April) can currently be invested in a maxi-ISA, where the funds may be used to purchase individual equities or bonds, or collective funds such as unit trusts, OEICs or investment trust shares as well as 'risk-controlled' products that meet specific 'stakeholder' rules.

The accumulation of the capital to repay the mortgage is dependent on the performance of the investments chosen. We looked earlier at the relative risks of different types of investment: if the borrower is exposed heavily to equity markets through ISAs/PEPs, the long term returns could be greater than for other types of investment, but equally the level of risk is greater with equities. A mix of different backing investments, such as bonds and equities, could be considered.

A client could make his ISA/PEP contributions on a **monthly basis** or by **annual payments**. The ISA/PEP holder might wish to phase the eventual encashment.

The ISA/PEP has **no fixed term** so, if the investment grows sufficiently, the outstanding capital may be repaid early. The continuation of ISAs and PEPs is subject to future government policies.

The lender may require that there is **level term life assurance policy** in place to cover the life or lives of the borrower.

An ISA or PEP **cannot be assigned** to the lender.

ISA contributions do not attract **tax** relief on payment into the ISA. However, capital gains within the ISA are tax-free.

There is no longer repayment of the 10% tax credit deemed to have been paid on dividends received in an ISA or PEP. However, there is no further tax to pay on dividends, as there would be for a higher rate taxpayer on non-ISA/PEP dividends received.

3.4 Other investments

As mentioned earlier, a borrower may have **other types of investment** that will be accepted by the lender as the basis of an interest only mortgage.

Some lenders do not require the borrower to provide evidence of investments prospectively being available for the future repayment of the loan, particularly if the ratio of the loan to the value of the house (**loan-to-value ratio or LTV**) ratio is low, and the borrower's credit standing is high. Therefore, the borrower might not have specific investments held in order to repay a mortgage.

This may be a viable strategy depending on the individual's circumstances and attitudes. The borrower may wish to retain a loan at approximately the same nominal value through its term, until the house is eventually sold and the **house proceeds** are used to repay the loan.

4 Other personal loans

4.1 Introduction

Personal loans that are not secured on property come in various forms. Given the lack of security, the risk for the lender if the borrower defaults is greater. It is partly because of this that rates of interest on unsecured borrowing are generally higher than for mortgages. Another reason for higher rates on unsecured borrowing than on mortgages is that amounts of unsecured borrowing tend to be smaller, and therefore the costs of servicing the loan may be relatively higher than for mortgages. At the highest range of the interest rate scale are companies offering loans to customers with low credit ratings and collecting payments by personal visits to the customers' homes.

4.2 Current account overdraft

One option is the **current account overdraft.** The current account holder applies for an overdraft limit. The bank or building society will assess the customer's record and credit history and may authorise a specified limit for a specified time. The customer will pay interest, typically on a daily basis, on the amount by which they overdraw on the current account. If the customer exceeds authorised overdraft limits, a higher interest rate may be charged, and the banking institution may impose further charges because the account conditions have been breached.

4.3 Credit card borrowing

A customer may alternatively borrow through their **credit card** account. The account will have an authorised credit limit. Interest is charged on the balance on the account, following purchases of goods and services made on the card account, normally after an initial interest free period depending on the credit card statement date. If the full balance is paid off each month, no interest is charged. Interest is charged on any outstanding balance. If cash advances are taken on the card, these normally attract interest charges from the date of the advance.

4.4 Store cards

Store cards are similar to credit cards except that their use is restricted to purchases made in a particular store or stores. Interest rates may be higher or lower than the rate applying to a customer's standard credit card.

4.5 Unsecured personal loans

Unsecured personal loans are available to provide a specific sum, for example for car purchase. The customer makes regular payments of capital and interest. As with a mortgage, with level repayments, early payments consist mainly of interest, while later payments include a greater proportion of capital repayment.

Unsecured personal loans are **less flexible** than credit card or overdraft borrowing: for the latter two types of borrowing, the customer pays interest only on the amount drawn, which may fluctuate up and down according to the customer's day-to-day and month-to-month circumstances. This can mean cost savings compared with the personal loan, for which the amount on which interest must be paid is determined by the repayment schedule.

4.6 Hire purchase (HP)

With **hire purchase**, the customer does not own the item being purchased (for example, a car) until all the payments have been made. The HP company can claim the goods back if the customer defaults on making payments.

If the customer has paid a third or more of the value of the goods, the HP company would have to get a court order to claim the goods back. The customer may still owe payments to the company in these circumstances.

HP can be a more expensive purchase method than a personal loan or credit card. However, it may be easier for an individual to obtain HP than to obtain credit from a bank or credit card company, particularly if their credit status is relatively low.

4.7 Secured loans

Some lenders will provide loans secured on a customer's house. If there is already a mortgage on the house, this security will be in the form of a second charge on the property.

Interest rates for such secured loans may only be slightly less than rates for unsecured loans. A better option may be for the individual to seek a **further advance** from their **mortgage** lender, which might be at the same rate or at a rate close to that of the customer's existing mortgage.

4.8 Interest-free credit

Interest-free credit deals are offered by many stores, for example on consumer goods such as refrigerators or televisions.

The customer takes the goods, and is given a specified time to pay – perhaps six months. If the payments are not made on time, then interest charges become payable, generally for the whole of the period.

Thus, the 'interest-free' feature is really a way of avoiding interest if the goods are paid for by a specified time. The credit provider expects that many customers will not repay within the specified period, and the provider will therefore earn interest on many of the contracts.

4.9 Credit unions

Credit unions can offer a relatively cheap way to borrow, for those eligible to join them. Credit unions are not allowed to charge more than 1% per month (12.68% annual equivalent).

Credit unions are co-operative organisations and are now FSA-regulated. All members of a particular credit union must have a 'common bond', such as living or working in the same place, working for the same employer, sharing the same occupation, or belonging to the same trade union, housing association, church or other association.

Someone must normally have saved with the Credit Union for a specified period before they can borrow, and the borrowing is usually limited to three times the amount the customer has saved.

5 Commercial loans

5.1 Introduction

Commercial lending is offered by banks and building societies.

Commercial loans include:

- Business **loans**
- **Overdrafts**
- Commercial **mortgages**, including **buy-to-let** mortgage loans

Lending may be offered to companies, to partnerships or to individuals for commercial purposes.

The following types of facility are possible.

(a) **Overdraft facility**. A company, through its current account, can borrow money on a short-term basis up to a certain amount. Overdrafts are repayable on demand.

(b) **Term loan**. The customer borrows a fixed amount and pays it back with interest over a period or at the end of it.

(c) **Committed facility**. The bank undertakes to make a stipulated amount available to a borrower, on demand.

(d) **Revolving facility**. The facility is renewed after a set period. Once the customer has repaid the amount, the customer can borrow again.

(e) **Uncommitted facility**. The bank, if it feels like it, can lend the borrower a specified sum. The only purpose of this is that all the paperwork has been done up front. The bank has no obligation to lend.

5.2 Loans to businesses

Term loans are available from banks to cover medium to long-term finance requirements involving capital expenditure. Interest rates on term loans may be fixed or variable. Lenders make additional charges for arranging the loan and also for effecting any security.

The lender cannot call in a term loan before the end of the term unless the borrower has defaulted in making a repayment or is otherwise in breach of the lending arrangements.

Sometimes a substantial amount of the borrowing is not subject to regular repayments (to keep them down) but is repaid in one lump sum at the end of the term (a '**balloon payment**').

Lending to finance working capital. Lending money, usually on overdraft, to finance some of the working capital of the business (its normal trading assets, including **stocks** of goods held and **debtors**: the amounts it is waiting to receive from customers) is quite normal. However, when the intended purpose of an advance is to finance a big increase in stock-holding or debtors, the bank will consider the liquidity of the business, and whether the customer will need more and more financial assistance from the bank as time goes on.

A loan to set up a **new business venture** should normally be viewed in the context that all new ventures are risky. While many do succeed, a considerable number of them fail to make profits and survive.

5.3 Amount borrowed

The lending proposition made on behalf of the customer should state exactly **how much** the customer wants to borrow. This might seem self-evident, but there are two important points to consider.

(a) The banker will check that the customer is not asking for **too much**, or **more than** is **needed** for the particular purpose. This is especially important with requests for an overdraft facility. Clearly this consideration is linked in with the customer's assets and ability to repay.

(b) The banker checks that the customer has not asked for **less** than he or she really needs. Otherwise the bank may later have to lend more, purely to safeguard the original advance.

The bank's lending policy will indicate limits on the amount of certain loans and the amount which must be paid 'up front' by the customer.

5.4 Repayment terms

The likelihood that the advance will be repaid is the most important requirement for a loan. A bank will not want to lend money to a person or business who has not got the resources to repay it with interest, even if it also has **security** for the loan. Security for the loan gives the lender the right to take certain assets if the borrower defaults, but security should be treated as a **safety net**.

The timescale for repayment is very important. Overdrafts are technically repayable **on demand** (though it is rare for a bank to insist on this without first having discussed a different timescale). Other loans might be payable in instalments, especially loans to acquire assets.

5.5 Security for lending

The **security for a loan** should have the following characteristics.

(a) **Easy to take**. The bank will want to have, or to obtain easily, title to the secured property so that it may be sold and the loan repaid.

(b) **Easy to value**. The security should have an identifiable value which:

- Is stable or increasing, and
- Fully covers the lending plus a margin

(c) **Easy to realise**. The ideal security is one which can readily be sold and converted to cash. Banks prefer readily realisable security for the following reasons.

- The administrative costs are thereby kept to a minimum.
- There is less danger of deterioration (say, of premises) between the time of default and that of realisation.
- A quick pay-off reduces the length of time over which interest accrues on the unpaid advance.

A **floating charge** 'floats' over a specified type of asset of the company (usually stock). The charge does not prevent the borrower from selling or otherwise dealing with those assets.

5.6 Personal guarantees

Often, in its search for security, the bank will ensure that a business loan is supported by a **personal guarantee**. Such requirements are mainly a concern of smaller or medium sized businesses, largely run by their owners.

For example, Mr Badger is Managing Director of Setts Ltd. Setts Ltd has an overdraft arrangement with the bank, but Mr Badger has to give a personal guarantee of the overdraft. This means that if Setts Ltd fails to pay its debt **to the bank**, the bank can call in the guarantee, and Mr Badger will have to pay the debt out of his own resources.

5.7 Overdrafts

Where payments from a current account exceed income to the account for a temporary period, the bank finances the deficit by means of an **overdraft**. It is very much a form of **short-term lending**, available to both personal and business customers.

By providing an overdraft facility to a customer, the bank is committing itself to provide an overdraft to the customer whenever the customer wants it, up to the agreed limit. The bank will earn interest on the lending, but only to the extent that the customer uses the facility and goes into overdraft. If the customer does not go into overdraft, the bank cannot charge interest.

The bank will generally charge a **commitment fee** when a customer is granted an overdraft facility or an increase in his overdraft facility. This is a fee for granting an overdraft facility and agreeing to provide the customer with funds if and whenever he needs them.

5.8 Swinging account

With lending to support normal trading finance is that the amount of the overdraft required at any time will depend on the **cash flows of the business**: the timing of receipts and payments, seasonal variations in trade patterns and so on. An overdraft will increase in size if the business writes more cheques, but will reduce in size when money is paid into the account.

There should be times when there will be no overdraft at all, and the account is in credit for a while. In other words, the customer's account may well **swing** from overdraft into credit, back again into overdraft and again into credit, and so on. The account would then be a **swinging account**. The overdraft bridges the gap between cash payments and cash receipts.

When a business customer has an overdraft facility, and the account is always in overdraft, then it has a **solid core** (or **hard core**) instead of swing.

Example: Overdraft

The accounts of Blunderbuss Ltd have the following record for the previous year.

Quarter to	Average balance £		Range £		Debit turnover £
31 March 20X5	40,000 debit	70,000 debit	20,000 debit		600,000
30 June 20X5	50,000 debit	80,000 debit	25,000 debit		500,000
30 September 20X5	75,000 debit	105,000 debit	50,000 debit		700,000
31 December 20X5	80,000 debit	110,000 debit	60,000 debit		550,000

These figures show that the account has been permanently in overdraft, and the hard core of the overdraft has been rising steeply over the course of the year (from a minimum overdraft of £20,000 in the first quarter to one of £60,000 in the fourth quarter).

If the hard core element of the overdraft appears to be becoming a long-term feature of the business, the bank might wish, after discussions with the customer, to convert the hard core of the overdraft into a **medium-term loan**, thus giving formal recognition to its more permanent nature. Otherwise annual reductions in the hard core of an overdraft would typically be a requirement of the bank.

5.9 Hire purchase and leasing

Hire purchase and **leasing** arrangements are flexible methods for businesses to acquire a variety of assets such as **plant, machinery and vehicles**. The arrangements can greatly assist cash flow, as they do not require the usual large down-payment associated with acquiring such assets.

5.10 Commercial mortgages

As with personal mortgages, a **commercial mortgage** is a loan secured on a property purchased by a business. The property could comprise offices, stores or warehouse or factory units.

Commercial mortgages are typically available for any time period between 5 to 25 years. The maximum length of the mortgage is typically 20 years for newer properties and 15 years for older properties.

As with personal mortgages, the percentage of the property value that a provider will be prepared to lend will depend on the lender's assessment of the customer's earning prospects (in this case, the business) and of the quality of the security (the property).

A sole trader will bear all the responsibility and potential liability of a mortgage in the trader's name. In a partnership with unlimited liability, all of the partners involved are jointly and individually responsible. With a company structure, the directors could be liable if the mortgage is not repaid. The lender might require personal guarantees from the directors.

A business might form a separate business entity to arrange the mortgage and then lease the building to the operating company. This could protect the operating business if there is a default on the mortgage.

5.11 Buy-to-let mortgages

A loan to an investor who uses a mortgage to buy a house for the purpose of letting is often called a '**buy-to-let**' mortgage.

Buy-to-let mortgages are considered to be more risky for the lender than mortgages to owner-occupiers. Accordingly, the buy-to-let investor may typically have to put up around 10-15% or more as a deposit.

The interest rates are likely to be higher than for owner-occupier loans, but both interest only and repayment mortgages are available for buy-to-let.

The amount that the mortgage provider will lend is likely to be based on the expected **rental yield** (annual rent as a percentage of the property price) from the property. The investor's **other income** may also be taken into consideration.

The buy-to-let investor is able to set off the mortgage interest payments and other expenses against rent received for tax purposes.

Key chapter points

- With house purchase being the largest transaction most people undertake, people usually obtain a mortgage to help them to buy a house.

- A personal or commercial mortgage is a loan given on the security of a property. If the borrower defaults on repayments, the lender can re-possess the property and sell it to repay the debt.

- The two main types of mortgage are repayment mortgages and interest only mortgages.

- With a repayment (or 'capital and interest') mortgage, each repayment consists of interest and a capital repayment.

- The capital element of an interest only mortgage does not reduce over the term, if repayments are kept up at usual levels. The borrower may repay an interest only mortgage using the proceeds of sale of the house, the value of investments such as ISAs/PEPs or an endowment policy, or the tax-free lump sum from a personal pension plan.

- Mortgage products are now available with various features, including fixed interest rates for a period, caps and collars. Offset mortgage plans set off mortgage loan balances against credit balances on current accounts or savings accounts, so that interest will only be charged on the net figure.

- Other forms of personal borrowing, such as unsecured loans or credit card borrowing, usually carry higher rates of interest than a mortgage loan.

- Forms of commercial borrowing, for sole traders, partnerships or companies, include overdrafts, term loans and mortgages.

Chapter Quiz

1   What are the two main types of mortgage? .... (see para 1.3)

2   Give three examples of repayment vehicles for an interest only mortgage. ....(1.5)

3   What is a cap and collar mortgage? ....(2.4)

4   Why are endowment policies now rarely used as repayment vehicles for new mortgages? ....(3.1)

5   Outline how hire purchase (HP) works. ....(4.6)

6   What is the maximum interest rate that a credit union may charge a borrower? ....(4.9)

7   What is a swinging account? ....(5.8)

8   What is the relevance of rental yield in relation to obtaining a buy-to-let mortgage? ....(5.11)

1 Budgeting

1.1 What is a budget?

Budgeting is an organised way of managing one's money. It can be described as setting out and totalling all of the various items of **income** and **expenditure** one has, using weekly, monthly or yearly figures.

Constructing a simple **spreadsheet** on a computer is an easy way to set out such a budget.

A financial adviser will often collect information on the client's monthly income and expenditure through a **fact-find** interview about the client's circumstances.

1.2 Categories for a budget

Exercise: Budgeting

Set out the categories of income to include in a standard budget sheet that would apply to individuals with different circumstances.

(The FSA Consumer Help web pages suggest ten categories of income. The first category is:

Earnings from your job or self-employment)

Then, compare your listing to the FSA Consumer Help listing given below.

The Financial Services Authority's **Consumer Help** section, on its website, suggests the following categories for a personal budget.

Your income

Earnings from your job or self-employment
Less tax and other deductions
Pensions from former employers or your own plans
State pension
Child benefit and tax credits
Other state benefits
Interest from savings accounts
Income from shares, unit trusts etc
Other income from investments
Miscellaneous

Your spending

Mortgage, rent, home maintenance
Council tax and water rates
Fuel and power bills
Food and non-alcoholic drinks
Alcohol
Tobacco
Clothing and footwear
Household goods
Home insurance, telephone, other household services
Medicines, toiletries, hairdressing, other personal items
Motoring, fares, other travel
Going out, holidays, other leisure
Life insurance, medical insurance
Regular savings
Loan repayments (other than mortgage)
Miscellaneous

In practice, the categories chosen can be tailored to suit the particular circumstances, whether they are those of a student, a family with children or a retired professional, for example.

1.3 Taking action

What **action** should be taken as a result of the budgeting exercise?

The FSA puts it in these simple terms, in advice aimed directly at the consumer:

- If spending exceeds income, there is an income shortfall: cut back on spending to keep it within income.
- If income exceeds spending, you could put your surplus income towards achieving your financial goals.

Certainly, you will have many clients who have not systematically set out a budget of their personal circumstances. Those clients that do know how they spend their money will generally have better control over their personal finances than those who do not budget.

Preparing such a budget may suggest to a **client** their own ideas about how they would like to change how they spend their money.

An **adviser** may also be able to point out ways in which expenditure might be reduced, particularly where financial planning aspects are involved. For example, if there are borrowings, there may be ways of re-arranging these so that the overall interest burden is lower. A further advance might be sought on a mortgage, at relatively low cost, to replace higher-cost credit card, personal loan or other borrowings. In this type of case, the costs of re-arranging loans should be considered.

Clients who rely heavily on **investment income** should find a budgeting exercise a useful way of indicating whether, given their current income needs, they will be able to maintain the real value of their income in the future.

In budgeting incomes and expenditures, it can be useful to check what the outcome will be if current incomes and expenditures continue.

Budgeting can also be an excellent aid to planning possible changes in an individual's circumstances. For example:

- What will the impact be on a family's finances if a daughter is sent to a fee-paying school for her two final years of schooling? A budget covering the years concerned will help to show whether this can be financed from income, or whether loans may be required or investments may need be sold.

- What will be the effect of a salary earner switching to part-time working? Expenditure may be affected as well as income: travel-to-work costs may be lower, although there could be additional costs if the person is planning to take up new interests as part of the change in lifestyle.

2 Borrowing

2.1 Introduction

We saw in Chapter 1 of this Study Text how the financial system plays a role in channelling funds from those who have a **surplus** to invest to those who wish or need to **borrow**.

In Chapter 4, we looked at the main types of **mortgages and other loans** that are available, and you may wish to briefly review that Chapter in considering **borrowing as an area of financial advice.**

2.2 Advising on borrowings

Individuals commonly take on a high level of borrowings at the time when they buy a house, and so decisions about mortgages are significant. A buy-to-let investor may be borrowing money to buy several properties.

Financial advisers may be involved in helping clients with **mortgage choices** and, if an interest only option is being considered, the choice of an appropriate **repayment vehicle** for the mortgage will be a part of this.

Re-mortgaging – the process of switching a mortgage to a new lender without moving home – has become increasingly popular. As the mortgage market has become more competitive, lenders have been keen to encourage mortgage borrowers to switch borrowings away from other lenders to them. Incentives such as free legal and survey fees are sometimes offered to re-mortgaging customers.

- Re-mortgage business can be attractive to the lender because the borrower will already have a track record with the previous lender, and the average loan-to-value ratio on re-mortgages will generally be lower than for new loans, since the value of the house will probably have risen since the borrower first bought the property.

- For borrowers, re-mortgaging is an opportunity to 'shop around' for the best deal, and may also be treated as an opportunity to take out a larger loan than before, perhaps to finance other spending such as purchase of a car. (This is the process of **equity withdrawal**.)

Advice on borrowing is however more than just a matter of advising on the selection of mortgage and loan products. The borrowings that a client has, or potentially could have, is a matter that can be reviewed in the light of the client's overall financial circumstances.

For example:

- Is there scope for re-organising or re-scheduling borrowings, to reduce their overall cost? (Consider: interest rates, arrangement and other costs arising from changing loans.)

- If the client has savings as well as a mortgage, should some of the savings be applied to make a part-repayment of the mortgage? (Mortgage providers often now allow part-repayments to be made easily, without penalty. If savings will earn a lower after-tax return than is being paid on the loan, a repayment will save money. An offset mortgage – see Chapter 4 – could be the answer. The client's need or desire to keep some savings available, for example in an emergency, is an aspect to consider here.)

3 Investment and saving

3.1 Introduction

Access to a varied range of different forms of **investment** is wider than it has ever been. Equally, along with the great variety of client circumstances you may encounter, people have different attitudes to risk and they have different levels of interest and available time in managing their financial affairs.

The variety of client circumstances will include people at different stages of their lives. Some will have outgoings and commitments that preclude them from making significant regular **savings** from their income. Others may have disposable income that they wish to save and invest, possibly to meet some future need or savings target.

In Chapters 2 and 3 of this Study Text, we have examined the different classes of financial asset in which clients might hold investments. We also looked at methods of direct investment in various types of asset, and then at methods that do not involve direct ownership of the asset: collective investments and derivatives.

3.2 Advising on investment and saving

To be able to give sound financial advice on investment and saving, the adviser's knowledge of financial products, assets and markets needs to be put to work along with his or her knowledge of the client's circumstances.

There are various ways of building up the information about a client's circumstances that is necessary for the necessary financial advice to be given. The most comprehensive way of obtaining this information is through a formal **fact find interview** with the client. This will record information in a questionnaire format, which may be compiled on a laptop computer. The purpose is to collect sufficient facts about the client or prospective client for a properly considered and comprehensive recommendation to be made.

3.3 Client needs and plans

Savings and investment needs can be divided into **short and long-term needs**.

(a) The **short-term need** may be for a car or a holiday, for which an obvious type of investment will a deposit account, such as a bank or building society account.

(b) **Longer term needs** could include savings for retirement and school fees or providing capital for children as they reach adulthood. Those with longer to save might possibly choose an equity backed investment, such as an Individual Savings Account (ISA) or a unit trust savings plan. Those with a shorter period until they will require the funds may select safer deposit type schemes to reduce the risk of capital losses.

A client's investments may originate from existing funds, which might have come from a recent inheritance or other lump sum, or from savings from income.

How much can the clients afford to save? A budget will analyse income and expenditure. Having established the amount of disposable income, a financial adviser can discuss how much the client wishes to spend and how much to save. The adviser should not recommend a course of action in which the client becomes over-committed to a long term contract which carries penalties for cancellation or for reducing the level or saving.

The financial adviser should look to the **client's future**. He or she should ask: Do the client's circumstances look likely to change? Are there clear signs that the client's earnings may increase, say from a promotion at work or income from another source? If this is the case, a savings plan where contributions either increase automatically or by selection may be appropriate.

The client's own **aims and ambitions** for the future are very important, but they need to be realistic in line with the amount the client has available to save.

An important consideration is **ease of access**. This will influence the choice of type of savings or investment and is particularly relevant for any savings into an emergency fund. As its name implies, this is money which may be needed at very short notice, so it should not be tied up in accounts that do not permit easy withdrawals.

3.4 Attitudes and risk

In advising on savings and investments, the attitude of the client to **risk** is very important. The client must have risks properly explained, or his awareness must be checked. If the client's assets and the amount available to save are small, then the recommendation is most likely to be for a low-risk deposit-type schemes.

Risky investments have the potential to produce possibly high **rewards**, but also the potential to produce significant losses. The **risks** faced by an investor can be categorised as follows.

(a) **Capital risk** is the risk of losing part or all of the capital invested.

(b) **Shortfall risk** applies when there is a financial target, and this is the risk that the chosen investments will fail to meet the target amount.

(c) **Interest risk** is a term we can apply to interest-bearing investments and describes the risk that interest received will be lower than it might have been. For example, if a saver makes a long-term investment that locks into a fixed rate of interest, this may turn out to be relatively unfavourable if variable interest rates generally rise.

(c) **Inflation risk** describes the risk that rising prices will reduce the purchasing power of what is invested.

3.5 Clients' ethical preferences

A client may have **ethical preferences** that influence their savings and investment requirements. Clients have various opportunities to match their preferences with a range of collective investments.

- A client may want to avoid investments in certain industries or companies, for example those connected with armaments or tobacco. There are **ethical funds** that screen investments on ethical, social or environmental criteria and the adviser's task will be to present the relevant information on such funds being considered to the client, so that the client can decide if the investment is consistent with their preferences.

- While '**dark green**' funds adopt negative screening criteria, '**lighter green**' funds adopt positive criteria, choosing companies that adopt a positive approach to ethically sensitive issues.

- Some funds focus on a particular **theme**, such as renewable energy or public transport.

- A further approach for a fund is to choose the '**best of class**' companies that surpass other companies in their sector in respect of ethical, social or environmental issues.

3.6 Diversifying investments

If the client has a relatively large amount of money to invest, then a diversified **spread of types and terms of investment** may be recommended. If the amount were only small, it may not be economical or practicable to diversify widely.

Consider investments that are:

- Low risk
- Higher risk
- Easy access
- Fixed term

A **portfolio** made up of different **asset classes** may be constructed if there are sufficient funds, mixing lower-risk **deposits** or **bond** investments with higher-risk **property** and **equity** investments.

Existing investments and savings plans must be taken into account when giving advice for a new savings scheme. Any new recommendations should fit in, giving a good spread of type and risk.

3.7 Pound cost averaging

If a client is saving in an equity-backed investment, such as a unit trust or investment trust savings plan, the client should be made aware of the effects of **pound cost averaging.**

The following example explains the concept.

Example: Pound cost averaging

The client is investing a regular premium each month in, say, a managed fund. Each month his premium will buy units in this fund. However the price of the units will vary from month to month depending on the performance of the fund. The fund units purchased by a monthly contribution of £30 over a period of six months are as follows (prices in pence).

Month	Bid price	Units purchased*
August	208.40	14.395
September	201.20	14.911
October	210.50	14.252
November	201.40	14.896
December	181.40	16.538
January	182.30	16.456

*Contribution/Bid price

The price inevitably fluctuates through time. The number of units purchased by the same monthly premium will vary from month to month. Over the long term, the client will benefit from shorter term fluctuations in the market by buying more units when the price is low and buying fewer units when the price is high.

Now try the **Exercise** below.

Exercise: Pound cost averaging

Alana invests £30 per month in a unit trust savings plan. The prices (in pence) at monthly dates were as follows.

Month	Offer price
August	257.60
September	263.00
October	272.90
November	280.00
December	278.90
January	291.00

Calculate the number of units purchased on each occasion. Compare the total amount of units with the amount Alan would have purchased if she had invested a lump sum of £180 in November.

Solution

Month	Offer price	Number of units purchased
August	257.60	11.646
September	263.00	11.407
October	272.90	10.993
November	280.00	10.714
December	278.90	10.757
January	291.00	10.309

Total units purchased during the period are 65.826. If £180 had been invested in November, 64.285 units would have been purchased.

3.8 Tax situation

Whatever the level of **tax** paid by the client, the income tax and capital gains implications of all investments must be considered and advantage taken of any tax incentives or reliefs available.

4 Protection

4.1 Risk and protection

Life always involves **risk** of various kinds. There are many risks that we are prepared to take, and life could become dull if everything was certain. For example, someone may embark on a training course, bearing the risk that there may not be a job available to them when they qualify. If there is not, they may have borne considerable training costs, for no eventual return. An investor may take on the risk of investing in the stock market quite deliberately, preferring the chance of a better return from equities to a much safer deposit-based investment.

These examples illustrate how we may actively choose risks. There are other risks that are with us whether we like it or not: for example, risks of death, injury or loss of possessions.

Most of us want to be sure that the contents of our house, our TV and video recorder, and our car, are **protected against loss** by theft, fire or flood. We protect can ourselves against this financial loss by means of insurance. We pay a premium into a pool with others. In the event of an unexpected happening, such as our car being stolen or our carpet being burnt by a log from the fire, then a claim is paid. Because the insurer anticipates that only a proportion of those insured will need to make a claim, he can meet that risk and hopes to still make a profit. **Insurance** offers **protection** to those who are insured.

However, insurance against risks we cannot avoid is not the only option. A person can choose to '**self-insure**' some risks. This means that the person knowingly takes on the risk themselves, and is prepared to take on the consequences. The benefit for the person is that they do not then have to pay for insurance. For example, owners of older cars often take out insurance for 'third party, fire and theft' risks only – a cheaper option than comprehensive insurance. Third party cover meets legal requirements, but if the owner is at fault in an accident which damages the car, the owner must bear the loss themselves. Thus, the owner has self-insured this risk.

Many of us take out insurance for our physical possessions, but we should also consider whether we need to **protect our income** and that of our **clients** from adverse situations. What will happen to our families if our income ceases through **death, sickness** or **redundancy**?

When a person dies or is taken **seriously ill**, some sort of **financial problem** will usually result. On death, for example, the costs of a funeral will have to be met. If the person who dies is a person with a young family, the rest of the family will still have the problem of finding the money for all of the normal living expenses, such as food, clothes and energy, in changed circumstances. On top of that, if the husband and wife were buying a house with the help of a mortgage, the widow or widower will be faced with an outstanding loan.

Sometimes the financial difficulties which follow **long-term disability** are even worse as someone can lose their job if they are too ill to carry on working. The State may give some help, but it may well not be enough.

Index-linking of protection policies means keeping the amounts insured updated in line with price inflation. Premiums are likely to rise in line with the index-linking. Index-linking protects the policyholder from the additional risk of inflation.

4.2 Financial protection on death

There are three main potential **financial consequences** of a death.

- Loss of income
- What to do about debts (liabilities)?
- Tax liabilities created by death

These potential consequences create a need for two different types of life cover: one providing a **replacement income**, the other a **lump sum to repay debts, pay taxes or meet one-off expenses** such as funeral costs.

In the case of the death of someone who does not have earnings - and the most common example of this will be a non-working parent with young children – a working co-parent will still be faced with financial problems: who will care for the children while is at work, and how will they be paid? If the widowed parent wishes to give up work, their income will need to be replaced, to the extent that outgoing expenditures cannot be reduced.

We are therefore looking for a method which will provide financial help at the time when it is needed in order to replace income, repay debts (eg mortgage), pay taxes and at least live without financial worry. **Life assurance** fulfils this function.

4.3 Life assurance

Which term should be used: **life assurance** or **life insurance**? The activity started hundreds of years ago as 'life assurance', but in recent years the term 'life insurance' has also been in widespread common usage. For all practical purposes there is no longer any significant difference.

In exchange for taking on the liability to make payments following a death, someone with a life assurance policy must pay **premiums** to the insurance company (or 'life office').

The sum that is payable on a claim under a life assurance policy may be called either the **sum assured** or the **sum insured**.

The person whose death triggers off a payment under the policy is the **life assured** or the **life insured**.

The person who is initially the legal owner of the policy is referred to by one of the following terms: **policyholder**, **assured**, **insured**, **grantee**, **policy owner**.

When a person is applying for a life policy, they are known as either the **proposer** or the **applicant**.

If you were applying for a policy on your own life, then you would initially be the **proposer** and then, when the policy came into existence, you would become both the **policyholder** and the **life assured**.

Because the information on a life assurance contract application form is the basis of the assurance contract, it is very important to ensure that all information entered on the form is accurate.

The proceeds of a life policy will often be paid to the legal **personal representatives** of a person who has died. They will be either the **executors** or the **administrators** depending upon whether or not a will has been left by the deceased. If a policy has been temporarily transferred (**assigned**) to someone else (the **assignee**) then the assignee will receive the proceeds.

4.4 Term assurance

Term assurance, as the name implies, provides life assurance for a fixed term. The sum assured is payable only if the life assured dies within that period. There is no benefit payable on maturity or on cancellation. Premiums are payable throughout the term of the contract. The major advantage of term assurances is that they can provide high amounts of life cover for relatively low premiums.

4.5 Family income benefit policies

Instead of a term assurance paying out a lump sum on death, it is possible to have a policy that pays out an income over a specific term. A **family income benefit** policy is so-called because it is intended to replace the income which the life assured would earn for his or her family if alive.

Technically, rather than paying an income, these policies are written to provide a **capital sum payable by instalments** for the selected period: this ensures that the 'income' is tax-free.

In order to overcome the effect of inflation, it is possible to effect an **increasing family income benefit policy**.

- The **benefit increases each year by a set percentage**, say 5%, or the RPI (in which case premiums also increase).

- The **benefit remains constant**. When a claim arises, the benefit increases by an agreed amount.

4.6 Whole of life policies

A **whole of life policy** for which regular premiums are payable provides for the payment of a lump sum on death There are three different ways for deciding how much that lump sum will be.

- The sum assured may be fixed at the same level throughout: a **non-profit policy**
- The sum assured may be increased at regular intervals: a **with profits policy**
- The sum assured is linked to the value of investments: a **unit linked contract**

Non-profit policies are sometimes called **without profit** or **non participating policies**. The sum assured **is fixed** at the same level for the entire duration of the contract. There is a little demand for or take-up of such contracts now.

A **with profits policy** is sometimes referred to as a **participating policy**: it is a policy which shares in the profits of the insurance company.

4.7 Disability protection

If someone is disabled and consequently unable to work, there is a loss in potential **earnings**. A disabled person could also be facing additional expenses such as structural alteration of their house in order to convert a downstairs room into a bedroom (if they cannot get upstairs), or to widen doorways to take wheelchairs.

There may be some help from the State in the form of **income** but, rather like the State payments made on death, this may be little more than a minor solution to a major problem.

There are various forms of **disability protection** that can help to solve these problems (see below).

4.8 Accident and sickness insurance

Accident and sickness insurance is designed to provide benefits in the event of the death of or injury to the life insured resulting from an accident. The policy pays a lump sum on death or for serious disability, such as loss of a limb or one or both eyes. This type of policy also pays an income in the event of less serious disability, including temporary and partial disablement.

Income payments may be paid for a defined number of weeks, possibly up to 52 or 104 weeks. There may be a deferment period from the date of injury or commencement of illness during which no income will be payable This period is typically between one and seven days.

Unlike income protection insurance (IPI) (see below), which is a long-term type of contract, accident and sickness insurance policies are shorter term, and may be renewable after a term of one year only. At the end of each year both the insured and the insurer can choose not to renew the contract. This contrasts with IPI where, under most circumstances, the insurer cannot refuse to renew the policy.

4.9 Income protection insurance

The objective of **income protection insurance (IPI)** (also sometimes called by its older name, **permanent health insurance (PHI))** is to replace earnings lost through long-term illness or disability. This means that the benefit is not a capital sum but an **income**.

The principal factors to take into account in assessing clients' need for IPI are:

(a) Their **level of earnings**
(b) **Any other benefits** receivable

The main source of other benefits is the **state incapacity benefit** and (for employees) initially **statutory sick pay**. For employees, any continuing benefits from an employer must be taken into account.

An income will be payable during disability which aims to **replace at least some of the consequent loss of earnings.** The basis for the level of benefit is loss of earnings. If a person has no earnings, eg through unemployment or because he has sufficient investment income to live on, there cannot *normally* be payment under an IPI policy.

In the case of an employee who receives full salary for, say, six months from the time disability begins, there will be no payment under an IPI contract during that period of time. The reason is that an IPI income is intended to replace lost earnings and, in such a situation, no earnings have been lost.

The existence of IPI cover can ensure that clients do not have to take retirement benefits early in the event of disability. This would cause them to receive a lower pension than they would receive by delaying the pension's starting date.

IPI is usually more expensive for **women** than for **men**: this is because statistics and claims experience shows that females suffer more ill health than males.

4.10 Critical illness insurance

Serious illness can cause **financial problems** which arise for a number of reasons.

- The cost of primary health care
- A person giving up work to care for a spouse
- The cost of home help
- The cost of a holiday needed for recovery or convalescence
- The cost of home alterations, including installing a chair lift
- The cost of equipment for treating kidney failure at home
- The cost of transport for the disabled, eg adapting a car
- Cash needed to supplement an early retirement pension

The cause of the problems lie in the possibility of an illness or disability that may be serious enough **to alter a person's lifestyle**. The solution is a policy that pays a **lump sum** on the diagnosis of an illness specified in the policy: **critical illness insurance**.

Possible uses are to:

- Repay a mortgage
- Provide specialist care and equipment
- Modify a home or car
- Meet responsibilities of dependants
- Provide aid for older people (widows or widowers with no family to support them)

A **wide variety of illnesses** may be insured through critical illness policies, including the following.

- Alzheimer's disease
- Blindness
- Cancer
- Coronary artery disease
- Heart attack
- Kidney failure

- Major organ transplant
- Multiple sclerosis
- Paralysis
- Stroke
- Total permanent disability

AIDS (Acquired Immune Deficiency Syndrome) is generally a specific **exclusion**.

4.11 Unemployment insurance

The level of protection in the event of **redundancy** (involuntary unemployment) is limited. Insurers will typically only cover mortgage repayments for up to a maximum of two years. The Government is keen for insurance companies to expand this market. They wish to reduce the individual's reliance on the State to help meet mortgage payments.

The State benefit **contributions-based jobseekers' allowance** is only paid for the first 26 weeks. The longer-term unemployed will need to live on their redundancy payments, if any, then their savings and, when these are sufficiently depleted, the **income-based jobseekers' allowance**. Savings over £8,000 usually mean you cannot get income-based JSA.

4.12 Private medical insurance

Private medical insurance (PMI) generally covers the cost of **hospital care in a private hospital,** outside the National Health Service (NHS).

Premiums could be payable monthly or annually. Various levels of cover may be provided, and premiums may differ according to the range of hospitals covered.

PMI is often provided as a benefit to employees, and many employers consider that it is of benefit to them for employees who need hospital treatment to be treated as quickly as possible so that they can soon work as normal again.

PMI is also worth considering for a self-employed person. PMI cover could help in providing treatment more quickly than under the NHS, thereby minimising time spent off work and the resulting loss of income.

4.13 Long-term care insurance

Many elderly people need long-term care towards the end of their lives, and the costs of care can be substantial. **Long-term care insurance (LTCI)** was introduced into the UK in 1991. By 2002, there were approximately 45,000 policies in force.

Policies may be **protection-based** or **investment-based.**

Protection-based LTCI may be available as an option on a **whole of life policy**: the benefit is provided as an acceleration of the sum that would have been payable on death. With protection-based policies, there will be no surrender value.

Investment-based policies are based on the principle of building up a sum to cover potential long-term care costs.

4.14 Business protection

We have looked particularly at protecting clients' families and dependants. A further in which financial advice may be given is in protection of the financial viability of a **business** upon the death or incapacity of a partner or director, for example in the following types of situation.

    (a)   **Sole traders** (businesses owned by a single person)

- **Protection for the family**. If the sole trader dies, there will be loss of income. Many businesses will be worth little following the death of the sole proprietor.

- **Protection of income in the event of long-term disability**. If the sole trader cannot work, the business ceases to operate and receive revenue. Income protection insurance plays a vital role for income replacement.

    (b)   **Partnership** (businesses co-owned by business partners)

- **Protecting the business in the event of one partner's death**. The surviving partner will need sufficient funds quickly to be able to buy out the deceased partner's share of the business. He may not want to have to resort to expensive borrowings, which could seriously curtail the development of the business.

- **Protecting partnership income in the event of a partner's long-term sickness or a critical illness**. If a partner is sick for a long period, his ability to bring in income to the partnership ceases. At the same time, the firm may need to hire someone to carry out some of his work. The

sick partner may also, under the terms of the partnership agreement, have a continuing right to a share of the profits. The partnership must protect this loss of income.

(c) **Private limited companies**

- **Protecting the business in the event of a director's death**. The surviving directors will need sufficient capital to buy out the shares of the deceased director and to repay his loan account, if any. The alternative could be a member of the deceased's family sitting on the board and influencing the future of the company.

- **Protecting the company's income in the event of the long-term sickness or critical illness of a director**. The directors must protect themselves against any loss of income to the company and provide funds to employ a replacement during the director's absence.

(d) **Key employees of any business (sole trader, partnership or company)**. In all businesses there are key employees, eg the marketing manager, the computer programmer or the product development manager. If any of these employees dies suddenly or has a long-term sickness, there will be an immediate loss of income to the firm and a need to bring in a replacement as quickly as possible. This potential financial loss needs to be protected.

5 Retirement planning

5.1 Introduction

Longer life expectancies and lower birth rates than in the past have all contributed to the relative ageing of our population. There are more people who are over retirement age than in the past. With the population growing older and living longer on average, planning for retirement, when people need money to meet expenses, but no longer have their full working income, is an important issue at the level of national policy as well as for the individual.

The working population will be unable to contribute enough through national insurance contributions and taxation to maintain the growing numbers of elderly people by means of State benefits. Individuals and their advisers must include retirement planning as a key element of their overall financial planning.

5.2 How much income?

A starting point for a retirement planning evaluation is the **amount of income the client requires to live on in retirement**.

The first answer that the client gives may be unachievable. She may think that she would like an income of two-thirds of her original earnings. The cost of this, particularly if the client is trying to achieve it himself without any help from an employer, may be prohibitive.

For a personal or stakeholder pension, the income will be provided from the pension funds either by drawing down income from the fund, or by using the fund to buy from an insurance company an **annuity**, which provides an income for life.

The client must be asked to sit down and work out her **expected income needs** in retirement. In many cases, a mortgage will have been paid off. Perhaps the client will move to a smaller house which will involve lower outgoings. Will there still be dependant children from a second or third marriage?

5.3 Influencing factors

Having established how much income the client would like to achieve, the adviser can move on to establish, with the help of a **full fact find**, whether this is possible and **the means of achieving the client's aims**. It is sensible to plan towards a target pension of a percentage of final earnings and to review the situation each year to ascertain the proximity to the target. In making his recommendations, the adviser will take into account a number of factors.

5.4 Previous and current pension arrangements

It may be that the benefits from existing and previous pension schemes, together with the State benefits, will be sufficient and therefore there is no need for additional pension planning.

(a)   Checking on the client's **existing pension arrangements** and his entitlement to the State pension is the first stage in the assessment process.

(b)   The next step is to ascertain details of all previous pension schemes of the client, whether company schemes, retirement annuities or personal pensions.

(c)   If it is difficult to ascertain the information from the client, then the adviser must obtain his authority to write to the insurance companies concerned and the trustees of previous pension schemes, or even to trace old schemes through the Registrar of Pension Schemes.

(d)   When all the information is received, it needs to be analysed to ascertain the total values of the schemes, in particular if there are any benefits on death or if the pensions increase up to retirement age and/or in retirement.

(e)   A client's current pension scheme needs to be thoroughly researched. This can usually be done by means of the scheme booklet and the up-to date report and accounts.

5.5 Non-pension assets

The extent of a client's **non-pension assets** should be ascertained, as these are also relevant to retirement planning.

These assets might include company shares or property, for example. A client may wish to use such assets to provide for living expenses in retirement, and this may reduce the extent to which pension arrangements are required by the client.

5.6 Non-pension investment and saving

Retirement planning is more than just pensions planning. Pensions schemes provide a range of options for providing for retirement, but these vehicles are not the only method of providing for retirement years.

Some people who are owner-occupiers of a house may plan to 'trade down' to a smaller house with a lower value, and realise a capital gain on their previous house in the process. This capital, which would be tax-free, could form a part of provision for retirement years.

Savings and investment vehicles other than pension plans can be used for saving for retirement. **Individual Savings Accounts (ISAs)** and existing **Personal Equity Plans (PEPs)** offer tax-free capital gains, with greater flexibility than many pension arrangements in how and when proceeds can be used.

5.7 State pension

State pension provision comprises the basic **State pension** and the additional **State Second Pension** or **S2P,** which replaced the State Earnings Related Pension Scheme (SERPS) from 6 April 2002.

Most clients will be entitled to a **basic State pension**. However the amount will depend on the amount of national insurance contributions paid. For the year 2006/07, the full pension for a single person who has made sufficient contributions is £84.25 per week.

Many people, particularly women, will have had breaks in their working lives and will not be entitled to a full pension in their own right. Women may have to rely on their husband's contributions. However, there is now Home Responsibilities Protection (HRP), protecting State pension rights for those looking after children.

Some women have paid a **reduced national insurance contribution**. This entitles them to a pension based only on the husband's contributions. (This option is no longer available, but those paying the married woman's rate may continue to do so.)

The Pensions Act 1995 introduced a **state pension age of 65** for both men and women from 2020. This will be introduced over a ten year period, from 2010 for women born after 6 April 1955.

5.8 Additional State pension

Only those who have been **employed** at some time will be entitled to this benefit. Those who have *always* been self employed will not.

(a)   The **State Earnings Related Pension Scheme (SERPS)** started in 1978 and only those retiring after 1998 receive the full benefit. From April 2002, SERPS was replaced by the **State Second Pension (S2P)**. S2P provides enhanced benefits for the lower paid.

(b)   The benefits of the additional State pension are based on **earnings between two bands**, the National Insurance upper and lower earnings limits, known as middle band earnings.

(c)   **Earnings above the upper earnings limit** are not pensioned.

(d)   For those retiring between 1998 and 2000, the Department for Work and Pensions (DWP) revalued each of their band earnings in line with earnings inflation, took the best 20 years and then allocated a pension based on 1.25% × 20 = **25% of the inflation-proofed middle band earnings**. For those who had less than 20 years in the scheme, say 15, the calculation was 1.25% × 15 = **18.75% of the inflation proofed middle band earnings**.

(e)   From the year 2010, the maximum calculation will be reduced to **20% of middle band earnings** of the average revalued middle band earnings throughout the member's whole working life. This will be particularly disadvantageous for those who have had working breaks to study or periods of self employment.

(f)   Where State Pension Age falls between 6 April 2000 and 5 April 2009, the reduction is applied on a gradual basis in accordance with the following table.

Tax year in which State Pension Date falls	Maximum SERPS as % of band earnings
1999/2000	25%
2000/2001	24.5%
2001/2002	24%
2002/2003	23.5%
2003/2004	23%
2004/2005	22.5%
2005/2006	22%
2006/2007	21.5%
2007/2008	21%
2008/2009	20.5%
2009/2010 or later	20%

(g)   Clients may have **contracted out of S2P/SERPS** either by membership of a company pension scheme or an appropriate personal pension. This may have been for some, or all, of the potential years of membership of S2P/SERPS.

(h)   In addition clients employed between 1961 and 1975 may be entitled to a very small state pension known as the **graduated scheme**.

(i)   The state pension scheme benefits are **complex** and it would be very difficult for anyone to calculate correctly a client's benefit without help. It is a worthwhile exercise for the adviser or the client to write to the Department for Work and Pensions for a forecast of state pension entitlement, as this will include basic, graduated and S2P/SERPS benefits.

5.9 Age

The **age at which the client wishes to retire** is important. The adviser should ascertain the age at which the client wishes to retire – is it 65, 60, or some other age? Retirement planning should be considered in the context of the normal retirement age under the client's contract of employment, if the client is in a long-term job.

The adviser should discover if the client wishes to **retire early** at say 50 or 55. Is this likely to be a reality or just a dream? The adviser will need to stress the expense of planning for early retirement. Advisers must be aware that the reverse can happen. Many directors of family companies have **no intention of retiring,** certainly not before the age of 70.

It is important to take into account the age of the **client's spouse or partner**. It is unlikely that one will wish to retire without the other, so the retirement planning must be dovetailed if possible. If the client is older than the spouse, there may be a greater requirement to provide for adequate pensions for a widow or widower.

The **current age of the client** is also significant. If he or she is young he has many years to achieve his objectives. The older the client, the fewer the years and the more expensive the exercise becomes. Many insurance companies provide leaflets emphasising the effect of 'delay' in pension planning.

5.10 Income

Current income and outgoings should be analysed to ascertain the income available for investment into pensions or other retirement planning investments. If income is likely to increase on a regular basis, some form of indexing of premiums should be considered.

In looking at the **client's outgoings,** it may be discovered that, because of current commitments, such as school fees, she is unable to fund sufficient pension at the present time. It would then be useful to advise the client of how many years she can afford to delay if she wishes to achieve his aim – also, the increased amounts which would then be involved to provide an adequate pension benefit.

If the client only has a small amount of spare income to commit to her financial needs, it is important that the **needs are prioritised**.

(a)   Cover for dependants
(b)   Protection of income in the event of sickness
(c)   Mortgage requirements
(d)   Pension
(e)   Savings
(f)   Investment

If the client is a director of his or her own company, then the discussion will centre around the amount which the **company can contribute** on his or her behalf; also the ability of the company to afford this from a cashflow point of view and to maintain the contribution level in the future. Often an adviser is called in when the company has had a good trading year. Before deciding on a level of contribution, it is important to ascertain whether this can be maintained in future, perhaps less profitable, years.

HMRC rules limit the amount of contributions on which tax relief can be received, but these limits became much more generous from 6 April 2006, after which, broadly speaking, 100% of earnings can be paid into pension schemes. There are also, from 6 April 2006, new lifetime limits on the total value of pension funds receiving tax advantages.

5.11 Dependants

The **cost of dependants**, particularly children, can limit the amounts available to contribute to pension. It is also important to stress to clients that they must not, if at all possible, be **dependent on others for their pension provision**. Too often in the past, women in particular have taken the view that they did not have to fund a pension in their own right because their spouse had made adequate provision. This is a fallacy. Changes in circumstances, such as a divorce or death of the spouse, can leave the client with no provision at all. The situation on divorce is changing. Pension benefits are now being taken into account in the settlement including splitting the fund.

The client should ensure that in the event of **death prior to retirement**, his or her spouse, partner or dependants are sufficiently covered. If life policies are not already in force this can be covered by pension life assurance and the return of the fund from the pension arrangement.

In designing the pension arrangements for a particular client care must be taken to ensure that any **dependants in retirement** will be properly covered, eg the spouse, partner or dependent children.

6 Estate planning

6.1 What is estate planning?

Someone's **estate** is the wealth they leave when they die. **Estate planning** is therefore concerned with how that wealth is passed on to beneficiaries, who may typically be children or grandchildren.

6.2 Inheritance tax

Some people will wish to find ways of passing wealth on during their lifetime, in ways that reduce the liability to **inheritance tax**. Careful planning can make this possible. It may be possible to make maximum use of the nil rate band, gifts and other exemptions. Inheritance tax is covered in more detail in the Chapter on *Taxation*.

Steps taken to reduce tax liabilities should not dominate planning for a client so much that the steps taken prevent the client from achieving the outcomes he or she wants.

Whatever the client's plans and wishes are, a client should have a properly drafted **will**.

6.3 Financial products

Another aspect of estate planning is to consider financial products that can meet **inheritance tax liabilities** that will fall due.

Life assurance products can be very useful for this purpose. A **whole of life policy** will pay out on death, just when the funds are needed to meet the liability.

If a life assurance policy is **written under trust**, this will ensure that:

- Proceeds will normally be free from inheritance tax
- Premiums are usually exempt as gifts
- Proceeds will be paid without delays in obtaining probate

For a married couple, inheritance tax is likely to have most impact on the death of the second person (the surviving spouse). A whole of life assurance on a joint life second death basis written under tryst for the beneficiaries would then be appropriate.

If the client dies within seven years of making a gift, the value will be included in the estate for inheritance tax purposes, with tapering relief applying. To mitigate any inheritance tax liability in these circumstances, a gift *inter vivos* seven-year decreasing term assurance can be used to protect the recipient against the potential inheritance tax liability if the donor of the gift dies within the seven-year period.

Some **investment products** make use of a **trust** in order to reduce inheritance tax liability. Lifetime gifts may be made into a trust for the benefit of children or grandchildren, and the trust assets may be invested.

Some people may choose to pass on wealth by making regular lifetime gifts to children or grandchildren. **Savings products** could be used, either in the name of the beneficiary or under trust.

Long-term care insurance, designed to meet some or all of the costs of nursing care if required, could be used as a way of preserving wealth that would otherwise be quickly depleted if such care were needed. Given the relatively high care costs involved and the proportion of people requiring it, such insurance can involve significant outlay.

7 Tax planning

7.1 Introduction

In the previous section of this Chapter on estate planning, we have been looking broadly at some of the ways in which inheritance tax effects may be reduced or mitigated. Inheritance tax planning is, of course, one aspect of tax planning.

7.2 Tax planning points

In giving financial advice in other aspects, there are of course tax considerations to be borne in mind:

- Is the client a non-taxpayer, starting rate (10%), basic rate (22%) or higher rate (40%) taxpayer?

- Are all personal allowances for income tax purposes being used?

- What is the likely capital gains tax position, and is there a way for the client to make use of annual CGT exemptions, or any brought forward capital losses that can be set against capital gains?

- What is the tax position of financial products being considered? Are proceeds exempt from tax? Are there planning steps that can ensure that tax effects are mitigated?

- At the **end of a tax year**, key issues are whether an individual wishes to top up **pension plans** or **ISAs,** for which there are limits on contributions within a tax year.

7.3 Tax-free?

Note that just because a product has no tax to pay on maturity does not mean that it is truly 'tax-free'. An **endowment policy** will often carry no tax liability for the policyholder at the time of surrender or maturity, but the life company has already deducted tax at source.

On the other hand, when a qualifying endowment policy is sold to someone else (a '**traded endowment policy**'), the **purchaser** will be liable to capital gains tax on any subsequent gain made.

7.4 Tax planning in context

As with estate planning, it is important to consider tax planning in the light of all the client's circumstances and needs, and in the context of all of their plans and wishes.

Any **tax advantages** should not be sought at all costs, without considering other aspects. For example, there will be no benefit to a client if a particular financial product carries a tax advantage which is cancelled out by the effect of higher charges on that particular product, or by exposure to **investment risks** that the client would not otherwise wish to be exposed to.

We look in more detail at UK tax rules later in this Study Text.

8 The client review

8.1 The need for review

The adviser is concerned with identifying and satisfying client needs. This is not just a 'one-off' process. Clients will have a continuing need for financial advice. Their circumstances will change, and there may need to be a review of whether products initially recommended continue to be suitable.

Regular **reviews** of client circumstances will enable the adviser to make best use of future business opportunities with that client. For the client, there are the benefits of the advice arising from the review.

8.2 Review dates

Many financial advisers conduct client reviews **annually**. This may fit well with the client's needs, if pay or bonuses are reviewed annually for example, or to fit in with the accounting cycle of a business. A review at the time of a client's birthday is another possibility: some life assurance risks are assessed in annual steps linked to the birth date.

Client reviews should not be restricted to **pre-determined review dates**. Clients' circumstances may change in unpredictable ways. An individual may be made redundant, or may start a new job. There could be a change in family health circumstances, or a new baby may be expected. These are examples of changes that could have a significant impact on financial planning, and so the client should be encouraged to seek advice and appropriate review of their circumstances, when such events occur.

Events in the financial world may produce an opportunity for the adviser to contact the client to review their effect on his or her circumstances.

- For example, **new tax rules** may be announced, or investment conditions may change, for example if there are significant movements in share prices.

- A **new tax year** can present possible opportunities, for example relating to ISA investments and pension contributions.

It may be most appropriate for an adviser to agree with the client that there will be an annual review date, but with the proviso that either client or adviser may make contact if an additional review is appropriate.

Key chapter points

- Budgeting involves a detailed examination of income and expenditure. This is a great help in financial planning.

- The fact find is a way of building up as full a picture as possible of the client's circumstances.

- Borrowing can take various forms and can be for various reasons, but borrowing for house purchase is often the most significant borrowing that an individual takes on.

- In investment and saving, client needs must be researched. Recommendations should be for products and investments appropriate to the client's attitudes.

- Protection against various risks is possible. There are various kinds of life assurance, including ASU (accident, sickness and unemployment insurance), income protection insurance, critical illness insurance and private medical insurance.

- Financial advisers are involved in clients' retirement planning. Pensions schemes or other investment products may be used in retirement planning.

- Estate planning is concerned with passing on wealth, and tax efficiency is often a consideration. Financial products of different kinds may be used to fund an anticipated inheritance tax liability.

- An adviser should always be alert to possible tax implications of a client's financial decisions, so that the adviser's recommendations take account of possible tax savings, within the context of the client's overall needs and plans.

- Regular (eg, annual) client review is a valuable process for both client and adviser, and ideally both client and adviser should get in contact with the other if changing circumstances suggest the need for a review at any time.

Chapter Quiz

1 List the seven financial advice areas we have considered in this Chapter. ....(see Chapter Topic List)

2 Define 'budgeting'. .... (see para 1.1)

3 What is meant by re-mortgaging? ....(2.2)

4 What is pound cost averaging? ....(3.7)

5 What are generally the most significant implications of a death occurring? .... (4.2)

6 What does IPI aim to do? ....(4.9)

7 'Retirement planning is pensions planning.' Do you agree? ....(5.6)

8 What is estate planning? ....(6.1)

9 What are the three rates of UK income tax? .... (7.2)

10 What is meant by client review, and why should an adviser conduct a review? ....(8.1)

chapter

6

Giving financial advice

1 Collecting client information

1.1 'Know your customer'

You will be well aware of the need to possess a lot of **information** about your client before you can give them advice. This need is reflected in one of the basic requirements of the regulatory regime: to **'know your customer'**. In the context of advising customers, this is also referred to as **'factfinding'**. This refers to obtaining sufficient information about a customer's personal and financial situation, before giving advice.

The process of obtaining this information is not only essential in ensuring that you give suitable advice on a current issue. It can also reveal further areas where you might help your clients in the future.

In the context of **anti-money laundering requirements** (discussed further later), **'know your customer'** refers to the collection and use of information about a customer over and above obtaining basic evidence of identity.

1.2 Communication techniques

Good **communication skills** are important for the financial adviser. Much of the information the adviser acquires is likely to be by interviewing – asking questions of – the client.

You should appreciate the difference between objective **factual information** and evaluative statements which express opinions or feelings. The latter type of statement may be expressed in terms of someone's hopes, wants or plans.

Examples of factual information

- Disregarding dividends, the Clearfield Unit Trust has grown in value by more than the FTSE 100 benchmark index over the three-year period to 31 December 2005.

- Brenda has fallen into two months' arrears on her mortgage payments.

Examples of non-factual statements

- Graham thinks that he should invest more of his portfolio in foreign stocks, in order to diversify risk.
- Matilda was disappointed by the service provided by her previous financial adviser.

Closed questions ask for a **specific** piece of **information**, for example a National Insurance number or a figure for the value of a property. Examples could be:

- Could you please tell me your address?
- Do you have any ISAs?

The answer to a closed question is typically a single word, or a short phrase, or 'Yes' or 'No'. The client may tire of having too much of this form of questioning quickly, and the questioner will not find out much about the client's views or feelings in the process.

Open questions give the client more opportunity to **express his views** or **feelings** in a **longer response**. Examples of open questions are:

- How do you feel about taking risks with your investments?
- What do you think are the most immediate financial needs to be addressed?

1.3 Client information

The first stage is to know the **essential information**. What is essential may sometimes seem to be limitless, but even the most obvious of information can have benefits.

To give an example, the client's **address** - obviously necessary for the purposes of correspondence and for general recording requirements - may reveal a different country of residence or domicile (although it is more likely that this information will be revealed through a specific question).

Details of a client's **children** may produce contacts which could lead to further business. Information regarding a client's **financial advisers**, such as accountant and stockbroker, can help you to establish contacts which will widen the circle of people who are aware of your services.

Information regarding whether or not your client is a **controlling director** may open up the possibility of providing a service for the client's co-directors or for the staff of the company.

Initially, however, the job is basically to obtain **all relevant information**. Although the question of what is relevant may be subjective, it is unlikely that you can safely omit any of the information that follows. You may well think of other items that should be included, but the following will be a guide.

Personal details

(a) Name, address and age of client. Age is useful knowledge for some investments, eg ISAs and NS&I products, and also for tax purposes, eg to establish entitlement to age allowance, and it is valuable for life assurance purposes and pension provision.

(b) National Insurance number and tax office / reference.

(c) Marital status - useful for establishing protection needs, and for tax purposes.

    (d)   Health - useful for protection needs, for life and disability cover.

    (e)   Domicile/residence, if not the UK.

Family details

Dependants - age and, for adult children, marital status
Other immediate family

Employment details

    (a)   Occupation
    (b)   Controlling director
    (c)   Employed by whom?
    (d)   Self employed

Financial advisers

    (a)   Bank manager
    (b)   Accountant
    (c)   Stockbroker
    (d)   Solicitor

Financial details

    (a)   **Assets**

        (i)   Cash (liquid assets, eg bank accounts, deposit accounts)

        (ii)   *Used*

            (1)   House
            (2)   Furniture
            (3)   Personal belongings
            (4)   Car
            (5)   Other

        (iii)   *Invested*

            (1)   Equities (revealing whether client is cautious or adventurous, or has short-term or long-term needs, or an active or passive investment approach)

            (2)   Unit trusts, OEICs and investment trusts

            (3)   Building society accounts

            (4)   National Savings & Investments

            (5)   Other

            (6)   How tax-efficient are the investments? (Current year ISA allowance used?)

    (b)   **Liabilities**

        (i)   Mortgage: details and repayment method. (Details can reveal whether a re-mortgage can be arranged more cheaply, but the client should take care regarding any redemption penalties on re-mortgage.)

        (ii)   Other liabilities

    The asset and liabilities information will now enable you to assess your client's **net worth**.

    (c)   **Income**

        (i)   *Earnings*

            (1)   Employee – salary, plus other remuneration package
            (2)   Self employed - profits

        (ii)   *Investment income*

            (1)   Interest

            (2)   Dividends

            (3)   Rents

        (iii)   *Pensions*

            (1)   State

            (2)   Occupational

            (3)   Personal, including stakeholder

            (4)   Annuities

(d) **Expenditure**

    (i)   Living expenses (these should be itemised so that nothing is missed)

    (ii)   Mortgage interest

    (iii)   School fees

    (iv)   Regular savings

    (v)   Expenditure on life assurance

(This will enable you to establish whether there is a surplus or a shortfall on income.)

(e) **Protection.** Full details of life cover and disability insurance

(f) **Pensions**

    (i)   Details of any occupational pension scheme including life/sickness/medical cover

    (ii)   Any personal pensions

    (iii)   Any preserved pensions

    (iv)   Any transferred pensions

(g) **Existing arrangements – wills and legacies**

    (i)   Has a will been made?

    (ii)   What are its main provisions?

    (iii)   When was it last reviewed?

    (iv)   Have any gifts been made in the last seven years?

    (v)   Are there any anticipated legacies?

Client's attitudes

(a) What is the client's **attitude to existing savings/investment/protection**?

(b) Are existing arrangements **sufficient**?

(c) Are they **suitable**?

(d) Have they been **reviewed recently**?

(e) Is the level of **investment risk acceptable** to a client?

(f) Is the client prepared to accept **more or less risk**?

(g) Are there any **constraints** on investment, eg ethical investments?

(h) Does the client consider that the **existing investments meet current needs**?

(i) **Do you consider that they meet current and existing needs**? (Remember that with long-term contracts such as life policies, surrender is not precluded but it must be recommended only when such a course is obviously suitable. This is likely to happen in very few cases, except perhaps with term assurance, where better terms may be obtained if premium rates have fallen.)

Client's objectives

The **client's objectives** and **expected liabilities** should be considered under headings such as the following.

(a)   Is the client expecting to buy **property** or move house or incur expenses for school fees or change jobs or buy a car or face major repairs?

(b)   What is the client's **timespan** for investments, ie short-term or long-term or both?

(c)   How **accessible** must the client's funds be?

(d)   What is the client's **current and future tax position**?

(e)   Are the client's needs for **income or growth** or both?

(f)   Does the client want any **personal involvement** in the direction of investment?

(g)   Does the client have **ethical views or preferences** which could influence their investment choices?

2 Recording and using information

2.1 The fact find

The information given in the previous section should be **recorded carefully and meticulously**. The standard method of doing this is the use of a questionnaire designed to ensure that all relevant information is sought. This questionnaire has become known as the **fact find**.

All advisers should make use of a **comprehensive fact find**. This can serve the function of helping to generate business for the adviser but it is also important from the compliance point of view. It ensures that a proper record is kept, that information was sought from a client, that it was either given or refused and, combined with documents recording recommendations made to a client, can confirm that the advice given to the client was sound and suitable.

An exception to the requirement to complete a fact find applies to **friendly society investment contracts** with premium levels of not more than £50 a year (£1 a week) for which fact finds are not required. This applies both to friendly societies and independent financial advisers.

2.2 Present client circumstances

The analysis of a client's current circumstances begins with an analysis of the financial figures for the client's current circumstances. This would show a list of the client's **assets and liabilities**, and reveal whether there is a surplus or a deficit. It will also include an **income and expenditure** account to reveal whether there is **surplus** income or a **shortfall**: this is effectively a budget (You will recall that we looked at budgeting in an earlier Chapter of this Study Text.)

- If there is a **surplus**, it will enable the client to put into effect at least some of any recommendations which involve an additional outlay.

- If there is a **shortfall**, this reveals the need for the client to take action not to increase liabilities and perhaps to reduce existing liabilities.

Current income needs should be measured and this will enable you to check whether or not the **protection** against death and disability is adequate to meet those needs.

2.3 Future client circumstances

You must also analyse the client's possible **changing circumstances**.

- What are the consequences, for example, of moving to another house or a prospective job change or children approaching fee paying school age?

- If the client is employed and is planning to become self employed, are any arrangements in hand for replacing company group life and disability cover with personal life and disability cover?

- Are arrangements in hand to ensure that finance is available to enable the move to take place?

2.4 Advising the client

In order to formulate a **recommendation** for a client, an adviser must always **identify and analyse the client's needs**.

Completing the **fact find** makes it much easier to assess current and future needs. You have all the information necessary regarding the client and you can quantify a client's protection needs against the existing provision and compare future income needs against expectations.

You can also assess the client's current and future **tax position** and evaluate the tax efficiency of existing investments.

After all this has been done, the chances are that **most clients will not be able to achieve all of their objectives**. This will mean prioritising their objectives according to their resources.

2.5 The financial planning process

For the purpose of applying the major factors which are relevant to formulating recommendations, we will use a **summary of the financial planning process** which needs to be followed from the time of the initial contact with the client to the point when a recommendation is made.

The six stages in the financial planning process are as follows.

(1)   **Obtaining relevant information**, ie completion of a **fact find**
(2)   **Establishing and agreeing** the client's **financial objectives**
(3)   **Processing and analysing the data** produced on the fact find
(4)   **Formulating recommendations** in a comprehensive plan with objectives
(5)   **Implementing the recommendations** as agreed with the client
(6)   **Reviewing and regularly updating** the plan

2.6 Fact find

An adviser must take into account all the **regulatory compliance requirements** that apply before dealing with the client (such as giving to the client a **business card**, an **initial disclosure document**, **menu** and **terms of business letter** – as discussed later) through the process to the stage where recommendations are given, when the reasons for those recommendations are required.

2.7 Objectives

The next stage is to establish with the client what are the client's **financial objectives**. We discuss this aspect further below.

2.8 Processing and analysing information

This covers the process discussed earlier of drawing up **statements of a client's financial position including assets and liabilities and cash flow**, and coming to conclusions based on that information.

2.9 Making a plan

The prime objective of the **comprehensive plan** is to make **recommendations** regarding the action needed to meet the client's stated and agreed objectives.

As well as **regulatory considerations,** the plan must **take account of economic conditions** which could affect the client, such as the possibility of redundancy, the prospects for a self employed person's business and the effect of inflation.

It should take account of a client's **current financial position**. Is there a surplus of assets over liabilities? If so, is the surplus in a form where it can be better used? For example, if you have a house valued at £80,000 with a mortgage of £50,000 the surplus of assets over liability, namely £30,000, is not in a form where it can be reinvested more efficiently. It may be possible to use the surplus as a method of borrowing but it cannot be reinvested directly.

If liabilities exceed assets then can **liabilities be rearranged**? For example if part of the reason is an expensive loan, can the loan be repaid (provided any repayment charges are acceptable) and replaced by a more effective loan such as borrowing on the security of a with profits policy where interest rates tend to be below average.

Such an action would reduce the client's total outlay by reducing the **total interest payable**.

How liquid are the client's assets? How much of the client's assets is in a form which can be turned into cash quickly, if necessary? Liquid assets would include bank and building society current and deposit accounts and NS&I (National Savings & Investments) products. On some NS&I investments, there may be a loss of interest on quick encashment, but the need for liquidity may outweigh the loss of interest.

Is the client expecting any **future inheritance**? If so, is there any way in which it can be arranged so as to eliminate or minimise inheritance tax?

The client's current **tax position** is of prime importance. Cash in ordinary building society accounts can be moved into ISAs up to the ISA contribution limits, for example.

The client's protection requirements will be affected not only by current needs but by **changing economic conditions**. Inflation could reduce the value of life cover with a fixed sum assured, whether the policy be for the purpose of protection against disability or death.

If a client with dependants has no existing financial planning arrangements – no retirement provision, no medium or long-term savings – then a **first priority** is some form of **life assurance** or **family income protection**.

State benefits may provide some protection against **disability and death** but, as we have already seen, they are very limited and the client's changing circumstances may reduce the importance of state benefits.

In view of the fact that the state disability benefit is at a fixed rate and is not earnings related, the **higher earning clients** will suffer all the more from a drop in earnings through disability.

Similar factors apply to **retirement planning** where the **State Second Pension (S2P)** is not sufficient to protect higher earning clients from a substantial drop in income at retirement in the absence of adequate pension arrangements. (Bear in mind that S2P rights do not accrue during periods of self-employment, and that those who contract out of S2P into non-State pension arrangements do not receive S2P.)

Fixed interest investments will be considerably affected by inflation and also by the client's tax position. From the tax point of view, a tax exempt investment is of less value to the non-taxpayer than to the higher rate taxpayer and the two factors need to be taken into account together in order to produce a suitable recommendation.

Inheritance tax liabilities will make it necessary to make the maximum use of exemptions such as the annual exemption or the normal expenditure exemption. Remember that making transfers to avoid inheritance tax may have the effect of reducing the client's income and that fact also must be taken into account.

Full account must be taken of the **client's attitude and understanding of risk** when it comes to arranging investments. Widows with small capital sum and whose only income is the state pension should not be advised to invest in futures and options! Equally, high net worth individuals with substantial excess of income over expenditure could spread their investments in a way which provides a balanced mix of caution, medium risk and high risk.

In taking account of any **ethical preferences** affecting investment choice that a client may have, the adviser needs to bear in mind the differences between funds. There are many **'ethical' funds**, but these cover a range of criteria, for example between **'dark green'** funds that use **negative criteria** to exclude companies to **'lighter green'** funds that use **positive criteria** to include companies that pursue positive policies on the environment or social factors. The adviser should ensure that funds chosen match the expressed concerns of the client.

3 Client circumstances and objectives

3.1 Client objectives

Any individual is likely to have a number of **objectives**, for which some financial provision may be required. Having a particular view of risk does not imply that the same attitude to risk should be applied to all of the individual's objectives.

An individual might have investments that they wish to use for specific purposes or objectives and which they cannot easily afford to bear a great degree of **shortfall risk**. In such cases, the individual may wish to choose low risk investments, so that they can be reasonably certain that their objective will be achievable by the desired date.

Examples of such purposes or objectives could include:

- Saving for a deposit on a house
- Payment of a child's school fees
- Payment of university costs
- Provision to cover care of a baby
- Replacement of a car

The same individual who has investment objectives such as those above might have other possibilities in mind for which the person would be prepared to tolerate a higher level of risk. The objective may be seen as less essential to the individual, and may be something that the person accepts that they will have to do without if investment returns are not sufficient.

Examples of purposes or objectives for which an individual might be prepared to take on higher risk include:

- Purchase of a vintage car
- A second home
- The possibility of an early retirement
- A 'dream' holiday

Of course, every individual is different, and the ways in which people rank their objectives and their risk tolerance in relation to different objectives vary. For one person, having enough money to spend on a comfortable home may take a higher priority than having the funds to travel widely. Another person may treat travelling as a higher priority than spending on a home.

In general, the objectives that an individual sees as having the highest priority are those for which they will want to take the lowest risk if they are investing to achieve those objectives. Lower priority objectives can generally be more easily foregone if investments suffer losses.

3.2 Factors shaping individual circumstances

There are various life stages, and people have differing financial needs. Every case is different, and there may be many variations in individual circumstances that cannot easily be fitted into easily formulated categories.

3.3 Wealth and investment exposure

When considering investment, the **wealth** of the investor is clearly an important consideration. If there is free capital to invest, then clearly it is sensible for the individual to take steps to make the best use of that capital.

It is possible, although not generally advisable, for someone with little wealth to gain exposure to investment markets, for example by **borrowing money to invest**, or by using investments such as derivatives or spread betting to gain a greater exposure than the individual's free resources. When investing in **risky assets** such as **equities**, a good principle is the often-stated one that **someone should only invest what they can afford to lose**. Someone who borrows to invest without having other capital to back it up if things go wrong, has the problem that they may end up with liabilities in excess of their assets.

An investor who uses instruments such as derivatives to increase their exposure should maintain other accessible resources (for example, cash on deposit) that can be used to meet losses that may arise. Clearly, it is also important that they understand the risks they are undertaking.

3.4 Life cycle, age and commitments

The **age** of an investor, the stage of **life cycle** that he is at, and his **commitments**, all affect the investor's risk profile.

Adventurous risk-taking may be unwise for someone with heavy financial **commitments**, for example to children and other dependants. Another aspect of an investor's commitments is that of how much time he has available: if he works full-time and has a family, there may be little time left for him to manage his own investments even if he has an interest and knowledge to do so, and his commitments may mean that he is more likely to wish to seek professional financial advice.

Individual circumstances may differ widely, but some aspects of common **life stages** encountered in different **approximate** typical **age groups** are described below.

- **Minors (under 18).** Someone who is under 18 may have very little in the way of direct investment needs as an individual. He is likely to be dependent on one or two parents and nobody is going to suffer financially if his bank balance runs out. A parent or grandparent who wants to give the minor a 'head start' is able to open a stakeholder pension for a child of any age.

- **Single and still young (18 to 30).** If your client is in his early or mid twenties, he may not yet have any dependants. There may be little need for protection products. The client may now be financially independent of his parents even if he is still living at home. Alternatively, your client may be renting a flat or possibly even buying a house. Such a client will probably not have accumulated much capital as he could be spending everything that he earns. He is also more likely to be an employee than to be self employed. Retirement planning is worth starting in this age band: the effect of compounding of returns means that investment in retirement savings from a relatively early age can pay off.

- **Married or cohabiting (20 to 30)** The client will have ceased to be dependent on parents at this stage and will be earning and either renting or buying a house.

- **Couple working but no dependants (20 to 30).** This is the time when a couple will be building up their income at the fastest possible rate before the expenses of looking after children begin.

- **One of a couple working, with no dependants (20 to 30).** The client's financial life could be a little bit more fragile. Dependence upon the earnings of one of the couple increases the possibility of difficulties if there is a fall in the earnings of the one person working.

- **One of a couple working, with dependants (25 to 40).** With all the earnings concentrated in the hands of one of the couple and with there being both a partner and at least one dependant to look after, the burden of dependency has now begun to reach its maximum with the welfare of an entire family. It is vital to consider protection issues in detail.

- **Married or cohabiting, with older children (35 to 50).** This is the point when the expenses are probably at their highest, even without school fees. Higher education costs can increase the burden especially if it takes the form of university. The couple may again have two incomes and possibly even have a higher net income despite the higher level of expenses.

- **After children: 'empty nesters' (45 to 60).** When children have left home, their parents have a higher net income as a result of lower expenses relating to children.

- **Retired (60 or 65 plus).** Retirement income may be significantly lower than when working, but there may be savings that have been built up. Investors may now have more free time, which they may or may not wish to devote to managing their own investments.

3.5 An individual's risk profile

The financial adviser must recognise that each client has their own views, aspirations and attitudes. **Attitudes to risk** vary widely, and accordingly investment choices vary widely too. Some individuals will be reluctant to take on any significant risk of loss of their capital while others are prepared to 'gamble' with their savings.

People are likely to take notice of the growth potential of an investment while some could be less willing to appreciate the risk involved. The adviser needs to take especial care to make such a client aware of risks.

Attitudes to risk vary according to the different objectives of the investor. An investor may have a core holding of deposits that he wishes to keep as an emergency fund, while he may be prepared to take greater risks with other funds he holds. If a client has a specific target for a particular investment – for example, to pay for children's education, or to pay for a vacation – then he may choose lower risk investments for the funds intended to reach that target than for other his other investments.

4 Making recommendations

4.1 Customer trust and confidentiality

The customer must have every reason to **trust** a financial adviser. Trust is gained through respect, and an adviser will be able to project the attitudes needed by professional presentation at all times, and through the way the adviser deals with customers.

Acting as a professional means that it should be clear in the way business is conducted that all relevant regulations are being adhered to. Regulations exist to **protect the consumer**, and a client will be reassured if there is no suggestion that regulatory rules might be breached.

If the adviser is trusted, the client will be more open about his or her circumstances, and a more satisfactory basis for giving financial advice will be created. The adviser must always treat personal information with the utmost **confidentiality**.

However, regarding confidentiality, all professional people need to be aware of the provisions of the **Proceeds of Crime Act 2002**. This Act requires a professional to disclose to the relevant authorities any information regarding possible crimes having been committed. These provisions mean that, by law, there are some circumstances – for example, if an adviser became aware of tax evasion having been committed – in which the professional requirement of confidentiality is overridden by the statutory requirement to breach that confidentiality by informing the authorities.

4.2 Suitability

Whether an investor is making his or her own **financial planning decisions**, or is being advised by a financial adviser, it may seem obvious to state that investments chosen should meet a test of **suitability**. An adviser clearly needs to follow the regulatory principle of 'Know your client' in order to be able to assess the suitability requirements of a client.

In more detail, the following guidelines should be followed by an adviser in making recommendations of **suitable** investments.

The aim should be to give conscientiously thought-out, considered advice, only in the best interests of the client.

Client needs should be quantified and the **shortfall** (if any) between needs and the client's existing arrangements should be assessed.

For each quantified need, the adviser should draw up a list of **suitable products** from those available.

From the list of suitable products, the most suitable should be identified: this can generally be achieved by a process of elimination.

The adviser must ensure that the client understands the disadvantages as well as the advantages of recommended products or courses of action, and the **risks** involved.

Where **past performance figures** are used to illustrate investment projections, it must be stated that past performance is no guarantee of future performance.

4.3 Customer understanding

It is a basic regulatory requirement that a firm should not recommend a transaction or act as an investment manager for a customer unless it has taken reasonable steps to help the customer **understand the nature of the risks** involved.

In the case of **warrants** and **derivatives**, the firm must obtain from the customer the appropriate **warrants and derivatives risk warning**.

If recommending to a private customer transactions in investments that are not readily realisable, the adviser should explain the difficulties in establishing a market price.

Following the recording of recommendations in a **report**, the adviser can check whether the client has read and understood the contents of the report, and can be asked whether he has any **questions** to ask about it.

4.4 Affordability and accessibility

The **affordability** of any investments and protection policies to be recommended for the client must be considered. The client's prospective disposable income should be ascertained in order to assess the affordability of regular contributions to policies and investment plans. Existing assets and policies, such as life assurance contracts and other savings need to be taken into account in quantifying the sizes of investments needed to meet client needs.

Some investments are constrained in their **liquidity** and **accessibility** in that they tie the investor in for a specified period. In some cases, the investment cannot be realised early even if the investor wishes it. In many other cases, early redemption may be possible, but at the expense of a penalty or a significant reduction in returns. It is sometimes possible to sell an investment before maturity on the open market, as for example with **traded endowment policies**. Although this can achieve a higher price than surrendering the policy to the insurance company, there is still likely to be a loss in the rate of return compared with retaining the investment until maturity. It is generally prudent to plan so as to avoid such '**forced selling**' of investments, so that the losses and costs incurred on such selling can be avoided or minimised.

Possible changes in a client's circumstances may change his or her investment needs. Is any course of action being considered adaptable enough to change to fit new changed circumstances? How easy is it for any investment contract or arrangement being considered to be cancelled? To the extent that most individuals must risk changes in their income (**income risk**), can the investment strategy accommodate salary changes easily? The adviser and client should consider these affordability questions, in the light of information about any investments or other financial products being considered.

4.5 Written reports to clients

Providing a **written report** to clients is an important part of the process of giving financial advice.

A written report provides a way of putting across **recommendations** that have already been made **orally** in meetings with clients. The written format makes some aspects of observations and recommendations easier for the client to understand.

Furthermore, providing a written report is clearly an important way of providing a **record** of what is being recommended, and on what key information it is based. A report in writing should avoid the potential for misunderstandings about the advice that has been given, thus acting as a safeguard for the adviser in justifying his work, as well as a document of record for the client.

The **parts of a financial planning report** to a client are typically as follows.

- A statement of the client's objectives

- A summary of the client's income and assets and other relevant circumstances or problems

- Recommendations, including any proposals for immediate action as well as longer-term suggestions for the client to consider in the future

- Appendices, including any data that is best presented separately, if appropriate

Product quotations, illustrations and brochures should be presented in an orderly way, possibly with an index listing the various items being sent to the client.

The **language** in the report should be phrased as concisely as possible. Jargon should be avoided except where necessary to explain points being made.

When a client has agreed a set of recommendations, there will be a considerable amount of work involved in arranging investments, along with any pension arrangements and protection policies also being taken out.

4.6 Monitoring and review

We mentioned the importance of regular reviews in the previous Chapter. **Regular review** of a client's circumstances, for instance on at least an annual basis, is important because it can take account of various changes:

- Changes to investor circumstances
- Changes in investor's attitudes and objectives
- The record of investment performance to date

A **fact find** for a client should be **updated** to reflect any changes in the client's circumstances if new advice is to be given to a client and time has elapsed since the fact find was carried out.

Although **annual review** might be appropriate for an investor who invests in funds (such as unit trusts and OEICs) and has therefore delegated fund management to professional fund managers, **more frequent review** may be more appropriate for an investor who has made direct investments, for example in equities and bonds.

More frequent review may also be prompted by an unexpected change in circumstances, such as a new job, or the loss of a job.

Monitoring a client's account circumstances from time to time will indicate whether there is a need for a more detailed comprehensive review. Monitoring for changes in client circumstances could be achieved by diarising dates for telephone calls that will enable you to talk with the client on a regular basis.

Key chapter points

- It is a basic requirement when giving financial advice to 'Know your customer'. All the relevant information on a client's circumstances is collected through the fact find.

- Information to be collected includes personal details, and information on a client's attitudes and objectives. A more useful interview will be achieved by asking open questions, and not just closed questions.

- Factors shaping clients' individual circumstances include the client's life cycle stage, age and commitments.

- Six stages in the financial planning process can be identified. (1) Information gathering – the fact find. (2) Establishing and agreeing client objectives. (3) Analysing the fact find information. (4) Formulating recommendations in a comprehensive plan. (5) Implementing the recommendations as agreed. (6) Review and update of the plan.

- Financial advisers' recommendations to clients must meet the requirements of suitability and affordability.

- Like any professional, a financial adviser must keep a client's details confidential, except where the law requires otherwise.

- Recommendations by a financial adviser are best backed up by a written report for the client to read.

Chapter Quiz

1   What does 'know your customer' mean in the context of anti-money laundering requirements? ...... (see para 1.1)

2   Give examples of a factual statement and a non-factual statement. ....(1.2)

3   Give examples of a closed question and an open question. ...._....(1.2)

4   Give examples of five questions designed to find out about a customer's attitudes and objectives. ...._.(1.3)

5   What is the fact find? ....(2.1)

6   Identify the stages in the financial planning process. ....(2.5)

7   What is 'S2P', and which two categories of individual will not receive it? ...._.(2.9)

8   What financial objectives might clients have (give three examples)? ...._....(3.1)

9   When might an adviser need to breach a client's confidentiality? ....…....(4.1)

10   How would you incorporate product quotations into a report to clients? ....…....(4.5)

BPP)))
PROFESSIONAL EDUCATION

Legal concepts

1 Legal personality

1.1 Introduction

A legal person possesses legal rights and is subject to legal obligations. In law, the term **person** is used to denote two categories of legal person.

- An individual human being is a **natural person**.
- The law also recognises **artificial persons** in the form of corporations.

A corporation, such as a limited company, is distinguished from an unincorporated association. An **unincorporated association** (for example a partnership) is not a separate legal entity; it does not have a legal identity separate from that of its members.

1.2 Artificial persons

A corporation is a **legal entity** separate from the natural persons connected with it, for example as members. Corporations are classified in one of the following categories.

Categories	Description
Corporations sole	A corporation sole is an **official position** which is filled by one person who is replaced from time to time. The Public Trustee and the Treasury Solicitor are corporations sole.
Chartered corporations	These may be **charities,** or professional bodies such as the Institute of Chartered Accountants in England and Wales.
Statutory corporations	Statutory corporations are formed by special Acts of Parliament. This method is little used now, as it is slow and expensive. It was used in the nineteenth century to form railway and canal companies.
Registered companies	Registration under the Companies Act 1985 is the normal method of incorporating a commercial concern. Any body of this type is properly called a company.

2 Companies, sole traders and partnerships

2.1 Companies and limited liability

The most important consequence of registration of an enterprise as a company is that a company becomes a **legal person distinct from its owners**. The owners of a company are its members, or shareholders.

A significant consequence of the fact that the company is distinct from its members is that its members therefore have **limited liability.**

The **company** itself is **liable without limit for its own debts.** If the company buys plastic from another company, for example, it owes the other company money.

The members (shareholders) own the business, so they might be the people who the creditors logically asked to pay the debts of the company if the company is unable to pay them itself. Limited liability prevents this by stipulating the creditors of the company cannot demand the company's debts from members of the company, for example if the company fails.

Although the creditors of the company cannot ask the members of the company to pay the debts of the company, there are some amounts that members are required to pay, in the event of a winding up.

Type of company	Amount owed by member at winding up
Company limited by shares	Any outstanding amount from when they originally purchased their shares.
	If the member's shares are fully paid, they do not have to contribute anything in the event of a winding up.
Company limited by guarantee	The amount they guaranteed to pay in the event of a winding up

Liability is usually limited by **shares**. Companies limited by guarantee are appropriate to **non-commercial activities**, such as a charity or a trade association which aims to keep income and expenditure in balance but also have the members' guarantee as a form of reserve capital if it becomes insolvent.

A company, as a separate legal entity, may also have liabilities in tort (eg, to pay damages for negligent acts) and crime. Criminal liability of companies is a topical area following recent disasters such as the Paddington train disaster.

It is currently extremely difficult to prosecute a company on criminal charges, as it is necessary to show a '*mens rea*', or controlling mind. Unless a company is very small it is difficult to show that the mind controlling the company was connected with the criminal act.

However, the Law Commission have issued proposals which include a charge of killing by gross carelessness, which it would be easier to charge companies with. There is, at present, no such criminal offence in the United Kingdom.

2.2 Evasion of obligations

A company may be identified with those who control it, for instance to determine its residence for tax purposes. The courts may also ignore the distinction between a company and its members and managers if the latter use that distinction to **evade** their **legal obligations**.

Gilford Motor Co Ltd v Horne 1933

The facts: The defendant had been employed by the claimant company under a contract which forbade him to solicit its customers after leaving its service. After the termination of his employment he formed a company of which his wife and an employee were the sole directors and shareholders. However he managed the company and through it evaded the covenant by which he himself was prevented from soliciting customers of his former employer.

Decision: An injunction requiring observance of the covenant would be made both against the defendant and the company which he had formed as 'a mere cloak or sham'.

2.3 Disqualified directors

Directors who participate in the management of a company in contravention of an order under the Company Directors Disqualification Act 1986 will be **jointly** or **severally liable** along with the company for the company's debts.

2.4 Unlimited liability companies

A company may also be formed with unlimited liability: its memorandum makes **no reference** to **members' liability**. If the company goes into insolvent liquidation, the liquidator can then require members to contribute as much as may be required to enable the company to pay its debts in full. An unlimited company can only be a private company since a public company is by definition always limited.

An unlimited company has two main advantages.

(a) It need not **file** a copy of its **annual accounts** and reports. There are some exceptions, the most notable of which being if the unlimited company is a subsidiary of a limited company.

(b) An unlimited company **may without formality purchase its shares** from its own members.

The unlimited company certainly has its uses. It provides a corporate body (a separate legal entity) which can conveniently hold assets to which liabilities do not attach.

2.5 Public companies and private companies

A **public company** is a company registered as such under the Companies Acts with the Registrar of Companies. Any company not registered as public is a private company: s 1(3). A public company may never be unlimited.

- A **public company (plc)** is limited by share or by guarantee, with a nominal share capital of at least £50,000, whose memorandum states that it is public and that it has complied with the registration procedures for such a company.

- A **private (Limited or 'Ltd') company** is a company which has not been registered as a public company under the Companies Act. The major practical distinction between a private and public company is that the former may not offer its securities to the public.

Private companies are generally small enterprises in which some if not all shareholders are also directors and *vice versa*. Ownership and management are often combined in the same individuals. In that situation, it is unnecessary to impose on the directors complicated restrictions to safeguard the interests of members and thus a number of rules that apply to public companies are reduced for private companies.

Only a **public company** can obtain a **Stock Exchange** or other investment exchange **listing** for its shares. This option is not open to private companies. Listed companies are sometimes referred to as **quoted companies** (because their shares are quoted publicly).

The following rules also apply to public companies.

(a) A **public** company must have at least **two directors**: a **private** company need only have **one director**.

(b) The rules on **loans to directors** are much **more stringent** in their application to **public companies** and their subsidiaries than to private companies:.

(c) A **public company**, except by ordinary resolution with special notice, may **not appoint a director aged over 70**.

2.6 Small companies

'**Small' companies** benefit from reduced legal requirements in terms of filing accounts with the registrar and obtaining an audit. The definitions of a small company for the purposes of accounting and auditing are different.

In accounting terms, a company is small if it meets two of the following criteria applicable for financial years ending on or after 30 January 2004:

(a) Balance sheet total of £5.6 million
(b) Turnover of £2.8 million
(c) Less than 50 employees

For the purposes of audit requirements, a company is small if it has a turnover of less than £2.8 million and a balance sheet total of less than £5.6 million.

2.7 Sole traders

Many small businesses start with someone becoming self-employed, as a **sole trader.**

In a sole tradership, there is no legal distinction between the individual and the business. The trader is personally liable for any debts of the business.

2.8 Partnerships (Partnership Act 1890)

Partnership was traditionally the normal organisation in the professions as most professions prohibit their members from carrying on practice through limited companies, and the Partnership Act 1890 set out law governing this form of business organisation.

In a partnership governed by the Partnership Act 1890, a partner is **personally liable** for all the debts of the firm (incurred while he is a partner and sometimes even after he has ceased to be a partner).

'**Partnership** is the relation which subsists between persons carrying on a business in common with a view of profit' (Section 1, Partnership Act 1890).

'Person' includes a corporation such as a registered company as well as an individual living person.

There must be at least **two** partners. If, therefore, two people are in partnership, one dies and the survivor carries on the business, he is a sole trader. There is no longer a partnership.

Until recently the maximum number of partners in a firm was 20, except for professional partnerships such as solicitors or accountants. The maximum was repealed in 2004, so there is now no limit on the number of partners that there may be in any firm.

Every partner is liable **without limit** for the debts of the partnership. It is possible to register a **limited partnership** in which one or more individual partners have limited liability, but the limited partners may not take part in the management of the business (Limited Partnerships Act 1907). The limited partnership is useful where, for example, one partner wishes to invest in the activities of the partnership without being involved in its day-to-day operation.

The **death of a partner** may itself dissolve the partnership. This is usually avoided by expressly agreeing that so long as there are two or more surviving partners the partnership shall continue.

2.9 A partner's authority as agent of the firm

Each partner is an **agent** of the firm when he acts in carrying on in the usual way business of the kind carried on by the firm, although his authority may be restricted by the other partners. (We discuss the concept of agency further later in this Chapter.)

The Partnership Act 1890 defines the apparent authority of a partner to make contracts as follows.

> 'Every partner is an agent of the firm and his other partners for the purpose of the business of the partnership; and the acts of every partner who does any act for carrying on in the **usual way business** of **the kind carried on by** the firm of which he is a member bind the firm and his partners, unless the partner so acting has in fact no authority to act for the firm in the particular matter, and the person with whom he is dealing either knows that he has no authority, or does not know or believe him to be a partner': s 5.

There is no formal statutory **supervision** of partnerships. Their accounts need not be in prescribed form nor is an audit necessary. The public has no means or legal right of inspection of the firm's accounts or other information such as companies must provide.

If, however, the partners carry on business under a firm name which is not the surnames of them all, say, 'Smith, Jones & Co', they are required to disclose the **names** of the **partners** on their letterheads and at their places of business. They are required to make a **return** of their **profits** for income tax and **usually** to **register** for Value Added Tax (VAT) purposes.

2.10 Limited liability partnerships

Under the **Limited Liability Partnership Act 2000** it is possible to register a **Limited Liability Partnership** (an **LLP**). A limited liability partnership combines the features of a partnership with the limited liability and creation of a legal personality more usually associated with limited companies. Many of the larger accountancy firms, for example, have taken advantage of this structure.

Every member of an LLP is an **agent** of the LLP. As such, where the member has authority, the LLP will be bound by the acts of the member.

3 Trustees

3.1 What is a trust?

A **trust** is an equitable obligation (see below for an explanation of 'equitable') in which certain persons (the **trustees**) are bound to deal with property over which they have control (the **trust property**) for the benefit of certain individuals (the **beneficiaries**).

The trustees may also be beneficiaries of the trust. An individual who transfers assets into a trust during his lifetime is known as a **settlor** and such trusts are known as **settlements**. A settlor may also be a trustee and/or a beneficiary. A trust may also be set up in a **will** and is then usually called a **will trust**. Where the trust is set down in writing, this document is called the '**trust instrument**'.

3.2 Trustees and beneficiaries: equitable interest

The word **'equity'** derives from the Latin word meaning justice or fairness.

Trusts are an invention of the law of equity. Originally the law of England was made up primarily of ancient customs which varied from one region to another. This was eventually compiled into a law which was uniform throughout England and known as the **common law**.

Over time, common law attained a definite shape but it did not tend to evolve sufficiently fast to cater for the changing needs of society. In particular, it tended to look at the form of a transaction (eg in a land purchase whose name appeared on the title deeds) rather than the substance (eg who provided the purchase money). It therefore became customary for individuals to appeal to the King's Chancellor in circumstances where the enforcement of common law would have been unduly harsh. The King's Chancellor was empowered by the King to give redress and relief from the full effects of common law where conscience indicated that this was appropriate.

Eventually definite principles were evolved and these were compiled into a system of rules. These rules became known as **Equity**. For example, equity would recognise the interest of the provider of purchase monies whether or not that person's name appeared on the title deeds.

Equity and common law frequently conflicted and in 1873 the Judicature Act provided that equity should override common law. The Act also provided that all courts could administer both types of law. The two types of law, however still remain distinct. Legal rights (those derived under common law) and equitable rights (those derived under equity) therefore need to be distinguished from each other.

Trusts encompass both types of interest. The **legal title** (ie, legal ownership) to the property in a trust will be held by the **trustees** whereas the **equitable (or beneficial) interest** will belong to the **beneficiaries**. For example land could be transferred to the trustees and the legal title would be in their names. Equity would recognise that the land was not transferred to the trustees for their own benefit but to be held for the benefit of the beneficiaries in accordance with the terms of the trust. If the trustees do not act in accordance with the terms of the trust, the beneficiaries may apply to the Court to enforce the trust.

4 Wills and intestacy

4.1 Wills

A **will** is a legal document which gives effect to the wishes of an individual (the testator, if male, the testatrix if female) as to how their estate should be distributed after their death. It appoints the persons who will have the responsibility for dealing with the estate (the executors) and gives instructions as to how the estate should be distributed.

A will must be signed in the presence of two witnesses. A **witness** or the **spouse of a witness** cannot benefit from a will. If a witness or the spouse of a witness is named as a beneficiary, the will is not made invalid, but that person will not be able to inherit under the will.

The **executors** (also called **personal representatives**) need to obtain a **Grant of Probate** from the Probate Registry to show they are entitled to **administer the estate**. Then they can collect the assets of the estate. The executors are responsible for settling all liabilities of the estate before paying out the money to the beneficiaries. The liabilities include funeral expenses, inheritance tax (in respect of which the executors must submit an account and pay any IHT due before obtaining the **Grant of Probate**), liabilities incurred while the testator was alive and expenses incurred during the period

of administration (ie while the estate is under the control of the executors). The estate cannot be paid out to the beneficiaries until all liabilities have been settled and the executors are satisfied that no claims will be made against the estate.

The assets comprising the estate are held by the executors on trust for the beneficiaries until they are distributed to them. Usually this will only last as long as it takes to administer the estate. However, longer term trusts are frequently created by wills. The trustees of these can be separate individuals to the executors and the trust terms can be the same as those of lifetime (*inter vivos*) trusts. Trusts are typically created to cater for minors. Another common use is the creation of a discretionary trust to use the inheritance tax nil rate band of the first of a married couple to die.

An important reason to effect a will is for a parent to indicate whom they would like as **guardians** to care for minor children. If this is not done (or if there are objections to the parent's choice), the guardians will be appointed by a court.

A will is made **invalid** if the testator **marries**, unless the testator expressly stated that the will was made in contemplation of marriage. If the testator **divorces**, bequests in favour of the **ex-spouse** no longer have effect.

4.2 Mirror and mutual wills

A husband and wife or an unmarried couple may make wills in similar terms. For example, the husband may make a will which leaves his estate to his spouse, if she survives him, failing that to their children. The wife's will leaves her estate to her husband, if he survives her, failing that to their children. Such wills are called **mirror or reciprocal wills**.

Under general legal principles, a will may be revoked at any time. This also applies to mirror/reciprocal wills. In particular, after one of the spouses has died, the other may alter his or her will, for example in favour of a new spouse.

Under the doctrine of **mutual wills**, two persons (often husband and wife) **make an agreement** that their property is to devolve in a certain way. For example, the agreement may specify that on the first of them to die, the deceased's property passes to the survivor, and after his or her death, the property of both of them passes to nominated beneficiaries, such as their children. The agreement must amount to a contract, not merely an understanding.

Clearly, this is very similar to the creation of mirror wills and it will be important to show that there was indeed an agreement to create mutual wills (which are effectively irrevocable dispositions), not merely mirror wills.

If it is decided that mutual wills have been made, the law will allow the ultimate beneficiaries to enforce the agreement.

4.3 Reasons for making a will

There are the following reasons for making a will.

(a) To arrange for beneficiaries other than those appointed under the intestacy rules to benefit. Unmarried partners and stepchildren cannot benefit other than by a will. Children of a previous marriage might also lose out if the testator remarries.

(b) To use tax reliefs and allowances

(c) To appoint guardians for minor children

(d) To create trusts to cater for the long term needs of the beneficiaries or to enable capital to skip generations

(e) To choose executors and trustees and to extend their statutory powers

(f) To specify funeral arrangements

4.4 Intestacy

An individual who dies without a will is known as an **intestate**. The estate of an intestate individual is dealt with under the Administration of Estates Act 1925 and the Intestates Estates Act 1952 as follows. What is stated about **spouses** below applies also to same-sex **civil partners** who have formed a civil partnership under the **Civil Partnership Act 2004**.

(a)   Where the intestate leaves:

- A surviving spouse (or civil partner) but no issue (children, grandchildren and so on) and no parent, brother or sister of the whole blood or issue thereof the surviving spouse takes the whole estate absolutely.

- A surviving spouse and issue: the surviving spouse take the personal chattels plus a statutory legacy of £125,000 (with interest up to payment). The residue, if any, is held 50% on trust for the benefit of the surviving spouse for life and thereafter on statutory trusts for the issue and 50% immediately on statutory trusts for the issue.

- A surviving spouse, no issue but one or more of: parent, brother or sister of the whole blood or their issue; the surviving spouse takes the personal chattels plus the remainder up to £200,000 (with interest up to payment) plus 50% of the residue absolutely. The other half is taken by the parents in equal shares and if none to the brothers and sisters of the whole blood or their issue on statutory trusts.

- Issue but no surviving spouse: the whole estate is held on statutory trusts for the benefit of the issue.

- No surviving spouse or issue: the estate is distributed as follows.

Relatives Surviving	Interest taken
Both parents	The whole in equal shares
One parent	The whole
Brothers and sisters of the whole blood (same two parents)	The whole on statutory trusts
Brothers and sisters of the half blood (one parent in common)	The whole on statutory trusts
Grandparents	The whole in equal shares
Uncles and aunts of the whole blood (same two parents as deceased's parent)	The whole on statutory trusts
Uncles and aunts of the half blood (one parent in common with deceased's parent)	The whole on statutory trusts
If no relative takes an absolute interest	The Crown takes the whole

(b)   Issue means children, grandchildren and so on. Adopted children are treated as children of their adoptive parents, not their natural parents. If a child predeceases the intestate person, that child's children takes his share, if more than one, equally.

(c)   A surviving spouse is one still legally married to the deceased. An ex-spouse has no rights under the rule of intestacy nor has an unmarried partner.

(d)   Under the statutory trusts, the entitlements of minor children are held on trust until they attain the age of eighteen years.

The **Law Reform (Succession) Act 1995** provides that a spouse must survive the deceased by 28 days in order to be entitled to a share. If the spouse dies within 28 days, distribution takes place as if there were no surviving spouse.

5 The law of contract

5.1 Elements of a valid contract

A contract is a legally binding agreement between mutually consenting two parties who intend to enter into a legal relationship.

There are **three essential elements** to look for in the formation of a valid contract: **agreement, consideration** and **intention.**

The first essential element of a binding contract is **agreement**. To determine whether or not an agreement has been reached, the courts will consider whether one party has made a firm **offer** which the other party has **accepted**.

In most contracts, offer and acceptance may be made **orally** or in **writing**, or they may be implied by the conduct of the parties. The person making an offer is the offeror and the person to whom an offer is made is the offeree.

In life assurance, the **proposal form** makes up the offer which the life assurance company can either accept at standard rates or on special terms, or reject. If the assurance company accepts on special terms, it is effectively rejecting the proposal and making a counteroffer, which the proposer then either accepts or rejects.

The second of the three essential elements of a contract is **consideration**. The promise which a claimant seeks to enforce must be shown to be part of a bargain to which the claimant has himself contributed.

Thirdly, an agreement is not a binding contract unless the parties **intend to create legal relations**. What matters is not what the parties have in their minds, but the inferences that reasonable people would draw from their words or conduct.

The requirements of standardisation in business have led to the **standard form contract**. The **standard form contract** is a document prepared by many large organisations setting out the terms on which they contract with their customers. The individual must usually take it or leave it.

5.2 Contract law and consumer protection

Many contracts are made between experts and ordinary consumers. The law will intervene only where the former takes unfair advantage of his position. The law seeks to protect the idea of **'freedom of contract'**, although **contractual terms** may be regulated by **statute**, particularly where the parties are of unequal bargaining strength.

In the second half of the twentieth century, there was a surge of interest in consumer matters. The development of a mass market for often complex goods has meant that the consumer can no longer rely on his own judgement when buying sophisticated goods or services. Consumer interests are now served by two main areas.

- **Consumer protection agencies**, which include government departments (the Office of Fair Trading) and independent bodies (the Consumers' Association).

- **Legislation**, for example, Consumer Credit Act 1974 and Unfair Contract Terms Act 1977 (see Chapter 15)

5.3 Form of a contract

As a general rule, **a contract may be made in any form**. It may be written, or oral, or inferred from the conduct of the parties.

For example, a customer in a self-service shop may take his selected goods to the cash desk, pay for them and walk out without saying a word.

However, certain contracts must be in **writing**, such as for the purchase of land and property.

5.4 Capacity to contract

Capacity to contract is the legal ability to enter into a contract.

Someone who is insane may have their capacity to contract limited by law.

Minors – that is, those under 18 – do not have unrestricted capacity to enter into contracts.

5.5 Legality of object

If you enter into an agreement with an accomplice to steal property, such a contract would be **illegal** and the contract would **not be valid**.

5.6 Utmost good faith

If you buy a used car from a private seller and find that it falls apart soon after you bought it, that usually is your problem. Provided that the seller answered honestly any questions that you asked, they were not obliged to volunteer information that you did not seek. The general principle here is: *caveat emptor* – the buyer beware.

However, if you make a proposal for insurance, including life insurance, you are expected to give to the insurance company **all relevant information** which will enable the company to assess the risk, eg if you are seriously ill or in a dangerous occupation or have a risky lifestyle, or whether you are a normal risk for which the company would issue a contract on standard terms.

This requirement to **disclose all relevant information** is fundamental to an insurance contract. If the rule is not observed the policy can be treated by the insurer as **voidable**. The requirement is termed **'utmost good faith'** or *uberrimae fidei*.

6 Agency

6.1 The agency relationship

'**Agents**' are engaged by '**principals**' generally in order to perform tasks which the principals cannot or do not wish to perform themselves, because the principal does not have the time or expertise to carry out the task. In normal circumstances, the agent discloses to the other party that he (the agent) is acting for a principal whose identity is also disclosed.

Agency is a relationship which exists between two legal persons (the **principal** and the **agent**) in which the function of the agent is to form a contract between his principal and a third party.

The relationship of principal and agent is usually created by mutual consent. The consent need not generally be formal nor expressed in a written document. **It is usually an 'express' agreement**, even if it is created in an informal manner.

When an agent agrees to perform services for his principal for reward there is a contract between them.

6.2 Examples of agency relationships

There are many examples of agency relationships which you are probably accustomed to, although you may not be aware that they are examples of the laws of agency. Some examples are as follows.

(a) **Partnerships.** A feature of partnerships is that the partners are agents of each other.

(b) **Brokers.** Any broker is essentially a middleman or intermediary who arranges contracts in return for commission or brokerage. For example, an **insurance broker** is an agent of an insurer who arranges contracts of insurance with the other party who wishes to be insured. However, in some contexts (for example, when the broker assists a car owner to complete a proposal form) he is also treated as the agent of the insured. Insurance, especially marine insurance, has complicated rules applicable to the relationship (insurer-broker-insured).

(c) **Appointed representatives of product providers.** A financial adviser who works as an appointed representative (tied adviser) for a product provider firm (such as a life office) is an **agent of the product provider firm**, while the firm is principal. The firm, as principal, is responsible for the acts and omissions of its appointed representatives (its agents) and must ensure that its agents comply with FSA rules.

(d) An **independent financial adviser (IFA)**, who offers advice on products from a full range of providers, is the **agent of his client** in respect of the advice or recommendations offered to the client. This is the case whether or not the IFA is a member or appointed representative of a **network**. The insurer or other product provider is not liable for the acts or omissions of the IFA, and the IFA owes no duty to the product provider. The IFA owes a duty of care to his or her client.

6.3 Obligations of an agent

Even if the agent undertakes his duties without reward, the agent has obligations to his principal.

(a) **Performance and obedience.** The agent must **perform** his obligations, following his principal's instructions with **obedience**, unless to do so would involve an illegal act.

(b) **Skill and accountability.** The agent must act with the standard of **skill and care** to be expected of a person in his profession and to be **accountable** to his principal to provide full information on the agency transactions and to account for all moneys arising from them.

(c) **No conflict of interest.** The agent owes to his principal a duty not to put himself in a in a situation where his own interests conflict with those of the principal; for example, he must not sell his own property to the principal (even if the sale is at a fair price).

(d) **Confidence.** The agent must keep in **confidence** what he knows of his principal's affairs even after the agency relationship has ceased.

(e) **Any benefit** must be handed over to the principal unless he agrees that the agent may retain it. Although an agent is entitled to his agreed remuneration, he must account to the principal for any other benefits. If he accepts from the other party any commission or reward as an inducement to make the contract with him, it is considered to be a bribe and the contract is fraudulent.

6.4 Authority of the agent

The **contract** made by the agent is **binding** on the principal and the other party **only if** the **agent was acting within the limits of his authority** from his principal.

7 Property

7.1 Real property

In legal terminology, **land** includes buildings and anything else which is permanently attached to the land.

Real property (also called 'realty') is land owned in perpetuity – in other words, **freehold property.** The mediaeval common law courts granted special remedies: the right of the dispossessed owner to have the land returned to him. For that historical reason, land in freehold ownership is in a category (real property) of its own.

Freehold property is distinguished from **leasehold property**. With leasehold property (in legal terminology, 'chattels real'), the right of a tenant (or lessee) will come to an end either by expiry of a fixed period (which may be as much as 999 years) or by termination by notice (and in other more unlikely events). When it terminates the landlord (or lessor) resumes possession from the tenant. The landlord is therefore said to have a 'reversion' which becomes possession when the lease terminates. While the lease continues, the tenant has possession but is usually required to pay a rent to the landlord.

A **lease** is a form of **contract**. If granted for a term of more than three years it must generally be in the form of a **deed**.

7.2 Personal property

Personal property – or **'personalty'** – is anything that is not **realty**, ie **real property** (freehold land). It is so called because the owner's claim could be satisfied by payment of the value instead of returning the property – his claim was against the wrongdoer personally and he could not automatically recover the property or thing.

Personal property comprises:

- **Leasehold land**, and
- Pure **personalty** (including chattels and things in action)

Banknotes and coins are 'things in action'.

These technical legal terms can be significant. For example someone (the **testator**) may by his **will** give his 'real estate' to A and his 'chattels' to B and his remaining personalty to C.

Moveable tangible property - generally called **chattels** – are literally those items of property of which ownership and possession can be transferred simply by delivery, such as furniture, books and jewellery.

8 Co-ownership of land

8.1 Forms of co-ownership

It is possible for more than one person to own land. If land is purchased or transferred to two or more persons, these persons become either **joint tenants** or **tenants in common**. (Note that this applies to owning freehold land outright, even though the word 'tenant' is used.)

Joint tenancy is where two or more people acquire land but no words of 'severance' are used. This means that the transfer does not state what share in the land each person has. The land is merely 'held by X and Y'. It is both legal and equitable co-ownership. **Joint tenancy** is a convenient and commonly used way for a husband and wife to own the matrimonial home.

Tenants in common have shares in the land. For instance, a conveyance may state that the land should go to 'P, Q and R equally' - each then owns one-third part of the interest. It is equitable ownership.

8.2 Significance of the type of ownership

The importance of the distinction is that if a **joint tenant** dies his interest lapses and the land is owned wholly by the survivor(s). He may not pass his interest on by **will**. The advantage is that only a limited number of interests can exist. The disadvantage is the fact that survival decides ownership. With tenants in common, each tenant can bequeath his interest which means that a house owned by tenants in common (A, B and C equally) will, if C dies and leaves his

interest to D, E, F and G, be owned by A, B, (one third part each) D, E, F and G (one twelfth part each). Whilst perhaps being fairer, this can be cumbersome!

The Law of Property Act 1925 achieved a compromise by providing that, where land is owned by two or more persons, no more than four of those persons hold the **legal estate** as joint tenants and trustees, for the benefit or **equitable interest** of themselves and other co-owners. Thus transfers can be effected by four signatures but the sale proceeds are subject to trusts so that all the owners get fair shares.

9 Powers of attorney

9.1 What is a power of attorney?

A **power of attorney** is a document made by a person ('the donor') which appoints another person ('the attorney' or 'the donee') or persons, to act for the donor in legal matters. An example of the use of a power of attorney is where the donee is given power to sign documents on behalf of the donor.

The power of attorney may be a **general** power, to allow the donee to act for the donor in all matters, or restricted to a **specific** act, for example to execute a specific document. In either case, the donor can still act himself. The donor is liable for the acts of the donee, for example, the donor would be bound by a document signed by the donee, provided that the donee has acted within the terms of the power of attorney.

9.2 Making a power of attorney

A general power of attorney should be in the form set out in S10 of the Powers of Attorney Act 1971. Briefly, this sets out the names of the donor and donee and states that the donee is appointed as attorney for the donor. The document must be executed as a deed. In general, this form cannot be used by trustees to delegate trustee powers. However, under S 1 of the Trustee Delegation Act 1999, it can be so used in the case where the trustee is a co-owner of land and also has a beneficial interest in the land eg where land is held in joint ownership, whether as tenants in common or joint tenants.

A limited form of power of attorney should be drawn up by a lawyer and specify exactly the powers being given to the donee. It should be formally executed (as a deed).

A **trustee** may delegate his powers by executing a power of attorney under the terms of the Trustee Act 1925 (as amended). The delegation can be for a period up to 12 months in length. Notice of the execution of the power of attorney must be given within 7 days to any person who has power to appoint trustees and to the other trustees.

9.3 Length of a power of attorney

An ordinary power of attorney (whether given as an individual or as a trustee) is only valid whilst the donor is capable of giving instructions. It can be revoked by the donor.

The power will also cease at the end of a time specified in it or when specific act has been carried out or if the donee dies or becomes incapacitated. Therefore it will cease to have effect if the donor becomes mentally incapacitated. For this reason, an **enduring power of attorney** may be advisable for many people, and it is probably a good idea to consider this at the same time as executing a **will**.

9.4 Enduring power of attorney

An **enduring power of attorney** (EPA) is a legal document by which a person appoints one or more persons to act for him as attorney. An EPA may act as an ordinary power, but it is also capable of having effect if the donor becomes mentally incapable of acting for himself.

If no enduring power of attorney is made before a person becomes incapable, it may be necessary to apply to the **Court of Protection** – a more cumbersome and possibly expensive procedure. The Court of Protection is intended to protect the finances of people who are no longer able to manage their own affairs.

The relevant **legislation** is the Enduring Powers of Attorney Act 1985 and the Enduring Powers of Attorney (Prescribed Form) Regulations 1990.

The EPA must be made when the donor is capable of understanding the nature and effect of creating an enduring power. The donor should understand that the donee will have complete authority over his affairs and will, in general, be able to do anything that the donor could have done. The donor should also understand that the donee's power will continue if the donor is mentally incapable and that it will not usually be possible to revoke the power once it has been registered (see below). The document must be in the prescribed form and executed as a deed.

It is usually advisable for more than one attorney to be appointed and for the attorneys to act jointly and severally (that is, they may act together or separately, as they choose). In this case, if one of the attorneys dies, the other can continue to operate the power.

The EPA may be general in nature or limited to specific transactions. It may also be limited to have effect only when the donor has become mentally incapable. It can be revoked by the donor if he has mental capacity to do this.

A **trustee** can make an EPA in relation to trust powers, within provisions of the Trustee Act 1925 (as amended).

9.5 Registering an enduring power of attorney

As soon as the donor becomes or is becoming mentally incapable, the donee must register the EPA with the **Court of Protection**. Until an application has been made, the donee may not use (or continue to use) the EPA. The donee must give notice of the intention to register to the donor and at least three close relatives of the donor (eg. spouse, children, parents). There are provisions dealing with the situation where the donor may be distressed by receipt of the notice, there are no relatives to notify or they cannot be traced. The donor and the relatives are entitled to object to the registration or to the attorney.

Once an application has been made, the donee has limited powers, for example to maintain the donor or prevent loss to the donor's estate. If there are no objections to the registration, it will take place 35 days after the last notice has been served. If the application fails, the attorney should consider whether an application for the appointment of Receiver should be made, under the Court of Protection.

After registration, the donee can make binding decisions about the donor's property. However, the donee must act reasonably and within the limits of the Enduring Powers of Attorney Act 1985. There are only limited powers to make gifts out of the donor's assets or to benefit people other than the donor. The EPA will continue until the death of the donor or until, for example, the death or mental incapacity of the donee.

Where there is no power of attorney, the Court of Protection may make orders concerning the person's property and may appoint a **receiver** with specified powers to manage the person's affairs with the authority of the court.

9.6 Mental Capacity Act 2005

The **Mental Capacity Act 2005** received Royal Assent in April 2005 but does not come into effect until **2007**.

The Act sets out a single **'decision-specific' test** for assessing whether a person lacks capacity to take a particular decision at a particular time. A lack of capacity cannot be established merely by reference to a person's age, appearance, or any aspect of a person's behaviour. Carers and family members gain a right to be consulted.

The Act deals with two situations where a designated decision-maker can act on behalf of someone who lacks capacity.

- **Lasting powers of attorney (LPAs).** This is like the current Enduring Power of Attorney (EPA), but the Act also allows people to let an attorney make health and welfare decisions.

- **Court appointed deputies.** The Act provides for a system of court appointed deputies to replace the current system of receivership in the Court of Protection.

The Act will replace the current statutory schemes for **enduring powers of attorney** and **Court of Protection receivers** with reformed and updated schemes.

- A new **Court of Protection** will have jurisdiction relating to the whole Act and will be the final arbiter for capacity matters.

- A new **Public Guardian** will be the registering authority for LPAs and deputies.

10 Bankruptcy

10.1 Introduction

From time to time, a client of a financial adviser might run into financial difficulties, and face **bankruptcy** or, in the case of a corporate client, **insolvency** proceedings. It is important for the financial adviser to have a broad understanding of the legal and financial implications for the client in these circumstances.

10.2 Bankruptcy

Bankruptcy occurs when an individual's financial affairs are taken over by a court. The individual's assets are transferred into a **trust** which is used to repay as much debt as possible.

The term 'bankruptcy' applies to individuals, not to companies. A sole trader or partner who owes money (a debtor) and is unable to pay the debt could be faced with bankruptcy proceedings.

Inability to pay a debt will occur when the individual cannot find the money. Inadequate cash flow, rather than a loss-making business, may be the problem. Typically, the business will have insufficient cash coming in to meet its various payment obligations, and will be unable to borrow more money. In this situation, the individual's business will have more current liabilities than liquid assets.

The current legislation dealing with bankruptcy is the **Insolvency Act 1986** as amended by the **Insolvency Act 2000** and (with effect from 1 April 2004) the **Enterprise Act 2002**.

10.3 Creditors' petition for a bankruptcy order

Bankruptcy proceedings against an individual begin with the presentation of a petition for a bankruptcy order to the court. (This could be the High Court or a County Court with power to deal with such proceedings.)

The petitioner is usually a creditor, or several creditors acting jointly. (However, a debtor may petition to have himself/herself declared bankrupt.) The court will not entertain a petition from a creditor unless the creditor is owed at least £750 (currently) on an unsecured debt.

A creditor's petition must allege that the debtor is unable to pay the debt or has very little prospect of being able to pay it. This inability to pay must be demonstrated in court by showing one of the following:

(a)   That a **'statutory demand'** (in the prescribed form) has been served on the debtor, requiring him or her to pay, and this demand has not been satisfied within three weeks

(b)   That a **judgement debt** (ie a payment ordered by a court or judge) has been returned unsatisfied, in whole or in part

In the time between the presenting of a petition for a bankruptcy order and the court's decision, the debtor may be tempted to dispose of some of his or her property, in order to put it outside the reach of the creditors. Under the Insolvency Act 1986, however, any disposal of property or payment of money after a petition has been presented will be **void** if the debtor is subsequently judged to be bankrupt, **unless** the court approves the disposal or payment.

10.4 Bankruptcy order

When a petition for a bankruptcy order has been presented, the court may decide to make a bankruptcy order, ie declare the individual bankrupt. The bankruptcy of the individual begins on the day this order is made.

When a bankruptcy order has been made, the Official Receiver takes control of the debtor's assets, as **receiver and manager**. The Official Receiver is an official of the Department of Trade and Industry (DTI) and an officer of the court.

The duty of the receiver and manager is to protect the bankrupt's property until a **trustee in bankruptcy** has been appointed.

10.5 Trustee in bankruptcy

The function of the **trustee in bankruptcy** is to get possession of and realise the value of the bankrupt's assets, and distribute them to the creditors, in accordance with the Insolvency Act.

Every bankruptcy is under the general control of the court, which has wide powers to control the trustee.

All property owned by the debtor on the date of the bankruptcy order, and any property acquired subsequently, passes to the trustee. The only items of property the debtor is allowed to retain are:

(a)   The tools of his/her trade
(b)   A vehicle, if one is needed for his/her trade or employment
(c)   Clothing, bedding and furniture belonging to the debtor and his/her family

10.6 Income payments order

As regards the income of a bankrupt person, the trustee is entitled only to the excess income above what is needed to support the bankrupt and his/her family. Income includes income from employment or holding office and profits from carrying on a business. The trustee can apply to the court, claiming for all such excess income to belong to the bankrupt's estate.

The court may then make an **income payments order**, permitting the debtor to receive an income from his/her trade or employment. However, the trustee may take any income in excess of what is considered reasonable.

10.7 Disposal of matrimonial homes

If the debtor owns his/her own **home**, and lives alone, lives with a co-habitee and/ or lives with adult children, the debtor's interest in the home passes to the trustee. The trustee will immediately obtain a court order for sale of the property.

If the **matrimonial home** is owned by the bankrupt's spouse or former spouse, the trustee should not normally have an interest in the property for the bankrupt's estate. However, if the property has been transferred by the bankrupt to the

spouse under suspicious circumstances, the trustee can apply to the court to have a claim on the property for the bankrupt's estate.

After one year from the date of the bankruptcy order, it is presumed that the needs of the creditors outweigh all other considerations, unless there are exceptional circumstances. As a consequence, after that time a court order can probably be obtained for the eviction of the debtor and his/her family, and for the sale of the home.

Under the Enterprise Act 2002, there is a limit of three years during which the trustee in bankruptcy can deal with the bankrupt's interest in the home. After this period it will revert back to the bankrupt.

Banks and other **lenders of mortgage finance** to buy a matrimonial home need to be aware of the potential problems in the event of the borrower's bankruptcy. Before granting a mortgage, the lender will ask about any potential legal or beneficial interest in the property of a person other than the borrower. The lender might insist that the mortgage should be in joint names. If one person is declared bankrupt, the other person remains subject to the mortgage, and is responsible for the mortgage payments in full.

10.8 Distribution of assets following a bankruptcy order

The job of the trustee is to dispose of the bankrupt's assets, and distribute the proceeds to the creditors.

The debts of the bankrupt person must be paid by the trustee in the following order of priority:

(a) The costs of the bankruptcy (including the professional fees of the trustee)

(b) Preferential debts. Preferential debts include:

    (i) Accrued holiday pay owed to employees

    (ii) Wages and salaries of employees due in the last four months before the bankruptcy order, subject to a maximum amount per employee (currently £800).

(c) Ordinary unsecured creditors. These can only be paid once the other categories of debt have been paid in full. If the proceeds from selling the bankrupt's assets are insufficient, these creditors are treated equally. For example, if there is £50,000 left over from the disposal of assets to pay ordinary unsecured creditors of £100,000, each unsecured creditor will receive 50p in the £1 on their unpaid debt.

Example: Creditors

A bankruptcy order was made against Peter Wilton. The trustee eventually disposed of his home, which was subject to a £170,000 mortgage, for £250,000. His other assets realised £200,000. Preferential debts were £25,000, the costs of bankruptcy were £15,000 and unsecured creditors totalled £500,000.

How much did unsecured creditors receive?

Solution

Realisation of:

	£
Home	80,000
Other assets	200,000
	280,000
Bankruptcy costs	(15,000)
Preferential debts	(25,000)
	240,000

Unsecured creditors will receive £240,000/£500,000 = 48p in the pound.

10.9 Voidable transactions by the bankrupt

A trustee in bankruptcy has a duty to obtain the most money possible in order to pay the bankrupt's creditors. If the bankrupt undertakes certain transactions that harm the interests of the creditors (or harm some creditors at the expense of others), the trustee can apply to the court for the transactions to be declared void.

10.10 Automatic discharge of bankruptcy order

Following the enactment of the Enterprise Act 2002, a bankruptcy order is normally discharged automatically **one year** after the date of the order. This means that the individual is no longer a bankrupt, and is free of debts, even if these have not been paid in full. Once the bankruptcy order has been discharged, any property subsequently obtained by the ex-bankrupt belongs to him/her, and does not vest in the trustee.

10.11 Bankruptcy Restriction Orders

Bankruptcy Restriction Orders (BROs) are designed to protect the public from a bankrupt whose conduct has been irresponsible or reckless. A BRO imposes restrictions that apply after a bankrupt has been discharged. The restrictions can apply for between 2 and 15 years.

11 Insolvency

11.1 Introduction

The law on **corporate insolvency** in the UK is similar in many respects to the law on bankruptcy. The courts responsible for administering corporate insolvency law are the High Court (Chancery Division) and the county courts. (This chapter deals with the law in England and Wales. The law in Scotland differs in some respects but the syllabus is tested on the basis of English law and practice. The **Insolvency Act 2000** and the **Enterprise Act 2002** have introduced major changes to corporate insolvency laws.

11.2 Aims of insolvency law

The purpose of insolvency law is to govern what should happen to the property of a company that is insolvent. The basic aims of the law are to:

(a)   **Protect** the creditors of the company
(b)   **Balance** the interests of competing groups
(c)   **Control or punish** directors responsible for the company's financial collapse
(d)   **Encourage** 'rescue' operations

11.3 Tests of corporate insolvency

There are two tests of corporate insolvency as follows.

(a)   **Inability to pay debts when they fall due.** A company can be the subject of a winding-up petition if it fails to pay an undisputed debt, currently of more than £750.

(b)   A **'balance sheet test'.** A company can be deemed insolvent if its liabilities exceed its assets.

It is important to be able to establish whether a company is solvent or insolvent.

(a)   It is often a requirement for a company to be deemed insolvent for insolvency proceedings to be started.

(b)   In the case of a voluntary liquidation, the liquidation cannot be initiated by the members (company shareholders) if the company is insolvent.

11.4 Types of insolvency proceeding

There are three types of corporate insolvency 'officials', depending on whether a company goes into **administration, receivership** or **liquidation.**

(a)   **Administration. Administrators** are officers of the court. They may be appointed under an administration order or may be appointed by companies and directors without a court order. The purpose of an administration is to provide a better way of realising the company's assets than could be achieved by a liquidation or receivership (see below), when the company is in financial difficulties.

(b)   **Receivership.** In most cases, **a receiver is appointed out of court by a debenture holder (usually a bank)** in pursuance of powers to do so contained in the debenture. A receiver is concerned principally with the interests of the secured creditors who appointed him and will try to take control of the charged assets. If the receiver is appointed under a debenture giving a general floating charge over the company's assets, he will be an **administrative receiver** and take over the management of the company's property. EA 2002 has largely abolished administrative receivership, in favour of a more streamlined procedure than there used to be for appointing an administrator.

(c)   **Liquidation.** A **liquidator** acts mainly in the interests of **unsecured creditors** and **members** (shareholders) of the company. Liquidators of insolvent companies might be appointed either:

(i)   Under a voluntary liquidation arrangement, or
(ii)   Following an unsecured creditor's petition to the court for liquidation of the company

Liquidation means that the company must be dissolved and its affairs 'wound up', or brought to an end. The assets are realised, debts are paid out of the proceeds, and any surplus amounts are returned to members. Liquidation leads on to dissolution of the company.

11.5 Fraudulent and wrongful trading

If, when a company is wound up, it appears that its business has been carried on with **intent** to **defraud creditors** or others, the court may decide that the persons (usually the directors) who were knowingly parties to the fraud shall be **personally responsible** for debts and other liabilities of the company: s 213 Insolvency Act 1986.

Key chapter points

- The law attaches rights to a person and imposes legal obligations on him. Legal persons include natural persons (individual human beings) and artificial legal persons (for example corporate bodies and local authorities).

- In a sole tradership, there is no legal distinction between the individual and the business.

- Partnership is defined as 'the relation which subsists between persons carrying on a business in common with a view of profit'. A partnership is *not* a separate legal person distinct from its members, it is merely a 'relation' between persons. Each partner (there must be at least two) is personally liable for all the debts of the firm.

- A company has a separate legal personality from its members, while a traditional partnership does not.

- The liability of company shareholders is limited. They may lose their investment, but will not normally be expected to pay more to creditors, if the company goes bust.

- A trust is an equitable obligation in which certain individuals (the trustees) are bound to deal with property over which they have control (the trust property) for the benefit of other individuals (the beneficiaries).

- A trust may also be set up in a will and is then usually called a will trust.

- A will is a legal document which gives effect to the wishes of an individual as to how their estate should be distributed after their death. It appoints the personal representatives who will have the responsibility for dealing with the estate (the executors) and gives instructions as to how the estate should be distributed.

- Three essential elements in any contract are: agreement (made by offer and acceptance); consideration (there must be a bargain by which obligations assumed by one party are supported by value given by the other); intention (the parties must have an intention to create legal relations).

- Agency is a relationship which exists between two legal persons (the principal and the agent) in which the function of the agent is to form a contract between his principal and a third party.

- Freehold land is termed real property. Co-ownership of land may be as joint tenants or tenants in common. With a tenancy in common, the shares of the property that each owns are specified. If a joint tenant dies, the property becomes wholly owned by the survivor.

- Powers of attorney are a form of agency. They allow a person to act in place of another person. They are particularly useful for older people who may not be able to manage their own affairs.

- Insolvency signals that a company cannot pay all of its debts. Insolvency law is designed to protect the creditors of the company, to balance the interests of competing groups, to control or punish directors responsible for the company's financial collapse, and to encourage 'rescue' operations.

- An insolvent individual can be declared bankrupt. Every bankruptcy is under the general control of the court, which has wide powers to control the trustee.

Chapter Quiz

1   What are the two types of legal person? .... (see para 1.1)

2   What is meant by the 'limited liability' of a company? .... (2.1)

3   What distinguishes public and private companies? .... (2.5)

4   What is an 'LLP'? .... (2.10)

5   Define a trust. .... (3.1)

6   What reasons are there for making a will? .... (4.3)

7   What are the three essential elements in a valid contract? .... (5.1)

8   Define the agency relationship. .... (6.1)

9   Distinguish real property and personal property. .... (7.1, 7.2)

10   What types of joint ownership are possible for two people who want to buy a house together? .... (8.1)

11   What are powers of attorney and enduring powers of attorney? .... (9.1, 9.4)

Taxation is a complex subject, and is covered here to the depth required for your examination. There may be particular rules for special situations that are not covered here because they are beyond the requirements of the syllabus. Clients may require specialist tax advice.

1 The scope of income tax

1.1 Individuals

Individuals are taxable on their **income for each tax year**. The **tax year** runs from **6 April** in one year to **5 April** in the following year.

Income for individuals includes **earnings from employment or self- employment** and **income from investments.**

1.2 Employees

The **earnings of employees** will include salaries, bonuses, commissions, fees, and benefits in kind such as a company car, cheap loans and the cost of private medical insurance.

Earnings for duties performed in the UK are subject to the **Pay As You Earn (PAYE)** system, under which the employer deducts tax before paying the net amount to the employee. The HMRC (Her Majesty's Revenue & Customs, which includes what used to be known as the Inland Revenue) issues a **Tax Code** to indicate to the employer how much estimated tax should be deducted.

1.3 Benefits in kind

Pay is not the only benefit which may be provided by an employer for employees. One of the additional types of **benefit in kind** is the provision of a **company car**, most commonly provided for senior managers and sales representatives. The value of private use of the car, and of fuel if used privately, is taxable.

The taxable benefit is based on a percentage of the list price subject to a maximum of £80,000 list price including VAT. The percentage varies between 15% and 35% depending on the car's carbon dioxide emissions.

In the case of **representatives**, a car is a necessary aid for them in their work. However they usually have the private use of a car when they are not using it on business and that private use is treated as a benefit in kind.

For senior managers, a company the car is less likely to be an essential part of their work and is more likely to be a **form of remuneration**. Other taxable benefits in kind include the value of **meal vouchers** in excess of 15p per day and the cost of **private medical insurance**.

The position is complicated by the fact that different rules apply to employees in two **different groups**. The two groups are (1) employees earning **£8,500 per annum or more** or directors of the company and (2) those who are earning less than £8,500 per annum ('excluded employees').

If an employee is not an excluded employee, then the employer must complete an HMRC **P11D form** giving details of all benefits and expenses payments.

Such **P11D employees** must pay tax on the value of benefits in kind whereas excluded employees are not liable for tax on many benefits. The deciding factor is whether or not an employee's pay and benefits in total reach the P11D level. Thus an employee whose pay is £8,400 a year and who has benefits in kind valued at £200 per year is classified as a P11D employee.

Expenses of an employee must be incurred **wholly, exclusively and necessarily** for their work (for example, subscriptions to a professional association) for them to be allowable against the employee's tax liability.

1.4 Termination of employment

Payment to an employee on **redundancy** is exempt from tax up to a limit of £30,000 including statutory redundancy pay.

1.5 Sole traders

A **sole trader** is a **self-employed** person, running a business. A self-employed person running his or her own business, which is not formed as a limited company, is a **sole trader** even if the person employs other people.

Sole traders pay tax based on the **profit** for their **accounting year**. The accounting year will be the one which ends in the current tax year.

A sole trader is taxed on **business income minus allowable expenses**. Then, the process is the same as for an employed person: other income is added to earnings and deducting the personal allowance.

Even if the sole trader retains profits in the business and does not draw them out, they are taxable as earnings. The fact that the trader has chosen not to draw and spend them does not change their status as earnings.

The sole trader's tax for each tax year will be based on the profits made in the business year which ended in that same tax year. For example, if the trader's business year ends on 30 June, then the tax liability for the fiscal year 2006/2007

will be based on the profit that the trader makes in the business year ending on 30 June 2006. This is known as the **current year basis**.

1.6 Donations to charity

A scheme of tax relief on gifts to charities by individuals applies to **'Gift Aid'** donations. A Gift Aid donation can be a 'one-off' gift or a regular gift to a charity. The taxpayer must make a Gift Aid declaration to the charity.

A Gift Aid donation is treated as though it was paid net of basic rate tax (22%). This amount can then be recovered by the charity. Higher rate relief is given to the taxpayer by extending his basic rate tax band by the grossed-up value of the gift.

Thus, if an individual who pays tax at the basic rate makes a gross charitable donation of £100, he can make a 'Gift Aid' declaration and so will pay (net) £78.

There is also income tax relief for gifts to charity of shares in quoted companies and land and buildings.

1.7 Charges

A charge is a payment by a tax payer which is allowed as a deduction. An example is a payment to use a patent (patent royalty).

A charge is deducted from income **before** tax is calculated. This means that the borrower is effectively relieved from paying tax on that part of his income which is used to meet the charge, ie he obtains tax relief.

1.8 Pension contributions

Payments to a **personal pension scheme** (including a **stakeholder pension**) are paid net of basic rate tax to the pension provider. For example, if the scheme member contributes £1,000 to his personal pension scheme in 2006/07, he will pay £780 and the pension provider will reclaim £220 from HMRC. This addition from HMRC applies even if the scheme member is a non-taxpayer: someone can contribute up to £3,600 gross (£2,808 net) to a pension scheme even if they have no earnings.

If the scheme member is a higher rate taxpayer, he or she will receive higher rate relief by extending his basic rate tax band by the gross amount of the contribution (eg in the above example by £1,000). This is similar to the treatment for Gift Aid donations.

Contributions to **occupational pension schemes** by an employee are deductible from earnings for tax purposes.

1.9 Residence

Someone who is physically present in the UK for six months in a tax year (a year from 6 April to 5 April) will normally be treated as **resident** in the UK and taxable on income and capital gains.

Someone who is in the UK for less than six months may still be liable for tax. Broadly, if someone is abroad only temporarily, or if they spend an average of three months a year in the UK for a four year period, then they will be treated as **ordinarily resident** and therefore liable to UK tax.

Income tax is payable by UK residents. If someone spends a period of time working abroad, they will normally be taxed on their overseas earnings by the country in which they earn the money. To prevent those earnings also being taxed in the UK, there exist a number of **double taxation agreements** with most countries of the world, generally stipulating that the earnings will be taxed only by the country in which they are earned.

Investment income from overseas will be taxed by the UK HMRC at the time the investor becomes entitled to it. If tax is deducted in the overseas country, it will be allowed as a credit against UK tax.

1.10 Domicile

Someone who treats the UK as their permanent home is classed as **UK domiciled**. Someone can be resident abroad but still domiciled in the UK even if the person has not set foot in the UK for years.

What tax consequences does domicile have? For **inheritance tax** purposes, if someone dies while they are domiciled in the UK, all of their assets anywhere in the world are chargeable to UK tax. If someone is not domiciled in the UK, then only their UK assets will be chargeable to tax. Someone who is UK-resident but not UK-domiciled will be charged to UK **income and capital gains tax** only on remittances made to the UK of investment income and capital gains.

You could therefore have someone domiciled in France but living and working in the UK. They would be subject to **income tax** and **capital gains tax**, but their assets outside the UK would not be taxable if they died while living in the UK.

However, HMRC deems people to be **UK domiciled** for inheritance tax purposes if they were one of the following.

(a) Resident for income tax purposes in the UK for not less than 17 of the 20 tax years up to the year of an inheritance-taxable event

(b) Actually domiciled in the UK within three years before an inheritance-taxable event

Domicile is something which we acquire at birth. It will usually be the domicile of our father but we can change it if we want. We can have only **one country of domicile** at a time, whereas we can be resident or ordinarily resident in more than one country in any one tax year.

1.11 Assessment of tax

Employees with simple tax affairs will not be asked to complete a Tax Return, as the PAYE deductions should be accurate. If an individual has more complicated tax affairs, he or she may need to complete a **self-assessment Tax Return**, to ensure that the correct tax liability is calculated. If there is income that has not been taxed, the individual must declare this to HMRC and complete a Tax Return.

If a Tax Return is issued, it must be completed and submitted by the **filing date**. This is the later of:

(a) 31 January following the end of the tax year which the return covers
(b) Three months after it was issued

The Tax Return includes a section for the taxpayer to compute his own tax payable (a **self assessment**), and this computation counts as an assessment to tax. The return and the balance of any tax payable are usually both due by 31 January following the end of the tax year. Payments on account of tax would have previously been made on 31 January in the tax year and on the following 31 July (ie 12 months and six months before the normal due date for the final payment). All capital gains tax (CGT) is payable on 31 January following the tax year, with no payments on account.

A taxpayer may choose not to complete the section of the return in which he works out his tax payable (the **self assessment**). HMRC will then make the **computation** and prepare an assessment. This counts as a self assessment made by the taxpayer, so the rules in this section relating to self assessments still apply. However, HMRC will not guarantee to have the work done in time for the taxpayer to pay the correct amount by the due date, unless the return is submitted by the later of:

(a) 30 September following the end of the tax year which the return covers
(b) Two months after it was issued

1.12 Penalties for non-compliance

Taxpayers filing tax returns late face maximum late filing penalties of £100 for returns up to six months late, then £200 if over six and up to twelve months late. Beyond twelve months, the maximum penalty is £200 plus 100% of the tax liability. A maximum penalty of £60 per day could be imposed if notice is given to the taxpayer.

Surcharges are imposed for tax paid late (but not payments on account by self-employed people). The surcharge starts at 5% for amounts more than 28 days late, increasing to 10% for payments more than six months late. Interest is charged on late payments on account.

1.13 Civil partnerships

As from **5 December 2005**, same-sex couples who obtain legal status as **'civil partners'** under the **Civil Partnership Act 2004** are treated **for all tax purposes** in the same way as a married couple. This treatment is not extended to common law partners.

2 Income tax allowances

2.1 The scope of allowances

Personal **reliefs** and **allowances** are deductions from an individual's income before tax is calculated, or deductions which reduce the tax on income. There is a list of current income tax rates and allowances in the **Tax Tables** at the end of this Study Text.

2.2 Personal allowance

All UK residents, including children, are entitled to a **personal allowance** in each tax year.

If a couple are living together and one of them does not have sufficient income to use up a personal allowance, the other can transfer assets to that person so that the income from those assets – previously taxable – will now no longer be taxable because it falls within the personal allowance. In order to do this, the **ownership** of assets must be totally transferred from one person to another: not everybody is willing to do that.

2.3 Age allowances

There are higher personal allowances called **age allowances** for those in the age brackets 65 plus and 75 plus.

If someone entitled to an age allowance has income over an annual sum known as the **income limit for age-related allowances**, the allowance is reduced gradually. The income limit is £20,100 for 2006/07. The rate is reduced by £1 for every £2 of income in excess of the limit.

The following example will show the effect of additional income for someone whose income exceeds the income limit. The reduction of £1 for every £2 excess will continue until the age allowance has fallen to the level of the ordinary allowance.

Example: Age allowance

A and B are aged 67 and single. A's income is at the income limit, while B's income is £200 higher than that. The effect of the income limit in each case is shown below.

	Example A £	Example B £
Income (all pension)	20,100	20,300
Age allowance	(7,280)	(7,180)*
Taxable income	12,820	13,120

* £7,280 – £200/2

Tax	Example A		Example B	
	£	£	£	£
	2,150 × 10%	215.00	2,150 × 10%	215.00
	10,670 × 22%	2,347.40	10,970 × 22%	2,413.40
	12,820	2,562.40	13,120	2,628.40

Notice the difference in income and tax.

	Income £		Tax £
Example A	20,100		2,562.40
Example B	20,300		2,628.40
Additional income	200	Tax	66.00

Income of £200 in excess of the limit results in extra after-tax income of only: £200 – £66 = £134.

2.4 Married couple / civil partnership allowance

The main **Married Couple's Allowance** was abolished from 6 April 2000, but the right to claim a couple's allowance remains for pensioners born before 6 April 1935. The amount of the allowance depends on whether at least one of the couple is aged 75 or over (at any time in the tax year). New marriages and civil partnerships meeting the age criteria will have an allowance based on the income of the highest earner.

The allowance is reduced by any excess over the income limit not used against the age allowance. The minimum amount available is £2,350 for 2006/07. The allowance available is then given as a reduction from tax payable at the rate of 10% (ie, the minimum amount of the reduction in 2006/07 is £235).

2.5 Blind person's allowance

A taxpayer who is registered with a local authority as a blind person gets a blind person's allowance (BPA) of £1,660 in 2006/07. The allowance is also given for the year before registration, if the taxpayer had obtained the proof of blindness needed for registration before the end of that earlier year.

3 Computation of income tax

3.1 Personal tax computation

An individual's income from all sources is brought together in a **personal tax computation**. We split income into **non-savings income, savings (excluding dividend) income and dividend income**. An income tax computation can be drawn up using three columns headed as follows.

Non-savings income £	Savings (excluding dividend income) £	Dividend Income £

Interest and dividends are **'savings income'**. All other income is **non-savings income**.

3.2 Statutory total income and taxable income

The total of an individual's income from all sources is the **statutory total income**. Once statutory total income has been calculated, personal allowances are deducted to arrive at **taxable income**.

Two allowances, the personal allowance and the blind person's allowance, are deducted from STI. The allowances come off non-savings income first, then off savings (excluding dividend) income and lastly off dividend income.

A taxable income computation can be set out as below.

Sue: taxable income for 2006/07

	Non-savings income £	Savings (excl dividend) income £	Dividend income £	Total £
Income from employment	36,000			
Building society interest (× 100/80)		1,000		
NS&I Savings Certificates interest		320		
UK dividends (× 100/90)			1,000	
Statutory total income (STI)	36,000	1,320	1,000	38,320
Less personal allowance	(5,035)			
Taxable income	30,965	1,320	1,000	33,285

Note that the **National Savings & Investments** interest Sue receives is received **gross**. Building Society interest and UK dividends must, however, be grossed up for inclusion in the income tax computation.

3.3 Income tax bands

The first step in calculating the income tax liability is to divide the total **taxable income** into three bands:

(i) The first £2,150 of income; this is called income in the **starting rate band**
(ii) The next £31,150 of income; this is income in the **basic rate band**
(iii) The remaining income over the **higher rate threshold** of £33,300

The rate of tax applied to the income in each band depends on whether the income is non-savings income, savings (excluding dividend) income or dividend income.

There is only **one set of income tax bands** used for **all three types of income**. These bands must be allocated to income in the following order:

(i)   **Non-savings income**
(ii)   **Savings** (excluding dividend) **income**
(iii)   **Dividend income**

Example: Personal tax computation

Zoë has total taxable income of £34,000. Of this £18,000 is non-savings income, £12,000 is interest and £4,000 is dividend income.

The first £2,150 of non-savings income is in the starting rate band. The remaining £15,850 of non-savings income is in the basic rate band. This leaves £15,300 (£31,150 – £15,850) of the basic rate band.

The next £12,000 of the basic rate band is used by interest income, leaving £3,300 (£15,300 – £12,000) of the basic rate band to be used by dividend income.

The remaining dividend income £700 (£4,000 – £3,300) is income above the higher rate threshold.

3.4 Computing the tax liability

The tax due on taxable income is calculated in three steps:

Step 1: Deal with non-savings income first:

Non-savings income in the starting rate band is taxed at 10%. Next any non-savings income in the basic rate band is taxed at 22%, and finally non-savings income above the higher rate threshold is taxed at 40%.

Step 2: Secondly, deal with savings (excl dividend) income:

Savings (excl dividend) income is dealt with after non-savings income. If any of the starting or basic rate bands remain **after taxing non-savings income** they can be used here. Savings (excluding dividend) income is taxed at 10% in the starting rate band. If savings (excluding dividend) income falls within the basic rate band it is taxed at 20% (not 22%). Once income is above the higher rate threshold, it is taxed at 40%.

Step 3: Thirdly, compute tax on dividend income:

Lastly, tax dividend income. If dividend income falls within the starting or basic rate bands, it is taxed at 10% (never 20% or 22%). If, however, the dividend income exceeds the basic rate threshold of £33,300, it is taxed at 32.5%.

Continuing Zoë's income tax computation from the Example above, the tax liability is:

Income tax	£
Step 1:	
Non savings income	
£2,150 × 10%	215
£15,850 × 22%	3,487
£18,000	
Step 2:	
Savings (excl. dividend) income	
£12,000 × 20%	2,400
Step 3:	
Dividend income	
£3,300 × 10%	330
£700 × 32.5%	227
4,000	
Tax liability	6,659

3.5 Computing the tax payable

We have seen above how to calculate the income tax liability on non-savings, savings and dividend income. Once this is done there are two final steps to be made in order to compute the tax payable:

Step 4

Deduct the tax credit on dividends from the tax liability. Although deductible, this tax credit cannot be repaid if it exceeds the tax liability calculated so far.

Step 5

Finally deduct the tax deducted at source from savings (excluding dividend) income and any PAYE. (PAYE is the tax deducted at source from an individual's earnings.) These amounts can be repaid to the extent that they exceed the income tax liability.

The resulting figure is the tax payable which is the balance of the liability still to be settled in cash.

Continuing the example of Zoë, above, and assuming all interest was received net of 20% tax:

	£
Income liability	6,659
Less tax suffered	
Tax credit on dividend (£4,000 × 10%)	(400)
Tax on interest (£12,000 × 20%)	(2,400)
Income tax payable	3,859

Below are some more examples of complete computations of income tax payable.

Examples: Further personal tax computations

(a)   Kathy has a salary of £10,000 and receives dividends of £4,500.

	Non-savings	Dividends	Total
	£	£	£
Earnings	10,000		
Dividends £4,500 × 100/90		5,000	
STI	10,000	5,000	15,000
Less personal allowance	(5,035)		
Taxable income	4,965	5,000	9,965

	£
Income tax	
Non savings income	
£2,150 × 10%	215
£2,815 × 22%	619
Dividend income	
£5,000 × 10%	500
Tax liability	1,334
Less tax credit on dividend	(500)
Tax payable	834

Some of the tax payable has probably already been paid on the salary under PAYE.

The dividend income falls within the basic rate band so it is taxed at 10% (*not* 22%). The tax credit on dividend income is deducted from the tax liability. Remember that the deduction can reduce the tax payable to £NIL but any excess tax credit cannot be repaid.

(b) Jules has a salary of £20,000, business profits of £30,000, net dividends of £6,750 and building society interest of £3,000 net. He pays a copyright royalty of £2,000 and makes a gift aid donation of £780 (net).

	Non-savings £	Savings (excl dividend) £	Dividend £	Total £
Schedule D Case I	30,000			
Earnings	20,000			
Dividends £6,750 × 100/90			7,500	
Building society interest £3,000 × 100/80	–	3,750	–	
	50,000	3,750	7,500	
Less charges	(2,000)			
STI	48,000	3,750	7,500	59,250
Less personal allowance	(5,035)			
Taxable income	42,965	3,750	7,500	54,215

Income tax	£
Non savings income	
£2,150 × 10%	215
£31,150 × 22%	6,853
£1,000 (£780 × $\frac{100}{78}$) × 22%	220
£8,665* × 40%	3,466
*£2,150 + £31,150 + £1,000 + £8,665 = £42,965	10,754
Savings (excl. dividend) income	
£3,750 × 40%	1,500
Dividend income	
£7,500 × 32.5%	2,438
	14,692
Less tax credit on dividend income	(750)
Less tax suffered on building society interest	(750)
Tax payable	13,192

Savings (excl. dividend) income and dividend income fall above the basic rate threshold so they are taxed at 40% and 32.5% respectively. The basic rate band is extended by the gross amount of the gift aid donation. Copyright royalties are deducted as a charge on income (paid gross).

4 Capital gains tax

4.1 Basic rules of CGT

When a person buys an asset and sells it at a profit, the difference between the two is taxed as a capital gain (subject to reliefs that are available, as we shall see below).

An individual pays capital gains tax (CGT) on his net chargeable gains (his gains minus his losses) for a tax year, less unrelieved losses brought forward from previous years and the annual exemption.

Individuals are liable to CGT on the disposal of assets situated anywhere in the world if for any part of the tax year of disposal they are resident or ordinarily resident in the UK, subject to the provisions of any international double taxation agreements.

There is an **annual exemption** for each tax year. For 2006/07, it is £8,800. It is the last deduction to be made in the calculation of taxable gains.

Taxable gains are chargeable to capital gains tax as if the gains were an extra slice of savings (excluding dividend) income for the year of assessment concerned. This means that CGT may be due at 10%, 20% or 40%. The rate bands are used first to cover income and then gains.

Example: Capital gains tax

In 2006/07, Jennifer has the following income, gains and losses. Her chargeable gain is not eligible for taper relief (see later). How much capital gains tax is payable?

	£
Salary	32,910
Chargeable gains	25,900
Allowable capital losses	8,000

(a)   Jennifer's taxable income is as follows.

	£
Salary	32,910
Less personal allowance	(5,035)
Taxable income	27,875

(b)   The gains to be taxed are as follows.

	£
Gains	25,900
Less losses	(8,000)
	17,900
Less annual exemption	(8,800)
Taxable gains	9,100

(c)   The tax bands are allocated as follows.

	Total	Income	Gains
Lower rate	2,150	2,150	0
Basic rate	31,150	25,725	5,425
Higher rate	3,675	0	3,675
		27,875	9,100

(d)   The CGT payable is as follows.

	£
£5,425 × 20%	1,085
£3,675 × 40%	1,470
Total CGT payable	2,555

4.2 Losses

Allowable losses are deductible from chargeable gains in the tax year or accounting period in which they arise and any loss which cannot be set off in this manner is carried forward for relief in future periods. Losses **must** be used as soon as possible. Losses may not be set against income.

Allowable losses brought forward are only set off to reduce current year chargeable gains less current year allowable losses to the annual exempt amount. No set-off is made if net chargeable gains for the current year do not exceed the annual exempt amount.

Examples: Capital gains tax losses

(a)   George has chargeable gains for 2006/07 of £10,000 and allowable losses of £6,000. As the losses are **current year losses** they must be fully relieved against the £10,000 of gains to produce net gains of £4,000, despite the fact that net gains are below the annual exemption.

(b)   Bob has gains of £13,000 for 2006/07 and allowable losses brought forward of £6,000. Bob restricts his loss relief to £4,200 so as to leave net gains of £(13,000 − 4,200) = £8,800, which will be exactly covered by his annual exemption for 2006/07. The remaining £1,800 of losses will be carried forward to 2007/08.

(c)   Tom has chargeable gains of £5,000 for 2006/07 and losses brought forward from 2005/06 of £4,000. He will leapfrog 2006/07 and carry forward all of his losses to 2007/08. His gains of £5,000 are covered by his annual exemption for 2006/07.

4.3 Married couples and civil partnerships

A husband and wife are taxed as two separate people. The same applies to same-sex **civil partnerships**.

Each has an annual exemption, and losses of one of the couple cannot be set against gains of the other.

Disposals or gifts **between spouses** or **civil partners** who are living together give rise to **no gain and no loss**, whatever actual price (if any) was charged by the person transferring the asset to the other.

4.4 The basic CGT computation

A chargeable gain (or an allowable loss) is generally calculated as in the following example.

	£
Disposal consideration (or market value)	X
Less incidental costs of disposal	(X)
Net proceeds	X
Less allowable costs	(X)
Unindexed gain	X
Less indexation allowance (see below)	(X)
Indexed gain	X

Taper relief may then apply (see below).

Incidental costs of disposal may include:

(a)   Valuation fees (but not the cost of an appeal against the HMRC's valuation)
(b)   Estate agency fees
(c)   Advertising costs
(d)   Legal costs

155

These costs should be deducted separately from any other allowable costs (because they do not qualify for any indexation allowance if it was available on that disposal).

Allowable costs include:

(a) The original cost of acquisition
(b) Incidental costs of acquisition
(c) Capital expenditure incurred in enhancing the asset

4.5 Indexation

Indexation was introduced in 1982. The purpose of having an indexation allowance is to remove the inflationary element of a gain from taxation.

The Finance Act 1998 abolished indexation allowance given to disposals by individuals, trusts and personal representatives for periods after 6 April 1998. For gains realised on or after 6 April 1998, indexation allowance is given for the period up to 5 April 1998 but not thereafter. For assets acquired on or after 1 April 1998 no indexation allowance is available on their disposal.

Indexation is calculated from the month of acquisition of an asset, or March 1982 if later.

The indexation factor is:

$$\frac{\text{RPI for month of disposal} - \text{RPI for month of acquisition (or March 1982)}}{\text{RPI for month of acquisition (or March 1982)}}$$

The calculation is expressed as a decimal and is rounded to three decimal places. The indexation factor is then multiplied by the cost of the asset to calculate the indexation allowance. If the RPI has fallen, the indexation allowance is zero: it is not negative.

Example: Indexation

An asset is acquired on 15 February 1983 at a cost of £5,000. Enhancement expenditure of £2,000 is incurred on 10 April 1984. The asset is sold for £20,500 on 20 December 2006. Incidental costs of sale are £500. The indexation factors between February 1983 and April 1998 and April 1984 and April 1998 are 0.959 and 0.835 respectively.

Calculate the chargeable gain.

Indexation allowance is:

	£
0.959 × £5,000	4,795
0.835 × £2,000	1,670
	6,465

The computation of the chargeable gain is as follows.

	£
Proceeds	20,500
Less incidental costs of sale	(500)
Net proceeds	20,000
Less allowable costs £(5,000 + 2,000)	(7,000)
Unindexed gain	13,000
Less indexation allowance	(6,465)
Indexed gain before taper relief (see below)	6,535

4.6 Indexation and losses

The indexation allowance on a disposal cannot create or increase an allowable loss. Thus if there is a gain before the indexation allowance, the allowance can reduce that gain to zero, but no further. If there is a loss before the indexation allowance, there is no indexation allowance.

4.7 Taper relief

For gains realised by individuals, trusts and personal representatives on or after 6 April 1998, **taper relief** applies.

The taper reduces the amount of chargeable gain according to how long the asset has been held for periods after 5 April 1998. The taper is more generous for business assets than for non-business assets.

The taper on **business assets** is as follows.

Number of complete years after 5 April 1998 for which asset held	% of gain chargeable
0	100
1	50
2 or more	25

The taper on **non-business** assets is:

Number of complete years after 5 April 1998 for which asset held	% of gain chargeable
0	100
1	100
2	100
3	95
4	90
5	85
6	80
7	75
8	70
9	65
10 or more	60

Non-business assets acquired before 17 March 1998 (Budget Day in 1998) qualify for an **addition of one year** to the period for which they are treated as held after 5 April 1998.

For example, someone buys a non-business asset on 1 January 1998 and sells it on 1 July 2006. For the purposes of the taper, the person is treated as if he had held the asset for nine complete years (eight complete years after 5 April 1998 plus one additional year).

The taper will be applied to net gains that are chargeable after the deduction of any losses of the current year or brought forward losses. The annual exemption will be deducted from the tapered gains. The allocation of losses to gains for this purpose will be on the basis that produces the lowest tax charge.

4.8 Business assets

A **business asset** can be broadly defined as:

(a) An asset **used for the purposes of a trade** carried on by an individual (either alone or in partnership) or by a company of that individual

(b) An asset **held for the purposes of any office or employment** held by that individual with a person carrying on a trade

(c) **Shares in a trading company** held by an individual where either the company is not listed on the Stock Exchange or the individual is employed by the company or holds at least 5% of the shares. Shares listed on the **Alternative Investment Market (AIM)** qualify as business assets.

If an asset qualifies as a business asset for part of the time of ownership, and part not, the business part and the non-business part are treated as separate assets calculated by time apportionment over the period of ownership of the asset (not just complete years).

However, if the asset was acquired before 6 April 1998, only use on or after that date is taken into account.

If the asset is owned for more than ten years after 5 April 1998, only the use in the **last ten years** of ownership is taken into account.

Taper relief applies to each gain separately but the period of ownership for taper relief purposes is taken to be the **whole period of ownership** of the asset.

4.9 Rollover relief

A gain may be 'rolled over' (deferred) where it arises on the disposal of a business asset which is replaced. This is **rollover relief**. A claim cannot specify that only part of a gain is to be rolled over.

All the following conditions must be met.

(a) **The old asset sold and the new asset bought are both used only in the trade** or trades carried on **by the person claiming rollover relief**. Where part of a building is in non-trade use for all or a substantial part of the period of ownership, the building (and the land on which it stands) can be treated as two separate assets, the trade part (qualifying) and the non-trade part (non-qualifying). This split cannot be made for other assets.

(b) The old asset and the new asset both fall within one (but not necessarily the same one) of the following classes.

(i) Land and buildings (including parts of buildings) occupied as well as used only for the purpose of the trade

(ii) Fixed (that is, immovable) plant and machinery

(iii) Ships, aircraft and hovercraft

(iv) Goodwill

(v)   Satellites, space stations and spacecraft

(vi)   Milk quotas, potato quotas and ewe and suckler cow premium quotas

(vii)   Fish quota

(c)   Reinvestment of the proceeds of the old asset takes place in a period beginning one year before and ending three years after the date of the disposal.

(d)   **The new asset is brought into use in the trade on its acquisition** (not necessarily immediately, but not after any significant and unnecessary delay).

4.10 Exempt assets

The following are **exempt** from capital gains tax.

- The individual's own home (principal private residence)
- NS&I Savings Certificates
- Gilts (government stocks)
- Qualifying corporate bonds (see definition below)
- Betting winnings
- NS&I Premium Bond prizes
- Qualifying life assurance policies (if still owned by the original policyholder)
- Chattels (tangible movable property) sold for £6,000 or less

A **qualifying corporate bond (QCB)** is a security (whether or not secured on assets) which:

(a)   Represents a 'normal commercial loan'. This **excludes** any bonds which are **convertible** into shares (although bonds convertible into other bonds which would be QCBs are not excluded), or which carry the right to excessive interest or interest which depends on the results of the issuer's business

(b)   Is expressed in sterling and for which no provision is made for conversion into or redemption in another currency

(c)   Was acquired by the person now disposing of it after 13 March 1984, and

(d)   Does not have a redemption value which depends on a published index of share prices on a stock exchange.

Permanent interest bearing shares issued by building societies which meet condition (b) above are QCBs.

4.11 Calculation of CGT on shares

If the investor makes a capital gain on the realisation of a share it may be subject to capital gains tax, and this is how it will be calculated.

The basic calculation for **capital gains tax** is:

Profit =   Proceeds (less sale expenses) less original investment less indexation allowance up to April 1998, less taper relief from April 1998

The profit thus calculated could become subject to capital gains tax if:

- After taking into account the capital gains tax indexation allowance and taper relief, the individual's gain is in excess of the annual exemption (£8,800 for 2006/07), or

- The gain is below the annual exemption but the investor has already made use of this in other transactions

There are methods of reducing the capital gain.

- The investor may have other capital losses including losses brought forward which could be offset.

- The investor may consider transferring the holding into a spouse's name prior to sale if the spouse has not used up his or her annual exemption.

4.12 Matching rules for sales of shares

Shares present special problems when computing gains or losses on disposal.

Matching rules determine which shares have been sold and so work out what the allowable cost on disposal should be.

Share disposals are matched with acquisitions in the following order.

(a) Same day acquisitions
(b) Acquisitions within the following 30 days
(c) Previous acquisitions after 5 April 1998 identifying the most recent acquisition first (a LIFO basis)
(d) Any shares in the **FA 1985 pool** (shares acquired between 6 April 1982 and 5 April 1998)

Example: Share disposals (1)

Catherine acquired the following shares in X plc.

	No of shares
1.4.90	10,000
1.9.98	5,000
10.11.01	7,000
30.12.06	2,000

On 11.12.06 Catherine sells 12,000 shares. With which acquisitions is Catherine's share disposal matched?

Solution

Catherine will initially match the disposal with the 2,000 shares bought on 30.12.06 (bought in next 30 days) She will then match with the other post April 1998 acquisitions on a LIFO (Last In, First Out) basis, so the 7,000 shares bought on 10.11.01 and 3,000 of the shares bought on 1.9.98 are deemed to be sold. 2,000 of the shares acquired on 1.9.98 and the FA 1985 pool of 10,000 shares remain.

Example: Share disposals (2)

June made the following purchases of ordinary shares in Read plc, a quoted company.

Date	Number	Cost
		£
15 May 2004	1,800	1,900
1 March 2005	1,000	1,260

On 30 September 2006 she sold 1,600 of the shares for £14,000. The shares were not a business asset for taper relief purposes.

Compute the capital gain after taper relief or allowable loss on the sale of June's shares.

Solution

Match post April 1998 acquisitions on a 'last in first out' (LIFO) basis:

1 March 2005

	£
Disposal proceeds (£14,000 × $\frac{1,000}{1,600}$)	8,750
Less: cost	(1,260)
Gain	7,490

15 May 2004

	£
Disposal proceeds (£14,000 × $\frac{600}{1,600}$)	5,250
Less: cost (1,900 × $\frac{600}{1,800}$)	(633)
Gain	4,617

The total chargeable gain on the sale of June's shares is £12,107 (£7,490 + £4,617). No taper relief is due in respect of either of the disposals (held for less than three complete years).

The rule of matching share disposals with acquisitions within the following 30 days prevents a shareholder from carrying out **bed and breakfasting** of shares, as used to be possible several years ago. 'Bed and breakfasting' refers to selling and then repurchasing (typically the next day, hence the term 'bed and breakfasting') the same shares in order to 'crystallise' a capital loss, or a gain, to make efficient use of the individual's annual exemptions while keeping an investment in the same shares.

For someone wishing to crystallise a gain or loss but to retain similar investments, possible alternatives to 'bed and breakfasting' are:

- 'Bed and ISA': repurchase of sold shares within an Individual Savings Account, where they will be sheltered from CGT

- 'Bed and spouse': repurchase of the same shares as those sold, by the investor's spouse or civil partner

- Repurchase of shares similar to those sold, for example shares in the same sector, if such shares can be identified

4.13 Bonus issues of shares (scrip issues)

When a company issues **bonus shares,** all that happens is that the number of shares of the original holding is increased.

Since bonus shares are issued at no cost there is no need to adjust the original cost. Instead the numbers purchased at various times are increased by the bonus. The normal matching rules will then be applied.

4.14 Rights issues

The difference between a **bonus issue** and a **rights issue** is that, in a rights issue, the new shares are paid for and this results in an adjustment to the original cost. As with bonus issues, rights shares derived from shares in the 1985 pool go into that holding and those derived from post 5 April 1998 holdings attach to those holdings. The number and cost of each of right issue is added to each holding as appropriate.

The length of the period of ownership for taper relief purposes depends on the date of acquisition of the original holding **not** the date of acquisition of the rights shares.

For the purposes of calculating the indexation allowance, expenditure on a rights issue is taken as being incurred on the date of the issue and not on the date of acquisition of the original holding.

4.15 Collection of CGT

Gains, and (if the taxpayer chooses to compute the tax) the CGT, are shown on the individual's **tax return**. The taxpayer must pay that tax on 31 January following the tax year. There are no interim payments on account, as there are for income tax.

5 Inheritance tax

5.1 Introduction to inheritance tax

Inheritance tax (IHT) is primarily a tax on **wealth** left on **death**. It also applies to **gifts within seven years of death** and to certain **lifetime transfers of wealth**.

IHT is different from income tax and CGT, where the basic question is: how much money has the taxpayer made? With IHT, the basic question is: how much has he given away? We tax the amount which the taxpayer has transferred - the amount by which he is worse off. If the taxpayer pays IHT on a lifetime gift, he is worse off by the amount of the gift plus the tax, and we have to take that into account.

We will see that (for 2006/07) the first £285,000 of transfers is taxed at 0% (the **nil rate band**), and is therefore effectively tax-free. To stop people from avoiding IHT by, for example, giving away £1,425,000 in five lots of £285,000, the IHT rules look back seven years every time a transfer is made to decide how much of the nil rate band is available to set against the current transfer.

5.2 Transfers of value and chargeable transfers

Inheritance tax (IHT) is a tax on gifts or '**transfers of value**'. There are two main chargeable occasions:

(a)   Gifts made in the lifetime of the donor (**lifetime transfers**)
(b)   Gifts or transfers on death, for example when property is left in a will (**death estate**)

Inheritance tax cannot arise unless there is a **transfer of value**. This is any '**gratuitous disposition**' made by a person which results in his being worse off – that is, he suffers a **diminution in value** of his estate.

The sale of an asset at its **open market ('arms' length') value** will **not** give rise to an IHT charge.

The measure of a gift is always the loss to the transferor (the diminution in value of his estate), not the amount gained by the transferee.

Inheritance tax arises on any **chargeable transfer**. A chargeable transfer is any transfer of value not covered by an exemption.

5.3 Chargeable persons

Individuals and **trustees of settled property (trust property)** are **chargeable persons** for IHT purposes.

5.4 The scope of the IHT charge

All transfers of assets (worldwide) made by **persons domiciled in the UK** (that is, persons regarding the UK as their permanent home), whether during lifetime or on death, are within the charge to IHT. For individuals not domiciled in the UK, only transfers of UK assets are within the charge to IHT.

IHT becomes payable on **death** only, except in the case of chargeable gifts to businesses or to discretionary trusts, when a **lifetime** charge at a tax rate of 20% can apply. We do not need to go into the calculation of tax on chargeable lifetime transfers here.

Trusts terminology

Note the following terminology relating to trusts.

- When there is a **trust, trustees** deal with the **trust property** over which they have control for the benefit of other individuals, who are the **beneficiaries**.

- An individual who transfers assets into a trust during his lifetime is known as a **settlor** and such trusts are known as **settlements**. A settlor may also be a trustee and/or a beneficiary.

- **Life interest trusts** (or '**interest in possession**' trusts) are trusts in which beneficiaries ('**life tenants**') are entitled to the enjoyment of the income during their lifetime after which further beneficiaries ('**remaindermen**') may become entitled to the income and/or the capital.

- **Accumulation and maintenance (A&M) trusts** are trusts enabling a settlor to give property to young people with conditions attached preventing them from having access to income and/or capital at too young an age.

5.5 Spouses and civil partners

Spouses, or **civil partners** in the case of a same-sex civil partnership, are taxed separately. On the death of one spouse or civil partner, it is necessary to value his or her estate. That estate includes only the property (or share of property) actually belonging to the deceased. Each spouse or civil partner has the benefit of the **nil rate band** (the £285,000 band on which IHT is at 0%), exemptions and reliefs independently of the other spouse or civil partner.

Transfers between spouses or civil partners (whether or not living together) are **exempt**. Two simple **planning points** follow from the exemption for such transfers.

(a) A married couple or civil partnership may avoid IHT on the first death if each makes a **will** leaving most or all of his or her property to the other.

(b) A couple should consider making **lifetime transfers** between themselves so as to achieve, as far as possible, estates of equal value. If they should die together, the combined estate will then enjoy the full benefit of two nil rate bands.

5.6 Family maintenance

Expenditure on **family maintenance** is not within the scope of IHT. An example of this would be school fees paid for a child.

5.7 Potentially exempt transfers and chargeable lifetime transfers

A **lifetime transfer** made by an individual to another individual is a **potentially exempt transfer (PET)**. This means that such transfers will not incur a lifetime liability to IHT.

A PET is treated as being exempt from IHT when made, and will remain so if the transferor survives for at least seven years from making the gift. If the transferor dies within seven years of making the gift, it will become chargeable to death IHT.

A lifetime transfer to a **discretionary trust** is a **Chargeable Lifetime Transfer (CLT).**

Changes to IHT and trusts were announced in the 2006 Budget (and are expected to pass into law following publication of this Study Text). The new rules as announced in the Budget are incorporated below.

From **22 March 2006**, the IHT rules for discretionary trusts were extended to:

- **Interest in possession (IIP) trusts**, and
- **Accumulation and maintenance (A&M) trusts**

These rules provide that:

- Payments into such trusts are **chargeable transfers** and may therefore be subject to an immediate 20% IHT charge, and

- A **periodic charge** of up to 6% is applied every 10 years

- When funds are removed between the 10-year anniversaries, there will be an **exit charge** proportionate to the periodic charge

A&M trusts which were **set up before 22 March 2006** and which provide for trust assets to go to a beneficiary absolutely at age 18 will enjoy the previous more favourable IHT treatment, whereby lifetime transfers into the trust are treated as **PETs**. The terms of trusts may be changed to take advantage of this treatment if the change is made by 6 April 2008.

IIP trusts created before 22 March 2006 also continue to have the previous favourable IHT treatment whereby transfers into the trust are PETs, until the interest in the trust property ends. Any property remaining in trust at that time will be treated as newly created settled property. If the beneficiary is alive at the time of termination, this will constitute a chargeable transfer. If the interest terminates on death, the settled property forms part of the beneficiary's estate and the trust property comes under the new rules. Periodic and exit charges will apply. There are exceptions relating to charities.

Furthermore, the new 2006 rules do not apply to:

- Trusts created for disabled persons (whether created on death or in the settlor's lifetime)

- A&M trusts set up on death by a parent for a minor child who gains full entitlement to the trust assets at age 18

5.8 Tax on lifetime transfers

There are two aspects of the calculation of tax on **lifetime transfers**:

(a) Lifetime tax (at 20%) on **chargeable lifetime transfers (CLTs)**, and

(b) Additional death tax on CLTs and on potentially exempt transfers (PETs) where the transferor dies **within seven years** of making the transfer.

The rate of death tax is 40%, but the longer the transferor survives after making the transfer, the lower the death tax. This is because a **taper relief** applies to lower the amount of death tax payable as follows.

Years between transfer and death	% reduction in death tax
3 years or less	0
More than 3 but less than 4	20
More than 4 but less than 5	40
More than 5 but less than 6	60
More than 6 but less than 7	80

Death tax on a lifetime transfer is payable by the **transferee**.

5.9 Exemptions

There are various **exemptions** available to eliminate or reduce the chargeable amount of a lifetime transfer or property passing on an individual's death.

- Some exemptions apply to both lifetime transfers and property passing on death
- Other exemptions apply only to lifetime transfers (including PETs becoming chargeable on death within seven years)

5.9.1 Exemptions applying to lifetime transfers only (including PETs)

Small gifts exemption. Outright gifts to individuals totalling £250 or less per donee in any one tax year are exempt. If gifts total more than £250 the whole amount is chargeable. A donor can give up to £250 each year to each of as many donees as he wishes. The small gifts exemption cannot apply to gifts into **trusts**.

Annual exemption. The first £3,000 of value transferred in a tax year is exempt from IHT. The annual exemption is used only after all other exemptions (such as for transfers to spouses/civil partners or to charities). If several gifts are made in a year, the £3,000 exemption is applied to earlier gifts before later gifts. Any **unused portion of the annual exemption** is **carried forward for one year** only. Only use it the following year after that year's own annual exemption has been used.

Normal expenditure out of income. IHT is a tax on **transfers of capital**, not on **dispositions of income.** A transfer of value is exempt if:

(a) It is made as part of the normal expenditure of the transferor
(b) Taking one year with another, it was made out of income, and
(c) It leaves the transferor with sufficient income to maintain his usual standard of living

As well as covering such things as regular presents, this exemption can cover **regular payments out of income under deeds of covenant**, and the **payment of life assurance premiums on a policy for someone else**. In general there should be evidence of a prior commitment or a settled pattern of expenditure: *Bennett v IRC 1995.*

Gifts in consideration of marriage or civil partnership are exempt up to:

(a) £5,000 if from a parent of a party to the marriage or civil partnership
(b) £2,500 if from a grandparent or a remoter ancestor of one of the parties to the marriage or civil partnership
(c) £1,000 if from any other person

The limits apply to gifts from any one donor for any one marriage or civil partnership.

5.9.2 Exemptions applying to both lifetime transfers and transfers on death

Transfers of value between spouses or civil partners are **exempt** provided the transferee is domiciled in the UK at the time of transfer. The exemption covers gifts between them, settlements during their lifetimes under which the settlor's spouse or partner has an interest in possession, property passing under a will or on intestacy, and settled property where the transferor has an interest in possession.

The exemption:

- Applies whether or not the spouses or partners are living together
- Ceases to apply on divorce

If the **transferor** spouse or civil partner is domiciled in the UK but the **transferee** is not domiciled in the UK the exemption is limited to a cumulative total of **£55,000**, but any gift in excess of the £55,000 cumulative total can qualify as a PET. If neither spouse or partner is domiciled in the UK, there is no limit on the exemption.

A further exemption relating to spouses is available, known as the **surviving spouse exemption**. Where one spouse died before 13 November 1974 and passed property to the surviving spouse not absolutely but with an 'interest in possession', there would have been a charge to estate duty. Consequently, since such a transfer would now be exempted under IHT rules, where the surviving spouse dies with an interest in possession in such property, or transfers such an interest during his lifetime, the property is left out of account for IHT purposes. In addition, any income earned before the transfer but not yet received by the trustees on such property is deemed to be part of the settled fund so that this also avoids a charge to IHT.

Transfers (whether outright or by settlement) **to charities** which are established in the UK are wholly exempt from inheritance tax.

Gifts to a qualifying political party are exempt. A political party qualifies if, at the General Election preceding the transfer of value, either:

(a) At least two members were elected to the House of Commons, or
(b) One member was elected and the party polled at least 150,000 votes.

Gifts for national purposes are also exempt. Eligible recipients include museums, art galleries, the National Trust, universities, local authorities and Government departments.

Gifts of **land** to **housing associations** are exempt.

Maintenance settlements can be made free of inheritance tax if they are for the upkeep of historic property.

5.10 Valuation of assets

The **value** of any property for the purposes of IHT is the price which the property might reasonably be expected to fetch if sold in the open market at the time of the transfer.

5.11 Quoted shares and securities

The **valuation of quoted shares and securities** is easy: the Stock Exchange daily official list gives the closing bid and offer prices of all quoted securities. Inheritance tax valuations are done on the basis of the **'quarter up rule'**, taking the bid price plus a quarter of the difference between it and the offer price. Thus if the closing price for a particular day is 300 – 304p the inheritance tax valuation is 300 + (304 – 300)/4 = 301p.

An alternative to the quarter up rule is available. Each day certain bargains on the Stock Exchange will be 'marked' and the alternative is to take the average of the highest and lowest **marked bargains**, ignoring bargains marked at special prices.

The rule for valuation of quoted securities is therefore to take the **lower of:**

(a)   The value on the quarter up basis, and

(b)   The average of the highest and lowest marked bargains for the day, ignoring those marked at special prices

Valuations for transfers on death must be **cum dividend** or **cum interest**, including the value of the right to the next dividend or interest payment.

Example: securities quoted ex interest

If someone owned £10,000 12% Government stock (interest payable half yearly) quoted at 94-95 ex interest, the valuation would be as follows.

	£	£
£10,000 at 94.25		9,425
Add ½ × 12% × £10,000	600	
Less income tax at 20%	(120)	
		480
		9,905

Units in authorised **unit trusts** are valued at the managers' bid price **(the lower of the two published prices).**

Note that shares listed on the **Alternative Investment Market (AIM)** are **exempt** from IHT when they have been held for **two years**. This is discussed further later in this Chapter.

5.12 Unquoted shares and securities

There is no easily identifiable open market value for shares in an **unquoted** company. The **Shares Valuation Division** of HMRC is the body with which the taxpayer must negotiate. If agreement cannot be reached, appeal lies to the Special Commissioners and then to the courts.

5.13 Life assurance policies

Where a person's estate includes a **life policy** which matures on his death, the proceeds payable to his personal representatives must be included in his estate for IHT purposes. But where a person's estate includes a life policy which matures on the death of someone else, the open market value must be included in his estate.

If an individual takes out a policy on his own life, pays some premiums and then decides to give the policy to someone else by assignment or by declaration of trust, he makes a potentially exempt transfer (PET).

The value transferred is the greater of:

*   The premiums or other consideration paid before the transfer of the policy, and
*   The open market value of the policy at the date of transfer.

If an individual writes a policy **in trust**, or **assigns** a policy, or makes a subsequent declaration of trust, the policy proceeds will not be paid to his estate but to the **assignee** or to the **trustees,** for the trust **beneficiaries**. The proceeds will, therefore, not be included as part of his free estate at death. It is common to write policies in trust for the benefit of dependants to avoid IHT. In many cases, these transfers will be exempted as normal expenditure out of income.

5.14 The death estate

An individual's **death estate** consists of all property to which he was beneficially entitled immediately before death, with the exception of **excluded property**. The estate also includes anything acquired as a result of death, for example the proceeds of a **life assurance policy**.

(In studying the following, note the **trusts terminology** given in the Box earlier in this section.)

The estate at death may include:

(a) **Free estate** (which means everything not within (b) or (c) below).

(b) **Property given subject to a reservation**. This is property given away before death, but with strings attached. For example, someone might give away a house but continue to live in it.

(c) **Settled property in which the deceased has had an interest in possession**. Settled trust property of this type is treated, for IHT purposes, as though the life tenant owned the trust capital.

It is important to keep the three classes of property separate, since the primary responsibility for payment of tax depends on the type of property.

(a) Tax on the **free estate** is payable by the **personal representatives** (executors or administrators).

(b) Tax on **property given subject to a reservation** is payable by the **person in possession of the property**.

(c) **Tax on settled property** is payable by the **trustees.**

The whole of the death estate will be chargeable to tax, subject to reliefs (such as business or agricultural property relief) and any exemptions which may be available on death.

In particular, if property passes to the deceased person's spouse or civil partner (outright or to a trust in which the spouse or partner has an interest in possession) this will be an exempt transfer.

A transfer to any other person, eg. children, will be chargeable to IHT, whether this is made outright or to any type of **trust**.

5.15 IHT and pension schemes

There is normally **no charge to IHT** on **death benefits from a pension scheme**, including the realisation of the value of the pension fund, which are received by the spouse, civil partner or financial dependant of the scheme member.

If the scheme members dies after age 75 and, instead of taking an annuity, is drawing an **alternatively secured pension**, then any transfer lump sum payment (to another scheme member) will generally be subject to IHT except where the payment is received by a spouse, civil partner or financial dependent of the scheme member. Death benefits paid to charity are free of IHT.

There are similar rules where an ASP death benefit is payable on the subsequent death of a spouse, civil partner or financial dependant.

The **scheme administrator** will be responsible for accounting for and paying IHT due.

5.16 Calculating tax on the death estate

To calculate the **tax on the death estate**, use the following **Steps**.

Step 1   Look back seven years from the date of death to see if any chargeable lifetime transfers have been made. If so, these transfers use up the nil rate band available for the death estate. Work out the value of any nil rate band still available.

Step 2   Compute the gross value of the death estate (see further below).

Step 3 Any part of the death estate covered by the nil rate band is taxed at 0%. Any part of the death estate not covered by the nil rate band is charged at 40%. Deduct any relevant reliefs from the death tax.

Step 4 Where relevant, divide the tax due between personal representatives, the person in possession of a gift subject to a reservation (see below) and trustees (where applicable).

Example: Tax on death estate

Laura dies on 1 August 2006, leaving a free estate valued at £400,000.

Laura had made a transfer of value of £123,000 to her sister on 11 September 2005. The amount stated is after all exemptions and reliefs.

Compute the tax payable on Laura's death by her personal representatives.

Solution

Death tax

Note: There is no death tax on the PET which becomes chargeable as a result of Laura's death as it is within the nil rate band at her death. However, it will use up part of the nil rate band, as shown below.

Step 1 Lifetime transfer of value of £123,000 in seven years before 1 August 2006 (transfers after 1 August 1999). Nil rate band of £(285,000 − 123,000) = £162,000 available.

Step 2 Value of death estate is £400,000.

Step 3 *IHT*

	£
£162,000 × 0%	0
£238,000 × 40%	95,200
£400,000	95,200

Step 4 The tax payable by Laura's personal representatives is £95,200.

5.17 Debts and funeral expenses

The rules on debts are as follows.

(a) Only debts incurred by the deceased **bona fide and for full consideration** may be deducted.

(b) The debts must be such as an executor could pay without making himself personally liable for a misuse of the assets of the estate. Thus gaming debts are not deductible but statute barred debts are, provided the executor pays them.

(c) **Debts incurred by the deceased but payable after the death may be deducted** but the amount should be discounted because of the future date of payment.

(d) Rent and similar amounts which accrue day by day should be accrued up to the date of death.

(e) **Taxes to the date of death may be deducted** as they are a liability imposed by law.

(f) **Debts incurred by the executor are not allowed.**

(g) **If a debt is charged on a specific property it is deductible primarily from that property**: thus a mortgage on freehold property is deductible from that freehold.

169

(h) Debts contracted abroad must first be deducted from non-UK property (whether or not the value of that property is chargeable to inheritance tax). If the foreign debts exceed the value of the foreign property the excess is allowed as a deduction from UK property provided it represents debts recoverable in the UK.

Reasonable **funeral expenses** may be deducted.

(a) What is reasonable depends on the deceased's condition in life.

(b) Reasonable costs of mourning for the family, and the cost of a tombstone, are allowed.

5.18 Gifts with reservation

There are rules to prevent the avoidance of IHT by the making of **gifts with reservation**. Without these rules, incomplete lifetime gifts would escape the charge to IHT by being PETs but would also reduce the individual's estate at death. The value of the assets could thus escape tax entirely, despite the original owner deriving some benefit from them up to his death.

An obvious **example** is a gift of a home to the donor's children but with the donor continuing to live in it rent free. Another example is a gift of income-producing assets but with the income continuing to be received by the donor.

Property given subject to a reservation is property where:

- Such property is not enjoyed virtually to the entire exclusion of the donor, or
- Possession and enjoyment of the property transferred is not bona fide assumed by the donee.

'Virtually to the entire exclusion' would, for example, allow a donor occasional brief stays in a house he had given away without creating a reservation, but spending most weekends in the house would create a reservation.

Where a **gift with reservation** is made, it is treated in the same way as any other **gift** at the time it is made (as a PET or a chargeable lifetime transfer, as appropriate). However, special rules apply on the **death of the donor**.

(a) If the reservation still exists at the date of the donor's death, the asset is included in the donor's estate at its value at that time (not its value at the date the gift was made).

(b) If the reservation ceases within the seven years before death, then the gift is treated as a PET made at the time the reservation ceased. The charge is based on its value at that time. The annual exemption cannot be used in calculating the value of this PET.

If the gift could be taxed as a PET when made, as well as taxed under (a) or (b) above, it will be taxed either under (a) or (b), or as a PET when made (but not both), whichever gives the higher total tax.

A gift will **not** be treated as being with reservation:

(a) If full consideration is given for any right of occupation or enjoyment retained or assumed by the donor, and the property is land or chattels. For example, an individual might give away his house and continue to live in it, but pay a full market rent for doing so.

(b) If the circumstances of the donor change in a way that was unforeseen at the time of the original gift and the benefit provided by the donee to the donor only represents reasonable provision for the care and maintenance of the donor, being an elderly or infirm relative. This exception only applies to interests in land.

5.19 Business property relief (BPR)

Business property relief (BPR) is applied to the value of **relevant business property transferred**, to prevent large tax liabilities arising on transfers of businesses.

Relevant business property for 100% IHT relief:

(a) Property consisting of a business or an interest in a business (such as a partnership share)

(b)   Unquoted securities of a company giving the transferor control of the company immediately before the transfer

(c)   Any unquoted shares (not securities) in a company

Relevant business property for 50% relief:

(a)   Quoted shares in or securities of a company giving the transferor control of the company immediately before the transfer

(b)   Land or building, machinery or plant of the business

Shares or securities on the **Alternative Investment Market** count as **unquoted.**

BPR is only available if the relevant business property:

(a)   Was owned by the transferor for at least the two years preceding the transfer, or

(b)   Replaced other relevant business property where the combined period of ownership of both sets of property was at least two out of the last five years. In this situation relief is given on the lower of the values of the two sets of property.

Some businesses are **non-qualifying** for BPR purposes. BPR is not available if the business consists wholly or mainly of:

(a)   Dealing in securities, stocks and shares (except for discount houses and market makers on the Stock Exchange or on LIFFE)

(b)   Dealing in land or buildings

(c)   Making or holding investments (including land which is let)

Shares in holding companies, where the subsidiaries have activities which would qualify shares in them for BPR, are eligible for relief.

5.20 Agricultural property relief

Agricultural property relief (APR) is available on the agricultural value of agricultural property. The agricultural value is the value the property would have if it were subject to a perpetual covenant prohibiting its use other than as agricultural property.

APR works like BPR in reducing the value being transferred by a certain percentage before any exemptions.

The percentage reduction in agricultural value is, in most cases, 100%.

6 Stamp duty on securities

6.1 Stamp duty and stamp duty reserve tax

An investor who buys shares in individual companies ('equities') must pay **stamp duty** or **stamp duty reserve tax (SDRT)** which is paid via the broker and will be shown on the broker's **contract note** recording the purchase. Most share purchases are made through **CREST**, which stands for: Certificateless Registration of Electronic Stock and Share Transfers.

(a)   0.5% **SDRT** is payable on the amount of purchases of UK equities settled through CREST, rounded up to the nearest 1 penny.

(b)   0.5% **Stamp Duty** is payable on purchases of UK equities not settled through CREST, rounded up to the nearest £5.

(c)   Stamp duty on stocks registered in the Republic of Ireland is charged at 1%.

6.2 Collective investments

Collective investments are treated as follows.

(a)   Shares in UK **investment trusts** are listed equities and so attract stamp duty or SDRT as shown above.

(b)   Purchases of shares in Open Ended Investment Companies (**OEICs**) and units in **unit trusts** do not incur stamp duty.

7 Tax planning and advice

7.1 Tax planning

Tax planning refers to the process of organising one's affairs so as to take best advantage of tax rules.

The practice of organising one's affairs so as to minimise tax liabilities, within the constraints of the law, is sometimes called **tax avoidance**. To make changes to one's affairs in order to avoid tax that one might otherwise have to pay is a legal activity, provided that no tax rule is being breached. However, caution is necessary with some of the more complex ways of taking advantage of tax rules: the **HMRC** may raise objections to schemes whose main objective is tax avoidance.

Tax evasion, on the other hand, is illegal. Tax evasion means failing to disclose one's affairs fully to the tax authorities, or breaching tax rules in other ways so as to evade the payment of tax. Penalties can be severe, and conviction for tax crimes could carry a prison sentence.

7.2 Confidentiality and disclosure

As a financial adviser, you have a general professional duty to maintain the **confidentiality** of your clients' affairs, including clients' tax affairs. You will often be in a position in which you have a great amount of detailed information relating to clients' finances.

In spite of the professional reasons for maintaining confidentiality, there are circumstances in which **disclosure** of information of clients' affairs is required. The requirement concerns situations in which a financial adviser becomes aware that information held on a client indicates possible breaches of the law. The legal provisions on this are included in the **Proceeds of Crime Act 2002**.

It is a criminal offence under the Proceeds of Crime Act 2002 for anyone working in a regulated financial firm not to report any dealing that they suspect, or ought to suspect, involves the proceeds of crime. This would include an act of tax evasion by an individual. The report should be made to the firm's **Money Laundering Reporting Officer (MLRO)**. The MLRO must report appropriate cases to the **National Criminal Intelligence Service (NCIS)**.

7.3 Selecting a tax planning strategy

A **tax planning strategy** should recognise that:

- The after-tax returns from different investments can be affected by tax rules
- Taxation should therefore be considered when choosing investments and how they are held

Favourable tax status should not however be treated as the first priority, over and above the choice of investments appropriate to the individual's risk profile and objectives. Possible tax savings should not generally be used a reason to choose bad investments.

7.4 Investment tax planning

Giving **tax advice** can be a specialist matter and may require the involvement of a qualified tax adviser. It is additionally important for the financial adviser to be familiar with the tax rules concerning the adviser's field of work. There is hardly an area of investment where tax considerations do not play a part.

Some particular **investment tax planning** points are set out in the following paragraphs.

7.5 Personal allowances and spouses / civil partners

The general position on allowances has been set out earlier in this Chapter. **Husband and wife**, and those in same-sex **civil partnerships** are taxed as separate people.

7.6 The year of marriage

In the year of marriage or the year of establishing a civil partnership, the married couple's / civil partners' age allowance for those eligible will be the full amount less 1/12 for each complete tax month during which the couple were unmarried. A tax month runs from the 6th of one month to the 5th of the next month.

7.7 The year of death

The deceased person will get their full tax-free personal allowance for the year of their death. They will also get a full year's entitlement to any blind person's or married couple's allowance for the full year.

7.8 Jointly owned property

Where spouses or civil partners jointly own income-generating property, it is assumed that they are entitled to equal shares of the income.

If, in fact, the couple are not entitled to equal shares in the income-generating property (other than shares in close companies), they may make a joint declaration to HMRC, specifying the proportion to which each is entitled. These proportions are used to tax each of them separately, in respect of income arising on or after the date of the declaration.

7.9 Spouses' and civil partners' marginal rates of tax

If one spouse's or civil partner's **marginal rate of tax** (the rate on the highest part of his or her income) is higher than the other's marginal rate, it could be chosen to transfer income-yielding assets to the individual with the lower rate.

7.10 Children's tax position

There is legislation to prevent the parent of a minor child transferring income to the child in order to use the child's personal allowance and starting and basic rate tax bands. Income which is directly transferred by the parent, or is derived from capital so transferred, remains income of the parent for tax purposes.

This applies only to parents, however, and tax saving is therefore possible through gifts from other relatives.

Even where a parent is involved, the child's income is not treated as the parent's if it does not exceed £100 a year.

This legislation is concerned with **gifts from a parent to a child.** It could be possible to use the child's personal allowance and starting and basic rate bands if the child is employed in the parent's trade.

The legislation does not apply to income from a **Child Trust Fund (CTF).**

7.11 Child Trust Fund (CTF)

The Government aims to promote positive attitudes to saving and to improve financial capability by funding a **Child Trust Fund (CTF)** account for each child born on or after 1 September 2002.

CTF accounts first became available from April 2005. The CTF is initially funded by a **Government contribution** (£250, plus an enhancement reflecting the child's age, plus £250 extra for lower income families who are within the Child Tax Credit threshold). There is a further Government contribution of £250 (plus £250 more for lower-income families) when the child is seven years old.

It will also be possible for **friends and family** (including parents) to contribute up to £1,200 a year to the account.

Child Trust Funds may include:

- Cash accounts
- Life products
- Collective funds (unit trusts and Open Ended Investment Companies)
- Equity-based schemes, including stakeholder or non-stakeholder investments and including self-selected equities

CTFs provide **asset diversification** and **'lifestyling'** options. ('Lifestyling' means switching progressively to less risky investments, as an investment gets closer to maturity.)

No income tax or capital gains tax is payable on the CTF. This applies even if parental contributions have been made.

The CTF will be held for the child until he reaches 18, when the money becomes available to the child and the tax benefit ceases.

The rules for CTFs involve the following provisions on **charges, access** and **terms.**

- The annual management charge is capped at 1.5% of the fund value.
- Penalty-free transfers between accounts and between CTF providers must be permitted (except for any stamp duty and dealing expenses resulting from the transfer).
- Minimum subscriptions must be set at a level of no more than £10.

7.12 Capital gains tax exemption

As we have seen, each individual has an **annual CGT exemption** (£8,800 for 2006/07). An investor with significant investments (outside the tax-free wrapper of ISAs) may choose to plan disposals of investments that are subject to CGT so as to make use of the annual exemption, using the rules set out earlier in this Chapter.

7.13 Use of ISAs

The use of **Individual Savings Accounts (ISAs)** as an investment wrapper is particularly important for individuals who could have a capital gains tax liability either now or in the future.

Higher rate taxpayers also benefit from the fact that they have no further tax to pay on dividends in a stocks and shares ISA.

7.14 Annuities

An **annuity** is a contract whereby a capital sum is paid to an insurance company, which in return pays a guaranteed income, either for a specific period or for the rest of a person's life.

The amount of income paid is based on the **investor's age**, ie the mortality factor, and interest rates on long-term gilts.

Purchased life annuities have a **capital element** and an **interest element**, with the split being pre-agreed between the HMRC and the insurance company.

(a)   The capital element is based on expectation of life tables and is **tax-free**.

(b)   The interest element is **taxable** (in the same way as interest on a bank account).

This means that a non-taxpayer can obtain a gross income from an annuity.

7.15 Pre-owned assets

If the gift with reservation rules do not apply, an **income tax** charge under **'pre-owned assets' rules** may apply (from **6 April 2005**) where individuals have entered into tax planning to reduce their inheritance tax liability without completely divesting themselves of the asset.

These could affect certain tax planning schemes involving the family home.

Key chapter points

- **Employed and self-employed individuals are liable to pay income tax. Some income is received in full with no tax deducted, while some income has tax deducted at source.**

- **All sources of income are aggregated in a personal tax computation. Some income is exempt from income tax and not included in the personal tax computation.**

- **All income in the personal tax computation must be included gross.**

- **Dividends are grossed up by multiplying by 100/90. Bank and Building Society interest is grossed up by multiplying by 100/80.**

- **Income is divided into non-savings income, savings (excluding dividend) income and dividend income.**

- **The personal allowance and blind person's allowance are deducted from Statutory Total Income to arrive at taxable income.**

- **There is one set of income tax bands which applies to all the income. Non-savings income is taxed first, then the savings (excluding dividends) income and finally dividend income.**

- **An individual pays CGT on his net taxable gains in a tax year. There is an annual exemption for each tax year.**

- **There needs to be three things for a capital gain to arise: chargeable person, chargeable disposal, chargeable asset. Disposals between spouses or civil partners are on a no gain/ no loss basis.**

- **Taxable gains are taxed as an extra slice of savings (excluding dividend) income.**

- Capital losses are deducted against gains in the same tax year. Excess losses are carried forward. Brought forward losses cannot reduce taxable gains below the annual exempt amount.

- Taper relief reduces gains. Taper relief is applied to net gains after the deduction of current year and brought forward losses.

- The percentage of gains taxable after deducting taper relief depends on the number of complete years after 5 April 1998 that the asset was held for. If the asset was held on 17 March 1998 an additional year is added to the number of years that it is treated as held for taper relief purposes.

- There are special rules for matching shares sold with shares purchased. Shares acquired after 5 April 1998 are matched on a last in first out (LIFO) basis. The FA 1985 pool contains shares acquired between 6 April 1982 and 5 April 1998. The FA 1985 pool is indexed to 6 April 1998.

- Bonus and rights issues are attached to the holding to which they relate.

- The length of the period of ownership for taper relief purposes depends on the date of acquisition of the original holding.

- Gilts and qualifying corporate bonds held by individuals are exempt from CGT.

- Inheritance tax (IHT) is a tax on gifts or 'transfers of value'.

- Transfers are accumulated for seven years so that the nil rate band is not available in full on each of a series of transfers in rapid succession.

- IHT is charged on what a donor loses. In some cases grossing up is required, to take account of the fact that the donor loses both the asset given away and the money with which he paid the tax due on it. Exemptions may apply, to make transfers or parts of transfers non-chargeable.

- The value of property for IHT purposes is the price which it should fetch if sold in the open market at the time of the transfer.

- There are rules to prevent someone making a gift 'with reservation' to avoid IHT, as well as new rules imposing an income tax charge on pre-owned assets.

- Stamp duty or SDRT is payable at 0.5% on the purchase of UK shares.

- There are various tax planning opportunities when an individual's investment strategy is being planned.

Chapter Quiz

1. What test applies for expenses of an employee to be allowable against tax? .... (see para 1.3)

2. On what period's profit is a self-employed person taxed in the current tax year? .... (1.5)

3. Who is entitled to age allowances? .... (2.3)

4. Distinguish statutory total income and taxable income. .... (3.2)

5. At what rates is CGT payable? .... (4.1)

6. What happens to capital losses which are not set off in the current tax year? .... (4.2)

7. What is meant by a 'business asset' for CGT purposes, and what is the significance of the term? .... (4.8)

8. What is the CGT treatment of gains on UK government stock and qualifying corporate bonds? .... (4.10)

9. What is the treatment for CGT purposes if shares are sold on one day and the same shares are repurchased on the next day? .... (4.12)

10. What is a transfer of value for inheritance tax purposes? .... (5.2)

11. What types of transfer by an individual are defined as potentially exempt transfers? .... (5.7)

12. A parent gives some money to his daughter on her marriage. What marriage exemption is applicable? ...... (5.9.1)

13. What is the significance of 'gifts with reservation'? .... (5.18)

14. What is the stamp duty regime for CREST-registered shares? .... (6.1)

National insurance and State benefits

1 National insurance contributions

1.1 Classes of NIC

There are four classes of **national insurance contribution (NIC)**:

    (a)   **Class 1**. Divided into:

        (i)   **Primary**, paid by employees
        (ii)   **Secondary Class 1, Class 1A and Class 1B** paid by employers

    (b)   **Class 2**. Paid by the self-employed

    (c)   **Class 3**. Voluntary contributions (paid to maintain rights to certain state benefits, such as the state retirement pension or sickness benefits)

    (d)   **Class 4**. Paid by the self-employed

1.2 NICs for employees

The **National Insurance Contributions Office (NICO)**, which is part of HMRC, examines employers' records and procedures to ensure that the correct amounts of NICs are collected.

Both employees and employers pay NICs related to the employee's earnings. NICs are not deductible from an employee's gross salary for income tax purposes. However, employers' contributions are deductible Schedule D Case I expenses.

'Earnings' broadly comprise gross pay, excluding taxable benefits which cannot be turned into cash by surrender (eg holidays). It also includes mileage payments over the approved amount (see below). No deduction is made for pension contributions.

An employer's contribution to an employee's approved personal pension or an approved occupational pension scheme is excluded from the definition of 'earnings'.

An expense with a business purpose is not treated as earnings. For example, if an employee is reimbursed for business travel or for staying in a hotel on the employer's business this is not normally 'earnings'. However, if an employee is reimbursed for his own home telephone charges the reimbursed cost of private calls (and all reimbursed rental) is earnings.

The rates of contribution for 2006/07, and the income bands to which they apply, are set out in the **Tax Tables** at the end of this Study Text.

Employees may participate in the state earnings-based pension (the **State Second Pension** or **S2P**): this is called being '**contracted in**, or alternatively '**non-contracted out**'. Alternatively an employee may be '**contracted out**' of S2P by having an alternative scheme that replaces S2P.

Non-contracted out employees pay main **primary contributions** of 11% of earnings between the **earnings threshold of £5,035** and the **upper earnings limit of £33,540** or the equivalent monthly or weekly limit (see below). They also pay additional primary contributions of 1% on earnings above the upper earnings limit.

Employers pay **secondary contributions** of 12.8% on earnings above the earnings threshold of £5,035 or the equivalent monthly or weekly limit. There is no upper limit.

There is a **lower earnings limit** of £4,368 (or the equivalent monthly or weekly limit). The significance of the lower earnings limit (LEL) is that '**nil rate contributions**' will be credited where the employee's earnings are between the LEL and the earnings threshold. These nil rate contributions 'frank' the employee's record and so create an entitlement to certain state benefits.

If an employee is in a **contracted out** employer's occupational pension scheme, reduced contributions are payable. Employee contributions at the main rate are 9.4% of earnings between the earnings threshold and the upper earnings limit. There is also a rebate of 1.6% on earnings between the lower earnings limit and the earnings threshold. There is an additional rate of 1% on earnings above the upper earnings limit.

Employer rates are also reduced for earnings between the earnings threshold of £5,035 and the upper limit.

If an employee **contracts out** of the state earnings related pension scheme through a personal pension, full contributions are payable but NICO pays a proportion of these contributions to the insurance company running the personal pension scheme.

1.3 Earnings period

NICs are calculated in relation to an **earnings period.** This is the period to which earnings paid to an employee are deemed to relate. Where earnings are paid at regular intervals, the earnings period will generally be equated with the payment interval, for example a week or a month. An earnings period cannot usually be less than seven days long.

NICs for employees are calculated on a non-cumulative basis, so only the earnings in the earnings period are considered. The monthly limits are the annual limit divided by 12.

Example: Primary and secondary contributions

Sally works for Red plc. She is paid £3,000 per month.

Show Sally's primary contributions for 2006/07, assuming she is not contracted out, and the secondary contributions paid by Red plc.

Solution

Earnings threshold £5,035 ÷ 12 = £420

Upper earnings limit £33,540 ÷ 12 = £2,795

Sally

	£
Primary contributions	
£(2,795 − 420) = £2,375 × 11% (main) × 12	3,135
£(3,000 − 2,795) = £205 × 1% × 12 (additional)	25
Total primary contributions	3,160

Red plc

	£
Secondary contributions	
£(3,000 − 420) = £2,580 × 12.8% × 12	3,963

1.4 Company directors

Special rules apply to **company directors**, regardless of whether they are paid at regular intervals or not. Where a person is a director at the beginning of the tax year, his earnings period is the tax year, even if he ceases to be director during the year. The annual limits as shown in the Tax Tables apply.

1.5 Class 1A NIC

Employers must pay Class 1A NIC in respect of most **taxable benefits** for example, **private medical insurance.** However, benefits are exempt if they are:

- Within Class 1, or
- Covered by a PAYE dispensation, or
- Provided for employees earning at a rate of less than £8,500 a year, or
- Included in a PAYE settlement agreement, or
- Otherwise not required to be reported on P11Ds

Employee contributions are not charged on benefits.

Class 1A contributions are collected annually in arrears, and are due by 19 July following the tax year.

1.6 NICs for the self employed

The **self employed** (sole traders and partners) pay NICs in two ways. **Class 2** contributions are payable at a **flat rate**. It is possible, however, to be excepted from payment of Class 2 contributions (or to get contributions already paid repaid) if annual profits are less than £4,465. The **Class 2 rate** for 2006/07 is **£2.10 a week.**

Self employed people must **register** with HMRC for Class 2 contributions within three months of the end of the month in which they start self employment. People who fail to register may incur a £100 penalty.

Additionally, the self employed pay **Class 4** NICs, based on the level of the individual's business profits.

Main rate Class 4 NICs are calculated by applying a fixed percentage (8% for 2006/07) to the individual's profits between the lower limit (£5,035 for 2006/07) and the upper limit (£33,540 for 2006/07). Additional rate contributions are 1% (for 2006/07) on profits above that limit.

Example: Class 4 contributions

If a sole trader had profits of £14,080 for 2006/07 his Class 4 NIC liability would be as follows. (Round amounts to nearest £1.)

	£
Profits	14,080
Less lower limit	(5,035)
	9,045

Class 4 NICs = 8% × £9,045 = £723.60 (main only)

Example: Additional class 4 contributions

If an individual's profits were £48,000, additional Class 4 NICs are due on the excess over the upper limit. Thus the amount payable in 2006/07 is as follows. (Round amounts to nearest £1.)

	£
Profits (upper limit)	33,540
Less lower limit	(5,035)
	28,505
Main rate Class 4 NICs 8% × £28,505	2,280
Additional rate class 4 NICs £(48,000 − 33,540) = £14,460 × 1%	145
	2,425

For Class 4 NIC purposes, **profits** are the **business profits taxable under Schedule D Case I or II profits, less:**

(a) **Trading losses**
(b) **Trade charges on income**

There is no deduction for personal pension premiums.

Class 4 NICs are collected by HMRC and are paid at the same time as the associated income tax liability. Interest is charged on overdue contributions.

1.7 Comparison of NICs for the employees and the self employed

The NIC burden on the **self employed** tends to be **lower** than that on **employees,** although the relative burdens vary with the level of income. The following example shows a comparison.

> **Example: Employed and self-employed**
>
> Two single people, one employed (not in a contracted out pension scheme) and one self employed, each have annual gross income of £18,000.
>
> Show their national insurance contributions for 2006/07.
>
> **Solution**
>
> | | Employed £ | Self employed £ |
> |---|---|---|
> | NICs | | |
> | Class 1: £(18,000 − 5,035) × 11% (main only) | 1,426 | |
> | Class 2: £2.05 × 52 | | 107 |
> | Class 4: £(18,000 − 5,035) × 8% | | 1,037 |
> | | 1,426 | 1,144 |
>
> The self-employed person is better off by £(1,426 − 1,144) = £282 a year.

1.8 National insurance contribution credits

Certain benefits are related to an individual's national insurance contribution record (see the next section of this Chapter).

In certain circumstances, an individual may be given credits instead of having to pay contributions. These circumstances include:

(a) Full weeks of unemployment or sickness
(b) Periods of entitlement to child benefit, maternity allowance or carer's allowance
(c) Periods of entitlement to statutory sick pay or statutory maternity pay
(d) Taking a course of approved training
(e) Being in receipt of Working Tax Credit

2 Benefits

2.1 Introduction

Individuals can claim State benefits for various reasons, and other benefits may arise from employment. We look at various benefits in this section.

The **Department for Work and Pensions** website **www.dwp.gov.uk** provides a useful reference point in its *Benefits and services A-Z* section.

Some of the **main rates of benefit** are shown in the **Tax Tables** at the end of this Study Text.

2.2 Benefits available following a death

2.2.1 Bereavement payment

Bereavement payment is a one-off **tax-free** lump sum payment of £2,000 (2006/07). It is available to widows and widowers whose late spouse made sufficient NIC contributions. Additionally, either the spouse must not have been entitled to retirement pension at the date of death or the claimant was under state pension age when the spouse died. (State pension age is generally 65 for men and 60 for women.)

2.2.2 Widowed parent's allowance (WPA)

Widowed parent's allowance is a weekly benefit available to widows and widowers whose late spouse or civil partner made sufficient NIC contributions. The claimant must be bringing up a child or expecting a baby.

Additional pension may be available under the State Second Pension scheme (S2P).

WPA is taxable (but child dependency increases are not taxable).

2.2.3 Bereavement allowance

Bereavement allowance is a taxable weekly benefit paid for 52 weeks after the death of the claimant's spouse or civil partner. It is available to widows and widowers whose late spouse or civil partner made sufficient NIC contributions. The claimant must be aged 45 or over at the death of the spouse or civil partner and not entitled to WPA.

A claimant aged 55 or over when widowed gets the full rate of bereavement allowance. Those aged between 45 and 54 get a reduced amount based on the claimant's age at the date of death of the spouse or civil partner. Once the claimant reaches state pension age he can claim state retirement pension and also state second pension inherited from the late spouse or civil partner.

2.3 Benefits following loss of income

2.3.1 Redundancy payments

An employee who has worked for a firm for two years or more will be entitled to receive a lump sum if made redundant. The sum will be payable by the employer.

The amount of the redundancy payment is determined by three factors: age, length of continuous employment with the employer and weekly gross pay.

(a)   You must be at least 20 years old and under 65 years old to claim.
(b)   You must have at least two years continuous employment. Service over 20 years is ignored.

You do not need to learn the detailed formula to compute the amount payable, and the following examples are for illustrative purposes only.

Employee age	Maximum payable
20	1 × one weeks pay
30	10 × one weeks pay
40	19 × one weeks pay

Additional voluntary payments may be made by an employer. A sum up to £30,000, including the statutory payments, will be **tax free**.

2.3.2 Jobseeker's allowance

Someone who has become unemployed may receive a **flat rate weekly payment** of Jobseeker's Allowance for the first six months of **unemployment**. A condition is that you are healthy and that you are actively job hunting at the time. After six months you may receive a sum similar to Income Support and subject to similar conditions.

The basic jobseekers allowance is **taxable**, except for additions for dependent children.

A family should ideally have **emergency funds**, equal to perhaps four to six months of income, to cope with unexpected contingencies such as unemployment. Having such an emergency fund would not affect **contributions-based jobseeker's allowance**, which is based on national insurance contributions having been made, but **income-based jobseeker's allowance** will not usually be payable to someone with savings of over £16,000 (2006/07).

The **risk of unemployment** may make it desirable to improve pension provision or long term savings while there are earnings.

2.3.3 Income support

Income support is a weekly payment made to those over 16 and under 60 who have an low income and work less than 16 hours per week. Income support is **not taxable**, unless the recipient is on strike during a trade dispute.

A number of factors are considered in the 'means test' used to establish entitlement, including the value of the claimants' **savings**.

- Savings of more than £6,000 (2006/07) usually result in a reduction in the level of income support paid.
- Savings of more than £16,000 (2006/07) usually mean that there is no entitlement.

Income support mortgage interest (ISMI) benefit is payable in only limited circumstances.

2.4 Benefits available on illness

2.4.1 Statutory sick pay (SSP)

When an employee is unable to work due to sickness or disability, then employers must make payments for time off sick to at least a minimum requirement. Under the **percentage threshold scheme**, employers can recover the cost of SSP if it amounts to 13% or more of national insurance contributions per month.

Statutory sick pay (SSP) is payable to employees who have been continuously sick for four or more successive days.

SSP is limited to a maximum period of 28 weeks. Different periods of sickness may be linked for this purpose if they are less than eight weeks apart. If incapacity continues after the end of the 28 week period then incapacity benefit may be claimed (see below).

It is not possible to receive SSP at the same time as incapacity benefit (see below), maternity allowance, or job seekers allowance.

SSP is a flat rate benefit, irrespective of the income of the recipient. However, the employee must earn at least enough for it to be relevant for NIC purposes - the lower earnings limit. If this requirement is not met then income support may be claimed which is a means tested benefit. SSP itself is not a means tested benefit.

SSP is **subject to tax and national insurance contributions**.

2.4.2 Incapacity benefit

Incapacity benefit is paid to claimants who have paid, or been credited with, sufficient NICs and who satisfy the relevant medical test of incapacity for work (see below). Incapacity benefit is also payable to young people aged 16 to 19 who have no contribution record and those aged 20 to 24 who were in education or training for three months immediately before they attained the age of 20.

Where there is no entitlement to SSP – for example where the individual is self employed, **short term incapacity benefit** is payable where because of sickness or disablement the individual is unable to work for at least four consecutive days.

During the first 28 weeks, the test for short-term incapacity benefit is inability to work in the claimant's own **normal occupation** - referred to as the **'own occupation' test**. This test also applies to SSP (see above).

From the 29th week onwards the test of incapacity for all persons, whether employed or self employed, is the inability to work in any occupation - referred to as the **personal capability** assessment.

Short term incapacity benefit is payable for up to 52 weeks but a higher rate of benefit is applicable from the 29th week onwards. From the 53rd week onwards **long term incapacity benefit** becomes applicable.

The incapacity benefits are **not means tested**.

Long term incapacity benefit ceases at state pension age.

If pension age is reached after incapacity has commenced then short-term incapacity benefit can continue for up to 52 weeks. Either the state retirement pension or short term incapacity benefit may be claimed.

Incapacity benefit paid for the first 28 weeks of sickness at the lower short-term rate is **not taxable. Other incapacity benefit** is **taxable**. There is also a non-taxable child dependent addition for short-term incapacity benefit at the higher rate and long-term incapacity benefit.

2.5 Benefits available to those needing long term care

2.5.1 Disability living allowance (DLA)

For entitlement to a Disability living allowance (DLA), there are no requirements as to payment of NICs and **neither is DLA in any way means tested**. DLA is tax-free.

Entitlement to DLA is for those who, because of illness or disability, develop care and mobility needs before age 65 and are thus too young to claim attendance allowance (see below). Where care and mobility needs arise beyond the age of 65 then attendance allowance is available.

The DLA payable to the claimant depends on two things:

- How much help is actually required, known as the **care component**, and
- The amount of difficulty a claimant has in getting around, known as the **mobility component**

The requirement for assistance with care must have existed for at least three months and must be expected to exist for a minimum future period of six months. However, claimants who are terminally ill do not have to satisfy the qualifying period.

There are three different rates of the care component dependent upon the degree of care needed. In addition there are two different rates of the mobility component.

Those who are entitled to the higher rate of the mobility component are exempt from paying road tax and will qualify for a disabled car badge.

If DLA is granted for three years or more recipients may also be able to obtain a car or wheelchair using the motability scheme. This scheme assists disabled people by offering contract hire or hire purchase facilities on the cars and wheelchairs.

2.5.2 Attendance allowance

Entitlement to attendance allowance is for those who have become disabled after the age of 65 and who require assistance. Additionally, entitlement applies where life expectancy is less than 6 months due to illness, or where a kidney machine is in use at home or in a self care unit at least twice a week. Attendance allowance is paid at one of two rates, depending on how much the claimant's disability affects him.

There is no test against the claimant's NIC record. **Attendance allowance** is **means tested** and **tax-free**.

Attendance allowance may be received even if there is nobody available to look after the claimant and is normally paid in addition to other social security benefits to which the claimant may be entitled. If the claimant lives at home and has no carer then receipt of attendance allowance may qualify the claimant for additional premiums under the rules for income support.

2.6 Benefits available to carers

2.6.1 Child benefit

Child benefit is a benefit paid to people bringing up children. A weekly amount is payable in respect of each qualifying child. Child benefit is not means tested and is not taxable.

Child benefit can be claimed by anyone bringing up a child who:

(a)   Is aged under 16

(b)   Is aged under 19 and is studying full time up to A Level, Advanced Vocational Certificate of Education (AVCE) or equivalent

(c)   Is aged under 18 and registered at the careers office for work or work-based training for young people

2.6.2 Carer's allowance

Carer's allowance (formerly called invalid care allowance) is a taxable benefit for those who spend at least 35 hours a week caring for someone who is in receipt of either attendance allowance or the disability living allowance at the higher or middle rate of the care component (see above).

There is no test against the claimant's NIC record. However, carer's allowance will not be paid if the claimant earns above a certain amount.

Benefit cannot be claimed where the person is in full time education for more than 21 hours a week or earns more than £79 per week after allowable expenses.

Where the claimant is in receipt of some other benefit at a lower rate, this benefit may be payable at an amount to make up to the weekly carer's allowance rate. There are further increases for adult and child dependants.

There is a non-taxable child dependent addition where the claimant has one or more dependent children.

2.7 Benefits available on retirement

2.7.1 National insurance retirement pension

If sufficient Class 1 or Class 2 NICs have been paid, then a full basic State **national insurance retirement pension (NIRP)** will become payable at State pension age. This is generally 65 for men and 60 for women. However, all individuals will have a State pension age of 65 by 2020.

An individual can make voluntary Class 3 NICs to make up a shortfall in their NIC record if they are eligible.

Credits of NICs are made for the purposes of the basic State pension in certain circumstances and in particular:

- Where the individual during a tax year was in receipt of carer's allowance or incapacity benefit.

- In respect of men who are unemployed, they will be given credits in respect of the tax year in which they reach age 60 up until the tax year before the age of reaching 65

2.7.2 State second pension

A **state second pension (S2P)** will be earned by those Class 1 NIC contributors who satisfy the entitlement conditions by having a sufficiency of such contributions paid at the contracted in rate.

Those who pay Class 2 NICs only, that is the self employed, earn no state second pension benefit.

A **widow or widower** may inherit state second pension from their late spouse.

Both the **NIRP** and **S2P** are **taxable**. There is a non-taxable child dependent addition to NIRP where the claimant has one or more dependent children.

3 Tax credits

3.1 Working tax credit

The **working tax credit (WTC)** is for people who are employed or self-employed who usually work for at **least 16 hours a week** and who have a **relatively low income**.

Employers have previously been paying the WTC to employees, following an instruction from HMRC, but from April 2006 it is to be paid directly by HMRC. The self-employed are also paid directly by HMRC.

In order to qualify for WTC, a person must be **over 16**, normally be working for at least **16 hours** per week, and either:

- Be **responsible for a child** or young person, or
- Have a disability

WTC will also be available to those **over the age of 25**, without children or disabilities, and who work at least **30 hours** per week.

WTC is made up of a number of elements, each of which has rules and conditions attached. WTC is **not taxable**.

Elements of working tax credit include the following.

- Basic element £1,665 (2006/07). This is the starting point which is available to each single claimant or to a couple.

- Additional couple's and lone parent element £1,640 (2006/07). This is paid in addition to the basic element where the claim is by a couple (including the unmarried) or by a single parent.

- 30 hour element £680 (2006/07). A couple with children is eligible for this if they jointly work at least 30 hours per week, provided that one of them works at least 16 hours. A childless couple cannot combine their hours to reach the 30 hour target.

3.2 Childcare

The **childcare element** of the WTC is paid to the main carer (not necessarily the main earner). Clearly, large amounts can be involved where a claimant is paying for child care. The costs of any registered or approved child care can be claimed, but this does not include any portion of the cost which is covered by vouchers.

- For one child, the weekly limit on the cost for which a claim can be made is £175 (2006/07).
- For two or more children, the limit is £300.

The maximum childcare element is 80% (2006/07), so that the maximum weekly tax credit for this part is 80% x £300 = £240.

Having added up the total entitlement from the above list, it may then be necessary to make a reduction. The annual first income threshold for WTC is £5,220. There is a reduction in credit of 37p per £1 of income above the threshold.

3.3 Child tax credit

The **child tax credit (CTC)** can apply to those with children who have a family income below approximately £58,000 (or more if there is a baby born in the year). It is payable to the **main carer** of a qualifying child. A child is a qualifying child until 1 September following their 16th birthday or if they are under 19 and in full time education. CTC is **not taxable**.

The CTC includes the following (at 2006/07 rates).

- Family element (one per family) £545
- Baby addition (child under one) £545
- Child element (in addition to baby element, paid for **each** child) £1,765

These are the maximum sums available, and will not be given in all cases.

Taper will reduce WTC before CTC but the income threshold for the start of CTC taper is £14,155. If no tax credit is payable after taper, then £545 (£1,090 if there is a child under the age of twelve months) is payable until income exceeds the second threshold of £50,000 pa. The excess of income over this limit then reduces this part of the CTC at the rate of £1 for every £15 of additional income.

The upper cut off point beyond which no CTC is due is therefore £58,175, or £66,350 in the year of a child's birth.

Example: Tax credits

Claire and Richard have a daughter aged 4 years and a baby son who was born on 6 April 2006.

Richard works full time and earns a salary of £14,800 each year. Claire does not work.

Their total entitlement to tax credits, ignoring income to begin with, is:

WTC

	£
Basic element	1,665
Additional couple's element	1,640
30 hour element	680
	3,985

CTC

	£
Family element	545
Baby edition	545
Child element (two children)	3,530
	4,620

The restriction by reference to income is: 37% x (£14,800 – £5,220) = £3,544.60

This reduces the WTC first, leaving a WTC award of £440.40, paid to Richard via his employer. The CTC paid to Claire (either weekly or monthly) will be £4,620.00.

If Richard had earned a salary of £54,000 instead, then there would be no WTC payable and, of the CTC paid to Claire, all but the family element and baby addition would have been tapered away.

These remaining two parts would then be restricted by reference to the second threshold of £50,000. The reduction would be 1/15 x (£54,000 – £50,000) = £267. Claire would receive a CTC of £1,090 – £267 = £823.

3.4 Pension credit

Pension credit is available to people aged 60 or over and replaced the Minimum Income Guarantee from October 2003.

Pension credit has two elements:

- **Guarantee Credit** (currently available from age 60)
- **Savings Credit** (available from age 65)

The **Guarantee Credit** is intended to ensure that those aged 60 and over an income of at least:

- £114.45 a week for a single person, or
- £174.05 a week for a couple

The Savings Credit is intended to go some way towards compensating for how the Guarantee Credit could penalise savings.

Savings Credit applies to those with an **income** equal to or more than the **state basic pension**, and provides an **additional benefit** of 60p for each £1 by which income exceeds this level, up to a maximum benefit of £17.88 per week (single pensioner) or £23.58 per week (pensioner couple). These maxima are reached when income equals the appropriate Guarantee Credit amount.

If income exceeds the appropriate amount, Savings Credit is **reduced** by 40% of the excess, until it ceases entirely.

Key chapter points

- **Employees pay Class I national insurance contributions (NICs). Employers pay Class I and Class IA NICs.**

- **The self employed pay Class 2 and Class 4 NICs.**

- **Various state benefits may be available on death, illness, disability, unemployment and retirement.**

- **State benefits are also be available to those with children and those who look after the disabled.**

- **Working tax credit is paid to working families with children or to those who are disabled.**

- **Child tax credit is paid to families with children, whether working or not.**

- **Pension credit is paid to people aged 60 or over to give them a guaranteed minimum income.**

Chapter Quiz

1	On what are Class 1A NICs paid?	(see para 1.5)
2	How are Class 4 NICs calculated?	(1.6)
3	Who is entitled to the bereavement payment?	(2.2.1)
4	Is SSP taxable?	(2.4.1)
5	Who is entitled to the disability living allowance?	(2.5.1)
6	Who can claim child benefit?	(2.6.1)
7	State two benefits that are available on retirement.	(2.7)
8	How is working tax credit paid?	(3.1)
9	What are 'Guarantee Credit' and 'Savings Credit'?	(3.4)

Economic influences on financial planning

1 Defining and calculating inflation

1.1 Defining inflation

The term 'inflation' is used to denote rises in prices. In economic terms, **inflation** can be defined as a **sustained rise in the general level of prices**.

Prices may be the prices of various things, from the prices faced by businesses in the prices of the materials they buy, to the prices we as consumers must pay for goods and services. In reviewing the general performance of the economy and in assessing how price rises affect individuals, we are particularly concerned with inflation in the prices of goods and services purchased by consumers.

When people talk about an inflation rate, they usually mean an increase in prices measured over a period of **one year**.

There is also the phenomenon of **asset price inflation.** 'Assets' here include houses, and house price inflation is an important aspect of asset price inflation.

1.2 Consumer price indices

Consumer price indices may be used for several purposes, for example as an indicator of inflationary pressures in the economy, as a benchmark for wage negotiations and to determine annual increases in government benefits payments. Countries commonly have more than one consumer price index because one composite index may be considered too wide a grouping for different purposes.

1.3 The Retail Prices Index (RPI)

One long-established measure of the general rate of inflation in the UK is the **Retail Prices Index (RPI)**. The RPI measures the percentage changes month by month in the average level of prices of the commodities and services, including housing costs, purchased by the great majority of households in the UK. The items of expenditure within the RPI are intended to be a representative list of items, current prices for which are collected at regular intervals.

The RPI was 186.7 in January 2004 and rose to 192.0 in January 2005. What was the annual percentage rate of inflation to January 2005, to one decimal place?

192.0/186.7	= 1.0284
$(1.0284 - 1) \times 100$	= 2.84%

After rounding, this gives an annual inflation rate of 2.8% to one decimal place.

Here are some more past values for the RPI.

December 1987	103.3
December 1995	150.7
December 2005	194.1

How has inflation eroded the purchasing power of money over the ten years to the end of 2005?

£1 $\times$ 150.7/194.1 = 77.6p

£1 in December 2005 bought as much as 77.6p would have bought ten years earlier.

Savings of £1,000 held for the ten year period would need to have grown to £1,000 $\times$ 194.1/150.7 = £1,288 to preserve their purchasing power over the period.

1.4 The underlying rate of inflation

The term '**underlying rate of inflation**' is usually used to refer to the **RPI adjusted to exclude mortgage costs** and sometimes other elements as well (such as the local council tax). The effects of interest rate changes on mortgage costs help to make the RPI fluctuate more widely than the underlying rate of inflation.

Up to late 2003, the UK government's target rate for inflation was defined in terms of **RPIX**, which is the underlying rate of inflation measured as the increase in the RPI excluding mortgage interest payments. Another measure, called **RPIY**, goes further and also excludes the effects of changes in Value Added Tax (VAT).

1.5 The Consumer Prices Index (CPI)

In December 2003, it was confirmed that the standardised European inflation measure, sometimes called the Harmonised Index of Consumer Prices (HICP), was to be used as the basis for the UK's inflation target. The UK HICP is called the **Consumer Prices Index (CPI)**.

The CPI excludes most **housing costs** that are included in the RPI, such as council tax and house price depreciation. Because housing costs have risen relatively rapidly in recent years, the annual rise in the RPI has generally exceeded the annual rise in the CPI.

The CPI is now used by the Government in setting its **inflation target** (annual rise in CPI of **2% or less**). However, pensions, benefits and index-linked gilts continue to be calculated using the RPI.

2 Effects of inflation

2.1 General effects

The overall general effect of inflation is that it **reduces the purchasing power of money**. If you have £100 and intend to spend it on bars of chocolate each costing £1, you will be able to buy 100 bars. If however, you have the same £100 but the price of bars of chocolate has gone up to £2 each you can buy only 50 bars with your money. The value of your money will have reduced as a result of the price increases.

The erosion of the value of money also **erodes the capital value of deposits** and also the capital in those investments whose value does not increase, such as National Savings & Investments (NS&I) Savings Certificates.

Inflation also erodes the value of interest received from **fixed interest** investments such as fixed interest gilts and fixed interest NS&I investments.

Those savings and investments that are **index linked** such as some gilts and NS&I products give protection against increases in the cost of living.

2.2 Spending

Inflation affects **personal financial plans**.

Inflation in prices affects how much we can buy with the money we have to **spend**. Inflation can lead to claims for pay increases which in turn can lead to higher costs which in turn can lead to higher prices which of course brings us back to higher inflation. Employees generally are better off in times of high inflation because pay rises often exceed the rate of inflation.

Retired people on fixed pensions are adversely affected by inflation. It reduces the value of the money that they have to spend without increasing the amount they have to spend. Those who are in a relatively better position are people whose retirement pensions are inflation-linked. Those who receive pensions that are subject to discretionary increases may be protected but the degree of protection will obviously depend upon the level of the increases.

If a pension increases by a fixed rate, that is it **escalates**, then whether or not the rate of escalation is greater than or less than the rate of inflation will be a matter of fortune - or misfortune. Many company pensions have some form of **inflation linking**.

2.3 Borrowing

An effect of inflation on **borrowers** is that it reduces the capital value of their debt. If interest rates do not increase too much, then borrowers will be in a relatively fortunate position. If somebody has **a fixed rate mortgage** at a rate that is less than the rate of inflation, then they will also be relatively fortunate.

3 Interest rates

3.1 The role of interest rates in the economy

Interest is a payment made for the use of someone's money for a period. Although there are many different interest rates in an economy, including lenders' mortgage and other loan rates, banks' base rates and yields on gilt-edged securities, interest rates in the economy tend to move up or down together.

(a) If some interest rates go up, for example bank base rates, it is quite likely that other interest rates will move up too, if they have not gone up already.

(b) Similarly, if some interest rates go down, other interest rates will move down too.

It is the general level of interest rates, but short-term interest rates in particular, that the government might try to influence.

3.2 The term structure of interest rates

The **term structure of interest rates** refers to the many different interest rates that there are. These various interest rates can be grouped into three broad classes, according to the length of time until the associated debts reach maturity.

- Short-term interest rates
- Medium-term interest rates
- Long-term interest rates

Longer term financial assets should in general offer a higher yield than short-term assets. This is because the investor must be compensated for tying up his money in the asset for a longer period of time.

3.3 Fixed interest rates

Financial products that carry **'fixed' interest rates** for a specified period include deposit products such as term accounts and bonds available from banks and building societies, and fixed rate mortgages. Fixed interest rates do not vary within the specified fixed rate period. The investor or borrower is not exposed to the risk of adverse changes in interest rates. At the same time, they will not benefit from favourable changes in interest rates during the term of the product. The **interest rate risk** during the fixed rate period is borne by the provider, for as long as the customer holds the product.

Fixed rate products can be particularly suitable for customers who do not want to be exposed to risk from changing interest rates. Such products give the customer a degree of certainty in their **affordability**, allowing the customer to budget for known outcomes.

Whether choosing a **fixed rate product** (for example, a deposit account, or a mortgage) is best for a customer who takes a view on how interest rates will move in the future will depend on how the fixed rate compares with variable rates on offer. For example, if the general sentiment in the market is that interest rates will rise during the next two years, then 2-year fixed rate mortgages may be on offer at higher interest rates than a comparable variable rate mortgage.

Fixed interest securities such as gilts and corporate bonds make interest payments that do not vary over the term of the security. However, as we saw in Chapter 2 of this Study Text, the capital values of such securities vary.

3.4 Variable interest rates

When a customer has a deposit or mortgage product with a **variable interest rate**, then he or she bears the risk of changes occurring in the interest rate on the product.

Although the product provider will generally need to change interest rates in line with general changes in interest rates in order to stay competitive, there may be no guarantee that the provider will track other interest rates. The customer may find that the product provider is slow to change rates in customers' favour. Some banks and building societies have been criticised for paying poor interest rates on types of savings accounts that are no longer marketed to new customers: existing customers may have a degree of 'inertia' about moving to a better product. Customers should be wary of **penalties** that could tie them into a product whose interest rate may become uncompetitive in the future.

Some providers have products that carry a guarantee that a specific general interest rates (for example, the Bank of England base or 'repo' rate) will be tracked: this is the basis of the **'tracker mortgage'**, for example. The mortgage provider may promise that the mortgage rate will not be more than x% higher than the Bank of England repo rate, for example. This provides reassurance to the customer that rates will not become less competitive in the future, relative to the market.

As noted above, a financial product that carries a variable interest rate will be subject to the effects of variations in the general level of interest rates such as those described in the following paragraph.

3.5 Variations in the general level of interest rates

The general level of interest rates is affected by several factors.

(a) **The need for a real return**. It is generally accepted that investors will want to earn a 'real' rate of return on their investment, that is, a return which exceeds the rate of inflation. The suitable real rate of return will depend on factors such as investment risk.

(b) **Uncertainty about future rates of inflation**. When investors are uncertain about what future nominal and real interest rates will be, they are likely to require higher interest yields to persuade them to take the risk of investing, especially in the longer term.

(c) **Changes in the level of government borrowing**. When the demand for credit increases, interest rates will go up. A high level of borrowing by the government is likely to result in upward pressure on interest rates.

(d) **Higher demand for borrowing from individuals**. If individuals want to borrow more, for example because they feel confident about their level of future earnings, then interest rates will tend to rise.

(e) **Monetary policy**. Many governments control the level of interest rates in order to control inflation.

(f) **Interest rates abroad**. An appropriate real rate of interest in one country will be influenced by external factors, such as interest rates in other countries and expectations about the exchange rate.

3.6 Effects of interest rate changes on investment performance

Returns on **deposits** are closely linked to other interest rates in the economy. If interest rates fall, keeping money on deposit will seem less attractive. However, this may reflect the fact that inflation has fallen. **Real interest rates** (that is, inflation-adjusted interest rates) may be of more concern to the saver than the quoted 'nominal' rates.

The relationship between the prices of **fixed interest securities** and interest rates is an inverse relationship. As interest rates are seen to rise, the prices of these securities fall. Suppose that a fixed interest security pays interest of 5% and is priced at £100. The yield is £5/£100 = 5%.

If interest rates now fall so that 4% is the expected return, then the holder of the security should now be able to obtain a price of around £125 for it. It still pays £5 and so at £125, it pays a yield at the new market rate of £5/£125 = 4%.

Lower interest rates will also reduce the yield in terms of company earnings which investors expect from holding company shares (**equities**). Equity investors are said to expect a **'risk premium'** for their investment, in excess of typical yields on deposits or fixed interest securities. If the yields on deposits and fixed interest securities fall while the risk premium is the same, the expected earnings yield (earnings as a percentage of the share price) from equities will be reduced, and equity prices will tend to rise.

Participants in the **equity markets** also generally favour lower interest rates because companies' profitability will be improved by lower borrowing costs for the company's debt and higher demand from consumers. Increased profits should feed through to higher dividend payments for shareholders. Accordingly, unexpected cuts in short-term interest rates are likely to cause a rise in share prices.

Key chapter points

- **Inflation is a sustained rise in the level of prices.**

- **Important measures of inflation in the UK are the CPI (for the Government's inflation target) and the RPI (for pensions, benefits and index-linked gilts).**

- **Inflation reduces the purchasing power of money and adversely affects those on fixed incomes, particularly.**

- **Interest rates on financial products may be fixed for a period, or they may be variable.**

- **Fixed interest rates make budgeting easier: the outcome is known in advance.**

- **Variable rates are subject to changes in the wider economy. They are also subject to product providers' policies on how it will vary its rates. In assessing the suitability of variable products, any penalties or notice periods should be considered carefully, in case the product becomes relatively less attractive in the future.**

- **The prices of fixed interest securities vary inversely with interest rates in the economy. If expected interest rates in the economy rise, a fixed rate security (such as a gilt) becomes less attractive and its price falls.**

Chapter Quiz

1   Give a definition of inflation. .... (see para 1.1)

2   What is meant by the 'underlying' rate of inflation? .... (1.4)

3   What is the CPI? .... (1.5)

4   What is the main difference between the CPI and the RPI? .... (1.5)

5   How do fixed interest rates affect clients' budgeting? .... (3.3)

6   Explain how interest rates are set for a 'tracker' mortgage product. .... (3.4)

7   State three factors which affect the general level of interest rates. .... (3.5)

8   Give two reasons why lower interest rates might lead to higher equity prices. .... (3.6)

Part B:
Regulation and ethics

The regulatory framework

1 The FSA regulatory regime

1.1 From self-regulation to statutory regulation

For many years up to the mid-1980s, a system of **self-regulation** prevailed in the UK financial sector. Against the background of a number of financial scandals, the need for changes in the law was reviewed. This review gave rise to the Financial Services Act 1986. This Act introduced a system of **'self-regulation within a statutory framework'** for the financial services industry, with financial services firms authorised by Self-Regulatory Organisations (SROs).

When the Labour Party gained power in 1997, it wanted to make changes to the regulation of financial services.

A series of new financial scandals, including the following, had added weight to the political impetus for change.

- The **Maxwell** group – assets from the Mirror Group Pension Scheme were used to prop up the Maxwell business empire, giving rise to new pensions legislation (Pension Act 1995) and changes to the corporate governance regime.

- **Barings** and the Nick Leeson affair – a lack of internal controls at the bank created a situation where a single trader exposed the bank to large financial losses. The new FSA regime focuses on senior management responsibilities.

- **Guinness** – there was evidence of bolstering of the Guinness share price in a bid situation. The new FSMA 2000 regime introduces the offence of **market abuse**.

- **Pension mis-selling** – many employees were wrongly advised to leave their occupational pension schemes. An estimated 2.2 million people were affected, with a compensation bill variously estimated to be between £15 billion and £35 billion.

The 1986 Act was replaced by the **Financial Services and Markets Act 2000**, under which the **Financial Services Authority (FSA)** was set up.

The **Financial Services and Markets Act 2000 (FSMA 2000)** created the **Financial Services Authority** as a single statutory regulatory authority for the financial services industry. It is illegal under FSMA 2000 to engage in unauthorised investment business in the UK.

1.2 FSA as the single statutory regulator

As the UK's **single statutory regulator** for the industry, the FSA:

(a) Brings together regulation of investment, insurance and banking
(b) Brings a move from contractual to statutory regulation
(c) Makes the UK the only major developed country with such a system

The FSA is not a government agency. As stated earlier in this Study Text, it is a private company limited by guarantee, with HM Treasury as the guarantor. The FSA is financed by the financial services industry. The Board of the FSA is appointed by the Treasury and the Chancellor of the Exchequer is ultimately responsible for the regulatory system for financial services under FSMA 2000.

The FSA:

- Is the authorising body for these carrying on regulated activities
- Is the regulator of exchanges and clearing houses operating in the UK
- Approves companies for stock market listing in the UK
- Is a rule making body
- Undertakes supervision
- Has wide powers of enforcement

With the implementation of FSMA 2000 at date 'N2', the FSA has responsibility for:

- Prudential supervision of all firms, which involves monitoring the adequacy of their management, financial resources and internal systems and controls, and

- Conduct of business regulations of those firms doing investment business. This involves overseeing firms' dealings with investors to ensure, for example, that information provided is clear and not misleading

Note that the term '**firm**' is used generally by the FSA to apply to an authorised person, whether the person is an individual, a partnership or a corporate body.

1.3 The FSA's approach to regulation

The FSA seeks to adopt a **'risk-based' approach** to regulation. This means that it focuses its attention on those institutions and activities that are likely to pose the greatest risk to consumers and markets. The approach is intended to recognise the responsibilities of consumers themselves and of firms' management. The FSA considers it both **impossible and undesirable** to remove **all risk and failure** from the financial system.

In the FSA's risk-based approach, there is a focus on the extent to which firms pose a risk to the FSA's ability to meet its objectives. A firm's relationship with the FSA, the resources it devotes to regulation of the firm and any programme of

PROFESSIONAL EDUCATION

risk mitigation that may be put in place, will be based on a **grading system**, according to the judged level of risk involved.

In its 2006/07 Business Plan, the FSA signalled its intention to shift, through time, towards more reliance on higher-level **principles**, with fewer **rules**. A '**twin approach**' has been heralded by the FSA, combined '**risk-based**' and '**principles-based**' aspects. We will look at the important Principles for Business of the FSA soon, below.

The FSA's desire to have fewer rules must be seen in the context of EU obligations which require certain rules to be in place, and the need to protect consumers effectively.

The FSA initiative on '**Treating Customers Fairly**', which we discuss later, is an example of the Authority's emphasis on principles.

We explain the FSA's approach in more detail later in this Study Text.

1.4 FSA's statutory objectives

The FSA's **four statutory objectives**, as set out in FSMA 2000, are as follows (with BPP comments in brackets).

    (a)   To **maintain confidence** in the UK financial system. (The FSA is concerned with the **stability of firms** and the **stability of markets**.)

    (b)   To promote **public understanding** of the financial system, including: **awareness** of the benefits and risks associated with different kinds of investment or other financial dealing, and providing appropriate **information and advice**. (The emphasis is on consumers protecting themselves.)

    (c)   To secure the appropriate level of **protection for consumers**, bearing in mind:

        (i)   The different levels of risk that come with different kinds of investment or other transaction

        (ii)   The differing experience and expertise of consumers

        (iii)   Consumers' needs for accurate advice and information, and

        (iv)   The principle that consumers should take responsibility for their decisions. (This principle has marked a move back towards the principle of *caveat emptor* – 'let the buyer beware'.)

    (d)   To contribute to **reducing financial crime** (by reducing the possibility for a regulated person to carry on a business whose purpose is connected with financial crime).

1.5 FSA enforcement powers

The FSA *Enforcement Manual* details the FSA's powers of:

    (a)   **Investigation**, which are broadly similar to pre-existing regulators' powers. If you are the subject of an investigation, you do **not** have a **right to silence**. However, because of human rights legislation, your answers are not admissible in human rights or market abuse proceedings.

    (b)   **Varying permission** to carry out regulated activities.

    (c)   **Redress for consumers.** The FSA can require firms to compensate consumers.

    (d)   **Discipline**, through fines, warnings or censure.

    (e)   Specific powers in relation to **market misconduct**. In relation to **market abuse**, the FSA can act against anyone.

The FSA has powers to take **regulatory** action and both **civil** and **criminal** action against a person whom it discovers to have committed a criminal act under FSMA 2000.

The FSA adopts a **'top-down'** approach to enforcement: it will first look to **senior management** before going down the organisation to the person who has apparently acted wrongly.

The FSA may conduct, without notice, **compliance visits** with which a firm must of course cooperate.

The FSA's wide-ranging powers under FSMA 2000 include the following.

- **Section 138** of FSMA 2000 gives the FSA powers to make general rules it considers necessary or expedient for investor protection

- **Section 167** allows the FSA to investigate an authorised person

- **Section 177** imposes penalties of up to six months' imprisonment or a fine of £5,000 for failure to co-operate with an investigation

- **Section 176** gives the FSA powers to enter the premises of an authorised person if they have a warrant

1.6 Risks for consumers

The FSA has identified the following **consumer risks** in the financial services industry.

(a) **Prudential risk** – for example the risk of a company collapsing through poor management

(b) **Bad faith risk** – the risk of loss due to mis-selling, non-disclosure, fraud and misrepresentation

(c) **Complexity/unsuitability risk** – the risk that a customer chooses unsuitable products through lack of understanding

(d) **Performance risk** – the risk that investments do not provide the returns that had been hoped for

The FSA has a **Consumer Panel** to monitor how the FSA fulfils its objectives in relation to consumers.

1.7 Mystery shopping

The FSA uses **mystery shopping** as a means of protecting consumers. This involves posing as a consumer to establish what a firm would say to a 'genuine' consumer. Telephone calls and meetings of the FSA's mystery shoppers may be recorded. The FSA plans to conform to the Market Research Society Code of Practice in its mystery shopping activities.

1.8 Market abuse and insider dealing

The FSA regulatory regime has brought with it the new offence of **market abuse**, complementing existing legislation covering insider dealing and market manipulation.

The FSA's **Code of Market Conduct** applies to any person dealing in certain investments on recognised exchanges and does not require proof of intent to abuse a market.

Section 123 of FSMA 2000 gives statutory powers to the FSA to impose unlimited fines for the offence of **market abuse**. **Section 165** gives the FSA powers to require information, and requires anyone to cooperate with investigations in to market abuse. As a civil offence, market abuse will be assessed on a **balance of probabilities**. The criminal law requires proof of guilt and, in the past, criminal convictions for **insider dealing** and financial fraud have been few. Insider dealing involves trading on the basis of information which is not available to the public, and is illegal.

Market abuse could consist of:

(a) Knowingly buying shares in a takeover target before a general disclosure of the proposed takeover (a form of **insider dealing**)

(b)   Market distortion: dealing on an exchange just prior to the exchange closing with the purpose of positioning the share price at a distorted level in order to avoid having to pay out on a derivatives transaction

(c)   Posting an inaccurate story on an internet bulletin board in order to give a false or misleading impression

These provisions relate particularly to participation in equity (shares) markets. Detailed rules introduced into the FSA Handbook during 2005 follow the common EU approach to market abuse and insider dealing as reflected in the EU **Market Abuse Directive (MAD)**.

New measures introduced with MAD to help detect market abuse and prevent it happening include:

- **Insiders' lists:** issuers and advisers must keep lists of persons with access to inside information

- **Suspicious transactions reporting:** firms must report transactions to the FSA if there is a reasonable suspicion that market abuse might have taken place

1.9 Capital adequacy

As already mentioned, the FSA supervises the **prudential standards** of regulated firms, including the soundness of firms' **financial resources**. Regulating the **capital adequacy** of firms should minimise the risk of consumer loss or market disruption.

The FSA regulates approximately 7,500 investment firms, from large investment banks to financial advisers operating as sole practitioners. The **Interim Prudential Sourcebook for Investment Businesses (IPRU(INV))** is the part of the FSA Handbook which sets out provisions to ensure the capital adequacy and prudential standards of investment firms, as a 'transitional' measure until a single Integrated Prudential Sourcebook is developed to cover all regulated firms.

IPRU(INV) sets out **minimum capital and other risk management standards** which are broadly similar to those that existed under previous regulators.

The general requirement is that a firm must:

- Have and maintain at all times financial resources of the kinds and amounts specified in, and calculated in accordance with rules, for different categories of firm, set out in detail by the FSA, and

- Be able to meet its liabilities as they fall due.

An IFA firm must in particular have 'financial resources' of at least £10,000 at all times.

Firms are generally required to have **Professional Indemnity Insurance**. If PII cover is cancelled or cannot be renewed, the FSA must be informed.

Proper records of financial resources must be kept, and must be available on request if the FSA requires them.

The FSA is working with the European Union and the industry to develop policies for implementing a new **capital requirements** framework via the **EU Capital Adequacy Directive**. This will cover the revised requirements of the Basel Committee on Banking Supervision (known as 'Basel 2').

1.10 FSA Principles for Business

The FSA's eleven **Principles for Business** of the FSA are a general statement of **authorised firms' obligations**.

FSA Principles for Business		
1:	**Integrity**	A firm must conduct its business with integrity.
2:	**Skill, care and diligence**	A firm must conduct its business with due skill, care and diligence.
3:	**Management and control**	A firm must take reasonable care to organise and control its affairs responsibly and effectively, with adequate risk management systems.
4:	**Financial prudence**	A firm must maintain adequate financial resources.
5:	**Market conduct**	A firm must observe proper standards of market conduct.
6:	**Customers' interests**	A firm must pay due regard to the interests of its customers and treat them fairly.
7:	**Communications with clients**	A firm must pay due regard to the information needs of its clients, and communicate information to them in a way which is clear, fair and not misleading.
8:	**Conflicts of interest**	A firm must manage conflict of interest fairly, both between itself and its customers and between a customer and another client.
9:	**Customers: relationships of trust**	A firm must take reasonable care to ensure the suitability of its advice and discretionary decisions for any customer who is entitled to rely upon its judgment.
10:	**Clients' assets**	A firm must arrange adequate protection for clients' assets when it is responsible for them.
11:	**Relations with regulators**	A firm must deal with its regulators in an open and cooperative way, and must disclose to the FSA appropriately anything relating to the firm of which the FSA would reasonably expect notice.

The Principles are important as bases for the FSA's more detailed rules, and we shall be referring back to some of the Principles later. Furthermore, the Principles are becoming increasingly significant as the FSA seeks to reduce the number of rules it imposes.

Although the Principles may be invoked when the FSA disciplines firms, they cannot themselves give rise to actions for damages.

Example: Applying the FSA Principles

Controversy about the FSA's move to a 'principles-based' approach was heightened when a fine of £13.9 million was imposed on Citigroup after a series of bond trades. The regulator stated that Citigroup had not breached specific rules, such as rules governing deliberate distortion of markets. Instead, Citigroup was found to be at fault because it had breached broader principles. It had breached Principle 2 by not considering to a sufficient extent the consequences of its trading strategy on the 'efficient and orderly operation' of markets. It had breached Principle 2 by not having appropriate risk management and approval systems in place.

2 FSA Handbook

2.1 Introduction

The **FSA Handbook** applies to all regulated firms. The Handbook contains both **high level requirements** applicable to all firms and **specialist sourcebooks** for particular types of firms. A single integrated sourcebook covering all firms may only be created when European standards are agreed.

2.2 Rules and guidance

The FSA Handbook can be found online at **www.fsa.gov.uk**. As well as the full Handbook, the FSA has issued an **Overview for small IFA firms** which focuses on key aspects that IFAs need to know. This is available on the FSA web site at **www.fsa.gov.uk/ifas**.

Note the following points if consulting the Handbook.

(a) An 'R' symbol in the Handbook denotes a **Rule**, which **must** be followed.

(b) 'E' stands for **Evidential Provision** indicating evidence of compliance or non-compliance with a linked rule. An Evidential Provision is not actionable.

(c) **Guidance** is indicated by a 'G' symbol and is not binding. A firm cannot be disciplined merely because it has not followed Guidance.

2.3 Conduct of Business Sourcebook

The **Conduct of Business Sourcebook (COB)** forms part of the **FSA Handbook**.

The **COB** rules deal with the protection of customer, and differentiate between types of customers, with the purpose of enabling greater protection to be given to the most vulnerable.

We will be returning to look at the COB rules you need to know later.

3 Authorisation of firms

3.1 Introduction

Under the FSA regulatory regime, firms carrying on regulated activities are required to have **authorisation** to do so before undertaking any such activity. However, firms' ability to **maintain** appropriate standards depends on the quality of the individuals it has performing key roles.

The FSA can either grant authorisation or refuse it, at its discretion. Firms refused authorisation have a right of appeal to the **Financial Services and Markets Tribunal**.

Under FSMA 2000, the FSA is responsible for a single regime for **approval** of individuals carrying out **controlled functions** for **authorised firms**. As well as covering senior management, the **approved persons regime** importantly covers those giving **investment advice**.

In this section of the Chapter, we look at the authorisation process for firms before going on to look at the approval of individuals in the next section.

3.2 Regulated activities

Section 19 of FSMA 2000 provides that a person (where 'persons' includes firms) must not carry on a **regula ed activity** in the UK unless either:

- **Authorised**, or
- **Exempt**

Possible consequences of breaching this provision are:

- Criminal charges
- Contracts becoming voidable
- Claims for damages

In deciding whether **authorisation** is required, the following need to be considered:

Regulated activities

↓

Exceptions

↓

Exemptions

The scope of **regulated activities** is determined by the Regulated Activities Order and covers:

(a)   Dealing in investments
(b)   Arranging deals in investments
(c)   Managing investments
(d)   Advising on investments
(e)   Establishing or operating a collective investment scheme (eg unit trusts, investment trusts)
(f)   Establishing or operating a stakeholder pension scheme (SHP)
(g)   Safekeeping of and administering investments
(h)   Lloyds insurance business
(i)   Carrying out contracts of insurance
(j)   Funeral plan contracts
(k)   Accepting deposits
(l)   Residential mortgages (excluding buy-to-let mortgages)

Since 14 January 2005, the FSA has regulated **general insurance sales and advice** (covered in Chapter 1).

Investments covered by regulated activities are also listed in the Order:

(a)   Deposits
(b)   Contracts of insurance
(c)   Shares
(d)   Government and local authority securities
(e)   Instruments giving title to investments
(f)   Units in collective investment schemes
(g)   Options, futures and contacts for differences
(h)   Lloyds syndicate capacity and membership of syndicates

3.3 Exceptions

By exception, the following do not require authorisation:

(a) **Dealings as principal** – there is no need for authorisation where people are dealing in investments for themselves

(b) **Newspapers and the media** – however, 'tipsheets', whose primary purpose is to tip shares, are **not** an exception

(c) Acting as an **unremunerated trustee**

(d) **Employee share schemes**

(e) **Certain overseas persons**, for business solicited in the UK

3.4 Exempt persons

The **Exempt Persons Order** exempts from authorisation:

(a) Certain institutions, including **central banks** and **National Savings & Investments**, and **local government authorities**

(b) Certain **members of professions**, such as lawyers, accountants and actuaries. Member firms of **'Designated Professional Bodies'** (**DPBs**) – such as the major accountancy bodies, and the solicitors' Law Society – require **FSA authorisation** if they recommend the purchase of specific investments such as pensions or listed company shares to clients, approve financial promotions or carry out corporate finance business. If the firms' activities are **'non-mainstream' investment business**, only assisting clients in making investment decisions as part of other professional services, they are exempt from FSA authorisation but must obtain a **licence** from the DPB, under which they are subject to a light form of regulation.

Appointed representatives (ARs) of an authorised firm are also **exempt**, where the authorised firm (the 'principal') takes full responsibility for the AR's activities. An AR might be providing advice, or might only be acting as an **introducer**, distributing marketing material and making introductions. The principal, who is FSA-authorised and takes responsibility for regulatory compliance, could be a **product provider** or an **IFA network**.

3.5 Permissions

Firms must apply to the FSA for **permission** to carry out any regulated activities as set out in the legislation. A bank, for example, will need to apply for permission to accept deposits. Limitations or requirements may be imposed by the FSA, for example over whether it may deal with private customers, or over the level of financial resources it must have. Firms need one permission, covering all their regulated activities.

Authorisation by the FSA gives **permission** (often called a **Part IV permission**, after the relevant Part of FSMA 2000) to carry on one or more regulated activity subject to the following **threshold conditions**:

(a) The legal status of the firm
(b) Location of offices: both Head Office and Registered Office must be in the UK
(c) Adequacy of the firm's financial resources
(d) Suitability, mainly of systems and controls, with appropriate reporting lines being in place

3.6 Applying for authorisation

When applying for authorisation, a firm must disclose anything relating to the firm of which the FSA would reasonably expect notice.

Routes to authorisation for a firm are:

- Direct, or
- 'Passporting'

3.7 Passporting

The EU's **Investment Services Directive (ISD)** was introduced in 1996. Under this Directive, the FSA is able to authorise investment firms to conduct business throughout the European Economic Area (EEA). The ISD operates alongside the **Capital Adequacy Directive**, which sets out minimum levels of capital which firms must maintain.

Before 1996, the **Second Banking Co-ordination Directive** had been introduced (in 1996) to cover banks and some investment business (for example, portfolio management) in a similar way to the Investment Services Directive.

The process of **passporting** allows European firms to operate branches and to sell across borders throughout the EEA without the need for licensing in each separate jurisdiction. (The **EEA** comprises the countries of the **European Union** plus **Norway, Iceland** and **Liechtenstein**.)

A firm can be granted a 'passport' by the FSA either:

- For a branch operating in another EEA country, or
- For cross-border business, for example by telephone or by computer link

For applications by firms to open a branch, the FSA must consider the application and notify the regulator in the other country (the '**host state**') within three months. The host state has two months to respond, after which time the firm can start business in the host state.

For applications to carry out cross-border business, the FSA must respond and notify the host state within one month, and no time is allowed for the host state to respond.

The UK is one of the few states that have implemented the ISD. The ISD allows UK investment firms to passport firms into all other EEA countries – even those that have not implemented the ISD.

3.8 Home State and Host State responsibilities

For passported activities, responsibilities are divided between home State and host State as follows.

(a) **Home State responsibilities**

- Authorisation
- Capital adequacy
- Fitness and propriety
- Conduct of Business in the home state
- Client assets

(b) **Host State responsibilities**

- Conduct of Business in the host state

Exercise: Passporting

A bank X based in France and authorised by French authorities offers investment products to UK citizens through a website. A UK-based firm Y operates branches in Germany through which it offers non-protection life policies.

To which does 'passporting' apply?

Solution

It applies to both firms, X and Y.

3.9 Sections 23 – 25, FSMA 2000

Section 23 of FSMA 2000 imposes penalties of up to two years imprisonment or a fine of £5,000 for the offence of trading in financial services **without the required authorisation**.

Section 24 imposes similar penalties for someone describing himself (in whatever terms) to be an authorised person when he is not

Section 25 prohibits promotion of investments unless by someone who is authorised.

4 Approved persons and controlled functions

4.1 Introduction

Individuals who carry out **controlled functions** must have **FSA approval** to do so. Such persons are subject to **Statements of Principles** for approved persons and a **Code of Conduct**.

4.2 Controlled functions

Controlled functions include:

(a)   **Governing functions** (eg directors)

(b)   **Required functions** (eg Money Laundering Reporting Officer)

(c)   **Systems and controls functions** (eg senior personnel in internal audit)

(d)   **Significant management function** (eg heads of business units in larger firms)

(e)   **Customer functions** including:

    (i)   Advisory functions
    (ii)   Customer trading and investment management functions

The controlled functions (a) to (d) above – ie, all controlled functions that are not customer functions – are managerial in nature and are called **significant influence functions**.

The regime places significant emphasis on senior management responsibilities, and it can be expected that the new regulator will look to senior management in holding firms accountable for failures.

Importantly, **customer functions** include the activities of most **personnel advising customers** under the category of **advisory functions**.

Advisory functions include:

(a) Those who provide investment advice (or financial advice, as it is often known), including those not yet assessed as competent

(b) Advice to clients relating to corporate finance business

(c) Advice on pensions transfers and pension opt-outs

(d) Advice to underwriting members of Lloyd's

Exercise: Approved persons regime

Can you think of two examples of personnel in the financial services industry who are not subject to the approved persons regime?

Solution

Possible answers include:

- Someone dealing with execution-only transactions (where the customer has confirmed that they do not want advice)

- A bank cashier who accepts a deposit from a customer

4.3 The approval process

The **firm** applies for approval of individuals on a **prescribed form** which is submitted to the FSA's **Individual Vetting and Registration Department** and covers:

(a) Personal details

(b) Firm's details

(c) Details of the contractual arrangement between the candidate and the firm, for example whether the candidate is an employee or working under a contract of services

(d) Controlled functions for which approval is sought

(e) Confirmation that the candidate meets **training and competence** requirements

(f) Ten-year employment history

(g) Answers to questions on past convictions, judgement debts etc, to help establish if the candidate is **fit and proper**

(h) List of directorships and any additional information offered

(i) Signed declarations by the candidate and the firm

The firm is required to notify the FSA of any significant matter which might affect the candidate's fitness and properness **as soon as** the firm becomes aware of it.

The FSA must be satisfied that the candidate is fit and proper, and will process applications **within three months**. Temporary approval may be granted.

If the FSA proposes to refuse an application, interested parties may make representations to the FSA. They may subsequently refer refused applications to the independent **Financial Services and Markets Tribunal** which was set up under Section 132 of FSMA 2000, and can hear appeals against FSA decisions which:

(a) Prohibit an individual

(b) Refuse authorisation

(c) Withdraw authorisation

(d) Take disciplinary action

(e) Object to a change in control of an authorised person

(f) Withdraw approval of an individual in a controlled function

4.4 The 'fit and proper' test

Although not explicitly defined, **'fit and proper'** is assessed on the following criteria:

(a) **Honesty, integrity and reputation**, in the light of employment record and any criminal record, for example

(b) **Competence and capability**, based on experience and training

(c) **Financial soundness**, relating to court judgements or bankruptcy, for example, rather than a person's financial resources

Using similar criteria for granting approvals, the FSA has the power to **withdraw** approvals.

4.5 Statements of Principle for approved persons

Failure to comply with the **Statements of Principle for approved persons** constitutes an act of misconduct which may result in disciplinary action, but only where there is **personal culpability**.

The seven Principles are set out below. Principles 1 to 4 apply to all approved persons. Principles 5 to 7 apply to senior management only. (See earlier above for an explanation of **significant influence functions**.)

Statements Of Principle For Approved Persons

Statement of Principle 1

An approved person must act with integrity in carrying out his controlled function.

Statement of Principle 2

An approved person must act with due skill, care and diligence in carrying out his controlled function.

Statement of Principle 3

An approved person must observe proper standards of market conduct in carrying out his controlled function.

Statement of Principle 4

An approved person must deal with the FSA and with other regulators in an open and cooperative way and must disclose appropriately any information of which the FSA would reasonably expect notice.

> **Statements of Principles 5–7 apply to senior management only**
>
> **Statement of Principle 5**
>
> An approved person performing a significant influence function must take reasonable steps to ensure that the business of the firm for which he is responsible in his controlled function is organised so that it can be controlled effectively.
>
> **Statement of Principle 6**
>
> An approved person performing a significant influence function must exercise due skill, care and diligence in managing the business of the firm for which he is responsible in his controlled function.
>
> **Statement of Principle 7**
>
> An approved person performing a significant influence function must take reasonable steps to ensure that the business of the firm for which he is responsible in his controlled function complies with the relevant requirements and standards of the regulatory system.

4.6 Senior management arrangements, systems and controls

Rules are set out in the **Senior Management Arrangements, Systems and Controls Sourcebook (SYSC)** which forms part of the FSA Handbook.

Firms must:

- Clearly apportion responsibilities among directors and senior managers
- Ensure that adequate monitoring of the firm's activities is possible
- Allocate to the Managing Director or most senior person the function of dealing with the apportionment of responsibilities and overseeing the establishment and maintenance of systems and controls
- Take reasonable care to create and maintain systems and controls appropriate to the business

Firms must keep an up-to-date record of how **responsibilities** are apportioned between directors and senior managers, for example in the form of an **organisation chart** or diagram.

SYSC covers the issues a firm is expected to consider in establishing and maintaining systems and controls appropriate to the business. These include:

- The size of the firm
- The scale and complexity of its business
- The need to counter the risk that the firm might be used to further financial crime
- The need to establish and maintain compliance with regulatory requirements and record-keeping

Firms should have **clear reporting lines, clear delegation limits** and **clear management responsibilities.** There should be adequate **record-keeping**.

A larger firm may need to have a **separate risk assessment function**, to assess risks that the firm faces and to advise directors and senior managers on them. Risks of regulatory concern are those relating to the fair treatment of customers, the protection of consumers, confidence in the financial system and financial crime. An **internal audit function** may monitor compliance arrangements in a larger firm.

Firms should have arrangements to ensure **business continuity** in the event of unforeseen interruption (for example, a fire or a computer system failure).

Small and **large firms** are likely to have different kinds of systems and controls: the important point is that they should be 'fit for purpose'. With a sole practitioner, one person is responsible for all aspects of the firm's business, and in that case there should be adequate systems allowing that person to adequately monitor and manage the firm.

4.7 Code of Practice for Approved Persons

The FSA's **Code of Practice for Approved Persons** sets out examples of conduct which is seen by the FSA as contravening the **Statements of Principle for Approved Persons**. Some of the more important examples for the first four Principles are set out below.

Principle	Examples of non-compliance
1	Misleading or attempting to mislead a customer, the firm or the FSA, eg falsification of documents, misleading customer about risks of an investment.
2	Failing to give a customer, the firm, its auditor or its actuary information which the person knew or should have known they should have provided, eg failing to disclose charges or surrender penalties.
3	Market abuse.
4	Failure to report relevant matters internally, where internal reporting procedures exist in the firm.

4.8 Disciplinary sanctions

For non-compliance with any of the Principles, the FSA may:

(a)   Issue a public statement of misconduct ('naming and shaming')

(b)   Impose a fine

(c)   Withdraw approved person status, if fitness and properness are concerned, and thus prevent the person from carrying out controlled functions. The process is subject to a warning and decision notice procedure with a right of referral to the Financial Services and Market Tribunal by the individual.

4.9 Prohibition orders against individuals

Under Sections 56 to 58 FSMA 2000, the FSA can prohibit an **individual** who is not fit and proper from the whole industry or part of it.

(a)   A prohibition order under s56 FSMA 2000 leads to **criminal sanctions**

(b)   Authorised firms must take reasonable care to avoid employing **prohibited persons**. If they **fail** to do so, a **private person** who suffers loss has a right of action against the firm.

4.10 Injunctions and restitution orders

Under Section 380 FSMA 2000, the FSA can apply to the court for an **injunction** against an individual.

Under Section 382, the FSA or the Secretary of State can apply for a **restitution order** requiring an approved person in contravention of rules to pay amounts to the FSA following a loss by an individual or a profit accruing to the approved person.

5 Notification requirements

5.1 Introduction

FSA-authorised firms must notify the FSA of various matters. Such notifications help the FSA in monitoring the firm and enforcing rule and requirements.

5.2 Reporting requirements

A firm must submit the following reports to the FSA each year.

- **Annual questionnaire** (on a standard form) – yearly, within four months after the firm's accounting date

- **Complaints report** (on a standard form) – twice yearly, within one month of the end of each **reporting period**: 1 April to 30 September and 1 October to 31 March

- For firms that are not sole traders, a **controllers report** and a **close links report**

- Where relevant, a six-monthly **pensions transfer and opt-outs report** and/or a **significant management function report**

- A firm that is a **holding company** must submit **audited consolidated annual financial statements**

5.3 Serious regulatory impact

Matters having a **serious regulatory impact** should be notified. The following are such matters.

- If the firm fails to satisfy one or more of the threshold conditions for Part IV permission to be granted (as covered earlier)

- Any matter that could have a significant adverse impact on the firm's reputation

- Any matter that could affect the firm's ability to continue to provide adequate services to customers and which could result in serious detriment to a customer

- Any matter regarding the firm that could result in serious financial consequences to the financial system or to other firms

5.4 Principle of Business 11

In line with **Principle for Business 11** (set out earlier), the following would require notification to the FSA:

- Any proposed restructuring, reorganisation or business expansion which could have a significant impact on the firm's risk profile or resources (including starting a product or service, and entering into or changing a significant outsourcing arrangement)

- Any significant failure of the firm's systems or controls

- Any action that significantly ('materially') changes the capital adequacy or solvency of the firm

- Significant breaches of rules and requirements under FSMA 2000

6 Whistleblowing

6.1 Facilitation of whistleblowing

A further measure to encourage proper and ethical conduct in the industry comprises the steps that the FSA has made to make '**whistleblowing**' possible. Employees can contact the FSA if they are concerned about something that is relevant to their functions, by any of the following methods:

- Telephone, on 020 7066 9200
- Email: **whistle@fsa.gov.uk**
- Letter, to the Authorisation Enquiries Department at the FSA

6.2 Public Interest Disclosure Act

Employees are protected by the **Public Interest Disclosure Act 1998** if they:

- Have raised the matter internally within the firm and remain concerned by the lack of response, or felt unable to raise the matter internally

- Reasonably believe the matters raised to be substantially true

- Reasonably believe that the FSA is responsible for the issue in question

Exercise: FSA Principle for Business

Fill in the blanks below in the FSA's **Principles for Business**. Check your answers with the table earlier in the Chapter.

FSA Principles for Business	
1: **Integrity**	A firm ....
2: **......... , ... and diligence**	A firm must conduct its business with due ..... , ... and diligence
3: **Management and ....**	A firm must take reasonable care to organise and control its affairs responsibly and ...., with adequate .... systems.
4: **Financial ....**	A firm must maintain adequate financial resources.
5: **Market conduct**	A firm must observe........................ of market conduct.
6: **Customers' interests**	A firm must pay due regard to the interests of its customers and treat them ....
7: **Communications with clients**	A firm must pay due regard to the .... needs of its clients, and communicate information to them in a way which is ...., ... and not ....
8: **Conflicts of interest**	A firm must manage conflicts of interest ...., both between itself and its customers and between a customer and ....
9: **Customers: relationships of ....**	A firm must take reasonable care to ensure the .... of its advice and discretionary decisions for any customer who is entitled to rely upon its judgment.
10: **Clients' assets**	A firm must arrange .... for clients' assets when it is responsible for them.
11: **Relations with regulators**	A firm must deal with its regulators in an .... and .... way, and must disclose to the FSA appropriately anything relating to the firm of which the FSA would ....

Key chapter points

- **The Financial Services Authority is the single statutory regulator for the financial services industry, with four objectives given to it by statute. These concern: maintaining confidence in the financial system, promoting public understanding of it, consumer protection, reducing financial crime.**

- **The FSA exercises prudential supervision of regulated firms, seeking to ensure that firms maintain adequate financial resources and the ability to meet its liabilities.**

- **The FSA directs its regulatory effort where it judges the risks to be highest (risk-based approach). It is seeking to reduce the number of rules it imposes, expecting firms to apply higher-level principles instead.**

- The FSA's Principles for Business underlie its rules, which are consolidated in the FSA Handbook.

- The FSA has wide-ranging powers, and its risk-based approach governs how it enforces its rules.

- It is a criminal offence to carry on a regulated activity, unless the person is authorised to do so, or is exempt from authorisation.

- Permission to carry out regulated activities may be direct, or 'passported' in the case of operations across borders throughout the European Economic Area.

- Individuals carrying out controlled functions need FSA approval as 'fit and proper' to do so, and are subject to a set of Statements of Principle for Approved Persons.

- The FSA has taken steps to facilitate 'whistleblowing' by employees, who can gain protection under the Public Interest Disclosure Act.

Chapter Quiz

1 What is the main implication of the FSA adopting a 'risk-based' approach to regulation? .... (see para 1.3)

2 What is meant by a 'principles-based' approach to regulation? ....(1.3)

3 What are the FSA's four statutory objectives? ....(1.4)

4 What is meant by 'prudential risk'? ....(1.6)

5 Outline five of the FSA's eleven Principles for Business. ....(1.10)

6 Across what borders may 'passporting' of permission to carry out regulated activities apply? ....(3.7)

7 Give three examples of 'controlled functions'. ....(4.2)

8 What is meant by a 'significant influence function'? ....(4.2)

9 What are the main criteria in assessing someone as 'fit and proper'? ....(4.4)

10 Outline some of the issues dealt with in SYSC. ....(4.6)

11 Give three examples of reports that firms must submit to the FSA. ....(5.2)

12 What is 'whistleblowing'? ....(6.1)

12

Rules on advising customers

1 Conduct of Business rules

1.1 To whom does COB apply?

The FSA's **Conduct of Business Sourcebook (COB)** applies to **all authorised firms**.

An **exception** is that COB does not apply generally to **authorised professional firms** (such as firms of solicitors, accountants and actuaries) in respect of their **non-mainstream regulated activities**. Professionals are regulated in these non-mainstream activities by their professional body, eg the Law Society and the Institute of Chartered Accountants in England and Wales.

1.2 The scope of COB rules

COB applies to firms in respect of **regulated activities**, except where specifically excluded. This covers **designated investment business** generally. Designated investment business includes:

- **Advising on investments**
- **Dealing in investments**

The COB rules do not apply to **deposits**, such as bank deposit accounts. Such accounts are covered by the banks' and building societies' own voluntary codes.

Where the COB rules require a communication, notice or agreement to be given **in writing** or where they refer to a **document**, a firm can comply with the rule using **electronic media**.

COB applies to activities carried out **in the UK** and also covers **business brought into the UK**, for a client in the UK.

1.3 No exclusion of liability

The FSA's Principle 6 *Customers' interests* requires a firm to pay due regard to the interest of customers and to treat them fairly.

A firm may not **exclude** the duties it owes or the liabilities it has to customers under FSMA 2000 or the regulatory system.

This means that **customers cannot sign away their rights** under the COB rules.

1.4 Right of action by private persons

Section 150 of FSMA 2000 gives a **right of action by a private person** (an individual not carrying an investment business, or a business not acting in the course of business of any kind) to sue for breaches of **Conduct of Business (COB) rules**.

Unlike the case of suing for negligence, or for breach of contract, to establish that there is a claim it is only necessary to show that there has been a **rule breach** and a **loss**.

Any person (not just private persons) has a right of action under Section 150 FSMA 2000 in relation to:

(a) COB rules prohibiting an authorised person from seeking to exclude or restrict any duty or liability

(b) COB rules seeking to ensure that investment transactions are not based on unpublished price-sensitive information

---

Exercise: COB rules

A journalist working for an investment magazine discovers that a financial services firm on which he is writing an article is in breach of the FSA's Conduct of Business rules. Can the journalist bring an action under Section 150 FSMA 2000?

Solution

The journalist has not suffered a loss, and so has no right of action under Section 150.

---

2 Accepting customers

2.1 Customer classifications

The task of bringing together the diverse rulebooks of the superseded Self-Regulatory Organisations, such as the SFA, IMRO and the PIA, resulted in much new material in the chapter of the COB rules on **accepting customers**. The need to create a single set of rules for all firms regulated by the FSA has resulted in new customer classifications.

Customers are classified as:

- **Market counterparties** (eg governments, other firms),
- **Intermediate customers** (eg large businesses, experts), or
- **Private customers** (eg individuals, small businesses)

The level of **protection** provided is differentiated by type of customer, based on their **size** and **knowledge**. Of the classifications above, private customers have the highest level of protection. The FSA's Conduct of Business (COB) rules generally apply to all dealings with **intermediate customers** and **private customers**.

Market counterparties include:

(a)   Central government bodies and agencies
(b)   Central banks
(c)   Supranational bodies (eg International Monetary Fund, World Bank)
(d)   State investment bodies
(e)   **Another firm**, or overseas financial services firm
(f)   An associate of the firm (with consent), but not if an occupational pension scheme
(g)   A large intermediate customer classified as a market counterparty

Intermediate customers include:

(a)   Local or public authorities
(b)   Large companies listed on a stock exchange
(c)   Body corporates or partnerships with called up share capital or net assets of at least £5 million
(d)   Trusts with assets of at least £10 million
(e)   **Another firm acting for an underlying customer**, if it is so agreed
(f)   Unregulated collective investment schemes
(g)   **Expert private customers** re-classified as intermediate customers

The category of **private customer** covers clients who are not market counterparties or intermediate customers. This category includes **individuals** who are not firms.

An **expert private customer** is:

- An experienced knowledgeable private customer
- Who, having received a warning
- Consents to treatment **as an intermediate customer** after having been given sufficient time to consider

The terms '**customer**' and '**client**' may generally be used interchangeably. The term '**consumer**' is also sometimes used: a consumer could be someone contemplating using financial services.

Before undertaking any work for a customer, an adviser must establish the correct customer classification.

Firms must **review the classification of a customer** as an intermediate customer or a market counterparty at least **every year** while it is doing business with the customer.

2.2 Differentiation of customer by service level

Different protections are given to customers depending on the **level of service** (**discretionary**, **advisory** or **execution only**, in descending order of protection level) they receive as well as their classification as **private** or **intermediate**, thus leading to six categories of customer as follows.

	Private	Intermediate
Discretionary	×	×
Advisory	×	×
Execution only	×	×

2.3 Terms of business and customer agreement

Customers generally must be provided with a firm's **terms of business**, '**in good time**' before designated investment business is conducted, setting out the basis on which the business is conducted.

Note that:

- **Terms of business** are one-way (unsigned)
- A **customer agreement** is two-way (signed)

The terms of business and client agreement requirements do not generally apply to **execution only** transactions, which are transactions where the customer does not wish to receive advice.

Where a private customer has made an **oral offer** to enter into an **ISA** or **stakeholder pension** agreement, a firm must provide a private customer with its terms of business **within five business days** of the offer.

In other cases, the firm must provide a **private customer** with its **terms of business before** conducting designated investment business with the customer.

The **terms of business** may comprise **more than one document**.

The firm must give **ten business days'** notice to the customer before conducting business on **amended terms**.

Where an **Initial Disclosure Document (IDD)** is provided under FSA rules which are explained further below, some of the more important terms of business will be included in the IDD, and a firm may choose to show its remaining terms of business on the back of the IDD.

2.4 Contents of terms of business

The **terms of business** or **customer agreement** should include provisions about:

(a) **Commencement** of terms of business

(b) The fact that the firm is **regulated or authorised by the FSA**

(c) Customer's **investment objectives**

(d) Any **restrictions** of the investments or markets the customer is seeking to use

(e) **Services** the firm will provide

(f) **Payment** arrangement for the firm's services

(g) For **packaged products** with **private customers**, disclosure of **status**, ie whether advice is:

(i) Independent

(ii) Restricted to packaged products of one product provider or marketing group (and whether **adopted packaged products** are included)

(iii) Given for discretionary portfolio management purposes

(h) Accounting arrangements

(i) Information on the right to withdraw, in the case of non-packaged ISAs or PEPs

(j) How fair treatment will be ensured if there is material interest or conflict of interest

(k) Soft commission agreements

(l) Risk warnings where relevant, eg for warrants or derivatives

(m) Any services relating to unregulated collective investment schemes

(n) Rights to realise a private customer's assets, if applicable

(o)   Complaints arrangements, including a statement that the customer may subsequently complain to the Financial Services Ombudsman

(p)   Compensation scheme arrangement

(q)   Arrangements for termination of terms of business, stating that:

    (i)   Termination is without prejudice to transactions already initiated, if this is the case
    (ii)   The customer may terminate by written notice, and when this takes effect
    (iii)   The form has termination rights, if so, and what the minimum notice period is

(r)   Arrangements for waiving the **best execution** rule, if applicable

3 Advising and selling

3.1 Adviser status under polarisation (up to 2005)

The **polarisation** rule dictated, in the past, that either an adviser must give advice on **a single product provider's** products, or they must be **independent financial advisers**, advising on the different products available across the **whole market**. Polarisation was abolished by **1 June 2005**, as discussed further below.

Polarisation resulted in many firms, for example estate agents and mortgage lenders, becoming **appointed representatives** (ARs) of a particular life office. In some cases, an AR (for example, a building society or a bank) actually owns the life office to which it is tied.

An **appointed representative** has only a **single principal** for investment business purposes. This ensures clear lines of accountability and responsibility for an appointed representative's advice.

An IFA can be the appointed representative of an **IFA network**, or of **another IFA**. In this case, the network, or principal, is responsible for the **training and competence** of the IFA and for ensuring compliance with FSA rules.

IFA networks are formed in order to facilitate authorisation and to provide marketing and other support to small IFA firms which might otherwise find the requirements of authorisation and compliance too onerous.

3.2 Depolarisation (since 1 June 2005)

In November 2004, the Financial Services Authority announced its new rules which abolished polarisation and introduced new rules designed to improve disclosure to consumers.

The new rules took effect on 1 December 2004, with a six-month transition period up to 31 May 2005. Since **1 June 2005**, all firms have been required to follow the new rules and '**depolarisation**' – the end of the old polarisation rule – became complete.

Under the new 'depolarised' regime, firms wishing to be regarded as **independent advisers** must offer advice encompassing the whole market or a whole market sector. Their clients must be given the option to pay by **fee**. If charging only by fee, the adviser can only retain minimal amounts of annual **trail commission**.

A major change is that **distributors** or '**multi-ties**' are able to emerge under the new regime, forming a new 'middle ground'. These are firms entering into agreements with two or more providers to sell the products offered or adopted by them.

Appointed representatives continue to have a **single principal**, except in the case of pure **introducers** of business. As a tied adviser, an appointed representative can only promote and sell a product within his host company's range. However, in the case of **stakeholder pensions**, the host company may '**adopt**' the products of one or more other providers, which can then be recommended by the company's tied agents.

3.3 'Keyfacts' disclosures

Abolition of polarisation means that firms must clearly explain to customers the scope of the advice or service they are offering, in new-style **'keyfacts' documents**. There are **Initial Disclosure Documents** which are to be provided to customers, and there are rules about disclosure in advertising and on stationery.

These changes have been backed up by a consumer education campaign. As part of its campaign, the FSA includes **consumer alerts** on the Consumer Help part of its website and uses leaflets, press activity and joint campaigns with organisations such as Citizens Advice Bureaux and through the Post Office. Firms are encouraged to send approved literature to consumers explaining the charges that have been made. This can all be used to support the introduction of the specific initial disclosure document which, along with certain other FSA required documents, will be recognisable by a **'Key Facts' logo**.

The following **'keyfacts' documents** are required:

- A **Menu**, and
- An **Initial Disclosure Document**

3.4 The menu

When a firm's representative makes initial contact with a private customer (unless the contact is by **telephone**) with the intention of advising on packaged products, the representative must give the consumer an information document, known colloquially as a **menu. Packaged products** comprise life policies that are not pure protection policies, stakeholder personal pensions and collective investments (such as unit trusts and OEICs).

The menu must also be given to a customer whenever the customer requests it.

The **menu** is entitled **'Key Facts: A Guide to the Cost of our Services'** and includes:

- A section on the FSA, and the purpose of the required menu
- A section in which the firm gives details of 'Our services'
- The payment options offered
- The maximum commission the firm is likely to receive for a transaction
- An indication of the market average commission

The **market average (MA)** is designed to give consumers a benchmark for what might be a competitive level of commission.

An adviser should not start charging until after the customer has been given a menu and has agreed the **payment option** for the client.

It is acceptable for a firm to have different 'menus', and firms are free to offer different charging structures to different groups of clients.

3.5 The Initial Disclosure Document

The new **Initial Disclosure Document (IDD)** must also be given on first making contact (except by telephone) with the private customer.

The **IDD** must be separate from the menu. The IDD is entitled **'Key Facts: About our Services'** and:

- States that the firm is regulated by the Financial Services Authority

- States whether advice is given only for a single provider's products, for a limited number of providers, or for the whole market

- Invites clients to ask for a list of products on which advice is offered

- Indicates whether a product provider has a shareholding of 10% or more in the advising firm

- Tells customers what to do if they have a complaint

- Gives detail of compensation arrangements through the Financial Services Compensation Scheme

As mentioned earlier, a firm may want to show its remaining **terms of business** on the back of the IDD.

Both the menu and IDD must carry the **keyfacts logo** as prescribed by the FSA, and this logo must not be used where its use is not mandated under FSA rules.

The FSA provides downloadable templates on its web site that firms can use for a **menu** and both a **retail investment IDD** and the **combined IDD (CIDD)**.

3.6 Statement of demands and needs

With the new initial disclosure requirements introduced on 14 January 2005, firms also need to provide the client with a **statement of his demands and needs** (except where these points are otherwise covered, in the **suitability letter**, which is explained later).

The **statement of demands and needs**:

- Should state simply and clearly why the personal recommendation is viewed as suitable, having regard to the client's demands and needs

- Is presented in a way which is for the firm to decide. (Simplicity and plain language, and concise and clear messages, are recommended.)

3.7 Status disclosure

When first contacting a private customer, a **provider representative** must disclose:

- The name of the firm

- Their status as an introducer or representative

- The fact that they can only provide advice on products of the firm and its marketing group, plus any adopted packaged products

When first contacting a private customer, an **independent financial adviser** must disclose:

- The name of the firm
- The fact that they provide independent advice

3.8 Information about the firm

The firm must inform private customers about:

(a) The firm's name and address
(b) The adviser's name and status
(c) The fact that the firm is authorised and regulated by the Financial Services Authority

This information can be given on a **business card**.

Letters and emails to private customers must state that the firm is '**Authorised and regulated by the Financial Services Authority**' (The abbreviation 'FSA' must no longer be used in this context)

If the firm is an **appointed representative** of a **network**, the following must be stated: '[Name of appointed representative] is an appointed representative of [firm] which is authorised and regulated by the Financial Services Authority'.

Of course, it would be convenient for this information to be included in the firm's **letterhead** and in standard wording sent out on all emails.

3.9 Record keeping

The general rule is that firms must keep **records** for the following periods:

(a)   Indefinitely, for pension transfers, pension opt-outs and FSAVCs
(b)   Six years, for life policies, pension contracts and stakeholder pensions
(c)   Three years in other cases

For example, records relating to a private customer's personal and financial circumstances in relation to a transaction for purchase of a unit trust or OEIC investment should be kept for a minimum of three years.

3.10 Know your customer

Someone **giving advice** to a private customer (or acting as an investment manager for a private customer) must:

(a)   Obtain relevant personal and financial information before acting: this process is generally known as **'fact-finding'**

(b)   **Warn** of adverse consequences, if the customer refuses to provide the necessary information

(c)   Conduct regular **reviews**, depending upon the client's particular stage of life and circumstances

The adviser should review the information regarding the particular customer each time the customer seeks advice.

3.11 Suitability requirements

A firm must take reasonable steps to ensure that it does not make a **personal recommendation** to a private customer to buy or sell a designated investment unless the recommendation or transaction is **suitable** for the customer having regard to information disclosed by him and other facts of which the firm is or ought reasonably to be aware.

For **tied advisers**, suitable advice is normally made possible by recommending a product from the provider's own range, given the rules on polarisation (prior to the expected abolition of polarisation). Any **packaged products** must have overall suitability for a client.

A **provider firm** making a personal recommendation to a private customer on a **packaged product** must seek to ensure that the product is the most suitable available from the products of the marketing group or the products adopted by the firm.

Bear in mind that the full definition of **packaged products** is:

(a)   A life policy (other than a pure protection policy)
(b)   A unit in a regulated collective investment scheme
(c)   An interest in an investment trust savings scheme, or
(d)   A stakeholder pension scheme

whether or not (in the case of (a), (b) or (c)) held within a PEP or an ISA.

In following the regulatory requirement of FSA Principle 6 *Customers' interests*, the adviser must pay due regard to customers' interests and must treat customers fairly. This Principle implies that the **interests of customers** must guide the adviser's proposals, and not the level of **remuneration** the adviser may receive.

3.12 The suitability letter

A **suitability letter** (called a **'reason why' letter** under pre-FSA rules) is required following a personal recommendation to a private customer on:

    (a)   A life policy
    (b)   A **stakeholder pension scheme (SHP)**
    (c)   Certain **pensions** transactions
    (d)   Regulated collective investment schemes

A **suitability letter** explains why the firm has concluded that the transaction is suitable, given the customer's circumstances.

The suitability letter must specifically justify any recommendation of:

    (a)   A personal pension scheme instead of a stakeholder pension plan

    (b)   A freestanding AVC (Additional Voluntary Contribution) pension scheme instead of an employer's own in-house AVC scheme

The suitability letter must be issued as soon as possible, and no later than the issue of the post-sale notice of the customer's right to cancel in the case of life policies or stakeholder pensions.

The suitability letter might form part of:

    (a)   A financial report to the customer, or
    (b)   A fact find document

3.13 Selecting a product provider

An independent adviser is under an obligation to select a suitable **provider** of an investment product in order to make a suitable recommendation to the client.

Factors that the adviser should take into account in selecting a **provider** include **financial strength** and **efficiency.**

One of the prime considerations in assessing financial strength of a provider is the **excess of a provider's assets over liabilities.** In the case of investment products, the consistency with which the provider has demonstrated investment performance over a period of years helps to indicate likely future financial strength.

The **sources of information** that an independent adviser may use when selecting the most suitable provider of an investment product include the following:

Factor	Source of information
Financial strength	Company reports, DTI returns, independent reports produced by specialist agencies
Product benefits	Product providers, independent publications, professional bodies
Fund performance	Product providers, independent publications, the Stock Exchange

3.14 Customers' understanding of risk

There is a **general obligation to disclose risks**, in accordance with the FSA's Principle 7 *Communications with clients* and Principle 9 *Customers: relationships of trust.*

One of the problems faced by advisers is that, if an investment performs less well than the client expected, there is a potential for a **complaint** against the adviser. This could arise if **risks** were not fully explained to the client, but it may also arise because the client has forgotten the fact that the risks have been explained.

An adviser must be fully satisfied that a client **understands** the nature of all risks associated with any transaction and explain the possibility of any future exposure to additional liability. This information must be given before recommending or entering into a transaction with a client. This applies especially to discretionary management of a client's assets.

Key Features Documents provide a way of explaining risks to clients.

There are also specific obligations to warn private customers of the risks of certain transactions, including **warrants and derivatives**, and **non-readily realisable investments**.

3.15 Excessive charges

As we have seen, FSA Principle 6 *Customers' interests* requires a firm to pay due regard to the interests of customers and to treat them fairly. Therefore charges to a private customer must not be **excessive**.

What is 'excessive'? The firm should consider:

    (a)   Charges on similar products in the market
    (b)   Whether charges could be an abuse of the customers' trust
    (c)   The extent to which charges are disclosed

3.16 Disclosure of charges and commission

There is an **obligation to disclose** to private customers:

    (a)   The basis or amount of charges
    (b)   Before business is transacted

For **packaged products** (remember: life policies other than pure protection policies, collective investment schemes and stakeholder pension schemes), the following must also be disclosed:

    (a)   Any remuneration payable to employer or agents
    (b)   Any remuneration or commission received by the firm

3.17 Inducements

FSA rules on **inducements** aim to ensure that firms' business arrangements do not conflict with its **duty to customers**, whom it must treat **fairly**. A firm should take reasonable steps to ensure that inducements are not offered, given, solicited or accepted by the firm itself, or by anyone acting on the firm's behalf, if this is likely to conflict with the firm's duty to customers.

Many firms will have explicit **policies** covering gifts which might be seen as inducements in certain circumstances.

Giving or receiving certain **indirect benefits** such as gifts, hospitality and promotional competition prizes is permitted.

Specified **reasonable indirect benefits** provided by **provider firms** to **independent intermediates** are permitted in the case of **joint marketing exercises** for **packaged products**.

These **reasonable indirect benefits** include:

    (a)   Generic product literature, if:

        (i)   The distribution cost is met by intermediaries
        (ii)   The intermediary's name is not more prominent than the provider firm's, and
        (iii)   The intermediary's broker fund is not promoted

    (b)   Freepost envelopes, if provided to all intermediaries

(c) Product specific literature, if:

    (i) The intermediary's broker fund is not advertised, or

    (ii) The intermediary's name is included, or

    (iii) The intermediary's name is only over-printed, and is less prominent than the provider's name

(d) Seminars, if open to all independent intermediaries

(e) Freephone links, if open to all independent intermediaries

(f) Technical services, such as quotations and projections

(g) Training facilities, if open to all independent intermediaries, including commercial travel and accommodation costs

3.18 Packaged products and 'soft commission'

Firms should not enter into the following types of **commission arrangements** for **packaged products** where commission must be disclosed.

(a) Commission on several transactions that is more than a single multiple of commission payable on a single transaction ('**volume overrides**')

(b) Commission in excess of that disclosed to the customer, unless due to higher contributions

(c) Arrangements to indemnify payment of commission where the recipient benefits if the commission becomes repayable

(d) Arrangements to pay commission other than to the seller firm, unless:

    (i) The firm has passed on the rights to commission, or

    (ii) Another firm has given advice to the customer, or

    (iii) The firm is a provider firm involved in a direct offer financial promotion involving an independent intermediary, who receives the commission

A **soft commission agreement** is an agreement which permits a firm to receive certain goods or services from another person in return for transacting designated investment business with or through that other person.

A firm must not deal through an intermediary under a **soft commission agreement** unless:

(a) There is a written agreement

(b) Best execution is achieved

(c) There is prior and periodic disclosure

(d) Goods or services provided are directly relevant to and assist the client

(e) When the firm acts as principal, commission must cover costs of execution and goods and services provided.

3.19 Treating customers fairly (TCF)

'**Treating customers fairly**' (**TCF**) is the name given to a project of the FSA which aims to ensure that firms meet the requirements of FSA **Principle for Business 6** to 'pay due regard to the interests of its customers and treat them fairly'.

Treating Customers Fairly is a key element in the FSA's retail agenda. The FSA wants retail markets for financial products and services to work more efficiently and effectively, and thereby to deliver through these markets a fair deal for consumers.

The FSA's retail agenda is built on four 'pillars':

- Capable and confident consumers
- Simple and understandable information for, and used by, consumers
- Well managed and adequately capitalised firms who treat their customers fairly, and
- Risk–based and proportionate regulation

The regulator's approach has been **not** to **define** precisely what constitutes treating customers fairly, but rather to **challenge** the senior management of firms to work this out for themselves, taking into account the particular types of business they undertake.

The FSA expects firms and their **senior management** to consider the implications of TCF for their business and to tackle any shortfalls which may be identified as a result. With the TCF project, the FSA hopes that senior management will embed TCF principles in their **corporate strategy**.

Based on the concept of the **product life cycle**, there are the following areas of focus.

(a) Product design (eg, literature can be tested on customers for understanding; complex products should be directed at appropriate groups of customers)

(b) Marketing practices (eg, financial promotions must be clear, fair and not misleading)

(c) The sales process (eg, does the process help to ensure that only products suitable for the customer are sold)

(d) Information and customer support after the point of sale (eg, do staff have access to the technical knowledge to answer customer's questions?)

(e) Complaint handling (eg, the firm should seek to understand the complainant's concern)

The **FSA** worked with more than 80 firms in 2004/05 looking at the systems and controls they have in place in a number of specific areas of their businesses. The FSA's supervisory work identified the following **specific issues** which could effect whether customers are treated fairly.

(a) Remuneration of sales staff, senior management and others (eg, a heavily commission-driven structure could create risks)

(b) Management of the interface between producer and distributor firms (eg, customers are better protected if distributors are supplied with good information)

(c) Taking TCF into account when firms consider strategic change (eg, some firms did not fully consider the impact on customers of a change of status on depolarisation)

(d) The role of management information in ensuring that customers are treated fairly (eg, regular reports to management on customer satisfaction and complaints trends)

Exercise: Treating customers fairly

For a financial product of which you have knowledge, consider if there could be instances where its sale might not involve treating customers fairly. Consider why and how this is occurring. Then consider how a firm might seek to ensure that such occurrences do not occur.

An example given by the FSA is that of sub-prime mortgages. The FSA reported that it knew of cases where a sub-prime mortgage product was sold even though the customer could have qualified for a prime product.

A **TCF review** by a firm should not be reviewed as an admission that customers are not being treated fairly by the firm. Instead, putting a positive or proactive interpretation on the process, it is an opportunity to find out where a firm already excels, and to identify areas in which improvements can be made.

PROFESSIONAL EDUCATION

4 Managing investments

4.1 Churning and switching

The following practices are prohibited when conducting investment business with or for a customer.

(a) For investments generally: **churning** – ie, dealing too frequently in the circumstances.

(b) For packaged products: **switching** between packaged products, **unless** the dealing or switching is in the client's best interest. Note that recommending the surrender of a life policy in order to switch into a new one could be against a client's interests because the surrender value could be relatively low compared with the expected maturity value, and there will also be charges on the new policy.

'**Churning**' refers to dealing or switching excessively, with the objective of increasing commissions earned. No definition of churning, for example in terms of the rate of dealing, is provided in the COB rules.

One of the major problems facing the industry has been accusations that clients have been recommended to cancel contracts in order to buy replacement products from the adviser's own provider (a form of **churning**). The client could suffer a substantial **financial loss** by cancelling a life assurance policy, especially if the policy is cancelled at an early stage.

An adviser who is recommending the surrender of a life policy should explain clearly the reasons for the recommendation and the effect on the policy and its benefits, and should keep careful record not only of the recommendations itself but of the reasons for it. There is a **general presumption** that existing life assurance policies should be allowed to continue.

4.2 Best execution

The requirement to carry out **best execution** mainly affects broker firms dealing directly in shares on behalf of customers, and is the requirement to obtain the **best price for a transaction of its type and size**. If an investor asks his broker to buy some shares, the broker must do so at the best price available at the time.

Exceptions to the rule are:

(a) Units in collective investment schemes
(b) Life policies

Intermediate customers may waive the right to receive best execution. They may wish to do this because obtaining stock at a particular time, for example when dealing in futures may be of more importance than the price.

Firms must also carry out **timely execution**, in other words they must deal as soon as is reasonably practicable.

Aggregation of deals may only be undertaken if:

(a) Each customer is not likely to be disadvantaged
(b) Each customer is informed orally or in writing of the possible disadvantage

There are rules which seek to ensure that customers are not disadvantaged by **personal dealing** carried out by employees of an FSA-regulated firm. The **firm** must seek to ensure that its duties to customers are not compromised.

4.3 Execution only

The term 'execution only' is a different thing from 'best execution', and it is important that the two terms are not confused. An adviser acts in an **execution only** capacity when he accepts the client's instructions to complete a transaction without requesting or receiving any advice. This is more likely to be the case in share dealing services, for which many brokers provide execution only services, than for products in life assurance and pensions.

An adviser providing an execution only service owes to the client a duty only to execute the transaction. This is when he can reasonably assume that the client is **not** relying on the adviser for advice or assessment of any transaction.

If an adviser is acting in an execution only capacity for a client the adviser must **keep adequate records** to make it clear that advice was neither given nor sought. This means that written and signed confirmation must be obtained from the client making it clear that the transaction was conducted without regard to any advice either having been given or offered.

Where a **product provider** sells on an execution only basis, the product provider should write to the client confirming the basis of the sale (ie that advice was neither sought nor given in respect of the transaction).

4.4 'Insistent customer' sales

A client may ask an adviser to effect a transaction which the adviser considers to be **unsuitable**. This may arise because the client does not agree with the adviser's recommendation. This situation has become known as an **'insistent customer' sale**. Extreme care needs to be taken that a full record is made of both the advice given and, if it can be established, the reason why the client is disregarding the advice. In these circumstances the rules relating to **execution only clients** should be used as a guide.

4.5 Limited advice

If a client asks for **limited advice** instead of a full financial review, then this is not treated as the same as 'execution only', since advice is still being given. The fact that limited advice was sought should be recorded in the fact find and should be confirmed in correspondence to the client.

The regulatory rules now provide for a level of '**basic advice**' to be provided on **stakeholder products**, enabling less qualified staff to sell such products. This is explained in Chapter 13.

4.6 Client assets

COB rules on **client assets** are designed to resolve the question: How do we protect clients if firms go insolvent? There are the following ways of providing such protection:

(a)   Putting assets into trust
(b)   Segregation of assets
(c)   Ensuring adequacy of the firm's resources
(d)   Procedures to reconcile assets held

The FSA's **Principle 10** *Clients' assets* states that a firm must arrange adequate protection for clients' assets for which it is responsible.

4.7 Client money rules

Client money rules cover money which the firm looks after and which is not its own. (Intermediate customers and market counterparties may **opt out** of these rules). The FSA generally requires a firm to place **client money** in a **client bank account** with an **approved bank**.

Key concepts:

(a)   **Segregation** of money into separate client accounts: a firm must normally hold client money separate from the firm's money.

(b)   **Trust** arrangements: for example, the bank at which a client account is held should confirm in writing that money in the client account is legally owned by the firm, but that the firm is not the beneficial owner of the money.

All **interest payments** must go to the client, unless the firm has notified the customer that different arrangements will apply.

Many Independent Financial Advisers (IFAs) have **no authority to handle client money**. In that case, they do not need to maintain client money accounts and they should ensure that the client makes cheques payable direct to the product provider.

5 Product disclosure and cancellation rights

5.1 Clear and fair communication

Note firstly the principle of clear and fair communication: **'When a firm communicates information to a customer, the firm must take reasonable steps to communicate in a way which is clear, fair and not misleading.'**

This important rule restates one of the FSA Principles for Business (Principle 7). Restating the Principle in COB enables a private customer to bring an action for damages under **FSMA 2000 Section 150** to recover a **loss** resulting from a **breach of the rule** by a firm.

5.2 Product disclosure rules

Chapter 6 of the COB rules, on **product disclosure and the customer's right to cancel or withdraw**, was closely modelled on the old Personal Investment Authority (PIA) rules.

5.3 Packaged products and ISA disclosure

Principle 7 *Communications with clients* states that due regard must be paid to the information needs of customers. The disclosure rules on packaged products and ISAs are intended to enable the **customer** to make a **comparative analysis** of **different packaged products** and Individual Savings Accounts (ISAs).

Note the emphasis on the **customers** themselves making comparisons between products, in an environment in which the general level of charges is being driven down in order to give better value to customers.

There are special disclosure rules covering:

- Packaged products – **Key Features** document required
- Cash deposit ISAs – **information document** required
- Variations on life policies
- Income withdrawals from pension schemes

5.4 Key Features

Key Features documents:

(a)   May be in electronic form only, if the firm conducts the business solely through electronic media

(b)   Must be produced to **at least the same quality** as associated sales and marketing material

(c)   Must be separated from other material, except for collective investment schemes or SHPs where it may be incorporated within other material if given due prominence

(d)   Must comply with the COB rules in content and format

5.5 The rationale of Key Features documents

A consumer review carried out by the FSA found that 48% of customers recalled being given a Key Features document (KFD), and only 8% had actually read the document – hence the perception that the Key Features requirement should be reviewed. Although originally designed to facilitate comparison between products of different providers, the purpose of KFDs has become more like that of summarising features of a particular product in easily readable form.

5.6 Stakeholder pension schemes: product disclosure

For **stakeholder pension plans (SHPs)**, the Key Features Document must be provided before a private customer completes the application, except where the SHP is sold on the personal recommendation of another firm.

The FSA has developed **decision trees** to help customers make decisions on stakeholder and other pensions. Such trees shift the emphasis towards allowing customers to make more informed choices. If the adviser takes a private customer through the decision tree process **by telephone**, he must check that the customer has a decision tree in front of him.

5.7 Key Features: packaged products

A product provider must provide a Key Features document (KFD), in hard copy or electronic format, for each of its **packaged products**.

- The document must be produced to the same standard as the provider's marketing material.
- The provider or IFA must give the KFD to a private customer before the application form is completed.

The rules are detailed. The Table below summarises required contents of **Key Features documents** for **packaged products**.

Contents of Key features: Packaged products

Title

'Key features of the (name of life policy/scheme/stakeholder pension scheme)'

Nature of policy/scheme

Prescribed headings:

- 'Its aims'
- 'Your commitment' *or* 'Your investment'
- 'Risk factors', giving a brief description

Description of the policy or scheme

The **description** is set out in the form of **questions and answers**.

In the case of stakeholder pension schemes (SHPs), the following should appear beneath or within the description.

PROFESSIONAL EDUCATION

'There is an annual *charge* of [y]% of the value of the funds you accumulate. If your fund is valued at £500 throughout the year, this means we deduct [£500 × y/100] that year. If your fund is valued at £7,500 throughout the year, we will deduct [£7,500 × y/100] that year.'

Tables and deductions summaries: life policies and CISs

For **life policies** of five years or more with a surrender value, a table called **The early years** is provided by the FSA, and figures showing the 'effect of deductions to date' and 'what you might get back' for the first five years of the life policy should be included.

The later years table covers similar data for the tenth and each subsequent fifth year of the policy.

The following statements must appear beneath the tables.

'What are the deductions for?'

'The deductions include [the cost of life cover, sickness benefits,] [commissions/ remuneration,] expenses, charges, any surrender penalties and other adjustments'.

'The last line in the table shows that over the full term of the policy the effect of the total deductions could amount to £x'.

And then either:

'Putting it another way, leaving out the cost of life cover (and sickness benefits) this would have the same effect as bringing investment growth from x% a year down to y% a year'

or:

'Putting it another way, if the growth rate were to be x%, which is no way guaranteed, this would have the effect of reducing it to y% a year'.

For **collective investment schemes (CISs)**, a table on *'How will charges and expenses affect my investment?'* is included, with the following statements underneath.

'The last line in the table shows that over [n] years the effect of the total charges and expenses could amount to £x';

'Putting it another way, if the growth rate were to be (x)%, which is in no way guaranteed, this would have the effect of reducing it to (y)% a year';

'Putting it another way, this would have the same effect as bringing investment growth from (x)% a year down to (y)% a year'.

Commission and remuneration

For SHPs, life policies and Collective Investment Schemes (CISs), information such as the following (for life policies), or alternative information on the cash value of commission must be provided.

'How much will the advice cost?'

'Your adviser will give you details about the cost. The amount will depend on the size of the premium and the length of the policy term. It will be paid for out of the deductions (or charges, if more appropriate)'

Further information

The following **further information** must be included in the key features.

(a) For life policies:

  (i) A clear indication, in one place, of the nature and amount or rate of any charges or expenses borne by the private customer, explaining any effect of reducing the investment

  (ii) 'Information for policy holders' as specified in the European **Third Life Directive**, including:

   (1) Name, state and address of the firm

   (2) Information about the commitment to the policy, including benefits, options, the term, termination methods, premium payments, surrender and paid-up values, unit definitions, cancellation rights, tax arrangements, complaints procedures and applicable law

   (3) Details of compensation arrangements

(b) For **CISs**, explanation of how to obtain further information about the scheme

(c) For **regulated CISs**, including those in PEPs/ISAs:

  (i) Information on where prices and other information can be found
  (ii) Names and addresses of the scheme manager and trustees, if any
  (iii) Explanation of cancellation and withdrawal rights
  (iv) Details of compensation arrangements
  (v) Summary of income tax and capital gains tax effects
  (vi) Details of where and how uninvested money will be held

(d) For **non-cash ISAs**, in addition to (a), (b) and (c):

  (i) Description of the nature of services provided for the private customer
  (ii) Comparisons with **CAT standards**, if it is stated that the ISA components comply with them
  (iii) A statement that ISAs' favourable tax treatment may not be maintained
  (iv) How and when statements will be sent
  (v) Termination of transfer arrangements
  (vi) Explanation of mini and maxi ISAs

(e) For stakeholder pension schemes:

  (i) Explanation of complaints arrangements
  (ii) Details of any compensation arrangements

Projections

Projections for life policies, collective investment schemes (CISs) and stakeholder pension schemes must comply with specific COB rules. The rates of return which must be used include standardised lower rates, intermediate rates and higher rates as follows.

Lower rate	*Intermediate rate*	*Higher rate*	
Life policies and CISs	4%	6%	8%
Pensions, ISAs, PEPs, friendly society schemes	5%	7%	9%

Projections must be:

(a) Clear, fair and not misleading
(b) Presented on the basis of uniform and consistent rates of return and methods of calculation

5.8 Rights of cancellation and withdrawal

Rights of **cancellation** and **withdrawal** by the consumer apply to various kinds of contract.

Where there is a right to cancel, the **product provider** must give written notice of this to the customer before the agreement is concluded **and** after it has been concluded.

The summary Table shown **on the next page** is based on the detailed Table from COB 6.7.15 in the FSA Handbook.

Note that:

- 'ICVC' refers to Investment Companies with Variable Capital (*remember:* this is the alternative term for Open Ended Investment Companies).

- An **Appropriate Personal Pension (APP)** is one which can receive contributions from contracting out of the State Second Pension (S2P).

- A **distance contract** is a contract marketed and concluded without the parties being physical present together – for example, by telephone or Internet.

5.9 Pre-sale notice

An **example of a pre-sale notice** is as follows. (The pre-sale notice below summarises information in the **post-sale cancellation notice**. The post-sale cancellation notice would be accompanied by a slip or form, or electronic equivalent, enabling the customer to exercise the right to cancel.)

'You will be able to cancel your [investment]/[contract] during a two-week period after concluding the agreement and receive a refund [in full/less a deduction for shortfall to reflect any fall in the markets in the interim]. You will be told of this right in more detail (including when it begins and ends, and how to exercise it) in documents that we will send you at the relevant time.'

5.10 Post-sale right to cancel

Where there is a **post-sale right to cancel**, the customer's money is invested throughout the period of reflection (7, 14 or 30 days, depending on the product), during which time the customer may suffer loss of capital ('**shortfall**') due to adverse market movements.

Except for distance contracts and cash deposit ISAs, the post-sale cancellation notice must be sent (by post or electronically):

- Within 8 days of concluding the contract (single payment pension contract, unit trusts, ICVCs/OEICs to which a shortfall applies)

- Within 14 days of concluding the contract (other investments)

If a firm does not give to a **retail customer** information about his cancellation rights, the contract remains cancellable and the retail customer will be not liable for any shortfall.

A post-sale information notice giving full details of the investment and of the commission payable to the adviser normally accompanies the cancellation notice.

Cancellable investment agreements			
	Post-sale right to cancel?	Pre-sale right to withdraw?	Maximum period of reflection
A. Contracts where the right arises regardless of means of sale.			
Appropriate personal pension (APP)	Yes [4]	No	30 days
Cash deposit ISA	Yes [4]	No	14 days
Life policy	Yes [1,4]	No [1]	30 days
Personal pension contract	Yes [1,4]	No [1]	30 days
Stakeholder pension scheme (SHP)	Yes [1,4]	No [1]	30 days
Certain variations of existing life policies, pension contracts and SHPs	Yes [1,4]	No [1]	30 days
B. Agreements where the right arises only if advice is given or if sold by distance contract.			
Unit trusts or OEICs/ICVCs (within an ISA or PEP):			
(1) Sold by distance contract	No	No	
(2) Sold otherwise, with advice	Yes [3]	No [3]	14 days
Other ISAs or PEPs:			
(1) Sold by distance contract	Yes [4]	No	14 days
(2) Sold otherwise, with advice	No	Yes [2]	7 days
Unit trusts or OEICs/ICVCs (outside an ISA or PEP):			
(1) Sold by distance contract	No	No	
(2) Sold otherwise, with advice	Yes	No	14 days

Notes:

1. For a pension annuity or pension transfer (and a relevant variation), the firm can, in certain circumstances, choose to provide the right to cancel through a pre-sale right to withdraw, even where there is no right to cancel.

2. There is no right to withdraw for a second ISA, or (for non-packaged product ISAs or PEPs) where the firm has declared that no such rights apply.

3. For unit trusts and OEICs within an ISA or PEP, the firm can choose to offer a 7-day pre-sale right to withdraw instead of a post-sale right to cancel.

4. There is no post-sale right to cancel for a distance contract where:

    (a) Price fluctuations outside the firm's control may occur during the cancellation period,
    (b) The contract has been fully completed, at the customer's express request, or
    (c) The contract is a successive operation, and there was an initial service agreement in place

BPP
PROFESSIONAL EDUCATION

5.11 Post-sale confirmation: life policies

Post-sale confirmation disclosing commission and its effects must be sent as soon as possible and no later than any post-sale notice under cancellation rules, in the case of **life policies**.

5.12 With-profit guides

Section 6.9 of the COB covers **with-profits guides**, whose purpose is explained in the following introductory text to such guides as prescribed by the FSA.

'All insurance companies, and the larger friendly societies, which market with-profits policies in the United Kingdom, are required to make available a guide containing information about the company or society and its with-profits fund. This is because the benefits under such polices depend in part, and sometimes to a considerable extent, on bonus additions which are made by the company or the society from time to time and which cannot be known in advance. It is therefore important that potential policyholders and their advisers should have access to information about the most important factors influencing such bonuses.'

'However, investors are advised that, in comparing a policy marketed by one company or society with other policies, it is unwise to place too much importance on any one factor. An over all view of all relevant elements will usually give a more realistic comparison: in particular, an examination of the history of a fund over a period of years will usually give a fuller picture than can be obtained from looking at the figures for just one year'.

Key chapter points

- The FSA Conduct of Business rules apply to authorised firms in respect of advising on and dealing in investments. Customers cannot sign away their COB rights, and they may sue for rule breaches if they suffer a loss.

- Different levels of protection are given to customers of different types, with private customers having the highest level of protection. An execution-only customer is one who has confirmed that he or she does not wish to receive advice.

- The polarisation rule has meant that an adviser must either be independent – offering recommendations for all products – or a representative dealing only in the products of a single company or group.

- Under 'depolarisation', which was completed by 1 June 2005, independent advisers may offer advice covering the whole market, or alternatively a market sector. Additionally, they must give the option of payment by fee. There is a new 'middle ground' of distributors or 'multi-ties', which are firms entering into agreements with two or more providers to sell their products. Appointed representatives (ARs) will continue to have a single principal unless they are pure introducers.

- An adviser must know the customer (through fact-finding) and must only recommend products that are suitable for the customer. The adviser must act in the customer's interests. There is a general obligation to disclose risks to the customer.

- Charges must not be excessive and must be disclosed to the client.

- Customers must be treated fairly. Excessively frequent dealing in investments (churning) is prohibited, and switching of packaged products is only permitted if it is in the client's best interests.

- Communications to the customer must be clear, fair and not misleading. Key features and other information documents are intended to help consumers make comparisons between different products.

- Customers have cancellation and withdrawal rights for some forms of investment. FSA rules set down maximum time limits for the 'cooling off' period allowed.

Chapter Quiz

1   What are the three main classifications of client or customer? .... (see para 2.1)

2   How does someone qualify as an 'expert private customer'? .... (2.1)

3   Explain what was meant by polarisation. .... (3.1)

4   Outline the main changes introduced in 2005 with 'depolarisation'. .... (3.3-3.6)

5   What is the definition of a 'packaged product'? .... (3.11)

6   Which FSA Principle for Business in particular is served by the rules on excessive charges?........................ (3.15)

7   Distinguish between 'churning' and 'switching'. .... (4.1)

8   What is the meaning of 'execution only'? .... (4.3)

9   What is the effect on customer's rights of re-stating one of the FSA's Principles for Business in the Conduct of Business rules? .... (5.1)

10 Which particular FSA Principle for Business is served by the product disclosure rules? .... (5.3)

chapter

13

Other aspects of financial services regulation

1 Financial promotions

1.1 Introduction

Financial promotion was a new concept when it was introduced under the new (post-November 2001) FSA regime. The concept of financial promotion is designed to encompass more fully a wider range of media, including the Internet, than the old Financial Services Act 1986 regime, which focused on **investment advertisements** and **unsolicited calls ('cold calling')**. The new rules also cover **solicited calls**.

A **financial promotion** is an invitation or inducement to engage in investment activity communicated in the course of business. (FSMA 2000, s21 (1))

The rules governing financial promotion:

(a)   Are directed at **regulated activities**, although they only affect deposits and general insurance to some extent

(b)   Are **media-neutral**, ie applying to all media of communication, including the Internet

Financial promotions may be communicated in:

(a)   Product brochures

(b)   General advertising (eg newspapers, television, websites)

    (c)   Mailshots (including by fax or email)

    (d)   Telemarketing, eg from call centres

    (e)   Written correspondence, telephone calls and face to face discussions with customers

    (f)   Sales aids

    (g)   Presentations

    (h)   Tip sheets (tipping shares or investments)

    (i)   Other publications containing non-personal recommendations

Section 21 of FSMA 2000 contains a **general prohibition on financial promotion**, except where they are issued or approved by an **authorised person** (eg a firm).

1.2 Exemptions

The following are **exempt** from the detailed promotion rules, but regulated firms must still take steps to ensure that such communications are **clear, fair and not misleading.**

Exemptions:

    (a)   Financial promotions to market counterparties (such as another firm, or a government body) and intermediate (ie non-private) customers

    (b)   One-off non-real time or solicited real-time communications (see below)

    (c)   Short form advertisements giving brief facts about a firm or product

    (d)   Personal quotations or illustrations

    (e)   Communications related to a takeover

Exemptions from the financial promotion and other COB rules also cover a number of types of promotions issued by an unauthorised person, including: generic promotions (eg for Investment Trusts generally), one-off communications and communications to 'sophisticated investors' and high net worth individuals in respect of unlisted securities.

1.3 Past performance details

If **past performance** is detailed in a financial promotion:

    (a)   Suitable text for the target audience must be shown, and

    (b)   A **warning** must be given that past performance will not necessarily be repeated

    (c)   A relevant and sufficient period must be covered

    (d)   Past data should not suggest that it constitutes a **projection**

For **packaged products**:

    (a)   The past performance data must cover the previous **five years**, or the whole period if the product has been offered for less than this.

    (b)   Comparative performance data should be stated:

        (i)   On an offer to bid basis, or

        (ii)   On an offer to offer, or offer to bid basis for comparisons with an index or movements in prices of units, or

        (iii)   On a single pricing basis, with allowance for charges

1.4 Real-time and non-real time financial promotions

COB distinguishes the following.

(a)   A **real time financial promotion** is communicated in an interactive dialogue.

*Example*s: personal visit, telephone call.

(b)   A **non-real time financial promotion** is non-interactive. The recipient of the promotion is not required to respond to it immediately.

Examples: newspapers, television.

Non-real time financial promotions must be **checked and approved** by the firm before they are used. The firm must keep a record of who checked it. Details must be given of:

(a)   The **firm**
(b)   An **address**, or a **contact point** from which the address can be obtained

1.5 Specific non-real time promotions

A specific non-real time promotion is one which promotes a particular investment or service, and must include details of:

(a)   The **nature of the investment or service**
(b)   The **commitment** required
(c)   The **risks** involved
(d)   The **service provider** (if not the firm approving the promotion)

Exercise: Financial promotions

Identify which of the following could communicate a financial promotion, and if so identify each as 'real time' or 'non-real time'.

(1)   Solicited phone call
(2)   Unsolicited telephone call
(3)   Internet 'chat' facility
(4)   A website showing an email address for contact

Solution

(1), (2) and (3) are 'real time'. (4) is non-real time: response is not required immediately.

1.6 Real-time financial promotions

The firm must try to ensure that an individual making a **real-time financial promotion** on the firm's behalf:

(a)   Does not make **untrue** claims

(b)   Identifies himself, the firm and the purpose of the financial promotion

(c)   If the time and form of communication were not agreed:

(i)   Checks that the recipient wishes to proceed (stopping, if not)
(ii)   Respects the recipient's wishes to end communication

(d)   Provides a contact point to a client with an appointment

(e)   Does not communicate at **unsocial hours** (before 9.00am or after 9.00pm, and all day Sunday unless agreed otherwise

(f)   Does not use an unlisted telephone number, unless agreed

1.7 Direct offer financial promotions

A **direct offer financial promotion** is a non-real-time financial promotion offering or inviting someone to enter into an agreement which specifies the manner of response or includes a form in which any response is to be made (for example by providing a tear-off slip).

A direct offer financial promotion must contain:

(a)   Sufficient information to enable an informed assessment of the investment or service

(b)   A statement that the firm is FSA-authorised

(c)   A statement that anyone with doubts about the suitability of the product should seek advice from the firm, or from an independent financial adviser if the firm does not offer advice

(d)   The full name of the person offering the investment or service

(e)   Details of charges or expenses

(f)   Commission or remuneration to third parties

1.8 Unsolicited real-time financial promotions

There are restrictions on uninvited calls, visits or interactive dialogue - often called **cold calling**. Financial promotion by such methods is only permissible in certain circumstances, including:

(a)   For recipients with an established existing customer relationship with the firm, where such unsolicited promotions are envisaged by the recipient

(b)   For investments not involving high volatility funds

(c)   In cases where general exemptions from financial promotions by regulated firms apply (see above)

In the early stages of an unsolicited telephone call, a prospective client must be offered an **opportunity to terminate** the call.

1.9 Financial promotions and the Internet

As already mentioned, the FSA adopts a **media-neutral approach**, to cover all media whether electronic or not, in its rules. Accordingly, Internet communications and moving images are governed by similar provisions to print-based media.

Specific issues affecting Internet **'e-commerce'** communications especially are as follows.

- Access to **key features** and **terms and conditions** is important. This could be provided by a clear hypertext link, not hidden in the body of the text. Perhaps a better approach would be to ensure that applicants must scroll through the relevant information.

- Firms are encouraged to include a hyperlink to the FSA's website **www.fsa.gov.uk**, which includes pages of specific relevance to consumers.

The FSA **Electronic Commerce Directive** (ECO within the FSA Handbook) also contains provisions for on-line business, including the following.

(a) **Basic information** – the firm's name, geographically-based address, email address and FSA registered number – must be easily accessible

(b) Information on **services** provided, and **how to place an order**, must be clear

(c) There must be ways for customers to **identify and correct input errors** before they place an order

(d) Orders must be **acknowledged** without delay, even if they are not accepted

The Electronic Commerce Directive removes restrictions on the international **cross-border** provision of services by electronic means, by introducing a 'country of origin' approach to regulation. This means that generally the regulatory requirements that apply in a firm's 'country of origin' will apply to any cross-border services that it provides electronically.

2 Money laundering and proceeds of crime

2.1 Introduction

Money laundering is the term given to attempts to make the proceeds of crime appear respectable by converting money obtained illegally into apparently legitimate funds.

The following three aspects have been identified in major money laundering operations:

- **Placement** of cash, for example through bank or building society deposit accounts, collective funds or life insurance policies

- **Layering**, which refers to the creation of a series of transactions designed to obscure the origins of the criminally obtained funds. There may be use of false names or fictitious transactions. The sheer complexity of the transactions can play a part in concealing the origin of the funds.

- **Integration** is the final process of converting the laundered money into an apparently legitimate portfolio of investments or what appears to be income from a legitimate business.

There is legislation to help in the prevention and detection of money laundering. The UK is a member of the **Financial Action Task Force** (FATF). The FSA is responsible for ensuring that authorised firms have controls that limit opportunities for money laundering.

The FSA has moved away from providing detailed rules on money laundering and the Money Laundering Sourcebook is being removed from the FSA Handbook, with effect from 31 August 2006.

A **Third Money Laundering Directive** of the European Union came into force in December 2005 and will therefore need to be implemented by December 2007. The third directive will extend EU anti-money laundering provisions to any financial transaction which could be linked to terrorism.

2.2 Identity checks and records

Anyone opening an account with a UK financial institution will be aware that steps are taken to check on their identity, to help prevent money laundering. An adviser must ensure the following to comply with the **Money Laundering Regulations 2003**, which came into force on 1 March 2004 (replacing the earlier 1993 regulations).

(a) **New clients must be required to prove their identity**. This is necessary when forming any business relationship, or when dealing with one-off transactions exceeding 15,000 euros or separate transactions that appear to be linked and in total exceed 15,000 euros (approximately £10,500).

No check is required if funds come from an EU bank or building society account in the applicant's name. Checks are also not required if the adviser is satisfied that:

(i)   Adequate checks have already been made

(ii)   The money is going into a pension scheme with neither surrender value nor facility for proceeds to be used as security for a loan

(iii)   Money is being used for an insurance policy where the single premium is not more than 2,500 euros (approximately £1,700) or the regular premium is not more than 1,000 euros (approximately £700) per year

(b)   **Adequate records must be kept**. Records must show evidence of a client's identity and details of transactions enacted by that person, and must be kept for **five years** after the business relationship ends.

(c)   **Internal reporting procedures must be maintained**. One person must be nominated to receive from staff any reports involving suspicions regarding money laundering activities, and that person must be able to investigate such reports and, where appropriate, inform and co-operate with the police.

There are requirements under the **Joint Money Laundering Steering Group's Guidance Notes** aimed at investment and insurance business. (The forms of identity required may be reviewed in the near future. The JMLSG concurs with an FSA Working Group in the view that anti-money laundering checks should be carried out on a risk-sensitive basis which recognises that most customers are not money launderers.)

The main requirements are outlined below.

(a)   **New accounts for new clients**.

(i)   Where possible, interview account holders personally

(ii)   Obtain **identification** documents (eg passport or driving licence), verify **address** (eg from utility bill, telephone directory or electoral register) and obtain date of birth

(b)   **Professional client accounts**. Advisers must be able to identify persons who open client accounts unless those persons are one of a small number of very specific exceptions such as an EU financial institution.

(c)   **Corporate client accounts**. Advisers must obtain the certificate of incorporation and a directors' resolution to open an account, and make a search at Companies House.

2.3 Financial exclusion

The FSA has issued guidance on the risks of **financial exclusion** of those without the standard form of evidence of their identity. If a person does not have a passport or driving licence, and does not have their name on utility bills, a firm may accept a letter from someone in a position of responsibility who knows the client to confirm the client's identity and permanent address, if they have one.

2.4 Money Laundering Reporting Officer

Every FSA-authorised firm must appoint a senior employee as the firm's **Money Laundering Reporting Officer (MLRO)** with authority to enforce compliance with money laundering regulations.

2.5 FSA Handbook

In a move towards more **principles-based regulation**, the FSA has removed detailed rules on money laundering from its Handbook, with the deletion of the Money Laundering Sourcebook from **31 August 2006**. The ML Sourcebook

contains, for example, a requirement that training must be carried out at least every 24 months for staff involved in transactions that could involve money laundering.

Money laundering provisions in the FSA Handbook are to be found in the Handbook section called **Senior Management Arrangements, Systems and Controls (SYSC)**.

A firm must take reasonable care to establish and maintain effective **systems and controls** for compliance with applicable requirements and standards under the regulatory system and for countering the **risk** that the firm might be used to further **financial crime**.

Firms must ensure that the systems and controls include:

- **Appropriate** anti-money laundering training for its employees
- Reports by the firm's **Money Laundering Reporting Officer (MLRO)** to senior management on the operation and effectiveness of the systems and controls, at least annually

2.6 Penalties

Note the following criminal **penalties** in relation to money laundering and its prevention.

(a) 14 years imprisonment, for knowingly assisting in the laundering of criminal funds

(b) 5 years imprisonment, for failure to report knowledge or the suspicion of money laundering

(c) 5 years imprisonment for 'tipping off' a suspected launderer. In this context, note that suspicions must be reported to the firm's **Money Laundering Reporting Officer**, who will decide whether to report to the **National Criminal Intelligence Service (NCIS)**. The suspected launderer must not be alerted.

2.7 Proceeds of Crime Act 2002

The **Proceeds of Crime Act 2002** extends provisions about money laundering and crime proceeds in ways that can affect regulated financial firms.

Sections 327-329 of the Proceeds of Crime Act 2002 make the following criminal offences:

- **Concealing**: to conceal, disguise, convert or transfer **criminal property** or to remove such property from the UK
- **Acquiring and using**: to acquire, use or possess criminal property
- **Arranging** – see below

It is a criminal offence for anyone to be involved in **arrangements** that they know or suspect would facilitate (in any way) **someone else** in acquiring, retaining, using or controlling the **proceeds of crime** generally. This is a wide-ranging provision, and so financial advisers should be careful that they do not fall foul of the law.

As stated earlier, it is a criminal offence under the Act for anyone working in a regulated financial firm not to report any dealing that they suspect, or ought to suspect, involves the proceeds of crime. The report should be made to the firm's **Money Laundering Reporting Officer**, who must report appropriate cases to the **NCIS**.

In most cases this will be after the transaction has taken place. Where the firm has advance notice of the transaction, it is protected against an allegation of '**assistance**' if it gets consent, or 'deemed' consent, from NCIS before it carries out the transaction.

It is a criminal offence for anyone to do or say anything that might '**tip-off**' someone else that they are under suspicion of acquiring, retaining, using or controlling proceeds of crime. That applies whether or not any report has been made to NCIS.

This means that a financial firm:

(a)   Must not, at the time, tell a customer that a transaction is being delayed because a report has been made under the Proceeds of Crime Act, and

(b)   Must not later (unless the NCIS agrees) tell a customer that a transaction was delayed because a report had been made under the Proceeds of Crime Act

2.8 Assets Recovery Agency (ARA)

The **Assets Recovery Agency (ARA)** was set up under the Proceeds of Crime Act 2002 in order to confiscate the proceeds of crime from criminals.

The ARA can obtain a court order giving them the power to sell a defendant's assets.

The ARA has wide powers to obtain financial information. The Agency could, for example, require trustees or managers of pension schemes to pay to the Agency the value of pension rights. The ARA's powers will override any scheme rules prohibiting the surrender or commutation of a pension. The member would lose rights under the scheme, following the payment to the ARA.

The ARA also has powers to **tax** gains from criminal conduct, taking over the function of the HMRC in respect of capital gains tax, corporation tax, national insurance contributions and inheritance tax in the cases involved.

2.9 The European Union Savings Directive

Agreement was reached during 2003 on the **European Savings Directive.** This Directive requires EU member states to exchange information automatically on the financial affairs of residents of other EU countries, or to levy a withholding tax. These measures are designed to prevent individuals from illegally concealing investments and savings from the proper legal authorities.

The European Savings Directive will affect EU citizens who hold investments offshore within the EU, or in Switzerland, a country that remains outside the EU and has been well known for having a banking system offering high levels of secrecy to account holders.

Two different mechanisms came into effect on 1 July 2005:

●   For most EU countries, including the UK, there is **automatic exchange of information** between their respective tax authorities.

●   Switzerland together with the three EU members Belgium, Luxembourg and Austria have instead introduced a **withholding tax** on cross-border interest payments via banks and paying agents responsible for crediting interest. The tax retained will increase in steps from 15% in 2005 to 20% in 2008 and 35% in 2011.

The new rules do not cover interest payments originating outside the EU and Switzerland, and they cover individuals but not **legal entities**.

The Directive covers bank accounts, interest bearing investments including investment funds whose assets are made up of at least 40% of bonds, money market instruments, government securities or corporate debt. Investments that pay a dividend or capital gains, such as shares, are currently exempt.

It would be legitimate for a person to neutralise the effects of the Directive by selecting **managers** to administer investments through an offshore company or trust, for example in conjunction with a tax exempt life wrapper to hold assets on a personalised basis.

3 Complaints and compensation

3.1 Grounds for complaint

There are various reasons why a client may complain to a **firm**. Not all of such reasons are **grounds for a complaint**. For example, poor investment performance alone is not normally grounds for a complaint.

Complaints may typically arise where:

- A firm makes excessive or unexpected charges
- A firm does not draw attention to a particularly strict condition in a contract
- A firm does not give adequate notice to a client about changes to a contract
- A client loses money because of a firm's slow administration
- A firm does not give adequate warning about risks of a product

Unresolved **complaints against the FSA** itself are investigated by an independent **Complaints Commissioner**.

3.2 Complaints procedures

FSA rules require that firms have effective **written complaints handling procedures**, which must cover the handling of any expression of dissatisfaction – whether oral or written, and whether justified or not.

- Availability of the procedures must be referred to in writing at the point of sale. The firm must display, in all branches or offices where customers have access, a notice stating that the **Financial Ombudsman Service (FOS)** covers the firm.

- A copy of the procedures must be provided to a complainant on request, or when a complaint is received

The **person** in the firm investigating a complaint must be:

- Competent
- Uninvolved
- With authority to settle the complaint

All of a firms' employees should be made aware of the firm's **internal complaints handling procedures,** which must cover:

- Receiving complaints
- Responding to complaints
- The appropriate investigation of complaints
- Notifying complainants of their right to go to the **FOS** where relevant

Complaints made to a regulated firm must be investigated by a **designated complaints handler**.

3.3 Complaint handling timescales

A complaint about an adviser should be directed at his or her firm, in the first instance.

(a) Complaints must be acknowledged, with a copy of the firm's internal complaints procedures and details of who will handle the complaint, within **five business days** (unless the complaint is resolved by the end of the next business day after receipt).

(b) By **four weeks** after receipt of the complaint, the firm should send a **final response** or a **holding response**. Any final response should include a copy of a leaflet about the FOS, and should cover:

- Summaries of the complaint and the investigation
- Details of any offer made and any time limit applying to the offer

- Information about the client's FOS rights

(c) By the end of **eight weeks**, the firm must have sent a **final response**, or a letter (ie, a '**further holding response**') explaining:

- Why a final response still cannot be given
- When such a response is likely
- The fact that the complainant may go to the FOS if dissatisfied with the delay

A **final response** is a response from the firm which either:

(a) Accepts the complaint and where appropriate offers redress or offers without accepting the complaint, or

(b) Rejects the complaint and gives reasons for doing so, and contains information about the right to refer the complaint to the FOS.

The **final response** 'starts the clock' in respect of the six month limitation period on the complainant taking the matter to the FOS.

Note that a '**closed complaint**' – one for which a **final response** has been issued – is not the same as a resolved complaint.

3.4 Records and reports

Records must be kept of all complaints for **three years** from the date of receipt, including:

(a) The name of the complainant
(b) The substance of the complaint
(c) Correspondence

Reports must be made to the FSA on a semi-annual (twice yearly) basis, detailing:

(a) The total number of complaints received

(b) The number of complaints settled within:

(i) Four weeks
(ii) Eight weeks

(c) The number of complaints outstanding

There must be a **complaints log** – even if there are no complaints!

3.5 Referral to FOS

The **Financial Ombudsman Service** has a responsibility to assist in resolving disputes between private customers and financial firms.

The following complainants are eligible to **refer a complaint to the FOS** if the complaint is not resolved after eight weeks:

- Private individuals
- Businesses with turnover < £1 million
- Charities with income < £1 million
- Trusts with net asset value < £1 million

The FOS does not cover **intermediate customers** or **market counterparties.**

The FOS is independent of government and financial firms and is required to take into account such matters as are 'fair and reasonable in all the circumstances'.

The rules which the FOS operates under mean that, except in certain exceptional circumstances, the FOS cannot deal with complaints made to the firm where:

- More than **six years** have passed **since the event** complained about, **and**

- More than **three years** since the person became aware of or could reasonably be expected to have become **aware** of the problem

The awards aim to restore the position customers could have been in if things had not gone wrong.

The Ombudsman may also (if appropriate) award **compensation** for suffering, damage to reputation, distress and inconvenience.

The **monetary award** that the FOS can make is subject to a maximum of:

- **£100,000**
- *Plus* reasonable interest
- *Plus* the complainant's costs (which will apply only unusually)

The FOS may **recommend** that a firm supplements the award with a further payment, if it considers more than £100,000 is required as fair compensation.

If the complainant accepts the FOS decision, it is **binding** on the respondent **firm**.

A customer who remains dissatisfied, even after the FOS has taken up the case, has the option of pursuing the matter through the **Courts**.

3.6 Compensation

What happens if a client loses money as a result of a financial services firm becoming unable to meet its claims under its contracts with clients?

There is a single compensation scheme for investors, known as the **Financial Services Compensation Scheme (FSCS)**, which was set up under Section 212 of FSMA 2000. The FSCS consolidated compensation schemes that operated previously into a single combined scheme.

This scheme is the final 'safety net' for eligible claimants of failed authorised UK firms. Private customers, except larger companies and partnerships, can claim.

The scheme comprises four sub-schemes. The compensation limits for these are as under previous arrangements except in the case of deposits, for which the limits are increased.

3.7 FSCS compensation limits

If it decides that the firm is unable to meet the claims against it, the FSCS can award compensation to each investor up to the following limits.

(a) **Insolvency of investment business firm** – 100% of the first £30,000; 90% of the next £20,000, ie £48,000 maximum (as formerly under the Investors Compensation Scheme)

(b) **Insurance company default** – compensation of at least 90% of the policy value for long-term insurance contracts. For general insurance contracts: 100% of first £2,000 and 90% of remainder of the claim, or 100% of the claim in full if subject to compulsory liability insurance (compensation formerly available through Policyholders Protection Board)

(c) **Loss of deposits following default by bank or building society** – 100% of the first £2,000; 90% of the next £33,000, ie £31,700 maximum (formerly the Banks' and Building Societies' Deposit Protection Schemes, which had lower limits)

The FSCS is **funded by a levy** on authorised firms. The FSCS has a duty to try to make arrangements for the continuity of long-term insurance policyholders' insurance by transfer of the business to an alternative insurer.

4 Mortgages regulation

4.1 Introduction

The FSA has established rules covering **advising on and arranging mortgages**. A Treasury review argued that the regulatory approach should focus on improving information for consumers, since many people experience difficulties in understanding mortgage products and making effective comparisons between them.

Mortgages regulation under the FSA started on **31 October 2004**. Those doing mortgage business need to be either directly authorised by the FSA or to be an appointed representative of an authorised firm. Anyone doing mortgage business who is not properly authorised is committing a criminal offence.

The new FSA rules will apply to firms advising on mortgage contracts entered into on or after 31 October 2004. Until that time, the voluntary **Mortgage Code** existed to protect consumers and was administered by the Mortgage Code Compliance Board.

Here, we cover some key aspects of the rules for the new mortgage regulation regime, as required for your syllabus.

4.2 MCOB

The FSA's new mortgage rules form a separate Sourcebook within the FSA Handbook called **Mortgages: Conduct of Business (MCOB)**.

MCOB applies to firms carrying on regulated mortgage activities and includes rules covering mortgage advice and mortgage arranging. Variations made to mortgage contracts entered into before 31 October 2004 are not subject to FSA regulation.

4.3 Types of firm

MCOB distinguishes four types of firm:

- Mortgage lenders
- Mortgage administrators
- Mortgage arrangers
- Mortgage advisers

A firm may be **directly authorised**, and is then responsible for its own compliance with MCOB and other FSA rules.

In the case of an **Appointed Representative**, it is the AR's principal who is authorised, and is responsible for compliance. The principal could be an IFA firm, or a network, or a mortgage lender.

An **introducer**, who only passes on 'leads' to an authorised firm for payment, does not need to be authorised.

4.4 Rules for mortgage firms

Firms doing mortgage business must comply not just with MCOB but with other relevant parts of the FSA Handbook as well.

As for investment business, a firm must ensure that its **communications** with customers are clear, fair and not misleading, having regard to the customer's knowledge of the mortgage contract.

You will recall that the FSA **Principles for Business** 1 and 6 require that a firm conduct its business with integrity and that it treats them fairly. A firm must not accept **inducements** which are likely to conflict with its duty to its customers, and it should take reasonable steps to ensure that any associate, even if unregulated, receives no such inducement. This does not mean that benefits cannot be provided to mortgage intermediaries to enhance service to customers, but they must not be such as to give rise to a likely conflict of interest.

Charges for a regulated mortgage contract should not be **excessive**.

Firms must avoid **high pressure sales** tactics such as presenting a mortgage deed for signature to a new customer at the same time as an illustration and offer document.

4.5 Types of sale

There are two **types of mortgage sale**, under the FSA rules:

- **Advised**, and
- **Non-advised**

A sale may be either:

- **Standard risk**, or
- **Higher risk**

A **higher risk mortgage** is a **lifetime mortgage**: lifetime mortgages are 'equity release' mortgages, allowing generally older persons to borrow in order to release equity in their house, with the lender being repaid the principal of the loan at a later date, usually when the borrower, or the last survivor of a couple, dies.

All other regulated mortgages are classed as **standard risk mortgages**.

4.6 Mortgages not regulated

Mortgage regulation covers standard owner-occupier mortgages generally but it does not cover:

- **Buy-to-let** (property investment) mortgages, unless the tenant is a member of the borrower's immediate family
- **Second charge loans**
- Loans to **limited companies**
- **Home Reversion Schemes** (Future regulation of these schemes is possible. For now, the rules governing the schemes are complex, and some loans normally treated as being in this category might be classed as regulated in practice.)

4.7 Affordability and suitability for advised sales

If advice is given, the firm must seek to ensure that any mortgage it recommends is **affordable**, appropriate to the customer's needs and the most **suitable** of those available within the scope of the services provided.

The **suitability** of a sale is not a matter only of **price**. Other factors, such as **flexibility** or **service quality**, can be taken into account.

A **suitability letter** may be provided to the mortgage customer, but there is no requirement to do so. In whatever form information is presented to the client, it should be possible for the adviser to show how a recommendation decision was reached and how it met the customer's individual needs.

4.8 Non-advised sales

If a customer does not wish to receive advice, the sale is 'non-advised'. In this case, a firm is required to use **pre-scripted questions** to obtain details of the customer's circumstances.

Firms must ensure that non-advised sales are closely monitored, to ensure that advice is **not** given to the client. The fact that advice is not being given should be made clear in writing.

4.9 Documentation requirements

As soon as contact is made with a client, the client must be provided with an **Initial Disclosure Document (IDD)**.

The IDD sets out basic details of the firm and its relationship with a client. It includes the firm's name and status, and details of the services that it offers and the cost of these services.

The advising firm must make it clear whether its service is based on the whole market, or on a single or a limited number of lenders.

If both mortgage and insurance business are being conducted with a client, a **Combined Initial Disclosure Document (CIDD)** can be provided to the client, after **general insurance regulation** comes into force on **14 January 2005**. The use of a CIDD is not compulsory: two separate IDDs could be used. The FSA provides templates for use as CIDDs.

Whenever information is provided to a client on a specific mortgage and mortgage amount, this information must be accompanied by a personalised **Key Features Illustration** (KFI).

A KFI must be given to the client with every recommendation and **prior to any mortgage application being made**.

A KFI provided by an intermediary must be accurate to within 1% for the monthly payment and total amount payable with the APR not understated by more than 0.1%.

4.10 Disclosure of commission

Any payment to an intermediary of £250 or more must be disclosed to a client. The amount of any commission payment will be stated on the KFI and it should always be brought to the client's attention.

4.11 Lifetime mortgages

As mentioned above, **lifetime mortgages** (**equity release** mortgages) are classed by the FSA as **'higher' risk** mortgages. Lifetime mortgages include **home income plans**, which are designed for older people (normally those over 60) who wish to make use of some of the capital tied up in their home.

There is a separate tailored regime with additional guidelines for advising and arranging lifetime mortgages. These guidelines require a greater level of disclosure and additional risk warnings.

Individuals advising on lifetime mortgages must be able to demonstrate that they have the skills required in this area. Advisers already covering this area under the previous voluntary Mortgage Code can be 'grandfathered' into the new FSA-regulated regime without taking additional examinations. However, firms must monitor ongoing competence of advisers in this area.

4.12 Self-certification mortgages

As we saw in an earlier Chapter of this Study Text, with **self-certification mortgages**, the lender makes a mortgage offer without verifying income information supplied by the borrower.

The FSA had considered making self-certification mortgages available only to the self-employed. However, following consultation the FSA has stated that self-certification can also be used by employed individuals in appropriate circumstances and when there is no reason to doubt the information provided by the client.

4.13 Consequences of rule-breaking

Although the requirements of KFIs are similar to existing requirements under the Consumer Credit Act 1974 (which we cover in Chapter 15 of this Study Text), the mortgage regulation regime is different in that failure to comply with the rules will not make the mortgage contract unenforceable, but it may expose the firm to enforcement action by the FSA.

If a customer suffers **loss** as a result of a failure by a firm to comply with MCOB rules, the firm could face:

- A complaint to the Financial Ombudsman Service leading to an award of compensation, or
- A claim by the customer for damages for breach of statutory duty

5 General insurance regulation

5.1 Commencement

14 January 2005 was the start date for **FSA regulation of general insurance sales and advice**.

Since that date, those who advise on or arrange general insurance need to be either:

- Authorised, or
- Exempt from authorisation (for example, if a firm is an appointed representative of an authorised insurer or intermediary)

It is not possible to be directly authorised for some activities, but be an appointed representative for other activities.

5.2 Scope

General insurance, for these regulatory purposes, means:

- General insurance contracts (for example, home insurance and motor insurance), and
- Pure protection insurance contracts, for example, critical illness, income protection and term life assurance, (but not long-term care insurance contracts, which will be regulated under separate future arrangements)

As for other regulated areas, individuals within authorised firms performing **significant influence** functions will need to be **approved** by the FSA as fit and proper to do so. General insurance firms will therefore be subject also to the FSA's Statements of Principle.

Authorised general insurance firms will be subject to regulations concerning financial safeguards, including requirements to maintain professional indemnity insurance and a prescribed minimum level of financial resources. They must belong to the **Financial Services Compensation Scheme**.

Conduct of Business requirements for general insurance are covered in the **Insurance Conduct of Business Sourcebook (ICOB)**, which forms part of the FSA Handbook.

5.3 ICOB

The **ICOB** (Insurance Conduct of Business) rules apply to **intermediaries**, including direct-selling insurers, and to **insurers** in their role as product providers.

For ICOB purposes, a **retail customer** is defined as someone acting outside their trade, business or profession; anyone else is a **commercial customer**.

ICOB includes rules on the following aspects of general insurance business.

- **Communications with customers**: firms must communicate information to customers in a way that is clear, fair and not misleading

- **Financial promotions** to retail customers (inviting or inducing customers to take out in insurance): the financial promotion must be clear, fair and not misleading. Firms are required to implement a **confirmation of compliance** exercise by an individual with appropriate expertise before a financial promotion is made.

- **Advising and selling** standards. Intermediaries must provide certain **information** about themselves and their fees, mainly at the pre-contract stage. **Suitability rules** apply when a firm makes a personal recommendation to buy a specific policy: the firm must assess the retail customer's demands and needs from all relevant information about the customer, and the customer must be provided with a **statement of demands and needs** containing the reasons for any personal recommendation.

- **Product disclosure**. In general, **insurers** (in their role as product providers) must produce product disclosure information and **intermediaries** (including direct-selling insurers) must provide this information to their customers. Product disclosure information required for retail customers encompasses the **policy document**, a **policy summary** (or **key features document**) covering the type of insurance and cover, and significant features, benefits and exclusions, **price information**, and information about **cancellation**, **claims handling** and **renewal**.

- **Cancellation** rules require that retail customers be given a cancellation period of **14 days** for general insurance contracts, starting from the day the contract is made or, if later, the day the customer receives the full policy documentation.

- **Claims handling**, which is the responsibility of **insurers**. For claims by retail customers, insurers must handle claims fairly and promptly, give the customer reasonable guidance, respond promptly to notification of a claim with information on claims handling, keep the customer informed about progress, explain why any claim is refused or not met in full, and settle the claim promptly once a settlement is reached. **Intermediaries** must act with due care and skill and avoid conflicts of interest when acting for a customer in respect of a claim.

ICOB prevents insurers from **refusing liability** to retail customers on the grounds of:

- Non-disclosure of a material fact that the customer could not reasonably be expected to disclose

- Misrepresentation, unless it was a deliberate or negligent misrepresentation of a material fact, or

- Breach of a warranty or condition, where the circumstances of the loss are unconnected to the breach (unless fraud is involved)

6 Advice on stakeholder products

6.1 The Sandler Review

The 2002 **Sandler Review** on medium and long-term savings suggested that it is the complexity of products that has mainly created the need for the great volume of FSA regulations. Simplified 'stakeholder' products could offer the possibility of:

(a) More 'guided self-help' for consumers, for example using a series of filter questions set by the FSA to screen out consumers for whom a product is unsuitable

(b) Advisers being able to give advice on a simplified suite of products without needing to train to the level needed to give the full range of regulated advice

6.2 Implementation

The **Sandler Review** proposals have been put into effect in legislation and in changes to the FSA Handbook which came into force on **6 April 2005**.

- These rules allow for firms to provide a **basic level of advice** on a range of '**risk-controlled**' stakeholder products.

- **Stakeholder products** are intended to provide a relatively simple and low-cost way of investing and saving.

6.3 The range of stakeholder products

The range of stakeholder products includes:

(a) **Stakeholder pension** schemes
(b) Stakeholder **Child Trust Funds (CTFs)**
(c) Stakeholder-compliant **deposit accounts**
(d) Stakeholder-compliant **collective investment schemes (CISs)**
(e) Stakeholder-compliant **linked long-term contracts**

To be a stakeholder product, a **deposit account** must have a minimum deposit amount set no higher than £10 per occasion. Interest must accrue at a rate not less than the Bank of England base rate minus 1 per cent per annum. The interest rate must be increased within one month of a change in the base rate. Withdrawals must be paid within 7 days, with no limit on frequency of withdrawals.

To meet stakeholder requirements, **collective investment schemes** and **linked long-term funds** must have no more than 60% of their value in listed equities, and must be appropriately diversified. The minimum contribution must be set no higher than £20. The scheme must be **single-priced** – with no spread between the buying and selling price of units.

Linked long-term contracts are assurance-based contracts. Where such contracts have **smoothed investment returns**, additional requirements apply. The fund must seek to meet a target range of investment return, which must be notified to the investor at the outset. However, no guarantee will be given. Full information must be made available about the policy and charges. The **basic level of advice cannot be provided** on smoothed linked long term products.

New medium term and pension stakeholder products have a **cap on charges** at 1.5% per year for the first ten years that the investor holds the product. After that, a cap of 1% applies. The charge caps will be reviewed by the Government in 2008. A **1%** charges cap continues to apply to stakeholder pension plans that were in existence **before 6 April 2005**, when the cap was raised to 1.5% for new plans.

6.4 Basic advice rules

The new requirements on **basic advice on stakeholder products** is designed to enable firms to provide **simple, quick and limited** advice to people interested in buying stakeholder products. The requirements include the following.

(a) An **Initial Disclosure Document (IDD)** is to be provided, and explained to the customer.

(b) The advice should be based on either a limited number of stakeholder product providers, or a single provider.

(c) The range of products should not include more than one of each of:

   (i) A collective investment product or linked life products
   (ii) A stakeholder pension
   (iii) A stakeholder Child Trust Fund

   (There can be more than one deposit-based product in the range. Also, a firm may operate with more than one range of stakeholder products. Proper records of the ranges must be kept, for six years.)

(d) Representatives are not to recommend one particular fund, and they are not to give advice on products outside the range while advising on stakeholder products. The firm must not hold itself out as giving **independent advice** when it is giving only basic advice on stakeholder products.

(e) Remuneration of representatives must not be likely to influence them to give unsuitable advice or induce them to refer customers to another firm.

(f) The sales process for basic stakeholder advice must use **scripted questions** put to the customer. Unless excluded at the preliminary stage, the customer must be sent a copy of the completed scripted questions and answers.

6.5 Scripted questions

A firm's scripted questions should be **short, simple and in plain language** that customers will understand. The customer should be able to **exit freely and without pressure** at any stage. There should be provision for the representative to **terminate** the sale process if no products are likely to be suitable or affordable for the customer.

A **software based system** may be most appropriate to provide prompts and support for representatives. It is permissible to **depart from the scripted questions** if it helps customers' understanding, if this is compatible with the representative's level of competence.

6.6 Affordability and suitability

Affordability may be assessed in a firm's scripted sales process by means of a threshold or indicator, for example where a customer:

(a) Has annual unsecured debt repayments of more than 20% of gross annual income
(b) Has four or more active forms of unsecured credit, or
(c) Has consistently reached his or her overdraft limit

Except in the case of stakeholder CTFs, the customer's **savings and investment objectives** should be ascertained, including:

- The importance of early access to amounts saved or invested
- Whether the customer wishes to save or invest for retirement
- Whether the customer wants to accumulate a specific sum by a specific date

The customer's **objectives** and **risk tolerance** will influence what may be recommended. For example:

(a)   If the customer wishes to save for the short term only, then a collective investment scheme (CIS), a linked life stakeholder product or a stakeholder pension would all be unsuitable and should not be recommended.

(b)   If a customer is not prepared to accept any risk of reduction of capital value, then a CIS or linked life stakeholder product should not be recommended. (However, in this case, a firm may invite the customer to consider his or her attitude to risk in the light of the effect of inflation on long-term savings.)

A stakeholder pension should not be recommended under the basic advice rules if the customer:

- Already has an occupational pension scheme
- Already has a pension to which he or she can contribute further
- Wishes to retire within five years

If appropriate, the customer should be given a warning about the desirability of meeting the following **other priorities** before making payments to a stakeholder product:

- Insurance protection for self or dependents
- Access to liquid cash in emergencies
- Reduction of the level of existing debt

The customer is only to be **recommended** to acquire a stakeholder product if the customer's answers and circumstances have been assessed, and (except for deposit-based products) the product is believed to be **suitable**. The adviser must reasonably believe that the customer **understands** the advice given.

When providing basic advice, the customer must not be advised on the contribution levels to a stakeholder pension needed to achieve a specific income in retirement.

6.7 Concluding the contract

Before concluding the contract, the representative is to:

- Explain the **aims, risks and commitments** sections of the **key features**, together with any other explanation of the product that will help the customer make an informed decision (except for a deposit-based product).

- Provide a **summary sheet** setting out amounts the customer wishes to pay in to the product, reasons for the recommendation and other relevant information including the customer's attitude to risk. (The summary sheet may be read through by telephone if the customer requests it, with the sheet being sent to the customer after the contract is concluded.)

- Explain that the recommendation is based on **limited information** and that the Financial Ombudsman may take this into account in determining any subsequent complaint.

Key chapter points

- Financial promotions must be issued or approved by an authorised person (eg a firm). Regulated firms must seek to ensure that communications are clear, fair and not misleading.

- A real-time financial promotion could be a personal visit or a phone call (including cold calling). The firm must take steps to ensure that unfair claims are not made and that rules governing the content and timing of the call are followed.

- There are important rules designed to prevent money laundering and to try to detect it when it does occur, and there are heavy penalties for contravention of the rules. FSA rules work alongside the guidance of the Joint Money Laundering Steering Group and the Money Laundering Regulations 2003.

- The Proceeds of Crime Act 2002 has introduced wider requirements, making it a criminal offence to be involved in arrangements involving the proceeds of crime generally.

- Firms must have written complaints procedures. The Financial Ombudsman Service (FOS) exists to deal with complaints that are not resolved by firms' own procedures. The FOS can make financial awards up to £100,000 to complainants.

- The Financial Services Compensation Scheme compensates investors and depositors up to specified limits where a firm undergoes financial failure and cannot meet the claims against it.

- Mortgage advice and sales, but not buy-to-let mortgages, have been regulated since 31 October 2004. Advised sales recommendations must be affordable and suitable for the client. With non-advised sales, pre-scripted questions must be used. Lifetime (equity release) mortgages have stricter rules, and are classed as 'higher risk'.

- Documentation provided to mortgage clients includes an Initial Disclosure Document (IDD) and a Key Features Illustration.

- Firms carrying out general insurance business have been subject to regulation by the FSA since 14 January 2005. Insurance Conduct of Business rules are intended to protect the customer and cover various aspects, including communications with customers, financial promotions, advising and selling, product disclosure, cancellation and claims handling.

- A simplified basic advice regime for a new, wider range of risk-controlled 'stakeholder' products started on 6 April 2005. Stakeholder products are intended to provide a relatively simple and low-cost way of investing and saving. Staff selling the stakeholder range of products must use scripted questions, and the firm must not hold itself out to be offering independent advice.

Chapter Quiz

Chapter topic list

Compliance monitoring and training

1 Monitoring by the regulator

1.1 Information received by the regulator

We have looked at the **notification requirements** for firms.

As we saw earlier, the FSA receives much information about authorised firms, and this includes:

(a) Accounts
(b) Auditors' reports
(c) Returns of banks, building societies and insurance companies
(d) Returns on complaints

1.2 Reactive enforcement

The FSA may **react** to the information it receives from firms and may decide to conduct further investigations in light of evidence it has received.

The regulator may also be alerted to problems by the **Consumer Panel** or the **Practitioner Panel**.

The **Director General of Fair Trading**, the **Complaints Commissioner** or the **Financial Ombudsman** may all make reports to the FSA.

1.3 The regulator's risk-based approach

We have already mentioned the FSA's risk-based approach to regulation.

The extent to which the FSA will carry out **checks** on the **compliance** of firms depends on the **type of business** transacted by the member and the perceived **risk** that a firm's activities involve. For example, a large firm of independent financial advisers with branches throughout the country may be subject to more stringent checks than a friendly society which deals with all business by post and has one product in its range.

The FSA uses an assessment of the risks to its four **statutory objectives** to prioritise its efforts and focus on the most significant **risks**.

The FSA's approach includes an **assessment of risks** at the firm level and at the consumer, product, market and industry levels. At the firm level, the FSA assesses the risk that individual firms pose to its objectives and decides its regulatory response to those risks.

The **level of supervisory intensity** depends on the regulator's assessment of:

- **Impact** (the effect on the statutory regulatory objectives if a risk occurs), and
- **Probability** (the likelihood of a risk occurring)

1.4 FSA supervision of small firms

A **small firm** with a simple business model, a local retail client base and no recent history of regulatory problems is likely to be **low impact** and its regulatory relationship with the FSA will reflect this. These firms will not have a dedicated FSA relationship manager but will have a contact point in the FSA's supervisory division. (In the case of small IFA firms, this is the **Investment Firms Division (IFD) Contact Centre**.)

An important part of the monitoring of low impact firms is the receipt and monitoring of returns and notifications. Firms submit the Returns required under the FSA Handbook (eg audited accounts, financial returns and complaints returns) which the FSA monitor in order to identify potential breaches of regulatory requirements.

The FSA does not carry out routine visits to small firms and there will normally be little contact with the firm on an individual basis.

- The monitoring may be limited to **desk reviews** if the firm's activities are seen as presenting a **low risk**. However, the regulator may make visits in response to risks identified from returns and other sources of information.

- In addition, the firm or its business will be covered from time to time by the FSA's sector-wide projects (**themes**) which monitor compliance standards in a class of firm, or firms as a whole.

1.5 Powers of enforcement officers and scope of visits

The FSA's **enforcement officers** have full authority to ensure that member firms have complied with the regulatory requirements.

FSA officers can choose to **visit** any member or any appointed representative of a member at any time without warning.

During their visits, FSA officers have the authority to **inspect** any of the firm's records which will enable them to make a judgment on the compliance with the regulatory requirements and effectiveness of the firm's procedures. They may institute such visits following the receipt of a complaint, or for other reasons.

FSA officers are entitled to receive **full co-operation** from the staff of the member and/or any appointed representatives.

2 Firms' compliance procedures

2.1 Record keeping

The basis for demonstrating compliance with regulations is the **keeping of adequate records**. These should cover all aspects of compliance, but the following will be examples of the principal categories of records that should be kept.

Area	Types of record
Dealing with clients	Copies of all fact finds
	Reasons for the recommendations made to clients
	The basis of those recommendations and the source of information
	Any agreements with clients
	Evidence that a transaction was on an execution only basis
	Evidence on any possible conflicts of interest and how they were handled
	Documentary evidence of transactions
Financial records	Daily records of income and expenditure, assets and liabilities
	Any other records to satisfy the FSA requirements
	Members holding clients' money must observe additional special regulations
	Firms must produce annual accounts but some may be required to produce information for the regulator more frequently depending on their category
Personnel records	Records of the appointment and dismissal of advisers and appointed representatives
	Records showing that adequate references were taken up before appointment
Advertising records	Copies of all advertisements
	Records of who authorised each advertisement
	Dates of publication for advertisements

Records must be **adequate for their purpose** and for the needs of the regulator. Ideally they should be in a standard format as this makes checking easier.

2.2 Record keeping periods

Bear in mind the general rules on the periods for which firms must keep records.

(a) Indefinitely, for pension transfers, pension opt-outs and FSAVCs (free-standing additional voluntary contributions arrangements, for pensions)

(b) Six years, for life policies, pension contracts and stakeholder pensions

(c) Three years in other cases

2.3 Compliance officer

All regulated firms must appoint a person to be responsible for ensuring that the company complies with regulations. That person - known as the **compliance officer** – must be an employee of the firm.

The compliance officer, in the case of a larger firm, may need a separate **compliance department** in order to meet the regulatory requirements. Although all the management of a company still retain legal liability for the company's activities, the prime responsibility for compliance rests with the board of a company or the partners. In practice, the day-to-day compliance requirements are monitored by the compliance officer. If that officer is not a partner or a member of a board of directors, then he should have direct access to a member of the board or the Chief Executive.

The overall responsibility of a compliance officer is to supervise the **compliance procedures** of the firm and ensure that the **rules are enforced**. This will involve the compliance officer ensuring that there are **regular checks** on the **keeping of records**, the **advice given** to clients and the contents of any **advertisements**.

A further role of the compliance officer is to provide an **advisory service** to all business areas within the firm and ensure that all the firm's advisers continue to be **fit and proper** for the purpose of giving investment advice.

The compliance officer must report **annually** to the board or partners and must liaise as required with the firm's regulator. Compliance procedures must be kept **regularly under review**.

2.4 IFA networks

Networks of advisors need to show the adequacy of their internal monitoring for appointed representatives, who must have a written contract.

3 Training and competence

3.1 The firm's commitment

The **firm's commitment** to training and competence should be that employees:

(a)   Are **competent**
(b)   **Remain** competent
(c)   Are appropriately **supervised**
(d)   Have competence **reviewed** regularly
(e)   Have a level of competence **appropriate** to the business

3.2 Recruitment

In recruitment for specified roles involving private customers, including giving **investment advice**, the firm must:

(a)   Take account of an individual's knowledge and skill for the role
(b)   Find out about the individual's previous relevant activities and training

3.3 Training

For advisers and other employees involved with private customers, the firm must determine training needs and organise appropriate timely **training**.

3.4 Attaining competence

Employees must pass 'appropriate' examinations before they can be assessed as competent. Otherwise, the employee may only engage in the relevant activity under appropriate supervision.

Employees permitted to work with private customers under supervision must first have passed a relevant regulatory module of an appropriate examination. On-the-job training is not sufficient.

For some activities, such as advising on packaged products, a period of up to two years may be spent under supervision before appropriate examinations are passed. In calculating time spent under supervision:

(a)   Time spent on (or overseeing) activities in different periods of employment are aggregated

(b)   Periods of 60 business days or more in which the employee is absent from engaging in or overseeing the activity are disregarded

For certain specialist advice, such as advice on pension transfers, these are specific exam requirements before the employee can engage in the activity. For pension transfers, the CII's G60 *Pensions* exam (or equivalent) must be passed before starting to give advice.

3.5 The Examination Review

A new framework of appropriate examinations is being developed by the Financial Services Skills Council (FSSC).

- Standards for appropriate examinations to assess those who will be carrying out particular functions are developed by the FSSC.

- Examining bodies (such as the Securities and Investment Institute, the Chartered Insurance Institute and the Institute of Financial Services) can then develop exam schemes in line with the FSSC's standards. The *UK financial services, regulation and ethics* exam for which this Study Text is written is based on FSSC standards.

The new qualifications framework being developed by the FSSC is the outcome of a wide-ranging Examination Review originally initiated by the FSA.

The Examination Review is eventually to cover all qualifications for financial services professionals with the aim of reflecting the needs of the sector in setting up a clear industry-wide, single qualifications framework.

The FSA began the Examination Review in 2001 after inheriting as many as 500 approved examination routes and a multitude of designations from previous regulatory bodies. It was considered that this task did not sit comfortably with its role as industry regulator. When the Financial Services Skills Council was formed in 2003, the FSA asked the Financial Services Skills Council to complete the Examination Review and to determine examinations that were appropriate to certain regulated activities.

3.6 'Appropriate' examinations

The Examination Review changed the requirement from 'approved' exams to 'appropriate' exams. Under the new 'appropriate exam' regime, lists of appropriate exams covering the common FSSC standards will be maintained, although a firm does not necessarily have to choose an exam from this list. It is open to a firm to devise its own 'appropriate examinations' and to present them to the FSSC for endorsement. In practice however, it is likely that the exam schemes developed by examining bodies will generally be used.

The FSA's training and competence rules make it clear that the responsibility for ensuring that individuals have passed a relevant examination rests with the individual's firm. The transition from 'approved' examinations to 'appropriate' does not change this requirement.

3.7 Maintaining competence

Firms must ensure that employees maintain competence in their activities, for example through **Continuing Professional Development (CPD)**. (See later in this chapter.)

3.8 Supervision

Employees who are not yet assessed as competent in an activity need to be appropriately supervised.

A firm must not permit an employee to **oversee** a regulated activity unless that employee has been assessed as competent. Supervisors of those giving advice on **packaged products** must have passed an appropriate examination and must have the technical knowledge and assessment and coaching skills to act as a supervisor.

3.9 Record keeping

Training records must be retained for at least **three years** after the employee leaves the firm although, for pension transfer specialists, records must be retained indefinitely. The FSA's requirement to keep records of skills and technical training is designed to ensure that all advisers maintain competence appropriate to the activities they undertake.

4 Key performance indicators

4.1 The role of KPIs

Key performance indicators (KPIs) provide ways of measuring the quality of the advice provided by an individual adviser. These factors are not always easy to measure. Their impact can, nevertheless, be important. For example, the adverse publicity that an organisation may receive as a result of poor advice being offered could have a lasting and measurable impact on its reputation and credibility.

The FSA rules do not specify KPIs. It would, however, be difficult to monitor performance adequately without them. Many firms' KPIs are based on those suggested originally by the PIA:

- Fact find completion
- Persistency and cancellations (see below)
- NTUs (not taken-ups)
- Range of advice provided
- Complaints from investors

Other KPIs that could be used include:

- Sales production levels
- Following money laundering prevention rules
- Suitability of advice

Whatever criteria are used, it is important they are specific. For example, what does **fact find completion** actually mean? Unless there are accepted standards about what information must be collected, the approach to information not provided and so on, such a standard would not have a consistent meaning. Even with the criteria that are capable of being quantified the need to be specific remains. For example, the standard for acceptable **persistency** (see below) may be set at 90% or more but is that over a 12 or 24 month period or both?

4.2 Persistency

Persistency is an indicator of an individual adviser's performance. Persistency measures the proportion of policies remaining in force after a specified period of time. A loss of only 1 per cent of policies after one year of the policy being in place generally reflects good persistency. Some policyholders may cancel their policies because of major changes in circumstances, such as redundancy. However, a loss as high as 25 per cent of policies after one year would be cause for concern, as it indicates that policies may have been mis-sold.

In the case of life assurance policies, cancellation penalties can be severe and policyholders may lose much of their original outlay if they cancel early in the life of the policy.

Persistency can be calculated as follows.

Assume that the number of contracts commenced is CC and the number of contracts still in force after a specified period of time is CF.

Persistency = (CF/CC) × 100%

For example, 25 personal pension contracts are commenced through adviser A. 22 of the contracts remain in force after four years.

Adviser A's persistency rate in respect of personal pension plans after four years is (22/25) × 100 = 88 per cent

4.3 Records on persistency

Product providers must keep and report to the FSA persistency records broken down by product type and by sales channel, indicating figures for their own advisers and for business done through IFAs. The records should cover the first four years of contracts.

For persistency calculation purposes, a policy is in force at the end of the year if the first premium in the following year is paid.

Aggregate persistency data are compiled by the FSA.

5 Maintaining competence

5.1 CPD

Approved advisers must **maintain their competence**, a process sometimes called **Continuing Professional Development (CPD)**.

Many groups of professionals such as doctors, solicitors and accountants have recognised for some time the need for CPD, or CPE (Continuous Professional Education), as it is sometimes known. Its purpose is perhaps best remembered by looking more closely at the three words in the name.

(a) **Continuing:** CPD continues throughout an adviser's (and supervisor's) career once he or she is deemed competent. Competence is a continuous process, not a destination in itself.

(b) **Professional:** CPD is intended to help individuals to develop and broaden their professionalism. At the very least, it must help them to retain credibility as professionals. For example, auditing procedures for accountants have changed over the years and so an accountant who qualified 15 years ago would not be able, with having undertaken continuing development, to be able to act now in a competent manner.

(c) **Development:** This suggests a need not only to address the knowledge and skill required today, but also those skills or attributes required in the future.

5.2 CPD for the individual adviser

The actual activities conducted as part of CPD will be particular to each individual as everyone's needs differ. For CPD to be effective, it is the individual who therefore needs to take responsibility for their own development, although under the T&C scheme the supervisor is also responsible for the identification of development needs, the appropriateness of the CPD and its transfer to the workplace.

Key chapter points

- The FSA receives much information about firms and may make further investigations in the light of the perceived risks (reactive enforcement).

- Rather than monitor all firms and types of firm to an equal extent, the FSA assesses the risk of a firm's activities, and plans its monitoring activities accordingly.

- The FSA may make inspection visits without giving any notice. Desk reviews are another form of monitoring, for low-risk firms and activities.

- All firms must have a Compliance Officer.

- Training and competence rules are designed to ensure that individuals are competent in the work they do and are appropriately supervised.

- The firm must determine appropriate training needs. Appropriate examinations must be passed, such as the exams for those advising on packaged products. Those overseeing advisers must be assessed as competent.

- Specialist advisers include those providing pensions transfer advice; their approved examination must be passed before the specialist advice is given.

- Key performance indicators include persistency, which product providers must report to the FSA by product type and sales channel.

- Continuing Professional Development is a means of maintaining competence. All advisers need to keep up to date.

Chapter Quiz

1 On what criteria does the FSA base its risk assessment of the level of intensity required in supervising firms? .... (see para 1.3)

2 In what circumstances might the FSA consider a desk review appropriate? ....(1.4)

3 Who is responsible for ensuring that an individual giving advice has passed a relevant examination – the firm, the FSA or the FSSC? ....(3.6)

4 For what minimum length of time must training records be retained? ....(3.9)

5 What persistency records must be reported to the FSA? ....(4.3)

6 What is CPD? ....(5.1)

1 Unfair contract terms

1.1 Introduction

Earlier in this Study Text, we looked at features that make a valid contract. The consumer has some protection against contracts that may be unfair to him or her. For example, such protection is provided under legislation on **unfair contract terms**, which may include certain forms of **exclusion clause**.

1.2 Exclusion clauses in contracts

An **exclusion clause** may be defined as a clause in a contract which purports to exclude liability altogether or to restrict it by limiting damages or by imposing other onerous conditions. Such clauses are sometimes called **exemption clauses**.

There has been strong criticism of the use of exclusion clauses in contracts made between manufacturers or sellers of goods or services and private citizens as consumers. The seller puts forward standard conditions of sale which the buyer may not understand, but which he must accept if he wishes to buy. With these so-called **standard form contracts**, the presence of exclusion clauses becomes an important consideration.

The **courts** have generally sought to protect consumers from the harsher effects of exclusion clauses in two ways.

(a)   An exclusion clause must be properly **incorporated** into a contract before it has any legal effect.

(b)   Exclusion clauses are **interpreted** strictly. This may prevent the application of the clause.

For many years, the courts demonstrated the hostility of the common law to exclusion clauses by developing various rules of case law designed to restrain their effect. The **Unfair Contract Terms Act 1977 (UCTA 1977)** provides statutory safeguards designed to protect consumers, who generally have unequal 'bargaining power' in their dealings with organisations, including financial institutions.

1.3 Unfair Contract Terms Act 1977

When considering the **validity** of exclusion clauses, the courts have had to strike a balance between:

- The principle that parties should have complete **freedom to contract** on whatever terms they wish, and
- The need to **protect the public** from unfair exclusion clauses

The scope of UCTA 1977 is restricted in the following ways.

(a)   In general, the Act only applies to clauses inserted into agreements by **commercial concerns or businesses**. In principle, private persons may restrict liability as much as they wish.

(b)   The Act does not apply to some contracts, for example **contracts of insurance** or contracts relating to the transfer of an interest in **land**.

(c)   Specifically, the Act applies to:

(i)   Clauses that attempt to limit liability for negligence

(ii)   Clauses that attempt to limit liability for breach of contract

The Act uses two techniques for controlling exclusion clauses: some types of clauses are **void**, whereas others are subject to a **test of reasonableness**.

The main provisions can be summarised as follows:

(a)   Any clause that attempts to restrict liability for death or personal injury arising from negligence is **void**.

(b)   Any clause that attempts to restrict liability for other loss or damage arising from negligence is void unless it can be shown to be **reasonable**.

(c)   Any clause that attempts to limit liability for breach of contract, where the contract refers to standard terms or conditions, or where one of the parties is a consumer, is void unless it can be shown to be **reasonable**.

If a clause is not automatically void, it is subject to a test of reasonableness.

1.4 The statutory test of reasonableness

The term must be fair and reasonable having regard to all the circumstances which were, or which ought to have been, known to the parties when the contract was made. The burden of proving reasonableness lies on the person seeking to rely on the clause.

Contractual exclusion clauses in relation to **services** are not illegal but they are not enforceable if they are unreasonable.

Statutory guidelines have been included in the Act to make it easier to determine what is 'reasonable'. For instance, the court will consider the following.

- The relative **strength** of the parties' bargaining positions.

- Whether any **inducement** (for example, a reduced price) was offered to the customer to persuade him to accept limitation of his rights.

- Whether the customer **knew or ought to have known** of the existence and extent of the exclusion clause.

- If failure to comply with a condition (for example, failure to give notice of a defect within a short period) excludes or restricts the customer's rights, whether it was reasonable to expect when the contract was made that compliance with the condition would be practicable.

- Whether the goods were made, processed or adapted to the **special order** of the customer (UCTA 1977, Sch 2).

Smith v Eric S Bush 1989

The facts: A surveyor prepared a report on a property which contained a clause disclaiming liability for the accuracy and validity of the report. In fact the survey was negligently done and the claimant had to make good a lot of defects once the property was purchased.

Decision: In the absence of special difficulties, it was unreasonable for the surveyor to disclaim liability given the cost of the report, his profession and his knowledge that it would be relied upon to make a major purchase.

The Law Commission has been formulating proposals for replacing UCTA 1977. Among the proposals are the following:

(a) A **fair and reasonableness test** which requires that the term is:

    (i) Expressed in plain language
    (ii) Presented in a clear manner, and
    (iii) Accessible to the consumer

(b) A list of exclusion clauses which are considered **not** to be fair and reasonable.

1.5 Unfair Terms In Consumer Contracts Regulations

These regulations implemented an **EU Directive on unfair contract terms**. UCTA 1977 continues to apply and there are now three layers of relevant law.

- The **common law**, which applies to all contracts, regardless of whether or not one party is a consumer

- **UCTA 1977**, which applies to all contracts and which has specific provisions for consumer contracts

- **The regulations** (**UTCCR 1999**), which only apply to consumer contracts and to terms which have not been individually negotiated

The UTCCR 1999 regulations apply to contracts for the supply of goods or services.

(a) They apply to terms in consumer contracts. (A **consumer** is defined as 'a natural person who, in making a contract to which these regulations apply, is acting for purposes which are outside his business'.)

(b) They apply to contractual terms which have not been individually negotiated.

(c) There are a number of exceptions including contracts relating to family law or to the incorporation or organisation of companies and partnerships and employment contracts.

A key aspect of the regulations is the definition of an unfair term. An **unfair term** is any term which causes a significant imbalance in the parties' rights and obligations under the contract to the detriment of the consumer.

In making an assessment of good faith, the courts will have regard to the following.

- The **strength of the bargaining positions** of the parties
- Whether the consumer had an **inducement** to agree to the term
- Whether the goods or services were sold or supplied to the **special order** of the consumer
- The extent to which the seller or supplier has dealt **fairly and equitably** with the consumer

The effect of the regulations is to render certain terms in consumer contracts unfair.

- Excluding or limiting liability of the seller when the consumer dies or is injured, where this results from an act or omission of the seller

- Excluding or limiting liability where there is partial or incomplete performance of a contract by the seller

- Making a contract binding on the consumer where the seller can still avoid performing the contract

Two **forms of redress** are available.

- A consumer who has concluded a contract containing an unfair term can ask the court to find that the unfair term should not be binding.

- A complaint, for example by an individual, a consumer group or a trading standards department can be made to the **Director General of Fair Trading**.

The application of the Unfair Contract Terms Act 1977 depends to a great extent upon whether there is a **consumer sale**. A contract between business operations is considerably less affected by the Act. Both types often have to satisfy a statutory test of **reasonableness**. The Unfair Terms in Consumer Contracts Regulations 1999 define what is meant by an **unfair term**.

1.6 FSA and unfair contract terms

The **Financial Services Authority** has the power to seek a Court **injunction** to prevent firms from using an unfair contract term. The injunction can be binding on other firms using similar terms. Most cases would, however, be settled by the firm undertaking to stop using the unfair term, before the matter goes to Court.

2 The OFT and the Consumer Credit Act

2.1 The Office of Fair Trading

The **Office of Fair Trading (OFT)** has the goal of helping make markets work well for consumers. Markets work well, the OFT states, 'when fair-dealing businesses are in open and vigorous competition with each other for custom'.

The OFT offers advice, support and guidance to businesses on competition issues and on consumer legislation. It also seeks to promote good practice in business by granting 'approved status' to Consumer Codes of Practice meeting set criteria. The OFT will pursue businesses that rig prices or use unfair terms in contracts.

Under the **Control of Misleading Advertising Regulations**, the OFT works with bodies including the Advertising Standards Authority in exercising its powers to seek injunctions to stop advertising that is deceptive or misleading.

2.2 Consumer credit licences

The OFT regulates the consumer credit market with the aim of ensuring fair dealing by businesses in the market. It operates a **licensing system** through which checks are carried out on consumer credit businesses and it issues guidelines on how the law will be enforced.

Through this licensing system, the OFT:

- Assesses applicants' fitness to hold a consumer credit licence and monitors the fitness of existing licence holders

- Issues and updates licences, and keeps public records of licensed businesses

Most businesses that are involved in the following activities are required under the **Consumer Credit Act 1974** to obtain a **consumer credit licence from the OFT**: offering goods or services on credit, lending money or hiring out goods to consumers, running a credit reference or debt collection agency or offer debt counselling, debt adjustment or debt collection services, or acting as credit brokers. Thus, for example, a **financial adviser** who offers **debt counselling or debt restructuring services** needs to be licensed.

Trading without a licence is a criminal offence and can result in a fine and/or imprisonment. An unlicensed company might not be able to enforce credit agreements in court, if the customer defaults.

2.3 The OFT and the FSA

The OFT has specific responsibilities under the Financial Services and Markets Act 2000 (FSMA 2000).

It is part of the role of the OFT to keep under review the activities and rules of the FSA with respect to competition issues.

If the OFT believes that FSA rules will impact adversely on competition, then it will report this to the FSA, the Treasury and the **Competition Commission (CC).** The CC is required to report on the matter to the Treasury, the FSA and the OFT. The Treasury must then decide on any further action, which could include requiring the FSA to change the rules concerned.

2.4 Consumer Credit Act 1974

One of the reasons for the passing of the **Consumer Credit Act 1974 (CCA)** was because credit agreements were being signed without individuals properly reading them and without their understanding them. Such agreements could then be legally enforced even though they might have been **unfair or contain exorbitant terms**.

The Consumer Credit Act does not itself ensure that credit agreements are reasonable. It aims to ensure that anybody who signs a credit agreement has the **opportunity to know what they are doing**.

2.5 Regulated business

Credit business where an agreement is in respect of credit of **up to £25,000** is **regulated** under the CCA. Activities covered by the Act include the introducing of clients to sources of finance and advising on methods of repayment of loans. Building societies mortgages and mortgages from other lenders who have a specific exemption are excluded. Loans to limited companies are excluded.

2.6 Cooling off, disclosure and procedures

People entering into credit agreements regulated under the CCA must be given a **copy of the agreement** for their own records **seven clear days before** the actual agreement is sent to them for signature. In addition they must have a **cooling off period** of seven further days in which they may change their minds and cancel the agreement. The lender must not contact the customer during this period.

The Act also regulates the procedures for the **enforcement** of an agreement and the requirement relating to the repayments of the credit given.

Any organisation giving credit needs a **licence** from the **OFT** to do so. This includes not only life companies but also tied agents who need their own separate licences, as they are not covered by the life company's licence.

The Act regulates how the **Annual Percentage Rate (APR)** must be calculated in order to show the full effect of the rate of interest being charged. The APR must be quoted prominently in **advertisements**.

3 CAT standards and ISAs

3.1 Charges, Access, Terms

CAT standards are intended to indicate that a product has **fair Charges, easy Access** and **decent Terms.**

CAT standards were introduced by the government to help consumers identify products which are straightforward and a reasonable deal. They can help the consumer when making comparisons between different financial products.

With the introduction of a wider range of **stakeholder products** – discussed earlier – stakeholder standards are replacing the concept of CAT standards.

Just because a product has a CAT standard does not mean that it is approved or that its performance is guaranteed by the Government: no such Government guarantee is implied.

CAT standards have applied to the following types of product:

- **Individual Savings Accounts** – but up to 5 April 2005 only
- **Mortgages**

The standards applying to **stakeholder pensions** also cover the three aspects: **charges, access** and **terms**..

3.2 Stakeholder pensions

Stakeholder pension plans (SHPs) were introduced in April 2001 and follow similar rules to personal pension plans, except that the following rules apply to SHPs.

- **Charges.** For new plans, charges are limited to 1.5% of the fund value pa for the first ten years and 1% pa thereafter. For plans started before 6 April 2005, a limit of 1% applies in all years.

- **Access.** The minimum contribution level must not exceed £20.

- **Terms.** Contributions can be raised or stopped without penalty. Transfers in or out attract no exit penalty.

3.3 Individual Savings Accounts

Individual Savings Accounts (ISAs) have been mentioned earlier in this Study Text. ISAs provide a tax-free 'wrapper' for limited amounts of **cash** savings and for investment in **stocks and shares**.

There has also been a **life insurance** component, but from 6 April 2005 this was combined into the stocks and shares component.

The stocks and shares component is able to hold eligible life insurance products and **medium-term stakeholder products**.

In a particular tax year, an individual investor may contribute **either** to a single '**maxi-ISA**', covering the different ISA components, **or** to separate '**mini-ISAs**', which are each for a single component only. It is not permitted to contribute to both a mini-ISA and a maxi-ISA in a single tax year. ISAs cannot be held **jointly**.

The ISA limits are summarised in the Table below. The limits for the tax year 2006/07 are expected to apply unchanged until 5 April 2009.

	ISA Component	2006/07
Mini-ISAs	Cash	£3,000
	Stocks and shares	£4,000
Maxi-ISA	Cash	£3,000
	Stocks and shares	£7,000 *less* amount invested in cash component

3.4 CAT standard ISAs

CAT standards were **withdrawn** for **new ISAs**, with effect **from 6 April 2005**. Existing CAT standard ISAs continue to operate under the same terms. However, providers should longer refer to CAT standards in marketing ISA products, and there is no need now for knowledge of what the ISA CAT standards were. The CAT standards have been withdrawn for ISAs because of the introduction of the new range of risk-controlled **stakeholder** suite of products, which was discussed in Chapter 13 of this Study Text.

3.5 CAT standards for mortgage products

The idea of 'CAT' standards covering **charges**, **access** and **terms** extends to **mortgages**, on a voluntary basis. A lender may decide to label a mortgage product as meeting CAT standards and must then meet the requirements set out below for that product. CAT standards for mortgages are not affected by the withdrawal of CAT standards for ISAs.

As indicated earlier, although the CAT standards are published by the Government, CAT standard mortgages do not carry a government endorsement or guarantee.

CAT-standard mortgages might not suit all borrowers and do not necessarily represent the best deal available. However, the CAT standards fulfil their role in providing a useful **benchmark** for customers when comparing different mortgage products available.

Both **capital repayment** and **interest-only** loans can qualify as CAT standard. Discounted, flexible and cash-back loans can also qualify provided they meet all the CAT standard conditions. (Cash-back loans include mortgages with free services such as valuation fees and solicitors' fees.)

3.6 Two sets of CAT standards

There are two sets of CAT standards for mortgages:

- Standards loans charging **variable interest rates**
- Standards for loans charging **fixed or capped interest rates**

For **variable rate** CAT standard mortgages:

(a) There is no arrangement fee.

(b) The interest rate is no more than 2% above Bank of England base rate. When the base rate falls, interest rates must adjust within a calendar month.

(c) There are no redemption charges at any time.

A lender offering a variable rate CAT standard mortgage may offer different interest rates to different borrowers, provided that all loans in the CAT standard range meet all the CAT standard conditions. For example a lender's CAT standard mortgage product might have **different margins against base rate** according to the **loan to value ratio** of the mortgage.

For **fixed or capped rate** CAT standard mortgages:

(a) Any booking fee must not exceed £150.

(b) The maximum early repayment charge is 1% of the amount owed for each remaining year of the fixed period, reducing monthly. There is no early repayment charge after the fixed or capped rate period, and no charge if the borrower stays with the same mortgage lender when moving home.

Example: CAT standard mortgage

A borrower is seeking a CAT standard mortgage with an interest rate that is initially fixed or capped for 3 years.

What would be the maximum early repayment charges for such a mortgage, in the following circumstances?

After two years, half of the outstanding balance of £50,000 on a loan is repaid, or

After two and a half years, all of the outstanding balance of £50,000 on a loan is repaid?

Solution

At the point of early repayment, the maximum charge is £500 per year of the fixed period still left eg:

(a) If half of the loan is repaid early at the end of the second year, with a year of fixed rate left to run, the charge will be:

1% of £25,000 = £250

(b) After 2½ years of the fixed rate period, with 6 months of the fixed rate period left to run, the charge will be:

0.5% of £50,000 = £250

Note: These examples show the maximum early repayment charge. A CAT standard mortgage may charge less than this but never more.

For **all CAT standard mortgages**:

(a) All **advertising and paperwork** must be straightforward, fair and clear.

(b) A customer must **not be required to buy any other product** to get a CAT standard mortgage.

(c) The lender must give at least **six months notice** if they can no longer offer the mortgage on CAT standard terms.

(d) A customer in **arrears** should pay interest only on the outstanding debt at the normal rate.

Lenders must make CAT standard mortgages available on the **same terms to both existing and new customers** provided they are creditworthy and propose to borrow on property the lender finds acceptable as security. (Existing customers may have charges to meet under the terms of a previous loan.) This means that existing customers must be eligible to **re-mortgage** to a CAT standard mortgage.

Lenders do not have to offer CAT standard mortgages to every borrower on every possible loan, but they should not **restrict** CAT standard mortgages to a privileged group.

The CAT standard does not set limits on loan to value ratios (ie minimum deposits compared to property value) or borrowers' income multiples (ie the maximum loan compared to the borrower's income). These are matters for the lender, taking account of the borrower's ability to repay the loan.

Lenders may set a **minimum loan size**. If they do, it must be **£10,000 or less** for a CAT standard mortgage.

3.7 Interest calculation and payment

With CAT standard mortgages:

    (a)   Lenders must calculate interest on CAT standard mortgages **daily**.

    (b)   All borrowers' payments, without exception, must be **credited in full** when they are cleared through the banking system, with interest adjusted accordingly. This means that the final repayment to close a CAT standard mortgage cannot include interest for any period after the date of the final payment.

    (c)   For monthly payments (including interest), the borrower may initially choose **any day** between the 1st and 28th of the month. (CAT standard loans may also permit **irregular payments**, eg in flexible mortgages.)

3.8 Portability

CAT standard mortgages should be **portable**. That is, lenders should let borrowers continue with their existing CAT standard mortgage product if the lender finds the borrower's new home acceptable as security and the borrower remains creditworthy.

This means, for example, that on moving home, the borrower should be able to continue with a fixed or discounted rate still running on a CAT standard mortgage, up to the amount of the mortgage on the original property.

Alternatively, the borrower can close the original mortgage and start a new mortgage on the new property on different terms, whether CAT standard or not. The lender may charge its normal terms for closing the original mortgage and the borrower may face costs such as legal fees for opening the new one.

The lender should offer the same mortgage product on the new property, although this may not mean exactly the same interest rate, for example if the mortgage product has different interest rates for borrowers in different circumstances.

The lender does not have to continue a CAT standard mortgage on the borrower's new property if a CAT standard mortgage would not normally be available on the new loan.

3.9 Fees, charges and commission

Brokers cannot charge borrowers introduction fees for CAT standard mortgages. Lenders can pay fees or commission to brokers if this is disclosed to customers.

CAT standard mortgages cannot have explicit **separate higher lending charges** (ie, for mortgage indemnity guarantees, mortgage indemnity insurance, or any other equivalent fee). Lenders may however charge a higher interest rate to borrowers with smaller deposits provided that all the other conditions (including the interest rate margin for variable loans and redemption charges for fixed loans) are met.

Lenders should send to each borrower with a CAT standard mortgage an **annual reminder of any ongoing fees**, including any sealing fees payable when a mortgage is fully paid off and any information about the charges if the borrower goes into arrears.

Lenders should give borrowers at least **three months notice of any upward variations** in fees or other terms not to the borrower's advantage, other than changes in interest rates.

4 Data protection rules

4.1 Data Protection Act 1998

Everyone is familiar nowadays with the fact that there is **data protection** legislation.

The **Data Protection Act 1998** replaced the earlier Data Protection Act 1984 and put into UK law the provisions of the **EU Data Protection Directive 1995**. The objective of the Data Protection Act is to **regulate the use of personal information.**

Some of the important features of the legislation are as follows.

(a)   Clarification of conditions under which data processing is lawful

(b)   Right given to everyone to seek redress at court for breach of the Act

(c)   Paper-based, microfilm and microfiche filing systems are encompassed by the Act, which covers information recorded in a 'relevant filing system' as well as in a computer system

(d)   The case of **Durant v FSA (2003),** dealt with the definition of a '**relevant filing system**'. This is a system that is so referenced or indexed as to enable the **data controller** to identify with reasonable certainty and speed relevant files and personal data without having to make a manual search for them. This means that some manual files will not be subject to the Data Protection Act.

4.2 Obligations under data protection law

There are various obligations for any organisation that keeps personal information, as follows.

- The organisation must have a **data protection policy**.
- **Personal data** must have been **obtained lawfully and fairly** and shall not be processed unless at least one of the **Schedule 2 conditions** is met (see below).
- In the case of **sensitive personal data**, the data subject's explicit consent is normally required. Sensitive data includes data on a data subject's racial or ethnic origin, religious or political beliefs, health or sexual orientation.
- Data must be **held and used** only for **lawful purposes.**
- Data should be used only **for the purposes for which it was originally obtained.**
- The data must not exceed what is **necessary** for the purpose for which it was obtained.
- Data must be **accurate** and must be **updated regularly.**
- Data must **not be kept longer than is necessary** for its lawful purpose.
- The person whose data is held is entitled to **access** to that information and has the right to correct it where appropriate. The **data subject** may be charged a **maximum fee of £10 for access** to their records, with a **maximum fee of £2** in the case of credit reference agency records. The person is also entitled to be told the source, purposes and recipients of the data. The 1998 Act requires **requests to be dealt with** 'promptly' and, in any event, within **40 days** of the request (along with any fee) being received.
- The data must be **protected** by appropriate technical and organisational measures against unauthorised or unlawful access and against accidental loss, destruction or damage.
- Unless the data is **exempt**, a data controller (such as a firm) processing personal data must **register** the holding of data with the **Public Register of Data Controllers** (the **Data Protection Register**), maintained by the **Information Commissioner**. Each register entry includes the name and address of the data controller, details of the data processed, the purpose and source for which it is held, and who has the right to see it.

    (As an *Exercise*, look up your firm, or your bank or another organisation, in the public register at www.informationcommissioner.gov.uk)

- Personal data must not be transferred outside the European Economic Area unless to a country or territory that ensures an adequate level of protection for the rights and freedoms of data subjects in respect of processing of personal data.

Personal data is any data relating to an identifiable living individual (the **data subject**).

There are **exemptions** for data controllers who only process personal data for:

- Staff administration (including payroll)
- Advertising, marketing and public relations (for their own business)
- Accounts and records of some not-for-profit organisations

There are also exemptions for:

- Processing personal data for personal, family or household affairs (including recreational purposes)
- Maintenance of a public register

The **Schedule 2 conditions** (see above) are that:

(a)   The data subject has given consent to the processing of the data

(b)   The processing is necessary in connection with a contract entered into by the data subject

(c)   The processing is necessary for the data controller to comply with legal obligations

(d)   The processing is necessary for public functions exercised in the public interest

(e)   The processing is necessary in pursuing the data controller's legitimate interests, provided that the processing does not prejudice the data subject's rights, freedoms or legal interests

4.3 Enforcement of the Data Protection Act

The working of the Data Protection Act is overseen by the **Information Commissioner**.

If the Information Commissioner considers that a data controller is in contravention of any of the data protection principles, the Commissioner can serve an **enforcement notice**. If the data controller fails to comply with the enforcement notice, he is committing an offence and could be subject to a **fine** of **£5,000**.

An offence is also committed if data is processed without prior notification.

An individual should take a **complaint** about a firm to the firm itself, in the first instance. If not satisfied with the outcome, the individual can approach the Information Commissioner with a **Request for Assessment**.

As mentioned earlier, the individual ultimately has the right to seek redress for a breach under the Act **through the courts**.

5 The Pensions Regulator

5.1 Introduction

The **Pensions Regulator** (PR) took over the role of the previous Occupational Pensions Regulatory Authority (OPRA) with effect from 6 April 2005.

The Pensions Regulator is now the regulator of work-based pension schemes in the UK, and it is financed by **levies** on pension schemes. A **work-based pension scheme** is any scheme that an employer makes available to employees. This includes all occupational schemes, and any stakeholder and personal pension schemes where employees have direct payment arrangements.

The PR has the following **statutory objectives**.

- To **protect the benefits of members** of work-based (occupational or personal pension) schemes
- To **reduce the risk** of situations arising that may lead to claims from the **Pension Protection Fund**
- To promote **good administration** of the schemes it regulates

Codes of practice published by the PR:

- Give practical guidance on compliance with the legal requirements on pensions
- Set out standards of conduct and practice for those providing and running pension schemes

The PR codes of practice are not statements of the law and there are no penalties for failing to comply with them.

5.2 Powers of the Pensions Regulator

The PR's top priority is to tackle risks to members' benefits. They plan to focus resources on identifying and reducing risks, working with pensions schemes to solve problems.

Created under the **Pensions Act 2004**, the PR has wider powers than OPRA and seeks to adopt a new proactive and risk-focused approach to regulation.

- All schemes are required to complete an annual return to the PR giving detailed information about the scheme, and the regulator has powers to require anyone to provide information and to inspect premises. Refusal to cooperate is an offence.

- Trustees, scheme managers, scheme administrators, advisers and employers are required to report in writing information about breaches of the law and potential risks to the scheme, if they are material. This is called **'whistleblowing'**.

- Possible **late payments of contributions** by the employer to the scheme are a particular area of scrutiny. If an employer cannot make contributions because the business is struggling, the PR can help trustees and the employer to reach agreement about levels of contributions to the scheme, and establish a long-term funding plan for the scheme.

- If there is not enough money in a scheme to provide benefits that members are expecting, the PR has powers to order the employer to **pay any shortfall** into the scheme.

- If companies are believed to have sought to avoid a shortfall on winding-up, eg through a corporate re-structuring, the PR can order individuals or companies involved to pay the shortfall.

- The PR can order scheme administrators to **improve the service** they provide to trustees, if the service is below standard.

- The regulator make seek to have any **money stolen** from a scheme returned.

- The PR can **suspend** a trustee, for example if they are involved in proceedings involving dishonesty, theft or insolvency. The PR can **prohibit** a person from being a trustee of a pension scheme if the person is in serious or persistent breach of their duties. The PR maintains a **register of prohibited trustees**.

- The regulator may **report** an **Independent Financial Adviser** or a **life office** to the FSA if they give misleading information to trustees or show insufficient knowledge.

- The PR has the power to **wind up** a scheme and can itself **appoint trustees** for a scheme if necessary to keep the scheme running. It can obtain an **injunction** from a court to prevent misuse of scheme assets.

- **Fines** can be imposed on trustees or employers by the regulator (up to **£5,000 for individuals** or **£50,000 for companies**).

Trustees and employers are required to give early warning of situations potentially leading to a claim on the Pensions Protection Fund.

- Trustees must report events relating to pension scheme funding –eg, reduction in the scheme membership

- The employer must report events relating to the firm's solvency –eg, changes in its credit rating

- Both trustees and the employer must report any proposal that would compromise the debt owed to the scheme on winding-up

Appeals against decisions of the PR can be directed to the **Pensions Regulator Tribunal**.

5.3 Pension Schemes Registry

The PR maintains a **register** of occupational pension schemes and personal or stakeholder pensions for employees.

The purpose of the registry is to help employees who have left their employment to trace schemes in which they have accumulated benefits. Tracing benefits can be difficult when schemes have terminated or companies have re-structured.

6 Code of Conduct and Principles [IFA Qualification only]

6.1 Introduction

This section is for students sitting the SII's IFA Qualification examinations, which may include questions on the SII's Code of Conduct and Principles.

Members of the **Securities and Investment Institute (SII)** are required to meet the standards set out within the Institute's Principles. In honouring these principles, members must act in a way that moves beyond mere compliance and supports the underlying values of the Institute.

Professionals within the securities and investment industry owe important **duties** to their clients, to the market, the industry and to society at large. Where these duties are set out in law or in regulation, the professional must always comply with the requirements in an open and transparent manner.

6.2 SII Principles

There are seven core **Principles** in the SII's Code of Conduct, and these Principles are set out below. The **stakeholders** to whom different Principles are relevant include **clients, firms, regulators, market participants** and the **SII member**. A material breach of the Principles would be incompatible with continuing membership of the Securities & Investment Institute.

The Principles

1. To act honestly and fairly at all times when dealing with clients, customers and counterparties and to be a good steward of their interests, taking into account the nature of the business relationship with each of them, the nature of the service to be provided to them and the individual mandates given by them.

2. To act with integrity in fulfilling the responsibilities of your appointment and seek to avoid any acts, omissions or business practices which damage the reputation of your organisation or which are deceitful, oppressive or improper and to promote high standards of conduct throughout your organisation.

3. To observe applicable law, regulations and professional conduct standards when carrying out financial service activities and to interpret and apply them to the best of your ability, according to principles rooted in trust, honesty and integrity.

4. When executing transactions or engaging in any form of market dealings, to observe the standards of market integrity, good practice and conduct required by, or expected of, participants in that market.

5. To manage fairly and effectively, and to the best of your ability, any relevant conflict of interest, including making any disclosure of its existence where disclosure is required by law or regulation or by your employing organisation.*

6. To obtain and maintain actively a level of professional competence appropriate to your responsibilities and to commit to continuing learning and the development of others.

7. To strive to uphold the highest personal standards, including rejecting short-term profits which may jeopardise your reputation and that of your employer, the Institute and the industry.

Principle 5 of the SII's Code of Conduct concerns **conflicts of interest**. On some occasions, if there is a conflict of interest, members may decide to decline to act.

SII members who find themselves in a position which might require them to act in a manner contrary to the Principles are encouraged to:

(a) Discuss their concerns with their line manager
(b) Seek advice from their internal compliance department
(c) Approach their firm's non-executive directors or audit committee
(d) If unable to resolve their concerns and, having exhausted all internal avenues, contact the SII for advice

Key chapter points

- The law on unfair contract terms addresses the issue of whether an exclusion clause in a contract is valid, but does not apply to insurance contracts. A clause that attempts to limit liability for breach of contract is void unless it can be shown to be reasonable. The relative strength of the bargaining positions of the parties will be considered in deciding what is 'reasonable'.

- The Office of Trading operates a system of licensing businesses that provide consumer credit. The OFT also works to keep markets operating as fairly as possible, and it seeks to stop advertising that is deceptive or misleading.

- The OFT has responsibilities under FSMA 2000 to keep the rules and operations of the FSA under review in relation to competition issues. The Competition Commission and the Treasury will become involved if the OFT makes a report on possibly anti-competitive FSA rules.

- The Consumer Credit Act covers credit agreements of up to £25,000 aims to ensure that somebody who signs a credit agreement has the opportunity to know what they are doing. People entering into credit agreements must be given a copy of the agreement for their own records. In addition they must be a cooling off period of 14 days.

- The government established voluntary CAT standards for ISAs (applying until 5 April 2005 only) and for mortgages. A mortgage provider can choose to market CAT standard products. The CAT standards are intended to indicate to consumers that a product has fair Charges, easy Access and decent Terms.

- The use of personal information is regulated by the Data Protection Act 1998, which put into UK law the provisions of the EU Data Protection Directive 1995. The Act covers paper-based as well as computer based information storage systems.

- The Pensions Regulator is the new regulator for work-based (occupational) pension schemes and has taken over from the former Occupational Pensions Regulatory Authority.

Chapter Quiz

1   Which UK regulations implemented the EU Directive on unfair contract terms? .... (see para 1.5)

2   What forms of redress are available in respect of unfair contract terms? ....(1.5)

3   Who operates the licensing system for consumer credit business? ....(2.2)

4   Who would become involved if the Office of Fair Trading reported adversely on FSA rules? ....(2.3)

5   How long is the cooling off period that must be allowed in credit business?....................................(2.6)

6   What is the purpose of CAT standards and which product types do they cover?...(3.1)

7   What do CAT standards lay down in respect of the portability of mortgages? ....(3.8)

8   Outline the scope of the Data Protection Act 1998. ....(4.1)

9   What information is maintained in the Public Register of Data Controllers? ....(4.2)

10 What are the Pensions Regulator's objectives? ....(5.1)

Practice Questions

Time allowed: 120 minutes

You may use the Tax Tables provided at the end
of this Study Text.

Questions

For each question, choose one option: A, B, C or D.

1 Which one of the following statements **most closely** describes the process of 'maturity transformation' provided through financial intermediaries?

    A   Depositors can invest and borrowers can borrow for various different lengths of time.

    B   Smaller amounts deposited are put together to make loans of larger size.

    C   Advice is given on how long a customer should invest funds.

    D   Risks of default on loans are pooled.

2 The most important target of the Monetary Policy Committee of the Bank of England in setting interest rates is:

    A   The rate of money supply growth

    B   The rate of consumer price inflation

    C   The pound/euro exchange rate

    D   The pound/US dollar exchange rate

3 Which of the following statements is **incorrect** regarding European Union law?

    A   An EU Directive has the force of law in member states without need of national legislation.

    B   EU Directives are issued to member governments.

    C   EU Regulations are formulated by the European Commission and authorised by the Council of Ministers.

    D   An EU Decision is immediately binding on its recipient.

4 Mr Feldman has a sum of capital which he does not want to place at risk. Which one of the following would be the **most suitable** investment?

    A   'Blue chip' shares

    B   Corporate bond fund

    C   Building society share account

    D   Open Ended Investment Company shares

5 The Alternative Investment Market is **best** described as:

    A   An exchange for trading in derivatives

    B   A money market for wholesale lending and borrowing

    C   A capital market for trading shares of smaller or newer companies

    D   A market for trading of junk bonds

6 An investor might avoid using bank deposit accounts for long-term investment because such accounts:

    A   Cannot pay interest gross to a non-taxpayer

    B   Have produced lower returns than asset-backed investments over long-term periods

    C   Are not covered by an investor compensation scheme

    D   Carry a relatively high level of risk of capital loss

7 The **most usual** key priority need in financial planning associated with someone becoming a parent is:

    A   Retirement planning

    B   Protection

    C   Savings and investment

    D   Tax planning

8 A bank account pays a positive real rate of return when:

    A   It pays interest above 0%

    B   It pays interest in excess of charges levied

    C   It pays interest in excess of the rate of inflation

    D   It pays higher interest than in the previous year

9   If rental yields on newly purchased residential property are rising, this could be because of:

   A   Rising rents, or falling property prices
   B   Rising rents, or rising property prices
   C   Falling rents, or falling property prices
   D   Falling rents, or rising property prices

10   A gilt-edged security is an investment **most** accurately described as:

   A   A loan to the UK Government
   B   A loan to a local authority
   C   A deposit account with one of the major High Street banks
   D   An equity investment in the Bank of England

11   Which of the following is **not** a feature of index-linked gilts?

   A   Interest payments indexed in line with the RPI
   B   The redemption payment is indexed in line with the RPI
   C   The indexation is calculated on the average of the previous eight months RPI
   D   The indexation is calculated up to the RPI measured at eight months before payment

12   An investment trust is:

   A   An open ended investment fund
   B   A private company limited by guarantee
   C   A public company which invests solely in unit trusts
   D   A public limited company which is closed-ended

13   The beta factor of a share is best described as a measure of:

   A   The extent to which total returns from the share will be reduced by taxes and charges
   B   The probability that the company concerned will be the subject of a takeover
   C   The volatility of the value of the shares relative to the market
   D   The risk that the share price will fall to zero

14   Which one of the following factors makes an equity-based unit trust investment **less** risky than a direct holding of shares in a company?

   In the case of equities unit trusts:

   A   The likelihood of capital loss is spread
   B   The investments are index-linked
   C   The units have a minimum capital value
   D   There is protection of capital

15   Which one of the following is exempt from income tax?

   A   Dividends from shares
   B   NS&I Premium Bond winnings
   C   Interest from NS&I Capital Bonds
   D   Rent from property

16   Andrew has received a net dividend of £80 together with a tax credit of £8.89. The investment is not held in an ISA or PEP. Andrew is retired, and his total taxable income after all allowances and deductions in 2006/07 before taking account of the net dividend will be £4,500. What will be his tax liability in respect of the dividend?

   A   He will be liable to pay a further £8.89 in tax.
   B   He will be neither liable for further tax nor entitled to a refund.
   C   He is unable to use the tax credit, and will be liable to pay a further £17.78 in tax.
   D   He will be able to claim a refund of £8.89.

17   'Re-mortgaging' is best described as a situation in which:

   A   A mortgage borrower switches to a new lender
   B   A mortgage borrower takes out a second loan on the mortgaged property
   C   A lender takes action on a mortgage account that is in arrears
   D   A lender transfers mortgage business to a new lender

18   Which of the following factors is **not** relevant to assessing the suitability of financial planning solutions for a client?

   A   The client's attitude to risk
   B   State benefits to which the client is entitled
   C   The time period to maturity for financial products chosen
   D   The structure of the commission payments made to the adviser

19   Capital gains tax will be potentially chargeable on gains made by individuals from the sale of which of the following, if held in the individual's name?

   A   Chattels valued at less than £6,000
   B   Gilt edged securities
   C   Listed company shares
   D   A private car

20   'Sub-prime' mortgage lending describes:

   A   Equity release and re-mortgage business
   B   Lending to applicants with low credit ratings or who cannot show satisfactory evidence of income
   C   Lending with a high loan-to-value ratio
   D   Lending on the security of repossessed properties

21   Which of the following types of investment is **not** subject to a maximum contribution limit in a single tax year?

   A   Personal pension plans
   B   Stakeholder linked long-term funds
   C   Individual Savings Accounts
   D   Stakeholder pensions

22   Which of the following provides the **most** appropriate form of cover for the future inheritance tax liability of an estate?

   A   Whole of life policy
   B   Income protection insurance
   C   Family income benefit policy
   D   Endowment policy

23   The **main** purpose in quantifying the disposable income of each prospective client is to determine:

   A   The affordability of products recommended
   B   The suitability of products recommended
   C   Their marginal rate of tax
   D   The most appropriate size of an emergency fund

24   Whilst performing the first client interview, your prospective client asks, 'Why does an adviser undertake a fact find?' You respond as follows:

   A   To decide whether an investment should be purchased or sold
   B   To enable investment performance to be measured
   C   To enable suitable advice to be given to a client
   D   To enable the facts to be established when a customer has a complaint

25   An adviser gives to her customer her firm's disclosure document entitled 'Key Facts: A Guide to the Cost of Our Services'. Which of the following does this document **not** normally include?

    A   Information about the regulator
    B   The maximum commission the firm is likely to receive from a transaction
    C   Details of charges incurred to date
    D   An indication of the market average commission

26   If a client refuses to supply relevant information, the action that should be taken by a financial adviser is to:

    A   Decline to act for the client
    B   Notify the Financial Services Authority
    C   Recommend the client to seek advice elsewhere
    D   Record the fact that information was not supplied

27   Concerning suitability requirements, which of the following is **false**?

    A   A firm may rely, without further enquiry, on information received from a customer intended to ascertain his investment objectives and financial position.

    B   A firm which has provided advice and sold a financial product has a responsibility continually to review the client's investments and to advise on their suitability.

    C   An employee of an authorised firm must not give investment advice (other than in an investment publication) to a private customer unless it is suitable for the customer concerned.

    D   An employee of an authorised firm must warn a customer who is advised by the firm if the customer gives instructions to make an unsuitable investment.

28   In connection with the law of contract, what is a life assurance company's 'consideration'?

    A   Acceptance of the payment of a first premium
    B   Payment of a death claim on production of a death certificate
    C   Confirmation that a proposal for life assurance has been accepted
    D   A promise to pay when a specified event occurs

29   To which of the following types of contract does the principle of utmost good faith *(uberrimae fidei)* apply?

    A   All contracts
    B   Consumer contracts
    C   Life assurance contracts
    D   Contracts for the sale of goods

30   One of the essentials of a valid will is that:

    A   The beneficiaries must be notified that they will have legal rights when the testator dies
    B   The witnesses to the testator's signature must not themselves be beneficiaries
    C   The will is stated to be valid in all circumstances unless the testator changes it
    D   The will can ensure that an estate is distributed in the manner laid down by the rules of succession

31   Which of the following statements about limited liability is **correct**?

    A   A main reason for converting a private company into a public company is to enable shareholders to gain the benefits of limited liability.

    B   By law, at least one director of a registered company must have unlimited personal liability for debts incurred by the company.

    C   If a limited company is unable to meet its liabilities, there may be circumstances in which the directors can be declared personally bankrupt.

    D   In the event of incurring business debts, an unincorporated sole trader can benefit from limited liability.

32 Nadia and John were married and lived in and owned a house as joint tenants. John has died without leaving a will. Which of the following is **true** in respect of the house?

A   It will now be owned outright by Nadia.

B   50% of the value of the house will be subject to inheritance tax.

C   A 50% share in the house will be inherited by their children in equal shares or, if they have no children, by Nadia, with the remaining 50% going to Nadia.

D   A 25% share in the house will be inherited by their children in equal shares or, if they have no children, by Nadia, with the remaining 75% going to Nadia.

33 Which of the following is **not necessarily** a feature of the relationship between an agent and a principal?

A   The agent receives payment from the principal.

B   The agent has a duty to avoid conflicts of interest with the principal.

C   The agent must hand over any benefit to the principal unless the principal agrees otherwise.

D   The agent must keep what he knows of the principal's affairs confidential even after the agency relationship ceases.

34 To be a fully binding agreement, which of the following attributes does a contract **not** necessarily need to have?

A   Offer and acceptance
B   Intention to create legal relations
C   Consideration
D   Expressed in writing

35 An attorney may be defined as:

A   A person who is not mentally capable of handling their own affairs
B   The person who takes possession of the assets of a bankrupt and distributes them to creditors
C   A person who has been given authority to act on another person's behalf
D   A person who signs documents but does not have the authority to enter into a contract

36 Amelia is a self employed fashion designer who started to trade on 1 June 1998 and whose financial year ends on 31 May. Her tax payable for the 2006/07 fiscal year is £10,000. For 2005/06, the amount payable was £8,000. Excluding any final balancing payment, what payments should she normally make?

A   £10,000 on 6 April 2007
B   £10,000 on 1 January 2008
C   £5,000 on 6 April 2007 and £5,000 on 6 October 2007
D   £4,000 on 31 January 2007 and £4,000 on 31 July 2007

37 Benefits in kind are normally taxable, but an employee will **not** be taxed on:

A   Private use of a company car
B   An employer's contribution to a personal pension
C   An interest free mortgage for house purchase
D   A loan at a preferential rate of interest

38   What is the effect on the tax liability and allowance entitlement of a single woman aged 70 when her gross income exceeds the income limit by £1,000?

A   Her personal allowance will reduce by 50% of the excess over her taxable income.

B   She will be unable to offset pension contributions against her gross income.

C   She can mitigate the reduction by investing in NS&I Income Bonds.

D   Her age allowance reduces by £1 for every £2 over the income limit, until it reaches the level of the personal allowance.

39   An investor makes purchases of (1) 5,000 shares in the Westward Follower plc Investment Trust at 200 pence each through CREST, and (2) 1,000 units in the Feeman Greville High Dividend Unit Trust at 300 pence each.

The investor will pay Stamp Duty Reserve Tax on the respective transactions as follows.

A   (1) £50 (2) Nil
B   (1) £50 (2) £15
C   (1) £100 (2) £Nil
D   (1) £100 (2) £30

40   Class 2 National Insurance Contributions are payable by:

A   A Civil Servant earning an annual salary of £29,000
B   A full-time director of a company in the defence contracting business whose annual salary is £72,000
C   An Administrative Assistant earning £17,000 per year and working for a charity
D   A freelance interior designer with annual profits of £11,000

41   Which of the following State benefits is **not** subject to tax?

A   National Insurance Retirement Pension
B   Child benefit
C   Jobseekers' Allowance
D   Invalid Care Allowance

42   When an employee is liable for Class 1 National Insurance contributions, the employer is automatically liable to pay:

A   Secondary Class 1 contributions
B   Class 2 contributions
C   Class 3 contributions
D   Secondary Class 4 contributions

43   Which one of the following is a **correct** description of inflation?

A   It is measured by the rise in the national average earnings index.
B   It is the rate at which the wholesale prices index increases.
C   It is when pay rises faster than prices.
D   It is the increase in the price of goods and services over a period of time.

44   By reference to which of the following is the UK Government's inflation target set?

A   Consumer Prices Index
B   Average Earnings Index
C   Retail Prices Index
D   Producer Price Index

45   Prices of gilts are **most** likely to fall if market expectations change so as to expect:

A   Lower interest rates
B   Higher interest rates
C   No change to interest rates
D   Early redemption of undated gilts

46   Which of the following could be said to be an advantage to the customer of a tracker mortgage based on a specified margin above the Bank of England repo rate?

A   The interest rate is fixed.

B   The customer knows what their future payments will be.

C   The customer knows that the interest rate will respond to general movements in interest rates in the economy.

D   The interest rate is capped.

47   Regulations regarding the marketing and promotion of investment products are the responsibility of:

A   The Department of Trade and Industry
B   The Office of Fair Trading
C   The London Stock Exchange
D   The Financial Service Authority

48   An example of prudential risk – as a form of consumer risk – is the risk of:

A   Collapse of a firm through poor management
B   Loss from mis-selling
C   Low investment returns
D   Customers choosing unsuitable products through lack of understanding

49   Which **one** of the following statements concerning an adviser's clients conveys objective factual information?

A   Michaela intends to increase her monthly contribution to her stakeholder pension scheme to £300.
B   Beryl's savings account balance has halved in the last two years.
C   Our clients are happier with repayment mortgages than they are with interest-only mortgages.
D   Andrew wants to avoid equity investments because of his attitude to risk.

50   The following statements are all true of the FSA, except which **one**?

A   The FSA is required to have a system to ensure persons are complying with their obligations when conducting investment business.

B   FSA rules are enforceable at law.

C   The FSA authorises people to conduct investment business.

D   All of the FSA's Statements of Principle for Approved Persons apply to those providing investment advice to customers.

51   When a firm advertises an investment which may fluctuate in value, a warning must be given on the advertisement of the possibility of a fall in value. This is a requirement of the:

A   FSA Principles for Business
B   Advertising Standards Authority
C   Department of Trade and Industry
D   FSA Conduct of Business Rules

52   The FSA's risk-based approach to the supervision of small firms is characterised by:

    I   Regular inspection visits to all authorised firms below a certain size
    II   The abolition of desk-based reviews
    III   Varying levels of supervisory intensity, depending on the regulator's risk assessment

    Choose which one option (A, B, C or D) is correct.

    A   I and II only
    B   I and III only
    C   II and III only
    D   III only

53   The Financial Services Authority's 'protection of consumers' objective requires that the Authority have regard to all of the following except which **one**?

    A   Differing degrees of risk involved in transactions
    B   Differing degrees of experience and expertise of different consumers
    C   Advisers' responsibility for the consequences of their clients' decisions
    D   Customers' needs for advice and accurate information

54   Which of the following are **not** exempt from authorisation by the Financial Services Authority?

    A   Local government authorities
    B   Self-employed appointed representatives
    C   National Savings & Investments
    D   Chartered accountancy firms recommending the purchase of specific investments

55   Which of the following is **not** a designated professional body?

    A   The Institute of Chartered Accountants in England and Wales
    B   The Institute of Actuaries
    C   The Financial Services Authority
    D   The Law Society England & Wales

56   A Disqualification Notice preventing an individual from working for an investment business is issued by:

    A   The Financial Services Authority
    B   HM Treasury
    C   The Department of Trade and Industry
    D   The Serious Fraud Office

57   'Mystery shopping':

    A   Is carried out by FSA staff prior to each monitoring visit
    B   Must be carried out by all authorised firms regularly
    C   Involves posing as a consumer to help establish what a firm would say to a 'genuine' customer
    D   Contravenes FSA regulations

58   Which of the following is correct regarding the Statements of Principles for Approved Persons?

    A   All apply to senior management only
    B   All apply to all approved persons
    C   Some apply to all approved persons and some apply to senior management only
    D   Some apply to all approved persons and some apply to those in customer functions only

59   Which of the following would **not** be an unsolicited real-time communication?

A   A personal call made without the explicit consent of the customer

B   A personal call made because the customer had given the firm his address

C   A telephone call made to sell units in a unit trust to a customer who had previously bought a life policy through the firm

D   A telephone call made to a customer to give regular updates on the composition of his investment portfolio being managed by the firm

60   The Conduct of Business rules apply to:

A   All authorised firms, except authorised professional firms in respect of certain regulated activities
B   Deposits and designated investment business
C   Firms' packaged products business only
D   Investment advice business only

61   Which of the following in an FSA-authorised firm would **not** generally need to be an approved person?

A   Money Laundering Reporting Officer
B   Chief Executive
C   Staff Training Officer
D   Pension Transfer Adviser

62   Which of the following is **not** specifically required of approved persons in the FSA's Statements of Principle for approved persons?

In carrying out his controlled function, an approved person must:

A   Act with integrity
B   Act with due skill, care and diligence
C   Observe proper standards of market conduct
D   Pay due regard to the interests of customers and treat them fairly

63   Which of the following **must** comply with the detailed Conduct of Business rules on financial promotions?

A   Communications by a regulated firm in connection with a takeover
B   A 'tipsheet' style publication, sent out via email by an FSA-authorised firm
C   Circulars sent by an IFA firm to high net worth individuals recommending unlisted securities
D   A personal illustration sent by a regulated firm to an intermediate customer

64   A firm of independent financial advisers publishes a quarterly newsletter for their clients. When they make a recommendation about a particular company's shares in the newsletter, the firm is prohibited from:

A   Including any investment advice in the recommendation
B   Dealing on their own account until a reasonable time after publication
C   Giving advice to any client who is affected by a topic covered in the newsletter
D   Discretionary dealing with any client's assets without specific client instructions

65   To give advice on pensions transfers, a person **must** pass an approved specialist pensions examination:

A   Before giving advice
B   Six months after starting to give advice, if working under supervision
C   Twelve months after starting to give advice, if working under supervision
D   Two years after starting to give advice, if working under supervision

66   'With-profits guide' refers to:

    A   A guide containing information about the insurance company or friendly society marketing a with-profits policy and its with-profits fund

    B   A guide published by the Financial Services Authority containing decision trees for use by consumers considering starting with-profits policies

    C   A guide containing rules on the percentage rates of return to be assumed in projections relating to with-profits policies

    D   A guide sponsored by the Financial Services Authority containing comparisons of performance of all with-profits policies available in the market

67   Who is responsible for sending out a cancellation notice?

    A   The product provider
    B   The compliance officer
    C   The financial adviser
    D   The Financial Services Authority

68   In the context of FSA regulation, which **one** of the following does the suitability rule require of a firm?

    A   Obtain independent confirmation of any information provided
    B   Take reasonable steps to obtain facts about a client's position
    C   Refuse to act for a customer who refuses to provide information
    D   Obtain bank references

69   'Churning':

    A   Is defined by the FSA as switching more frequently than annually for packaged products, and as dealing more frequently than monthly for other investments

    B   Is no longer be relevant following de-polarisation

    C   Is forbidden under FSA rules

    D   Is one of the disadvantages of excessive regulation

70   What is the most important consequence for regulated firms of the FSA's move to a 'principles-based' approach to regulation?

    A   Firms should have fewer detailed FSA rules to follow but must follow higher-level principles.

    B   Firms must formulate a set of principles and must disclose these principles to private customers before they do business.

    C   Firms can expect more regular compliance checks from the FSA, whether or not their activities are regarded as risky.

    D   Firms will decide which detailed rules to follow based on whether the rules are in accord with the firm's principles.

71   A notice advising a customer of the right to cancel a life assurance policy must normally be sent within how many days of making the agreement?

    A   7 days
    B   14 days
    C   21 days
    D   28 days

72   In order to become treated as an intermediate customer, a private customer must be all of the following, **except** which one?

A   Experienced and knowledgeable
B   In receipt of a warning
C   A 'high net worth' individual
D   Given sufficient time to consider their treatment as an intermediate customer

73   What are the restrictions on making unsolicited calls to non-private investors?

A   None.
B   They must only be made between 9am and 9pm and not on Sundays.
C   They must not relate to derivatives.
D   They can only relate to packaged products.

74   A broker firm F does business with an IFA firm which is doing this business on the instruction of an individual. Which of the following is **true**?

A   The IFA firm is a client of F, unless there is an agreement with F to treat the individual as its client.
B   Both the IFA firm and the individual are clients of F.
C   The individual is an indirect customer of the broker, and this relationship cannot be altered.
D   The individual is a client of F, unless there is an agreement to the contrary.

75   Which of the following will **not** be found in a key features document?

A   A description of the investment
B   Cancellation rights
C   Adviser's terms of business
D   Illustrations of returns

76   When recommending a stakeholder pension plan, the independent adviser acts as the agent of:

A   The product provider
B   His employer
C   The client
D   The Financial Services Authority

77   In life assurance, what will normally be the part of the contract which constitutes the 'offer'?

A   An insurer's acknowledgement of receipt of a proposal form
B   An advertisement in an insurer's shop window
C   A postal offer of life assurance with a free gift
D   A completed proposal form

78   You are telling a client about the stakeholder suite of products introduced in April 2005. Which word is **most** appropriate to describe such products?

A   Risk-free
B   Tax-free
C   Government-guaranteed
D   Risk-controlled

79   A separate tailored regime within the MCOB rulebook covers the following type of mortgage:

A   Buy-to-let mortgages
B   Personal pension mortgages
C   Self-certification mortgages
D   Lifetime mortgages

80   Malcolm is an appointed representative for the company Freeborn Merriweather. When advising Mrs Dent, a client, he concludes that there is no suitable product for Mrs Dent within Freeborn Merriweather's range.

Malcolm should:

A   State to the client that he has nothing suitable to offer
B   Offer to the client the best available Freeborn Merriweather product
C   Introduce the client to a representative for another company
D   Recommend a suitable product from another provider company

81   For anti-money laundering purposes, records showing evidence of a client's identity, and details of transactions enacted by that person, must be kept for the following minimum period after the business relationship ends.

A   Six months
B   Three years
C   Five years
D   Six years

82   A firm transacting business via the Internet must verify the following client information.

A   Name
B   Address
C   Name and Address
D   Either Name or Address

83   The Proceeds of Crime Act 2002 allows a firm to carry out a transaction and be protected from allegations of 'assistance' if:

A   The firm has established that the only offence possible being committed is tax evasion
B   The firm has obtained consent from the National Criminal Intelligence Service
C   The firm has explained its concerns to the customer
D   The firm does not stand to gain a material monetary advantage from the transaction

84   What is meant by 'layering' in the context of money laundering?

A   Taking out second mortgages on property
B   Trying to disguise the source of money through complex transactions
C   Theft of bank notes
D   Defaulting on mortgage payments

85   You are a financial adviser and you suspect that a customer may be involved in money laundering. Which of the following is correct?

A   You must tell the customer that you intend to report the relevant transactions.

B   You must report your suspicion to the National Criminal Intelligence Service.

C   You must stop all transactions of the customer and cease doing business with him.

D   Failure to report knowledge or suspicion of money laundering can result in a penalty of up to five years imprisonment.

86   The Financial Services Compensation Scheme is funded by:

A   A compulsory levy on authorised firms
B   Voluntary subscriptions by financial services firms
C   The Government
D   A charge made on clients' policies or accounts

87   A financial adviser has given advice as a result of which a client has suffered financial loss. The client's first step to recover her loss should be to approach **which** of the following?

    A   The regulator
    B   The Financial Services Compensation Scheme
    C   The firm that employs the financial adviser
    D   The Treasury

88   What is the **maximum** award that may be made by the Financial Ombudsman Service?

    A   £48,000 plus costs and interest
    B   £100,000 plus costs and interest
    C   £200,000 plus costs and interest
    D   £250,000 plus costs and interest

89   What is the maximum protection available from the Financial Services Compensation Scheme in the event of a deposit account loss through failure of the deposit taker?

    A   £18,000
    B   £20,000
    C   £31,700
    D   £33,000

90   An individual has made a complaint against a financial adviser. She has received a final response to her complaint from the adviser. Which of the following would **not** be included in this response?

    A   Acceptance of the complaint with an offer of redress
    B   Rejection of the complaint
    C   An offer of a payment to settle the matter, without the firm accepting the complaint
    D   A statement that the customer has three months in which to take the matter to the Financial Ombudsman Service

91   A customer asks for access under the Data Protection Act to data held in respect of her personal pension plan. Which of the following responses to the customer's request is **correct**?

    A   'The Data Protection Act entitles you to access to such data and requires that the product provider supplies this information free of charge.'

    B   'You may obtain access to the data, but we are permitted to make a charge of up to £2.'

    C   'You may obtain access to the data, but we are permitted to make a charge of up to £10.'

    D   'The Data Protection Act does not entitle you to access to data relating to personal pension plans.'

92   Which one of the following is **not** a requirement of the Data Protection Act 1998?

    A   Data must be kept only for as long as is necessary for its original purpose.
    B   The person whose information is registered must be allowed to see the information.
    C   Individuals must be given a copy of any agreement they sign.
    D   The Data Protection Register must reveal who is entitled to see data held on file.

93   Information on data processing by financial services firms can be viewed in a Data Protection Register maintained by:

    A   The Department of Trade and Industry
    B   The Information Commissioner
    C   The Financial Services Authority
    D   The Office of Fair Trading

94   Which financial services firms are required to register under the Data Protection Act 1998?

    A   All firms authorised by the Financial Services Authority
    B   All firms processing personal data, unless exempt
    C   All firms processing either corporate or personal data, unless exempt
    D   All firms processing computer-based personal data, unless exempt

95   Which of the following conditions does **not** necessarily apply to a firm processing personal data?

    A   Data must have been obtained lawfully and fairly.
    B   Data shall not be processed unless one of the Data Protection Act's Schedule 2 conditions is met.
    C   The data subject must have given consent to the processing of the data.
    D   Data must not be held longer than is necessary for its lawful purpose.

96   The case of Durant v Financial Services Authority is often cited with regard to data protection because it dealt in particular with:

    A   The enforcement of data protection law
    B   The definition of a relevant filing system
    C   The definition of sensitive personal data
    D   Data subject access

97   A firm of independent financial advisers offers a debt counselling service. Which of the following is correct?

    A   There is no requirement for the firm to obtain a consumer credit licence.
    B   The firm must obtain a consumer credit licence from the Financial Services Authority.
    C   The firm must obtain a consumer credit licence from the Office of Fair Trading.
    D   The firm must obtain a consumer credit licence from the Department of Trade and Industry.

98   To which of the following contracts made by a consumer does the Unfair Contract Terms Act 1977 normally apply?

    A   A contract with an overseas company doing business in the UK
    B   A contract with a private seller
    C   A contract to sell a house
    D   A contract of insurance

99   For which of the following product types do 'CAT' standards apply?

    A   Cash ISAs (Individual Savings Accounts)
    B   Stocks and shares ISAs (Individual Savings Accounts)
    C   Personal Equity Plans
    D   Mortgages

100   Which of the following products **cannot** be a stakeholder product?

    A   A deposit account with a minimum opening balance of £10
    B   A unit trust scheme with a spread of 2.5% between the selling price and the buying price
    C   A stakeholder pension plan with an annual management charge of 1.25% for new customers
    D   A Child Trust Fund Account

Answers

Answers

Notes are given for most answers.

1   A   The key word is 'maturity', which implies a length of time. Option B describes 'aggregation', another benefit of financial intermediation. It is true that risks are 'pooled' by intermediaries (Option D) but this does not describe maturity transformation. The advice process (Option C) is not relevant here.

2   B   The inflation rate is currently the key monetary policy target.

3   A   Directives require EU member governments to alter national laws to conform to the Directive within a specified period – usually two years.

4   C   A building society savings account will not put capital at risk. A 'share' account confers membership of the Society. The market prices of blue chip shares, corporate bond fund units and OEIC shares may all fall.

5   C   There is no minimum market capitalisation for a company to join the AIM, and no trading record requirement.

6   B   Bank deposits generally produce relatively low but steady returns, at low risk.

7   B   The consequences of death or incapacity of one of the parents can be significant. Therefore, protection needs become very important for parents.

8   C   From the investor's point of view, it is the net interest that matters. If this exceeds inflation, the investor has made a real rate of return.

9   A   Rental yields could rise because of rents rising or properties becoming cheaper to buy, or both.

10 A   Gilts provide a way for the Government to borrow money.

11 D   The coupon and redemption value are indexed according to the RPI from eight months before payment.

12 D   An investment trust is closed-ended and is a public limited company.

13 C   A share with a beta factor greater than 1 fluctuates more widely than the market.

14 A   The risk of capital loss is spread because there are various underlying investments made by the trust.

15 B   Premium bond prizes are completely exempt from income tax.

16 B   As Andrew is a basic rate taxpayer there will be no further tax liability. The tax credit of 10% satisfies the liability in full.

17 A   The term 're-mortgage' is used to refer to the process of taking out a loan with a new lender.

18 D   Commission payments made to the adviser do not affect whether a financial plan or product is suitable for the client.

19 C   Capital gains tax will be payable on listed company shares not in an ISA or a PEP. The other items listed are specifically exempt from CGT.

20 B   Sub-prime lending is likely to be at a higher rate of interest than for an applicant with satisfactory evidence of income and credit history.

21 B   Linked long term funds are part of the risk-controlled stakeholder suite of products.

22 A   A whole of life policy will pay out when needed – on death.

23 A   Assessing affordability is an important requirement for advisers.

24 C   The fact find is a regulatory requirement for the 'Know your customer' rule. Having information about clients enables the adviser to tailor advice to the client's requirements.

25	C	The 'menu' (Key Facts: A Guide to the Cost of Our Services) is presented on initial contact with a private customer. An adviser should not start charging until after the customer has been given a menu and has agreed the payment option.
26	D	The refusal should be recorded in the fact-find.
27	B	When the firm offers advice, the customer's current situation (and anticipated changes) should be considered. However this does not necessarily create an ongoing obligation, although there would be such an obligation if there is a discretionary management relationship.
28	D	Consideration from the life company is the provision of life cover, on the payment of a premium.
29	C	This is a general feature of insurance contracts.
30	B	Witnesses are excluded from benefiting under the will.
31	C	A private company can have the benefit of limited liability so A is incorrect. B is not true of companies; however in certain circumstances (fraudulent and wrongful trading) directors may be liable for a company's debts and hence face bankruptcy (C). An unincorporated sole trader cannot claim limited liability as he or she is not a separate legal entity. Therefore D is incorrect.
32	A	'Joint tenancy' (as opposed to a 'tenancy in common') means that the survivor inherits the property outright.
33	A	Reward is not a necessary feature of the agency relationship, although it is often present.
34	D	A contract does not have to be in writing for it to be binding, although a contract to sell land must be.
35	C	The attorney, who is given 'power of attorney' to handle someone's affairs, has the authority to enter into contracts.
36	D	Under self-assessment, the tax will be paid on the 31 January during the tax year (based on 50% of the previous year's assessment) with a further 50% on 31 July in the tax year following the current tax year. The final balancing payment will be due on 31 January following the current tax year.
37	B	Personal pension contributions by the employer are not taxable. This feature makes this benefit in kind very attractive to the employee.
38	D	When income is over £20,100 (2006/07), the personal allowance is reduced by £1 for every £2 that income is over this figure. However, the personal allowance given cannot fall below the £5,035 personal allowance.
39	A	SDRT is payable at 0.5% for investment trusts, as for other shares. There is no SDRT to pay on purchases of unit trusts.
40	D	Class 2 NI contributions are payable by self-employed people with sufficient earnings.
41	B	Child Benefit is not subject to tax or a means test.
42	A	Secondary Class 1 National Insurance Contributions will be paid by the employer.
43	D	Inflation is the increase of prices over time.
44	A	Before the CPI was used for the target, the RPI was used.
45	B	There is a generally inverse relationship between gilt prices and expected interest rates.
46	C	Having an interest rate which tracks Bank of England rates means that the lender is not free to set a variable rate of its own choosing.
47	D	The FSA, as overall regulator of the financial services industry, has this responsibility.
48	A	B is bad faith risk. C is performance risk. D is complexity/unsuitability risk.
49	B	An adviser should be able to identify what information is factual. Evaluative statements, and statements about feelings or about intentions, wishes or plans are not objectively factual.

50	D	The last three statements of principles for approved persons apply to senior management only.
51	D	The Conduct of Business (COB) rules form part of the FSA Handbook.
52	D	The level of supervisory intensity will depend on the regulator's assessment of risk. Monitoring may be limited to desk based reviews.
53	C	The matters concerned are set out in the legislation. There is no expectation that advisers be held responsible for the consequences of their clients' decisions. Instead, the general principle is noted that consumers should take responsibility for their decisions.
54	D	Members of Designated Professional Bodies, including the Institute of Chartered Accountants in England and Wales, need direct FSA authorisation in respect of mainstream investment business.
55	C	The Financial Services Authority is the lead regulator.
56	A	Disqualification notices are issued by the Financial Services Authority.
57	C	The FSA uses mystery shopping as a means of protecting consumers.
58	C	Principles 1-4 apply to all approved persons. Principles 5-7 apply to senior management only.
59	D	'Unsolicited' means 'without explicit invitation'. Just providing your address is not an invitation to receive calls. Update calls to existing customers are not unsolicited calls.
60	A	The COB rules do not apply to deposits, which are currently governed by the voluntary Banking Code.
61	C	Training is not specified as a 'controlled function'.
62	D	D is a requirement on *firms*, in the FSA's eleven Principles for firms.
63	B	The other options are all specifically exempted.
64	B	They must not deal as the effect of the letter could be to increase the share price. If the company holds the stock, there could be a conflict of interest.
65	A	A period under supervision before passing the exam is not permitted in this case.
66	A	With-profits guides are covered in the Conduct of Business Rules.
67	A	The provider should send it out. If the provider omits to do so, the client retains cancellation rights for 24 months.
68	B	In order to provide suitable advice, one needs to 'know the customer'. Note that there is no general requirement to obtain independent confirmation of the information.
69	C	Churning means dealing too frequently, given the particular circumstances.
70	A	The new 'principles-based approach will go hand-in-hand with the 'risk-based' approach. There will be fewer rules and more emphasis on higher-level principles.
71	B	The cancellation notice must be sent within 14 days of making the agreement.
72	C	There is not a requirement that the customer should have a high net worth.
73	A	Non-private customers can look after themselves.
74	A	The IFA firm will normally be a client of the broker.
75	C	The terms of business letter is issued separately.
76	C	The IFA acts as agent of the client. Note that a tied agent is an agent of the product provider.
77	D	A completed proposal form constitutes an offer in the legal contractual sense.
78	D	The word 'risk-controlled' is used in Government statements on the products.
79	D	'Lifetime mortgages' is a term referring to equity release products.

80   A   The 'best available' company product must not be offered, if unsuitable (B). A company representative must not recommend the product of another company (C and D). The representative should simply state that there is nothing suitable (A).

81   C   Records should be kept until at least five years after the client relationship ends.

82   C   Evidence of identity and address details will be required, as for other transactions.

83   B   The anti-money laundering rules are designed to allow transactions to go ahead, if to do so could help in apprehending criminals. Discussing the matter with the customer could constitute 'tipping off' – a criminal offence.

84   B   Layering is one of the stages of the money laundering process.

Placement means getting the money into the financial system.

Layering refers to separating the money from its illegal origin.

With integration, the process is complete, the money has been laundered and it looks as if it has come from a legitimate source.

85   D   Suspicions must be reported to the firm's Money Laundering Reporting Officer, who will decide whether to make a report to the National Criminal Intelligence Service. The adviser should not alert the suspected launderer, since this would hamper any investigation. 'Tipping off' a suspected launderer carries a penalty of up to five years' imprisonment.

86   A   The FSCS is funded by a compulsory levy on firms. It also has a duty to try to transfer long-term insurance business to new insurers, which may mean that clients do not have to be directly compensated.

87   C   Complaints should be addressed in the first instance to the firm concerned.

88   B   Costs will not usually apply, but 'reasonable' interest may be added to the amount awarded.

89   C   100% of the first £2,000, and 90% of the next £33,000 deposited.

90   D   The customer has six months to take the matter to the FOS, from when the response is issued.

91   C   A charge of up to £10 may be made by the data holder, or £2 in the case of credit reference agency information.

92   C   Providing a copy of all agreements is not a specified requirement of this Act.

93   B   The Information Commissioner maintains a public register of data controllers.

94   B   Exemptions include companies processing only staff administration data and marketing data.

95   C   Although the consent of the data subject is *one* of the Schedule 2 conditions, it is not a necessary requirement except in the case of sensitive personal data.

96   B   The case demonstrated that some manual files will not be subject to the Data Protection Act.

97   C   It is the OFT that issues consumer credit licences.

98   A   A contract with a business will normally be covered by UCTA 1977, but the other three types of contract are excluded.

99   D   CAT standards for ISAs were discontinued with effect from 6 April 2005.

100 B   Stakeholder collective investment schemes must be single-priced and so have no spread between buying and selling prices. A stakeholder deposit account must set its minimum deposit no higher than £10 per occasion. A new stakeholder pension plan may charge up to 1.5% per year for the first ten years A Child Trust Fund may be a stakeholder product.

Tax Tables

Income tax rates

2006/07		2005/06	
Rate %	Band £	Rate %	Band £
10	1 – 2,150	10	1 – 2,090
22	2,151 – 33,300	22	2,091 – 32,400
40	Over 33,300	40	Over 32,400

Income tax reliefs

		2006/07 £	2005/06 £
Personal allowance	– under 65	5,035	4,895
	– 65 – 74	7,280	7,090
	– 75 and over	7,420	7,220
Married couple's allowance	– 65 – 74 (see note 1)	6,065	5,905
	– 75 and over (see note 1)	6,135	5,975
	minimum for 65+	2,350	2,280
Age allowance income limit		20,100	19,500
Blind person's allowance		1,660	1,610
Enterprise investment scheme relief limit (see note 2)		400,000	200,000
Venture capital trust relief limit (see note 3)		200,000	200,000

Notes

1   Ages relate to the elder spouse or civil partner. MCA is available to only those couples where at least one spouse or civil partner was born before 6 April 1935. Relief is restricted to 10%.

2   EIS qualifies for 20% relief.

3   Tax relief is at 30% for VCT shares issued on or after 5 April 2006 (previously 40%).

Pensions

	Annual Allowance £	Lifetime Allowance £
2006/07	215,000	1,500,000
2007/08	225,000	1,600,000
2008/09	235,000	1,650,000
2009/10	245,000	1,750,000
2010/11	255,000	1,800,000

Working and child tax credits

Working tax credit	2006/07	2005/06
	£	£
Basic element	1,665	1,620
Couple and lone parent element	1,640	1,595
30 hour element	680	660
Childcare element of WTC		
Maximum eligible cost for 1 child	175 per week	175 per week
Maximum eligible cost for 2 children	300 per week	300 per week
Percent of eligible child costs covered	80	70
Child tax credit		
Family element	545	545
Baby addition	545	545
Child element	1,765	1,690
Tax credits income thresholds and withdrawal rates		
First income threshold	5,220	5,220
First withdrawal rate	37%	37%
Second income threshold	50,000	50,000
Second withdrawal rate	6.67%	6.67%
First threshold for those entitled to CTC	14,155	13,910
Income disregard	25,000	2,500

Capital gains tax

	2006/07	2005/06
Rate	Gains taxed at 10%, 20% or 40%, subject to level of income	Gains taxed at 10%, 20% or 40%, subject to level of income
Individuals - exemption	£8,800	£8,500
Trusts - exemption	£4,400	£4,250

Taper relief

Gains on business assets		Gains on non-business assets *	
Complete years after 5 April 98	% of gain chargeable	Complete years after 5 April 98	% of gain chargeable
0	100.0	0	100
1	50	1	100
2 or more	25	2	100
		3	95
		4	90
		5	85
		6	80
		7	75
		8	70
		9	65
		10 or more	60

* Non-business assets held on 17 March 1998 given additional year of relief.

Inheritance tax

Death rate %	Lifetime rate %	Chargeable 2006/07 £'000	Chargeable 2005/06 £'000
Nil	Nil	0 – 285	0 – 275
40	20	Over 285	Over 275

Reliefs

Annual exemption	£3,000	Marriage	– parent	£5,000
Small gifts	£250		– grandparent	£2,500
			– bride/groom	£2,500
			– other	£1,000

Reduced charge on gifts within 7 years of death

Years before death	0 – 3	3 – 4	4 – 5	5 – 6	6 – 7
% of death charge	100%	80%	60%	40%	20%

Stamp taxes

Stamp Duty Land Tax

Transfers of property (consideration paid)

Rate (%)	All land in the UK		Land in disadvantaged areas	
	Residential	**Non-residential**	**Residential**	**Non-residential**
Zero	£0 - £125,000	£0 - £150,000	£0 - £150,000	
1	Over £125,000 - £250,000	Over £150,000 - £250,000	Over £150,000 - £250,000	
3	Over £250,000 - £500,000	Over £250,000 - £500,000	Over £250,000 - £500,000	
4	Over £500,000	Over £500,000	Over £500,000	

New leases - Duty on rent

Rate (%)	Net present value (NPV) of rent	
	Residential	**Non-residential**
Zero	£0 - £125,000	£0 - £150,000
1%	Over £125,000	Over £150,000

The rate applies to the amount of NPV in the slice, not to the whole value.

Duty on lease premium is the same as for transfer of land (except special rules apply for premium where rent exceeds £600 annually).

Shares and securities

The rate of stamp duty / stamp duty reserve tax on the transfer of shares and securities is unchanged at 0.5% for 2006/07.

Retail prices index

	Jan	Feb	Mar	Apr	May	Jun	Jul	Aug	Sep	Oct	Nov	Dec
1982			79.4	81.0	81.6	81.9	81.9	81.9	81.9	82.3	82.7	82.5
1983	82.6	83.0	83.1	84.3	84.6	84.8	85.3	85.7	86.1	86.4	86.7	86.9
1984	86.8	87.2	87.5	88.6	89.0	89.2	89.1	89.9	90.1	90.7	91.0	90.9
1985	91.2	91.9	92.8	94.8	95.2	95.4	95.2	95.5	95.4	95.6	95.9	96.0
1986	96.2	96.6	96.7	97.7	97.8	97.8	97.5	97.8	98.3	98.5	99.3	99.6
1987	100.0	100.4	100.6	101.8	101.9	101.9	101.8	102.1	102.4	102.9	103.4	103.3
1988	103.3	103.7	104.1	105.8	106.2	106.6	106.7	107.9	108.4	109.5	110.0	110.3
1989	110.0	111.8	112.3	114.3	115.0	115.4	115.5	115.8	116.6	117.5	118.5	118.8
1990	119.5	120.2	121.4	125.1	126.2	126.7	126.8	128.1	129.3	130.3	130.0	129.9
1991	130.2	130.9	131.4	133.1	133.5	134.1	133.8	134.1	134.6	135.1	135.6	135.7
1992	135.6	136.3	136.7	138.8	139.3	139.3	138.8	138.9	139.4	139.9	139.7	139.2
1993	137.9	138.8	139.3	140.6	141.0	141.0	140.7	141.3	141.9	141.8	141.6	141.9
1994	141.3	142.1	142.5	144.2	144.7	144.7	144.0	144.7	145.0	145.2	145.3	146.0
1995	146.0	146.9	147.5	149.0	149.6	149.8	149.1	149.9	150.6	149.8	149.8	150.7
1996	150.2	150.9	151.5	152.6	152.9	153.0	152.4	153.1	153.8	153.8	153.9	154.4
1997	154.4	155.0	155.4	156.3	156.9	157.5	157.5	158.5	159.3	159.5	159.6	160.0
1998	159.5	160.3	160.8	162.6	163.5	163.4	163.0	163.7	164.4	164.5	164.4	164.4
1999	163.4	163.7	164.1	165.2	165.6	165.6	165.1	165.5	166.2	166.5	166.7	167.3
2000	166.6	167.5	168.4	170.1	170.7	171.1	170.5	170.5	171.7	171.6	172.1	172.2
2001	171.1	172.0	172.2	173.1	174.2	174.4	173.3	174.0	174.6	174.3	173.6	173.4
2002	173.3	173.8	174.5	175.7	176.2	176.2	175.9	176.4	177.6	177.9	178.2	178.5
2003	178.4	179.3	179.9	181.2	181.5	181.3	181.3	181.6	182.5	182.6	182.7	183.5
2004	183.1	183.8	184.6	185.7	186.5	186.8	186.8	187.4	188.1	188.6	189.0	189.9
2005	188.9	189.6	190.5	191.6	192.0	192.2	192.2	192.6	193.1	193.3	193.6	194.1
2006	193.4	194.2										

Indexation relief was frozen at 5 April 1998 and replaced by taper relief for individuals and trustees.

Main Social Security benefits

		2006/07 £	2005/06 £
Child benefit	– first child	17.45	17.00
	– subsequent child	11.70	11.40
Incapacity benefit	– short term lower rate	59.20	57.65
	– short term higher rate	70.05	68.20
	– long term rate	78.50	76.45
Attendance allowance	– lower rate	41.65	40.55
	– higher rate	62.25	60.60
Retirement pension	– single	84.25	82.05
	– married	134.75	131.20
Widowed parent's allowance		84.25	82.05
Bereavement payment (lump sum)		2,000.00	2,000.00
Jobseekers allowance (25 or over)		57.45	56.20

National Insurance contributions
2006/07 rates

	Weekly	Monthly	Yearly
Class I (employee)			
Lower Earnings Limit (LEL)	£84.00	£364.00	£4,368.00
Upper Earnings Limit (UEL)	£645.00	£2,795.00	£33,540.00
Earnings Threshold (ET)*	£97.00	£420.00	£5,035.00

Employees' contributions – Class 1

Total earnings £ per week	Contracted in rate	Contracted out rate
Below £97.00*	Nil	Nil
£97.01 - £645.00	11%	9.4%
Excess over £645.00	1%	1%
		1.6% rebate on earnings between LEL and ET

Employers' contributions – Class 1

Total earnings £ per week	Contracted-in rate	Contracted-out rate	
		Final salary	Money purchase
Below £97.00*	Nil	Nil	Nil
£97.01 - £645.00	12.8%	9.3%	11.8%
Excess over £645.00	12.8%	12.8%	12.8%
		3.5% rebate on earnings between LEL and ET	1% rebate on earnings between LEL and ET

*   Earnings threshold below which no NICs payable. There is a zero band between the lower earnings limit (£84 pw) and the earnings threshold (£97 pw) to protect lower earners' rights to contributory state benefits such as basic state pension.

Class 1A
(employers' contributions on most benefits)   12.8% on all relevant benefits

Class 2 (self-employed)
Flat rate per week £2.10
where earnings are over £4,465 pa

Class 3 (voluntary)
Flat rate per week £7.55

Class 4 (self-employed)
8% on profits £5,035 – £33,540;
1% on profits above £33,540

Index

Name: _____   Address: _____

_____

Email: _____   _____

Date: _____

Why did you decide to purchase this Study Text?
(Tick one box only)

How have you used this Study Text?
(Tick one box only)

☐ recommended by training department

☐ home study (book only)

☐ recommendation by friend/colleague

☐ on a course: at _____

☐ recommendation by a lecturer at college

☐ with 'correspondence' package

☐ saw advertising/website

☐ other _____

☐ have used BPP products in the past

☐ other _____

Have you used the BPP Passcards ☐ or i-Pass disk ☐ for this subject?   *Yes / No*

Your ratings, comments and suggestions would be appreciated on the following areas.

	Very useful	*Useful*	*Not useful*
Introductory section	☐	☐	☐
Main text	☐	☐	☐
Questions in chapters	☐	☐	☐
Chapter roundups	☐	☐	☐
Quizzes at ends of chapters	☐	☐	☐
Practice examination	☐	☐	☐
Structure and presentation	☐	☐	☐
Availability of Updates on website	☐	☐	☐

	Excellent	*Good*	*Adequate*	*Poor*
Overall opinion of this Study Text	☐	☐	☐	☐

Do you intend to continue using BPP study material?   ☐ Yes   ☐ No

Please note any comments or suggestions on the reverse of this page, or write by e-mail to FPQueries@bpp.com

Please return this form to: Financial Adviser Series Publishing Manager, BPP Professional Education, FREEPOST, London, W12 8BR

REVIEW FORM

Please note any further comments, suggestions and apparent errors below.